The Netscape LiveWire™ Sourcebook

Create and Manage a Java-Based Web Site

The Netscape LiveWire™ Sourcebook

Create and Manage a Java-Based Web Site

Ted Coombs

Jason Coombs

Don Brewer

WILEY COMPUTER PUBLISHING

John Wiley & Sons, Inc.

New York • Chichester • Brisbane • Toronto • Singapore

Publisher: Katherine Schowalter
Editor: Philip Sutherland
Managing Editor: Micheline Frederick
Text Design & Composition: Benchmark Productions, Inc.

This publication is designed to provide accurate and authoritative information in regard to the subject matter covered. It is sold with the understanding that the publisher is not engaged in rendering legal, accounting, or other professional service. If legal advice or other expert assistance is required, the services of a competent professional person should be sought.

Library of Congress Cataloging-in-Publication Data:
Coombs, Ted.
    The Netscape LiveWire sourcebook : create and manage a Java-based
web site / Ted Coombs, Jason Coombs, Don Brewer.
        p.   cm.
    Includes index.
    ISBN 0-471-15605-1 (paper : alk. paper)
    1. Netscape. 2. World Wide Web (Information retrieval system)
3. Java (Computer program language) I. Coombs, Jason. II. Brewer,
Don. III. Title.
TK5105.883.N48C66 1996
005.75--dc20   96-19455
                                                    CIP

ISBN 0-471-15605-1
Printed in the United States of America
10 9 8 7 6 5 4 3 2 1

CONTENTS

Chapter 1   **Introduction** 1
              Part I—The LiveWire Software Tools .2
                     Netscape Navigator Gold .3
                     Site Manager and the Build WEB Utility 4
                     Application Manager 5
                     Netscape Server Systems .7
              Part II—Building LiveWire Applications 7
              The JavaScript Language 8
              The LiveWire Object Framework 9
              JavaScript Database Access 10
              Part III—Producing Multimedia Web Content 11
                     Java Applets 11
                     Netscape Inline Plug-ins .13
                     Macromedia Director and Shockwave 13

Chapter 2   **Netscape Navigator Gold** **17**
              Navigator Gold Browser Environment 18
                     Internet Tools 19
                     Configuring Navigator Gold for E-mail and News 20
                     E-mail, Still Number One .21
                     File Transfer Protocol Capability 25
               Navigator Gold Editor Environment 27
                     Navigator Gold Editor Window 27
                     External Editors 44

Chapter 3   **The LiveWire Tool Set** **51**
              Site Manager 52
                     Bringing a Web Site Under Management 54
                     Link Management 60

Build WEB Utility 63
    Command-Line Build WEB Utility .64
Application Manager 67
    Adding Applications 68
    Managing Applications 69
Servers 70
    FastTrack Server 71
    Commerce Server 72
    News Server 72
    Catalog Server 72
    Proxy Server 72
    Mail Server 72
    LiveWire Pro 73

Chapter 4   **Writing JavaScript** **75**
Some JavaScript Basics 77
    JavaScript Variables, Operators, and Condition Statements 78
    Creating Functions 85
Event Programming 88
Programming with JavaScript Objects 90
    The JavaScript Built-in Functions .90
    The JavaScript Standard Objects 91
    Link 102
    Netscape Objects 113
Don't Go There! 117
Getting More Information 118

Chapter 5   **Client/Server JavaScript** **119**
JavaScript Everywhere 121
    Using the LiveWire Source Files .121
    Embedding JavaScript in HTML 122
JavaScript Server Functions 124
    write() Function 124
    redirect() Function 125
    defined() Function 125
    debug() Function 126
    lock() and unlock() 126
    flush () Function 126
    registerC() Function 127
    callC() Function 127
LiveWire Objects 127

Server Object 128
Project Object 131
Client Object 132
    Client Object Properties 132
    Maintaining the Client Object 133
Request Object 137
    Properties 137
Database Object 139
File Object 140
Running Your Web Application 143
Debug Function and Trace Utility 144
    Tracing 144
    Debugging 147
What the Future Holds 148

Chapter 6   **Using Databases in Your LiveWire Application** **149**
Introduction to Databases 149
The Database Object 150
    Connecting to the Database 150
    Tables 153
    Columns and Rows 154
    Relationships 155
Introduction to SQL 156
    Executing SQL in JavaScript 157
Data Handling 158
    Using the database.execute() Method 158
    Inserting Information into the Database 160
    Updating the Database 160
    Deleting Information from the Database 161
    Retrieving Information from a Database 161
    Database Column Types 163
Database Cursors 164
    Navigating Through the Data 164
    Inserting Rows with Cursors 166
    Updates with Cursors 167
    Deleting with Cursors 167
Support for BLObs 168
    Inserting BLObs into the Database .168
    BLObs as HTML Images 169
    Linking to BLOb Fields 169

On-Line Transaction Processing 170
  To Commit or Not to Commit 171
Database Error Handling 173
  Database Status Codes 174
Database Object Sample Application 175

Chapter 7   **Java Applets** **179**
Placing Java Applets in Web Pages 180
  Using ONETAG 183
  Functions in Applet Execution 184
  Applet Security Features 184
Java Developer's Kit 185
  Viewing and Debugging Applets 185
  Demo Applets 188
Various Java Applets 191
  IRC Utility 192
  Impressive and Useful Java Applets .198
  Just Gotta Scroll 224
  Just Plain Fun Applets 229
  Valuable Java Applet Sites 232
  When to Use Java Applets 233
Conclusion 234

Chapter 8   **Java Applet Creation Tools** **237**
Just-in-Time Compiler 237
Java Applet Animation 238
  The Easy Animator 239
  Corel WEB.MOVE 250
Java Visual Development Tools 264
  JFactory 264
  Java Applet Sample Code 268
  Other Java Visual Development Tools 277

Chapter 9   **Inline Plug-ins** **279**
Installing Plug-ins 280
  Challenges with Plug-in Installation .281
Deploying Inline Plug-ins 283
  Configuring Server for MIME Files 284
  UDP and Firewalls 285
VIPs (Very Important Plug-ins) 286
  Video Inline Plug-Ins 287
  Audio Plug-ins 296

Animation Inline Plug-ins 306
Document Viewing 309
Image Enhancement 317
OLE/OCX Controls 322
Virtual Reality Worlds 325
Combination of Plug-ins 328
Plug-ins with Java Applets 329
What If the User Doesn't Have the Plug-in? 329
Now It's Your Turn 332

Chapter 10   Understanding the Netscape Inline Plug-in Architecture **333**
Extending the Web with MIME 334
Understanding the Plug-in API 338
Demystifying Key Plug-in API Concepts 341
Handling Plug-in API Function Calls 353
Calling Navigator Functions from a Plug-in 379

Chapter 11   Building a Netscape Inline Plug-in **397**
Programming with the Netscape Plug-in SDK 398
Handling Plug-in Instance Initialization 398
Initializing Plug-in Display 404

Chapter 12   Shockwave **409**
Shockwave 409
Director 411
Interactive Web Lingo 416
Afterburner 418
Keep in Mind 418
Embedding Content in HTML 418

Appendix A   Installing and Configuring Netscape LiveWire Pro **421**
Installing the Netscape FastTrack Server 421
Installing Netscape LiveWire 426
Installing the Informix OnLine Database Server 428
Configuring Informix to Work with LiveWire 434

Appendix B   The transferRNA Plug-In **447**
Using transferRNA 448
Sending Files with transferRNA 449
Receiving Files with transferRNA 450
Where to Get transferRNA 451
Serving transferRNA 452

Index **455**

ACKNOWLEDGMENTS

We are constantly reminded that no matter how large the Internet becomes there *are* people behind all those computers. As it takes millions of people to make an Internet, it takes a lot of people to create a book. We had fun writing this book, and we'd like to thank some of the people who helped make this book fun for us, and a great book for you. Thanks to Phil Sutherland who spent long nights and weekends making this book happen. Thanks also for believing in us and our projects. Thanks to Len Feldman who is probably the busiest man we know. Without you letting us peer into the Netscape inner sanctum, this book would not be quite as interesting. Thanks also to Tim Hickman of Netscape for putting up with our never ending voice mail messages. We traded so many voice mail messages we forget if we ever really talked to you. A special thanks goes to Micheline Frederick who got to do all the grunt work. A big thanks to Bob Zurek for all his hard work tech editing the book while doing his job as the head of technology for Powersoft Corporation. We'd like to thank everyone at Waterside Productions for their help in making this book a reality. We would like to thank CTSNET of San Diego for providing our Internet connection while writing this book. Lastly and most importantly, we'd like to thank all the members of the Netscape developer community for sharing their insights through e-mail and newsgroups.

INTRODUCTION

N etscape, the company renowned for its innovative Internet technology and amazing business success, is once again pushing the Internet envelope. This time, Netscape is changing the way the World Wide Web looks and works in order to bring quality interactive multimedia content to every desktop. You are about to take part in the next generation of the Web using the new tools and capabilities developed by Netscape as part of LiveWire.

With the tools and techniques presented in this book you will be able to add exciting interactive multimedia content to your Web site and create sophisticated custom network software for both the Internet and your company intranet.

With the Netscape LiveWire application development architecture centered on Java, JavaScript, inline plug-ins, and Netscape server technology, developing for the Internet and intranets is straightforward and flexible. For the first time, programmers have access to an integrated set of network programming and rapid application development tools for building and deploying custom software and live content on the World Wide Web. This book refers to these custom creations as *Web* *application*s, and it assumes that you, as a software or content developer, want to discover and unleash the potential of LiveWire and all its related tools.

There are three significant parts to the LiveWire application development architecture. The first is the minimum set of software tools that together bear the LiveWire product name. These tools include Navigator Gold, Site Manager, Application Manager, and the Netscape Internet- and intranet-server systems such as the Netscape Communications and FastTrack servers.

The second part is a set of programming tools including the LiveWire object framework and the JavaScript language. The third part involves the use of Java applets and Netscape inline plug-ins to enable new content types and high-performance interactive and multimedia network applications.

Although many LiveWire components are valuable technologies all by themselves, the maximum benefit is realized only when all the Netscape development technologies are used together as a cohesive unit. In this book we cover all three significant parts of the LiveWire development architecture so that we can provide insight and instruction that will enable you to fully realize the potential of LiveWire. The following sections describe the three parts of this book and the three parts of the LiveWire application development architecture in more detail.

Part I— The LiveWire Software Tools

At the core of the LiveWire product is a set of software tools that greatly reduce the complexity of creating and managing a Web site. The software that you will use most often, *Netscape Navigator Gold*, serves as an HTML and JavaScript authoring tool and provides access to the LiveWire server features. Among the LiveWire server features, the *Application Manager* is the most visible component. LiveWire's Application Manager is used to deploy and manage Web applications and other LiveObject Web content. *Site Manager*, another LiveWire tool used to create Web applications, allows you to assemble the parts of a Web application into a single .WEB file and then deploy the .WEB file on the server. Site Manager also provides numerous Web application utilities such as an external link tester, a file and directory manager, and a menu-driven interface to the Build WEB utility.

Netscape Navigator Gold

To change the individual pages of a Web application, use edit mode, Navigator Gold's editor environment. Navigator Gold will retrieve files, including images, for you and save them to a local directory. This function makes it possible to change the Web page source file, test each link, and verify final layout of the page before updating the server. The Navigator Gold editor environment, shown in Figure 1.1, removes from the creation and maintenance of Web pages the tedium of HTML tag-syntax authoring. It also enables JavaScript authoring for both client-side and server-side JavaScript with visual color-coding indicators that differentiate the two types of JavaScript.

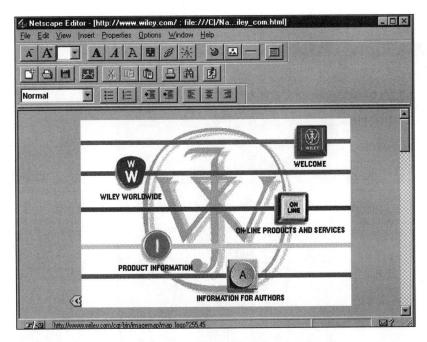

■■■■■■ **Figure 1.1** Author HTML pages and JavaScript code in the Navigator Gold editor.

Navigator Gold also provides a functional FTP client, including a little-known file upload ability, through an extension to the standard FTP URL type. Navigator Gold is covered in Chapter 2 of this book.

Site Manager and the Build WEB Utility

The LiveWire Site Manager is a stand-alone software tool that can be used only on the LiveWire server machine. Site Manager makes it easy to manage the many files that accumulate for each Web application. Figure 1.2 shows the LiveWire Site Manager user interface. The Site Manager menu gives you easy access to the *Build WEB* utility, an essential component of LiveWire that packages each file in a Web application into a single .WEB file.

The Build WEB utility is also available in a command-line version, which makes it easy to write batch files or even integrate the Build WEB utility into a MAKE file.

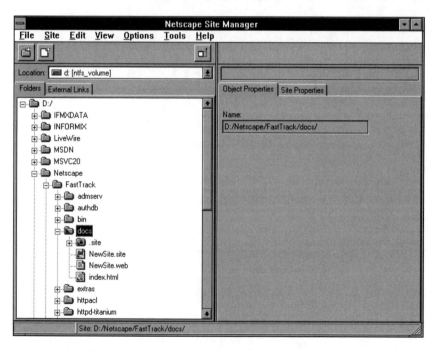

Figure 1.2 Use the Site Manager to administer LiveWire Web applications.

One other feature of Site Manager worth noting is a very useful link tester that will verify the links in a Web file, making it easy to locate and fix invalid links. Site Manager and the Build WEB utility are covered in Chapter 3.

Application Manager

Through the Application Manager, authorized users can modify, remove, stop, start, or run any of the Web applications deployed on a LiveWire site. Figure 1.3 shows how Navigator Gold is used to access the Application Manager. Chapter 3 of this book covers the Application Manager.

When you need to modify the properties of a Web application, the Application Manager provides an HTML form like the one shown in Figure 1.4. LiveWire operates as an extension to the Netscape FastTrack, Communications, or Commerce servers. As a result, the Application Manager can control the URL through which a

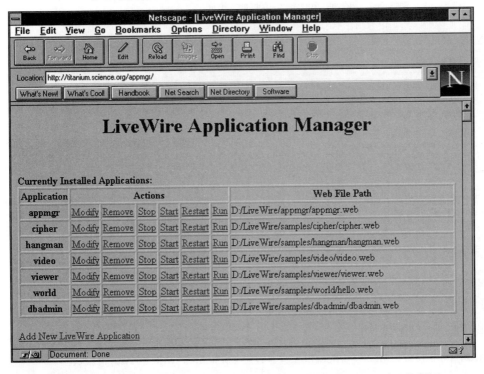

Figure 1.3 Use the LiveWire Application Manager to maintain Web applications.

given Web application is accessed by the end user. In the URI Prefix field of the
HTML form shown in Figure 1.4 you can see an example of this control where the
Web application is registered under the /newsite location. Separating the URL directory path from the physical directory path in this way enables a whole heap of distributed management abilities for your Web site. For example, the files for a Web
application could reside on a network drive somewhere else on the Internet instead
of residing locally on the same machine as the LiveWire server.

Any Web browser can be used to access the Application Manager, including the regular Netscape Navigator. Netscape Navigator Gold looks and acts just like the regular Netscape Navigator, except that Navigator Gold has an *edit mode* that makes
it possible to edit the content of a Web page.

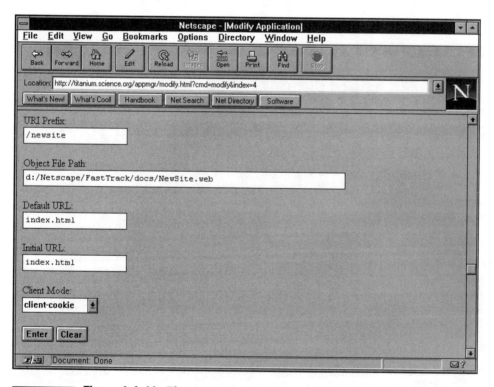

Figure 1.4 Modify properties of a Web application with the Application
Manager.

Netscape Server Systems

Netscape offers a comprehensive line of server systems ranging from the classic HTTP Communications server to the secure Commerce server and the SuiteSpot server package. Not all of the Netscape servers pertain directly to the LiveWire application development architecture, so we feature the ones that offer the most to serious Internet site developers. Because Netscape isn't a database company, the LiveWire Pro package is shipped with the Informix database server, and it is the one that we feature in the database development portions of this book. The Netscape FastTrack, Commerce, Communications, and News servers are featured in Chapter 3. For help installing the LiveWire system, the FastTrack server, and the Informix database see Appendix A.

Part II—
Building LiveWire Applications

LiveWire application development centers on the JavaScript language. A joint creation of Netscape and Sun Microsystems, JavaScript promises to become the scripting standard for the Web. Whether embedded in the HTML of a Web page source file or designed to stand alone as a .JS file, JavaScript provides a simple and powerful way to develop real Web applications. JavaScript is used in LiveWire both to produce interactive or dynamic Web page content and to create back-end processing. Part II of this book is devoted entirely to JavaScript.

As an extension to the JavaScript language, Netscape LiveWire provides an object framework that makes it possible to access databases and embed SQL in JavaScript code. The LiveWire object framework also simplifies Web application development through its *server* and *request* objects that enable LiveWire applications to communicate with other applications or exchange data with any Web browser. Thanks to the LiveWire object framework, writing back-end processing facilities that receive form data from a Web browser, access databases, or generate dynamic Web pages is simpler than ever. Say good-bye to complicated CGI scripts; JavaScript is easier and better for back-end processing in most Web applications.

The JavaScript Language

The JavaScript language brings real programming functionality to any Web page. Although used as the foundation for both client-side and server-side Web application development in LiveWire, the JavaScript language itself does not depend on LiveWire. It is through object extensions to JavaScript that Netscape has created the LiveWire object framework for server-side scripting and database access. The LiveWire object framework is the only aspect of JavaScript that is dependent on the LiveWire system; all other JavaScript that you create will work independently of the LiveWire server. To make use of the LiveWire object framework, you must know how to write JavaScript programs. Chapter 4 begins our coverage of the JavaScript language with a focus on syntax, which is similar to that for C and Java, yet still easy to learn, and the standard client-side JavaScript that is meant to execute in a JavaScript-enabled Web browser like Netscape Navigator.

If you're comfortable with HTML, JavaScript will seem like a natural extension to your existing Web pages. As shown in Figure 1.5, client-side JavaScript code is meant to be embedded right in your HTML Web page source file. When a JavaScript-enabled browser views a page with both JavaScript and HTML, the full functionality of the Web application is realized by the end user. Because Netscape is

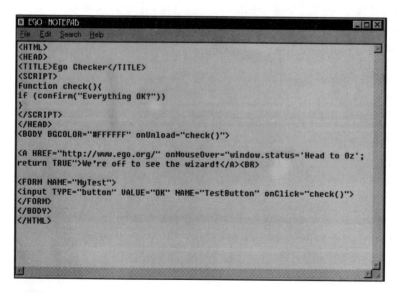

```
EGO - NOTEPAD
File  Edit  Search  Help
<HTML>
<HEAD>
<TITLE>Ego Checker</TITLE>
<SCRIPT>
function check(){
if (confirm("Everything OK?"))
}
</SCRIPT>
</HEAD>
<BODY BGCOLOR="#FFFFFF" onUnload="check()">

<A HREF="http://www.ego.org/" onMouseOver="window.status='Head to Oz';
return TRUE">We're off to see the wizard!</A><BR>

<FORM NAME="MyTest">
<input TYPE="button" VALUE="OK" NAME="TestButton" onClick="check()">
</FORM>
</BODY>
</HTML>
```

■■■■■■■ **Figure 1.5** Embed JavaScript right in any Web page HTML source file.

committed to providing new tools while maintaining compatibility with existing Internet standards, the JavaScript portion of a Web page source file is just ignored by any Web browser that does not speak JavaScript.

It is very likely that JavaScript will become the standard for scripting in the World Wide Web. Using JavaScript as part of your Web page, you can write scripts that manipulate form input before it is sent to the server or access objects and properties built into the Web browser. Client-side JavaScript programs even offer the ability to perform calculations or adjust the display and behavior of a page based on just about any condition. More than any other new Web technology, JavaScript promises to free you from the world of static HTML pages by providing real application functionality using the standard interface of a Web browser.

The LiveWire Object Framework

One of the most compelling reasons to purchase and use LiveWire is for its JavaScript-based object framework. Each of the LiveWire objects, which are accessible only to server-side JavaScript like that shown in Figure 1.6, serves a particular purpose. For example, the database object enables server JavaScript to access database servers. The request object is a dynamic object whose properties are set by the Netscape HTTP server when a Web browser submits a POST request. The request

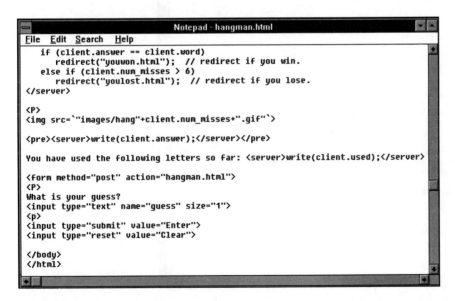

```
                          Notepad - hangman.html
File   Edit   Search   Help
     if (client.answer == client.word)
        redirect("youwon.html");  // redirect if you win.
     else if (client.num_misses > 6)
        redirect("youlost.html");  // redirect if you lose.
</server>

<P>
<img src=`"images/hang"+client.num_misses+".gif"`>

<pre><server>write(client.answer);</server></pre>

You have used the following letters so far: <server>write(client.used);</server>

<form method="post" action="hangman.html">
<P>
What is your guess?
<input type="text" name="guess" size="1">
<p>
<input type="submit" value="Enter">
<input type="reset" value="Clear">

</body>
</html>
```

■■■■■■■■ **Figure 1.6** Access any of the LiveWire objects using server JavaScript.

object replaces the Common Gateway Interface (CGI) standard for server JavaScript. Chapter 5 covers client/server JavaScript and the LiveWire object framework.

Server JavaScript appears in a Web page source file within <SERVER> and </SERVER> tags. The LiveWire server processes server JavaScript and sends the result to the Web browser. Server JavaScript is never sent directly to the Web browser as is client-side JavaScript.

JavaScript Database Access

The LiveWire object framework includes built-in access to database servers through the JavaScript database object. For many organizations, database application development for the Web is the single most important factor in the decision to create a Web site in the first place. When the JavaScript database object is combined with the other aspects of a LiveWire-based Web site such as Java applets and inline plug-ins, LiveWire becomes a mature solution for Internet database programming. Figure 1.7 shows a simple server JavaScript sample that uses the database object. The sample shown is part of the video sample provided with a LiveWire package.

```
Notepad - start.html
File   Edit   Search   Help
<html>
<head>
<title> Start Video Rentals </title>
</head>
<body>
<server>
if(!database.connected())
{
   theError = database.connect("INFORMIX", "ol_titanium", "informix", "
   write(theError);
}

if (!database.connected())
{
   write("Error: Unable to connect to database.");
}
else
{
   project.lastID = 0;
   cursor = database.cursor("select * from customer order by ID");
   while(cursor.next())
   {
   project.lastID = cursor.id;
   }
   cursor.close();

   redirect("home.html");
}
</server>
</body>
</html>
```

■■■■■■ **Figure 1.7** Use the LiveWire Database Object to embed SQL in server JavaScript code.

Notice the straightforward approach to database access and embedded SQL. The LiveWire database object provides support for cursors, online transaction processing (OLTP), and binary large object (BLOb) data types. With an object framework that was designed for Web development, the range of Web-oriented query output formatting features is impressive. For instance, a JavaScript object method is provided that will convert an image from a BLOb value into an <IMG> tag. Another feature allows JavaScript to automatically prepare a table layout from a multirow result set. JavaScript will even perform any necessary type conversion between database data types, such as VARCHAR, and the corresponding data type in JavaScript, such as a string. Database access in JavaScript is covered in Chapter 6 of this book.

Part III— Producing Multimedia Web Content

JavaScript is an ideal solution for both client- and server-side Web programming, but it doesn't attempt to address the needs of multimedia content producers. To round out its technology offering and enable true multimedia content publishing on the Web, Netscape LiveWire supports two additional interactive publishing solutions:

- Java applets
- Netscape inline plug-ins

Part III of this book features the use of Java applets and Netscape inline plug-ins to enable new content types and provide high-performance interactive and multimedia Internet applications via the World Wide Web. In this part, you learn how to utilize existing Java applets and Netscape plug-ins to immediately enhance your Web site with interactive or multimedia content. In addition to featuring useful technologies created by others, we show you how to create your own Java applets and inline plug-ins. Finally, we show you how to use Macromedia Director, one of the best authoring tools for Web content, to produce and publish amazing interactive multimedia on the Internet using a Netscape inline plug-in called Shockwave.

Java Applets

Java is a new technology created by Sun Microsystems that includes an innovative programming language, an interpreter that will execute platform-independent compiled byte code, and a *virtual machine* designed to be the operating system of small network appliances. The details of Java programming are outside the scope of this book, but the role of Java in LiveWire is so important that we devote two chapters to it.

Specifically, Chapter 7 shows you how to integrate existing Java applets into your Web site and features a number of useful applets that are available today on the Internet. Java applets are platform independent Java programs that have been compiled into a byte code format. Any Java-enabled Web browser can be used to execute any Java applet, regardless of the operating system on which the Web browser is running. With its advanced network communication abilities, built-in class library, cross-platform support, and unparalleled security features, Java promises to become an integral part of every Web application.

Chapter 8 shows you how to build your own Java applets using some of the best applet creation software available. Even if you're not familiar with Java programming, the applet creation tools featured in this book give you the ability to build useful animation applets without programming. When you learn to write Java programs, the visual Java development tools featured in Chapter 8 will increase your

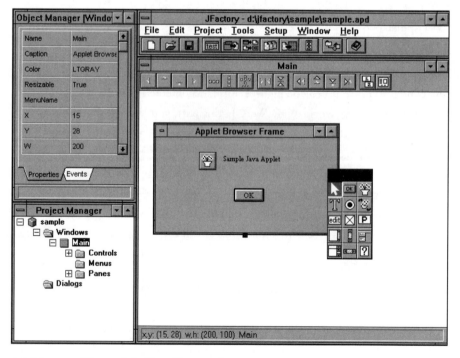

Figure 1.8 Use JFactory for visual Java development.

productivity and remove much of the burden of writing Java code. Figure 1.8 shows a sample of one such visual Java development tool called *JFactory*.

Whether you build your own Java applets or deploy content for your LiveWire site using existing applets created by others, it's important to understand what Java is and how to integrate it into the World Wide Web. This book explains everything you need to know, from the HTML tags added for Java applet support to the role of JavaScript in gluing together applets, inline plug-ins, and HTML on a single Web page.

Netscape Inline Plug-ins

The display of Web content has, until now, been limited to HTML. With the introduction of Netscape inline plug-in technology, it is now possible to create and deploy any type of content on the Web. More importantly, new content types can be viewed by anyone who is using a Web browser that supports Netscape plug-ins. Already we've seen new audio and video formats that allow you to embed real-time data streams right in a Web page. Many static image formats have also been implemented using plug-ins, so that your Web site is no longer limited to GIF or JPEG images for graphical display. A wide range of plug-in data formats now available will transform your Web site from an HTML-only wasteland into a digital, interactive art showpiece. Chapter 9 shows you how to create and deploy exciting content for your Web site through the use of existing Netscape inline plug-ins.

Plug-ins work by using the multipurpose Internet mail extensions (MIME) standard to enable new content subtypes. Figure 1.9 shows an Adobe Acrobat creation being viewed within Netscape Navigator through the Amber plug-in. Although many content types are already supported through plug-ins, there is still a need for more. By creating your own plug-in, you can enable custom content types for just your Web site or provide a new content type for general use on the Web. Chapters 10 and 11 cover the Netscape plug-in API and get you started creating your own plug-in MIME type.

Macromedia Director and Shockwave

By far the most exciting plug-in MIME type to emerge recently is the Macromedia Director plug-in called Shockwave. Shockwave makes it possible to view and interact with Macromedia Director productions on the Web. Figure 1.10 shows Shockwave in use within Netscape Navigator.

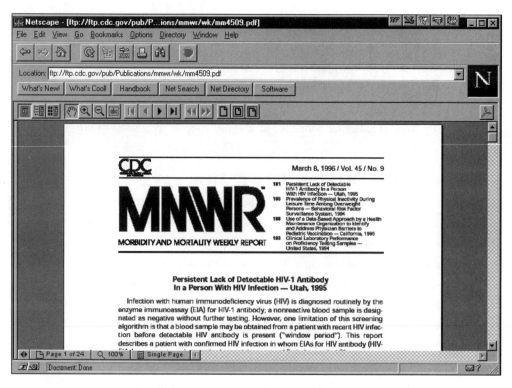

Figure 1.9 Embed Adobe Acrobat creations in your Web site using the Amber plug-in.

Macromedia Director includes a scripting language called Lingo. Through Internet extensions to Lingo, which are designed to work with Shockwave, it's possible to include hyperlinks and other Web features in a Director production. Director is emerging as one of the premier content authoring solutions for multimedia Web content, and a book on LiveWire wouldn't be complete without a guide to Shockwave. Chapter 12 shows you how to use the Macromedia Director authoring tool to create and deploy interactive multimedia content for the Shockwave plug-in.

The Netscape LiveWire product is clearly evolving quickly. However, we're confident that the technical content of this book will remain applicable and accurate for a long time. As with any computer book about a new software product, the beta version of the software was our only guide to the features

Figure 1.10 Use the Shockwave plug-in to deploy Web content created with Macromedia Director.

and functionality about which we've written. For this reason, and because the LiveWire product continues to improve during the beta test, there will probably be a few inaccuracies in this book when it is used with the production release of LiveWire. One of our goals in designing such a comprehensive guide to LiveWire was to focus on those aspects of the LiveWire development architecture that represent the most immediate value and that appear to us to be mature and stable components. As a result, we've minimized the impact that future changes to LiveWire might have on the accuracy of the material found in this book. To help address any remaining concerns about applicability of this book to the final release of LiveWire, we've established a Web site that will provide the most up-to-date information and highlight important changes in the LiveWire software:

http://www.science.org/netscape/

2

NETSCAPE

NAVIGATOR GOLD

Your HTML dreams have come true with Netscape Navigator Gold. Netscape has added visual HTML editor capability to the popular Navigator browser to create Navigator Gold. As you may have found, creating HTML has been awkward and inconvenient. The Navigator Gold editor presents you with a WYSIWYG (what-you-see-is-what-you-get) HTML editor, whereby a Web page is displayed as it would appear by someone using a Web browser. Navigator Gold gives you a visual development environment that looks and works similar to existing word processor programs. Just as you would in your favorite word processor, you can make text in your Web page bold, italic, or blinking, or you can change it to a different color with simple-to-use icons. Navigator Gold creates all of the HTML for you, allowing you to spend time developing and creating Web applications, instead of writing HTML. Navigator Gold allows you to do the following:

- Modify text by highlighting it and choosing an icon in a typical point-and-click fashion
- Quickly create hyperlinks with drag-and-drop capability

- Use the JavaScript properties function to identify *server* and *client* JavaScript, thus providing an easy, integrated programming environment for JavaScript
- Instantly publish a Web document after you create it

The combination of the browser and editor windows in Navigator Gold provides a platform for creating advanced Web applications. The browser portion of Navigator Gold is used to access sites in the same fashion as the Netscape Navigator. Bringing Web pages into your browser and then switching to edit mode, you can evaluate and edit them for your own use.

One way to use the browser/editor combination is to correct and enhance your Web pages. Load one of your Web pages with the Navigator Gold browser and fix misspelled words instantly, change colors, fonts, and layout by launching the Navigator Gold editor. Do the following to edit an existing Web page in Navigator Gold:

1. View a Web Page in your Navigator Gold browser.
2. Start the editor by clicking the **Edit** button. The Web page source file that you are viewing is then downloaded, saved, and displayed in the editor.
3. Make changes and enhancements to the Web page using the Navigator Gold editor.
4. Use the built-in FTP client capability of Navigator Gold to upload and replace the existing Web page source file on the HTTP server.

In Navigator Gold you can browse, edit, upload, and save your Web pages. With these versatile capabilities Navigator Gold is the cornerstone of the LiveWire development architecture. Navigator Gold serves many functions in LiveWire, from HTML editor to user interface for LiveWire application management to IDE for developing client/server JavaScript applications.

Navigator Gold Browser Environment

With the introduction of several new features in the Navigator browser, an exciting new realm of multimedia capabilities is possible on the Web. These multimedia enhancements, including inline plug-ins, Java applets, and JavaScript, allow for new content within Web pages as follows:

- The inline plug-in enhancement enables the Navigator browser to display MIME (multipurpose Internet mail extensions) content types within the browser window. These MIME types can produce animated graphics, inline streaming video or audio, or an endless range of OCX controls and other objects.

- Java applets can be used to spice up a Web document with scrolling text, a ticker tape of stock quotes, or even an integrated multiuser chat utility.

- JavaScript, the scripting language provided in LiveWire, allows your Web pages to include scripts that add interactive behavior or dynamic HTML features.

Inline plug-ins are executable programs that run right in the Navigator window, extending the abilities of the Navigator browser. Any type of MIME content, whether a video, a sound, or still graphic, can be experienced through one of the plug-ins provided by Netscape and by third-party software developers. If you have already downloaded a few plug-ins, it's a good idea to keep checking Netscape's site for any new ones that may have been added recently.

One of the most important features added to the Navigator browser is the new scripting language, JavaScript. JavaScript can be used on the client side to check form input before sending it to the server or do calculations on user input and instantly display the results. JavaScript can also be used on the server side, allowing for database access, or as a replacement for CGI.

Internet Tools

Netscape has incorporated many of the existing Internet protocols into the Navigator browser to make it a one-stop-shopping application for users on the Internet. In addition to the HTTP protocol that serves as the basis of the Web, the Navigator browser now has the ability to launch an e-mail client (SMTP), a news reader (NNTP), and a File Transfer Protocol (FTP) client. The features of each of these client protocols is enhanced within the Navigator browser because each also has the additional capabilities of the browser environment, including support for hyperlinks. The following are some of the benefits provided by the Navigator Gold browser:

- Views hyperlinks in your e-mail client and news reader
- Sends an attached URL right in your e-mail message or news posting

- Takes advantage of the built-in Netscape security
- Reads newsgroups on local or remote news servers
- Logs in and uploads files to any FTP server
- Switches to edit mode at any time with a single mouse click

Navigator Gold is your single most important Internet tool. For a site developer using LiveWire, it's important to become familiar with all that Navigator Gold has to offer.

Configuring Navigator Gold for E-mail and News

Before you can use either the Netscape e-mail client or news reader you must first configure Navigator Gold. Choose the **Options|Mail and News Preferences** option from the Navigator menu to access the Preferences window as shown in Figure 2.1. Use the Preferences window to configure Navigator for use on your computer.

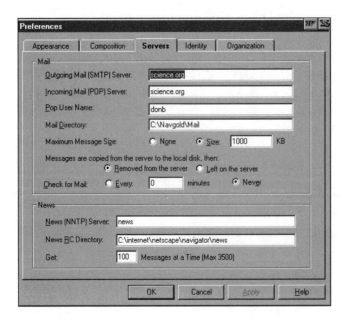

Figure 2.1 Enter your mail SMTP, POP, and NNTP servers to enable Netscape client ability.

In the Preferences window you need to enter the SMTP, POP, and NNTP servers to configure the e-mail client and the news reader before they will work correctly. Your Internet access provider or company network administrator will tell you the names of each of these servers.

E-mail, Still Number One

E-mail is the number one application on the Internet, far surpassing even the World Wide Web. Navigator Gold has its own built-in e-mail client that provides features that are useful to both Web users and developers. For example, if you want to share information about an impressive URL location you have just found, you can use the e-mail capabilities of Navigator to send a message that has the actual Web page attached, rather than just include the URL address in the message.

Before exploring these interesting e-mail features you must first launch the Navigator e-mail client by choosing the **Window|Netscape Mail** option from the Navigator menu. This menu option opens the e-mail client window shown in Figure 2.2.

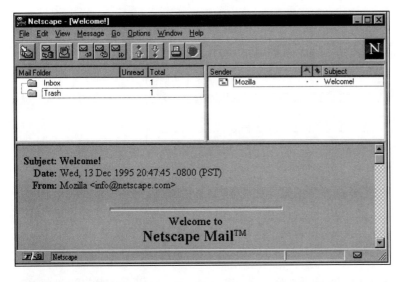

Figure 2.2 Use the Netscape e-mail client to send and receive e-mail.

You will find all the basic functionality here that you would expect to find in a typical e-mail client. Because the Netscape Mail client is integrated into Navigator, it gives you Web functionality, including support for hyperlinks. If someone sends you a Java applet as part of an e-mail message, the applet will run right in your mail client. Any MIME type for which your Navigator has an inline plug-in will even display in your mail message exactly as it would on a Web page.

The Navigator e-mail client conveniently displays the various mail folders in the top left window. The messages in a mail folder are shown in the top right window, and selected e-mail messages appear in a window near the bottom of your screen. The Navigator's e-mail client has an excellent message-sending interface. When you choose to send an e-mail message, the window shown in Figure 2.3 appears on your screen.

The window shown in Figure 2.3 is nearly identical to the new message windows in many other e-mail clients. Enter the following information to send an e-mail message:

- The e-mail address of the recipient
- The (optional) e-mail address of someone else who should receive the message
- A subject line explaining the topic of the message
- The e-mail message itself

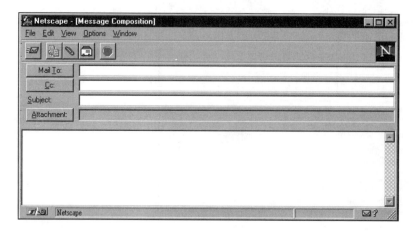

Figure 2.3 Enter the e-mail address of the recipient and then type the e-mail message.

Any URL addresses that you type in the e-mail message is automatically converted to a valid hyperlink when viewed by the recipient (provided the recipient is also using the Navigator e-mail client). This means that someone reading your e-mail in Navigator can launch a Web page, download a file using FTP or Gopher, or even access a newsgroup just by clicking a link in the e-mail message.

As with other e-mail clients, you can attach files so that Navigator encodes them using MIME or UUEncoding. First select the **Attachments** button from the window shown in Figure 2.3. This opens the Attachments window shown in Figure 2.4.

In the Attachments window you can see one of the Navigator e-mail client's features, the ability to attach URLs. It is much more convenient for someone reading your e-mail if you attach a URL rather than type it in the message. Someone receiving an e-mail message containing an attached URL does not need to launch the Navigator browser to view the URL. Instead, the recipient sees the contents of the URL displayed right in Navigator's e-mail client. Attach a URL document to your e-mail message by clicking on the **Attach Location (URL)** button, and then enter the desired URL location.

Anyone who receives an e-mail message from you that contains a URL attachment will see it displayed at the end of the e-mail message. Figure 2.5 illustrates a sample e-mail message with an attached URL.

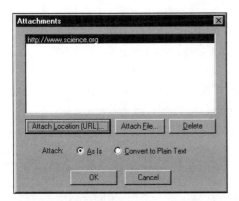

▰▰▰▰ **Figure 2.4** Choose the desired file or URL location to attach to your e-mail message.

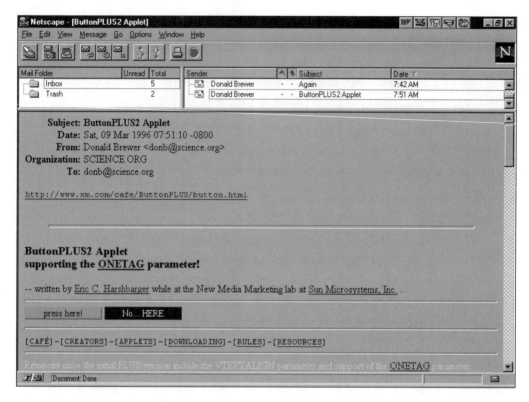

Figure 2.5 The attached URL is displayed in the e-mail client as part of the message.

The attached URL has all the Web functionality it would have if it were loaded in the Navigator browser window. This means that not only are the hyperlinks active, but also Java applets and MIME files will run in the e-mail client. Of course, you must have a plug-in installed that can handle the MIME type in order for the MIME content to be displayed correctly. This capability is truly an impressive feature of the Navigator Gold e-mail client.

You may have problems when you try to send a URL or file attachment to recipients who are not using the Navigator e-mail client. When they try to read a URL or file attachment with a conventional e-mail client, they will see either garbage or nothing at all in the e-mail message. It is Netscape's goal to create the best e-mail client available and thereby increase the number of people using it. When more people use the Navigator e-mail client, you'll begin to feel more comfortable sending URL and file attachments.

File Transfer Protocol Capability

Most Web developers are familiar with using a file transfer protocol (FTP) client to upload or download files from FTP servers. The Navigator browser now has the ability to function as an FTP client to send and receive files. This FTP capability is somewhat hidden in the browser environment, because its menu functions appear only when an FTP site has been contacted. You can't access the FTP capabilities with the **Window** menu selection as you do to launch the e-mail or news reader clients. The FTP capabilities become active only when you contact an FTP site by entering an FTP:// URL into the location field of the Navigator browser.

ftp://ftp.hostname/

When you contact an FTP server with the command shown, you are logged on as an anonymous user on that FTP server. You then have the ability to upload and download files on that FTP server, depending upon the current permissions for anonymous users. After you contact an FTP server, the **File|Upload File** menu selection appears as shown in Figure 2.6.

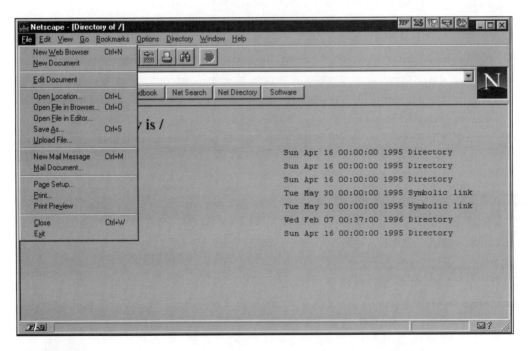

Figure 2.6 A new **Upload File** menu selection is created after an FTP server is contacted.

Choose the **Upload File** menu selection when you need to send a file from your local hard drive to the FTP server. Windows 95 users can upload files even more easily by first opening Windows Explorer and locating a file to upload, then dragging the file into the open FTP directory in the Navigator browser window. Navigator creates a pop-up window that asks you if you want to upload the file. If you answer "yes," the file is uploaded.

Rather than contacting an FTP server as an anonymous user, you can contact FTP servers with which you have a user account, using an FTP URL like the following:

ftp://username@ftp.hostname/

After you contact an FTP server in this fashion, a pop-up window will appear that allows you to enter your password. Figure 2.7 shows the Password Entry Dialog that appears in this circumstance.

After you enter the password, you can send or receive files as allowed by your current permissions. You can bypass your password entry in the pop-up window by including it in the FTP URL, as shown in the following example:

ftp://username:password@ftp.hostname/

Although Navigator gives you the ability to contact FTP servers with your username, it doesn't provide you with any way to close your account when you finish. This means that your FTP account will be closed by the FTP server with its built-in time-out function. Assuming your FTP account hasn't timed out, you can go to other FTP or other Web sites and still reconnect to the FTP server without reentering your password.

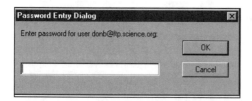

Figure 2.7 If you have a user ID other than anonymous, enter your password when contacting an FTP server.

Once you have logged onto an FTP site either anonymously or with a user account, you can navigate through the directories by clicking on the directory folders. When you've found a file you'd like to move from the FTP site to yours, double-click on it with your mouse to start the transfer process.

One of the main applications and an essential feature of the new Navigator Gold FTP client is to allow Web developers to upload Web documents to their HTTP server after they have edited them.

Navigator Gold Editor Environment

The Navigator Gold editor is a Web development tool that you will soon learn inside and out. Its capabilities free you from memorizing awkward HTML tag syntax and allow you to quickly insert and modify images, create or edit hyperlinks, and instantly modify text with simple point-and-click utilities. The Navigator Gold editor also allows you to write JavaScript code for both client and server JavaScript applications, and it will display them in different colors to differentiate the two types. When you run Navigator Gold, the first window that appears looks exactly like that of the Navigator browser, as shown in Figure 2.8.

At first glance Navigator Gold looks a lot like the regular Navigator, but the extra capabilities of Navigator Gold are provided through a separate window. The only difference in first appearance between the conventional Navigator browser and the Navigator Gold browser window is that Navigator Gold has an **Edit** button. Also, additional commands added to the File menu (see Figure 2.9) allow you to launch the editor.

These editor-related commands include the **Edit Document** and **Open File in Editor** menu options. Through these commands and the **Edit** button you can launch the editor capabilities of Navigator Gold.

Navigator Gold Editor Window

The easiest way to launch the editor window is to click on the **Edit** button found on the browser toolbar. When you do, Navigator Gold closes the browser window and launches the editor window. The document you were viewing in the browser window is then opened in the editor window. Before you can edit this document,

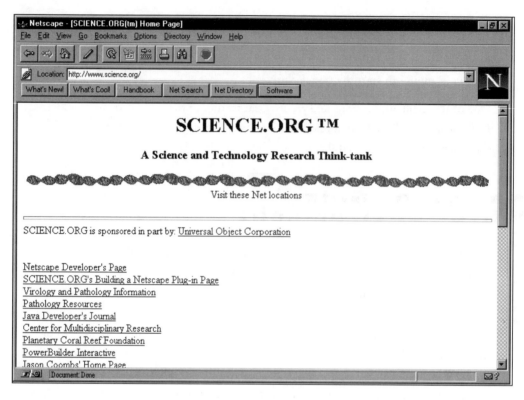

■■■■■ **Figure 2.8** The Netscape Navigator Gold browser window has an extra icon in the tool bar.

Navigator Gold opens a pop-up window, shown in Figure 2.10, that allows you to specify information about the document that will be edited.

The pop-up window allows you to choose to have the images associated with the Web document downloaded and determine how the hyperlinks should be handled. When you edit a document that is remotely located, you typically need to choose to have the images in the desired Web document downloaded onto your computer. The pop-up window also asks you either to maintain links or not to change the links. When you choose the **Adjust links to assist in remote publishing** option, Navigator Gold changes the *local links* into *remote links*. A local link is used in a Web document to refer to files that are located locally on the same computer system, while a remote link would be a URL address to a computer system somewhere else on the Internet. For example, if you wanted to edit Netscape's home page, many of the hyperlinks would be local links to files on its system and would look like the following:

Figure 2.9 Editor-related commands are added to the File menu.

file:///comprod/mirror/index.html

When the **Adjust links to assist in remote publishing** selection is chosen and you have Navigator Gold download Netscape's home page, this local file link would be changed into the following remote link:

http://www.netscape.com/comprod/mirror/index.html

As you can see, Navigator Gold recognizes the current URL address for the Web document that is about to be edited. Navigator Gold is smart about the way it handles URLs. When you move files between the server and your machine, the URLs are changed between local (relative) pathnames and absolute URLs.

When you don't choose the **Adjust links to assist in remote publishing** selection the local hyperlinks in a Web page are maintained as local links. This is preferable when you edit your own Web pages that will eventually be stored back on the server.

After you make the desired selections, you can choose either the **Save, Cancel,** or **Help** button as illustrated in Figure 2.10. When you select the **Save** button, the

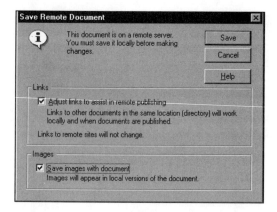

■■■■■■■ **Figure 2.10** Before editing a document, you choose to download images and retain current hyperlinks.

document you were viewing in the browser window will be loaded into the editor window after you save it with the desired filename. When you choose the **Cancel** button, you will go back to the browser window. Once you launch the Navigator Gold editor window it appears as shown in Figure 2.11.

If you are familiar with HTML code, you'll be happy to find out that there are no visible HTML tags in this development environment. Before Navigator Gold, when you created Web documents, you needed to describe every minute attribute of the document with the proper HTML tags. Navigator Gold does all the HTML work for you. The HTML tags still exist and can be seen if you choose **View|View Document Source**, as shown in Figure 2.12; they just aren't displayed in the editor.

The Navigator Gold editor writes HTML in the background while you create in the editor, allowing you to focus all your attention on the creation of your Web application. Notice that text and images appear in the editor window exactly as they would in the browser window. Creating Web pages using a visual development environment is the only way to modify a Web document and instantly know what it looks like in a browser. The JavaScript code is the one exception—Navigator Gold displays it as text instead of displaying the output generated by the JavaScript. This makes it possible to use Navigator Gold as your IDE for developing JavaScript applications.

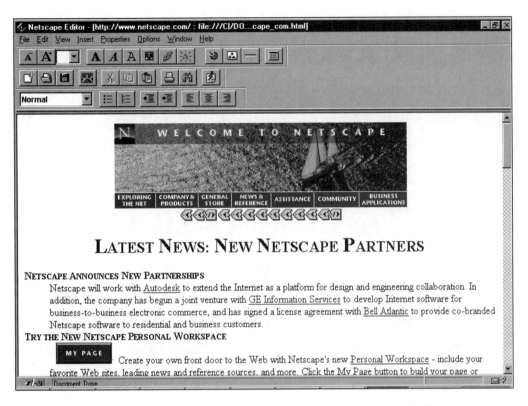

Figure 2.11 The Editor window is used to create and edit HTML pages.

Setting Editor Preferences

Before you begin to edit files with the Navigator Gold editor, configure the Options|Editor Preferences window. This preference window, shown in Figure 2.13, allows you to set defaults for creating and editing Web documents.

The **General** tab allows you to record your name as the author of the pages that are created and edited and to set other aspects of the editor's behavior such as designating the external HTML and image editors. The **Appearance** tab allows you to modify the color of the HTML elements in your Web page, such as hyperlinks and the background, when you select the **Use Custom Colors** option. Use the **Publish** tab to designate the link and image characteristics when saving remote documents, and to indicate a default publishing location.

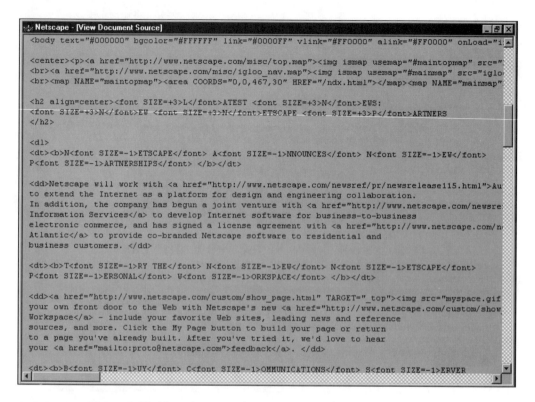

Figure 2.12 View document source to see the HTML tags.

Setting Document Properties

When you create a new document with the Navigator Gold editor, begin by defining the document properties. Select **Properties|Document** from the Navigator Gold menu to view the window that allows you to set the document properties. Switch between the three tabs to access the different properties: **General, Appearance,** and **Advanced.** Figure 2.14 displays how the window appears when you select the **General** tab.

In the input fields you can enter the basic information, such as the title and author, about the document being edited.

The **Appearance** tab adds simplicity to creating and developing Web documents. Now you don't have to remember the exact RGB value for the color you want for the background. Use the point–and–click interface to select a new background color. Figure 2.15 shows the Document Properties window that appears when you select the **Appearance** tab.

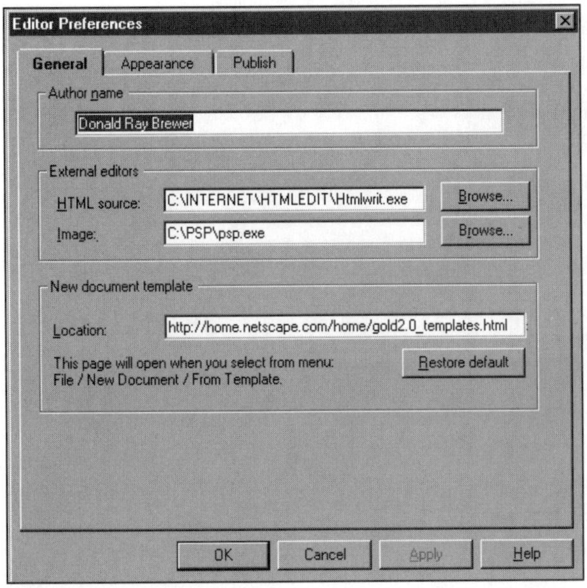

Figure 2.13 Editor preferences window.

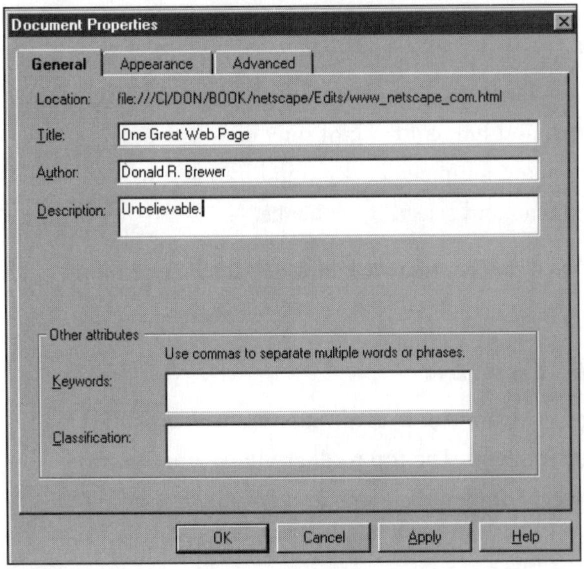

Figure 2.14 General document information entry fields.

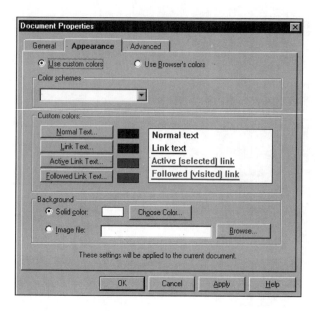

■■■■■■■ **Figure 2.15** Set the appearance characteristics in the Properties window.

This window allows you to change the conventional coloring schemes of Web documents. Hyperlinks no longer must appear as blue text, but they can appear in any color you desire. With the **Appearance** tab all color characteristics of the document being edited can instantly be changed. Check the **Use Custom Colors** radio button to select background, foreground, text, and link colors. Not only can you easily add colors to a document, but you can add an image background by selecting **Background|Image File** from the file menu and selecting an image.

Use the **Advanced** tab to define any Netscape system variables or user variables for the Web document you create.

Using the WYSIWYG Toolbar

The Netscape Navigator Gold editing environment is made easy with three WYSIWYG (what-you-see-is-what-you-get) toolbars. The top toolbar allows modification of the many properties of the Web page. Some of the icons in the toolbar give you great control over text formatting, allowing you to change text size, font, and color. Other toolbar icons let you insert or modify links and images.

To use the toolbar to modify text parameters, select the text you'd like to modify then choose the desired icon from the toolbar. You will see a complete set of file-handling icons. Choose to cut and paste, save, open new files, and find text in the file. For quick access to Web publishers, click the Web resources icon. Table 2.1 shows all the icons that appear in the toolbars in the editor window, along with a description of what each one does.

■■■■■■■ **Table 2.1** Navigator Gold Editor Toolbar Icons

Icon	Description
A⁻	Decreases relative font size of highlighted text
A⁺	Increases relative font size of highlighted text
+0 ▼	Displays or selects font size
A	Makes highlighted text bold
A	Makes highlighted text italic
A	Converts highlighted text to fixed width
▦	Selects font color of highlighted text
⌀	Makes a new link or modifies an existing link
⚡A	Removes all styles of highlighted text

Icon	Description
	Inserts a target in a Web page
	Inserts a new image
	Inserts a horizontal line
	Used to define object properties of the document
	Launches new editor window to create new document
	Opens new file to edit
	Saves file currently being edited
	Launches new browser window containing document currently being edited
	Cuts highlighted text
	Copies highlighted text
	Pastes highlighted text

▮▮▮▮ **Table 2.1** Continued

Icon	Description
	Prints current document
	Finds specific text in file being edited
	Used to publish documents after they have been edited or created
	Creates bullet point list
	Creates numbered list
	Decreases the indent of the highlighted text
	Increases the indent of the highlighted text
	Left aligns highlighted text
	Center aligns highlighted text
	Right aligns highlighted text

You may find the tools in the Navigator Gold editor familiar because they are very similar to the formatting tools in most word processing programs. Whether you're an experienced HTML guru or a beginner at building Web pages, you'll find Navigator Gold to be an excellent resource.

Creating Hyperlinks

Hyperlinks are among the key elements that have made the Web such an interactive and exciting information medium. The hyperlink can be an anchor to a remote document, a local document, or a target to a specific location in the current document. Here is an example of the conventional HTML code used to create a hyperlink to a remote document.

```
<A HREF="http://www.cnet.com/home.html">COMPUTER INDUSTRY</A>
```

The <A> tag is known as the anchor tag, and HREF is an attribute used to identify the URL address. When this simple HTML example is included in a Web document, the text COMPUTER INDUSTRY appears blue and underlined and is a hyperlink to ClNet's home page. A hyperlink can also be made to open a file available on your local server, as shown in the following example.

```
<A HREF="/images/shuttle.html">NASA MANNED VEHICLES</A>
```

The third type of hyperlink is known as an *internal anchor* within the current document. This type of hyperlink allows people navigating through your page to go directly to a certain location, referred to as a target, within your document. There are several steps to creating this type of anchor using Navigator Gold, as follows:

1. Place the cursor in the desired location for the target and choose the **Insert|Target** menu selection, or select the Target icon on the toolbar.

2. Enter the name of the target in the Target Properties window that is opened, and choose **OK.** The target should then appear in your Web document. In this example the target was named *Business Info.*

3. Place the cursor at the desired location for the anchor to the target. Choose the **Insert|Link** menu selection. This launches the Create Link window shown in Figure 2.16. Enter in the text that you want to appear for the link, and then select a named target. After you select **OK** the internal anchor to the target will be created.

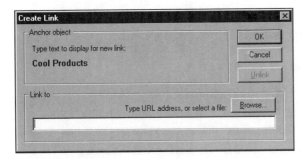

██████ **Figure 2.16** Dialog window used to create a new hyperlink.

████

When you view the HTML source code for this example, the Business Info target would appear as shown. <A NAME="Business Info">

████

Here is the HTML source code for the internal anchor produced in this example.

████

<A HREF="www.example.com#Business Info">

████

When creating a link, you can use two methods to determine what text will appear on the Web page as the hyperlink. Highlighting the text on the Web page before choosing **Insert|Link** from the Navigator menu will make the text appear automatically in the Properties window. Choosing **Insert|Link** from the Navigator menu without highlighting text allows you to enter text into the Properties window.

Navigator Gold also gives you the ability to edit existing hyperlinks. Highlight the link you would like to edit and choose **Properties|Link** from the Navigator menu. When the Properties window appears, you may choose to remove the link, or change the link to a different document.

Navigator Gold also features the ability to create links from pages currently loaded in the browser window. In the Navigator Gold browser window there is a link icon next to the URL location input field. To create a link to a Web page currently loaded in the browser window, simply drag the link icon to the editor window. The link is instantly created in the location that you dropped the link icon.

Using an Image as a Hyperlink

Images can be hyperlinks, too. Instead of clicking on boring text, you can allow visitors to your Web site to click on an image to activate a hyperlink. Click the **Make Link** button in the toolbar to launch the Properties dialog box. One of the differences between creating a link with an image rather than text is that the image filename instead of text is entered in the link dialog. When an image is selected and the **Make Link** button is clicked, the image filename will appear automatically.

When you modify an existing link, you must first select the desired image and click the **Make Link** button, or choose the **Properties|Link** menu selection. The Properties dialog box is launched, allowing you to make modifications.

Creating and Editing Images

On the Web the visual appearance of a page is often what makes it appealing to users visiting your site. Before Navigator Gold, when you wanted to add an image to your Web page, it was necessary to add the <IMG> tag to your Web page source file. The following shows a sample <IMG> tag.

```
<IMG SCR="earth.gif" ALIGN=TOP>
```

For those writing the <IMG> tag by hand, it was tough to know just how the Web page would look until they loaded the page into a Web browser. The Navigator Gold editor not only displays the image, but it also provides a way for you to add or modify images on a Web page. For you to add a new image to a Web page, you may either click on the **Image** button or choose **Insert|Image**. The window shown in Figure 2.17 then appears, allowing you to insert an image.

After you launch this window, it is a simple process to select the desired image file from the appropriate directory. This window also allows you to specify how text will be placed around your image. Text can be aligned with the top, middle, or baseline of the image. When you're done, click the **OK** button to place the image in the Web page.

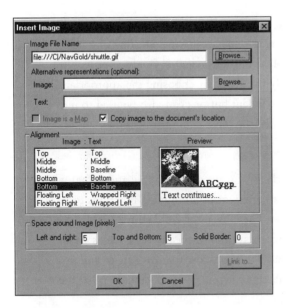

▰▰▰▰ **Figure 2.17** Dialog window to insert images on a Web page.

When you create hyperlinks, it is important to know the difference between a *relative link* and an *absolute link*. A relative link involves a hyperlink to a file that is located on the same machine as the Web page. It is called a relative link because it is relative to the location of the Web page. When the page to which you are linking is located on the same machine as the Web page you are editing, you should use a relative link.

An absolute link is a hyperlink that indicates the complete location of a page using a full URL. An absolute link URL includes the protocol prefix (such as http), the server name or IP address, and the full path to the file to which you are linking. Use the absolute link when linking to documents and objects located on another machine or somewhere else out on the Internet.

Once you have an image on a Web page, you can also position it to the left, right, or center part of the page by first selecting the image and then clicking on one of the buttons on the paragraph layout toolbar in the Navigator Gold editor window. You can center, left justify, or right justify the image by choosing the appropriate button. The **Increase Indent** and **Decrease Indent** buttons can also be used to move the image to intermediate positions between the three main justifications.

Creating JavaScript Code

JavaScript is one of the cornerstones of the new wave of Web applications that is changing the Internet, because it allows a variety of programming functions to be executed on both the client and the server. The Navigator Gold editor enables you to write JavaScript code in your Web documents and to specify the code as either client or server JavaScript. Chapters 4 and 5 explain how to create client and server applications in JavaScript. To write JavaScript code in a Web document using the Navigator Gold editor, do the following:

1. Start the Navigator Gold editor.
2. Enter the JavaScript code, leaving off the <SERVER> or <SCRIPT> tag. They are added automatically by Navigator Gold in step 5.
3. Highlight the JavaScript text by dragging across it with the mouse while holding down the mouse button.
4. Select **Properties|Character** from the Navigator Gold menu.
5. Select either **JavaScript (Server)** or **JavaScript (Client)** from the options in the menu.

When you choose the **JavaScript (Client)** menu option, the selected code will reappear colored red, and when you choose the **JavaScript (Server)**, the selected code will reappear colored blue in the editor window. Although JavaScript is visible in the Navigator Gold editor window, it will not appear in the Navigator browser. This is one of the few exceptions to the WYSIWYG feature of the Navigator Gold editor environment.

The Navigator Gold editor environment automatically places the appropriate HTML tag (either <SCRIPT> or <SERVER>) around the JavaScript code as it does with all the other document properties such as images and hyperlinks (Figure 2.18). Navigator Gold is also designed not to permit incorrect embedding, such as placing client JavaScript within server JavaScript.

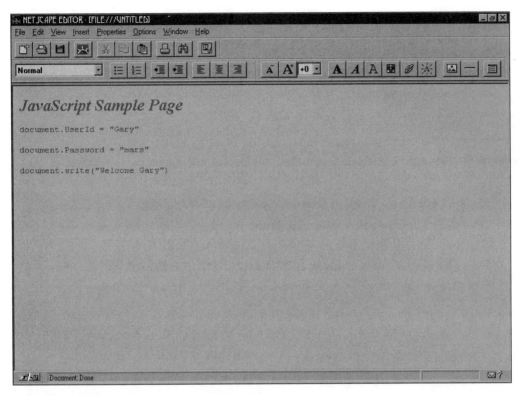

Figure 2.18 Insert JavaScript client and server code in Navigator Gold.

Right Click Wonders

The Navigator Gold editor features a quick and simple tool to modify objects in the editor window. When you want to modify objects in a Web document, position your mouse pointer over the object, such as a hyperlink or image, and click the right mouse button. This opens a pop-up menu within the editor that allows you to immediately access or edit the features of the object. The pop-up that appears when you right-click on an image is illustrated in Figure 2.19.

In this example, the image is also a hyperlink. Clicking on the image with the right mouse button reveals the ability to both modify the link and launch another browser window to verify the link. This right click edit capability is a very handy method to quickly edit the properties of objects in your Web page source files.

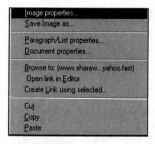

Publishing Document After Editing

Once you're satisfied with your newly created Web page, you'll want to see it on the Net. If you already have a Web publishing service, remember that you can use the FTP upload capabilities of Navigator Gold to send your file to the server. There's no need to deal with other FTP programs because everything you need is in one place.

Publish your Web page by selecting the **File|Publish** menu selection or clicking on the publish icon. The File|Publish window that appears allows you to designate the FTP server your documents will reside on, along with your username and password. Click **OK** and your edited documents will instantly be published on that FTP site.

External Editors

The Navigator Gold editor is an impressive and useful tool, but it does lack the ability to add or modify the actual HTML source code. Depending on your preference, this is either a feature or a bug. When you need to add or modify forms or frames, for example, you will need to load the file into a text editor to modify the actual HTML source code because the Navigator Gold editor doesn't provide a visual editor for these things. You will also need to use a text editor to add client-side JavaScript into HTML tags, as in the case of an HTML form with JavaScript event processing.

Navigator Gold allows you to designate an external HTML and image editor. Click on **Options|Editor Preferences** to open the Editor Preferences window. Select the **General** tab, and enter the filename and directory location of the external editors you want to use to edit the HTML source code and images.

If you are running Windows, you have a perfectly good HTML editor called Notepad, which you can normally find in your accessories folder. To activate your external HTML editor, choose the **View|Edit Document Source** menu selection. The external HTML editor will be launched with the desired document loaded. Make your desired modifications and save the document file. When you return to Navigator Gold, it will recognize that the document being viewed has been changed, and will ask if you want the document reloaded.

This external editor feature allows you to modify the HTML source code of your documents to include features and capabilities not presently supported in Navigator Gold.

Inserting HTML Tags

You may have noticed the unusual HTML tags that appeared under the Welcome to Netscaspe sailboat image in Figure 2.11. When the Navigator Gold editor encounters HTML source code that it does not support, such as forms, it produces these HTML tag icons. Each icon represents a line of HTML source code. When you move your mouse over an HTML tag the actual HTML source code is illustrated in the bottom left-hand corner of the editor window.

Choose the **Insert|HTML Tag** menu selection to add features such as forms and frames. When you choose this selection a window appears to allow you to enter a line of HTML source code for the feature to be added. Continue inserting HTML tags until you have entered every line of source code for the feature being added.

Adding Forms

As a LiveWire application developer, you will certainly want to create forms. You can add forms using either the HTML tag feature built into Navigator Gold, or the HTML external editor.

Adding forms to the document you've created in Navigator Gold is easy. First, make sure you've saved your Navigator Gold file. Once you're certain it has been saved, start your external HTML editor by choosing the **View|Edit Document Source** menu selection and begin by finding the <BODY> tag. If you have placed any text on your Web page, Navigator Gold will have created a <BODY> tag. Your form must be added after this tag; you can't add forms into the HEAD section of the Web page.

Start your form with the <FORM> tag, following it with all the form elements and text you need to create your input form. You can also include JavaScript in your form by adding it manually along with your form elements.

Figure 2.20 shows an example of a Web page that was downloaded into Navigator Gold and edited. You can see that this file includes a form between the <FORM> and </FORM> tags.

Even though Navigator Gold version 2.0 doesn't support the display and creation of forms in the editor window, it supports an external HTML editor and HTML tag feature. Using one of these methods you can create and edit the forms in your Web documents.

■■■■■■■■ **Figure 2.20** Sample HTML form syntax in a Web page source file.

```
<HTML>
<HEAD>
   <TITLE>Personal Information</TITLE>
   <meta name="GENERATOR" content="Mozilla/2.0GoldB1 (Win32)">
</HEAD>
<BODY bgcolor="#FFFFFF">


<H1>Personal Information</H1>


<FORM METHOD="Post" ACTION="http://science.org/bogus.html">
<PRE>     First Name:
<input TYPE="text" NAME="FirstName"
       SIZE="12" MAXLENGTH="35"></input>
 Last Name:
<input TYPE="text" NAME="LastName"SIZE="12" MAXLENGTH="35"></input>
 MI:
<input TYPE="text" NAME="MiddleInit" SIZE="2" MAXLENGTH="2"></input>


E-Mail Address:...
<input TYPE="text" NAME="EMail"
       SIZE="50" MAXLENGTH="50"></input>


Your Home Page:...
```

```
<input TYPE="text" NAME="HomePage"
        SIZE="55" MAXLENGTH="80"></input>


</PRE>
<P>
<input TYPE="submit" VALUE="Add to list"></input>
<input TYPE="reset" VALUE="Clear form"></input>
</P>
</FORM>
</BODY>
</HTML>
```

Adding Frames

Figure 2.21 shows an example of creating frames in an HTML file. You can see the <FRAME> tags included that specify which HTML files will be loaded into each frame window. Start your external HTML editor or use the HTML tag feature to

Figure 2.21 Sample HTML frame syntax in a Web page source file.

```
<HTML>
<HEAD>
<TITLE>Welcome to My Adventure</TITLE>
</HEAD>
<FRAMESET COLS=27%,73% > <FRAME SRC="toc.html">
<FRAME SRC="info.html" NAME="mainframe">
<NOFRAMES>
<H1>Welcome to my page!</H1>
Blah blah blah
</HTML>
```

add frames to your Web documents. When adding frames, you need to be aware of these three things: (1) Begin with a <FRAMESET> tag. This defines how many frames you will have in your window and how they are sized. (2) Define a file or image to open in each frame. (3) Include a <NOFRAMES> tag for the non-frames-enabled browsers that may access your page.

Once again, the Navigator Gold version 2.0 does not support visual frames design and layout, but you can use an external HTML editor to add the frame syntax manually.

Adding JavaScript into Form Elements and Tags

Because it isn't possible to edit form elements in Navigator Gold version 2.0, you will have to add JavaScript to form elements manually. You may also want to add JavaScript to some of the other HTML tags. Figure 2.22 shows a sample of JavaScript embedded in HTML tags, like the <BODY> tag and the <A> tag, and form elements like the button.

■■■■■■ **Figure 2.22** Sample client JavaScript embedded within HTML tags.

```
<HTML>
<HEAD>
<TITLE>Ego Checker</TITLE>
<SCRIPT>
function check(){
if (confirm("Everything OK?"))
}
</SCRIPT>
</HEAD>
<BODY BGCOLOR="#FFFFFF" onUnload="check()">

<A HREF="http://www.ego.org/" onMouseOver="window.status='Head to Oz';
return TRUE">We're off to see the wizard!</A><BR>
```

```
<FORM NAME="MyTest">
<input TYPE="button" VALUE="OK" NAME="TestButton" onClick="check()">
</FORM>
</BODY>
</HTML>
```

▬▬▬▬

Because Navigator Gold can add <SERVER> tags for you when you write server-side JavaScript, you don't need to use an external text editor to embed server JavaScript in your Web page. Use only the external HTML editor to add client-side JavaScript into your Web page source file.

Navigator Gold revolutionizes the generation and creation of Web source files. At the same time, the editor capabilities give you an environment to generate the JavaScript code that directs the execution of specific tasks in the server and client environments. Navigator Gold plays an important role in the LiveWire development architecture, acting as both an HTML editor and the core of the LiveWire IDE for creating Web applications.

3

THE

LIVEWIRE TOOL SET

Netscape has created the ultimate Web authoring and client/server application development tool set called LiveWire. This suite of tools is made up of several Netscape products that allow you to create Web pages, write client/server JavaScript applications, and manage all the files in a Web application on either your Internet or your intranet site.

LiveWire has something for everyone. Most importantly, it puts the power of Web publishing in the hands of the people who really need it. Companies, both large and small, have found that depending on a select group of people for all their computer needs is troublesome. This team usually becomes backlogged with work and sometimes loses touch with the users' actual needs. Recent changes in business computing have helped to change the model of centralized computer resource management, placing computer processing ability on the desktop and computer management responsibility with the individual user. This is what LiveWire does for Web publishing. It's no longer necessary to bring in the webmaster every time you want to change your company or departmental Web page. LiveWire makes creating powerful Web applications simple for anyone.

The LiveWire product contains a number of useful software tools. *Site Manager* is an integrated Web site management utility and launching point for the editing of Web page source files. The *Build WEB* utility will assemble all the pages in a Web application into a single .WEB source file that LiveWire understands. *Application Manager* is a Web-based tool for managing and debugging the Web applications registered with your LiveWire server. These three LiveWire tools and the Netscape server set are covered in this chapter.

Site Manager

Site Manager is a stand-alone program that can manage every piece and every page of your Web site. Some of the Web site management features provided by Site Manager include a link manager, which simplifies hyperlink management and enables invalid link detection, and a built-in set of automated Gurus, for generating typical Web sites. The Site Manager Gurus will immediately create the framework of a new Web site for you. After a Guru has created a framework for your site, all you have to do is customize the files created by the Guru and deploy your new Web site.

The Site Manager display is tab based and divided in half vertically. The left half contains a **Folders** tab with a tree control that displays files and directories present in the selected file system. The right half contains an **Object Properties** tab that displays properties associated with the item currently selected in the left half of the Site Manager. Figure 3.1 shows the standard Site Manager window.

Before you get started with Site Manager, take a moment to configure the default editor and browser to use when editing or viewing Web page source files. Choose **Options|Editor Location** from the Site Manager menu. Figure 3.2 shows the pop-up that appears, allowing you to enter the path for the editor to use. If you wish to use Navigator Gold as the editor for your Web page source files, enter the full path to the Navigator Gold executable followed by **-edit** as the single parameter. The -edit parameter tells Navigator Gold to start up in edit mode instead of browse mode.

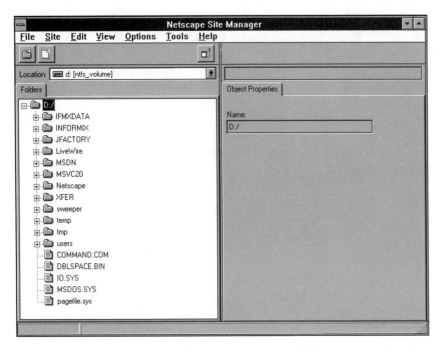

Figure 3.1 Site Manager provides a two-column, tab-based user interface.

Choose **Options|Browser Location** from the Site Manager menu to configure the default Web browser to use when viewing pages in your Web site. You may wish to use the regular Navigator browser instead of Navigator Gold, though either one will work. If compatibility with other browsers is important to you, you could even choose a browser other than Navigator to make it easier to test your Web pages in a browser other than Netscape's.

When you start Site Manager for the first time, no Web sites are under management. The first step in using the Site Manager is to begin managing a Web site through the process known as bringing a site under management. There are two ways to bring a site under management: either create a new site or begin managing an existing one. These two options are discussed next.

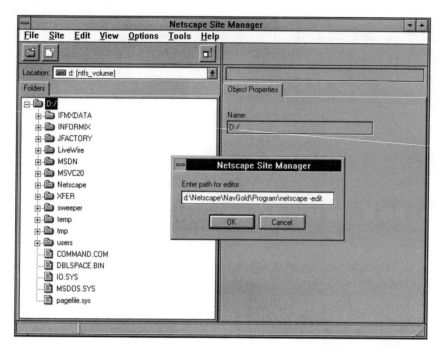

Figure 3.2 Configure Site Manager to edit Web page source files with Navigator Gold.

Bringing a Web Site Under Management

To create and manage a Web site from scratch, begin by selecting **Site|New Site** from the Site Manager menu. The Guru Template window shown in Figure 3.3 appears, allowing you to select a directory for the new site. The directory you choose in this step can be on any file system, even on a network drive. Note that the directory you choose must already exist, and it should be empty.

Click on the **Next** button after selecting a directory and then choose the kind of site you wish to create by selecting one of the radio buttons shown in Figure 3.4. Then select, from subsequent screens, the exact style of Web site that you want the Guru to create for you. Your options, grouped according to the four kinds of sites listed in Figure 3.4, are shown in Table 3.1.

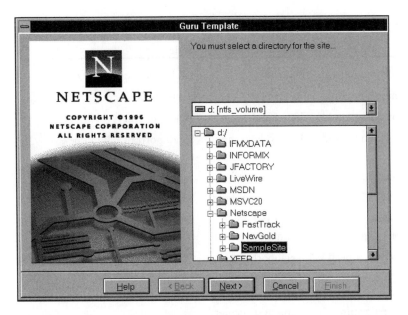

Figure 3.3 Choose a directory in which to create a new site.

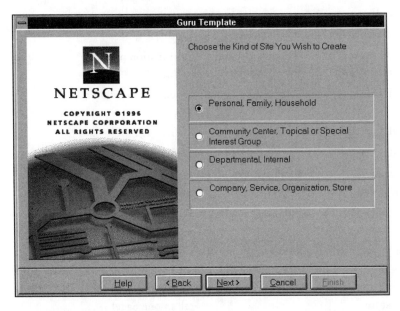

Figure 3.4 Select the kind of Web content to be created at the new site.

■■■■■■ **Table 3.1** List of Possible Guru Template Web Site Configurations

Kind of Site	Sub-kind	Style
Personal, family, household	Individual	All in one page
Personal, family, household	Individual	Professional
Personal, family, household	Individual	Wild and crazy
Personal, family, household	Family, household	Small portrait (all in one page)
Personal, family, household	Family, household	Family
Personal, family, household	Family, household	Shared household
Community center, topical or special interest group	Neighborhood, community center	Essential services (all in one page)
Community center, topical or special interest group	Neighborhood, community center	Community center
Community center, topical or special interest group	Neighborhood, community center	Virtual community
Community center, topical or special interest group	Topical or special interest group	Focused interest group (all in one page)
Community center, topical or special interest group	Topical or special interest group	Event production group
Community center, topical or special interest group	Topical or special interest group	Information provider
Departmental, internal		Essential information (all in one page)
Departmental, internal		Office organizer
Departmental, internal		Departmental site
Company, service, organization, store	Products	Product information (all in one page)
Company, service, organization, store	Products	Product centered
Company, service, organization, store	Products	Company centered
Company, service, organization, store	Sales	General information (all in one page)
Company, service, organization, store	Sales	Catalogs

◼◼◼◼◼ **Table 3.1** Continued

Kind of Site	Sub-kind	Style
Company, service, organization, store	Sales	Storefront
Company, service, organization, store	Services	Basic service information (all in one page)
Company, service, organization, store	Services	Offices
Company, service, organization, store	Services	Company or organization

Each of the possible Guru Template Web site configurations provides a different ready-made Web site. Experiment with a few configurations to see what each one has to offer. Setting up a new site with the help of a Guru template gives you a good starting point to which you can add Java applets, JavaScript code, and inline plug-in content. In most of the site configurations you'll find a considerable number of Web pages, all linked for you by the Guru.

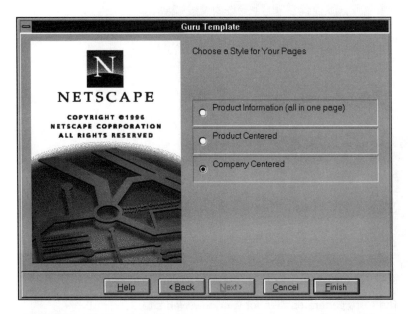

◼◼◼◼◼ **Figure 3.5** Choose a style for the pages of your Web site.

Choose a style for your new Web site when prompted to do so. Figure 3.5 shows a sample style selection found in the *Company, Service, Organization, Store* style group.

After selecting a style, click on the **Finish** button, and the Guru will generate all the files for your Web site and place them in the directory you chose for the new site (see Figure 3.6).

In addition to creating the files for your new Web site, the Guru automatically places the new site under management in the Site Manager. When a site is under management, its files are displayed in Site Manager with a small red triangle in the lower left corner. Figure 3.7 shows a Guru-generated Web site ready to be managed with Site Manager. Notice in Figure 3.7 that Site Manager now shows additional tabs in both the left and right halves of the display. We'll explore the functionality provided by the link-management tabs in the next section.

Use the **Site Properties** tab, located in the right half of the Site Manager, to set things like the output filename for the site's .WEB file and the default deployment area. To modify any file in the new site just click on the file and choose **Edit** from the File menu. Likewise, you can choose **File|Browse** to view one of the files in your

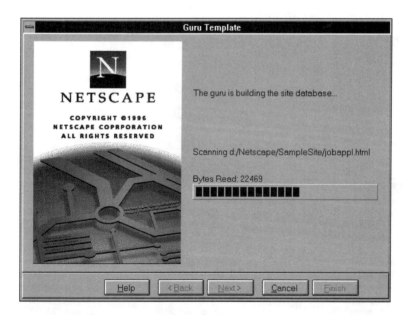

■■■■■■■■ **Figure 3.6** The Guru generates files for your new Web site.

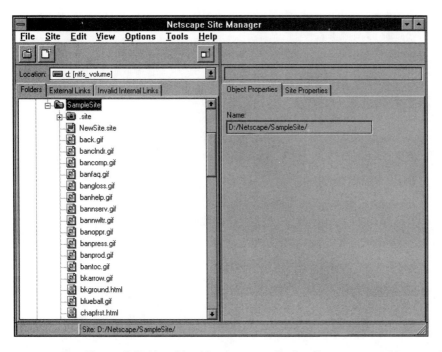

Figure 3.7 Use Site Manager to edit the files generated by your Guru.

Web browser. If you would rather see the <TITLE> of each Web page displayed in the Site Manager instead of the HTML filenames, choose **View|By Document Titles**, and Site Manager will display titles instead of filenames.

If you already have a Web site that you would like to bring under management, find and select the directory that contains unmanaged Web site files and choose **Site|Manage** from the Site Manager menu. Site Manager asks you to confirm the manage request before bringing the Web site under management. For example, if you choose to manage the FastTrack server document root directory with Site Manager, your new document root directory will look something like Figure 3.8 after Site Manager brings it under management.

If your existing Web site is already being served through your HTTP server, bringing the site under management does not disrupt the normal operation of your Web site. However, managed Web sites are typically not served by the HTTP server in addition to being served by LiveWire. If you wish to migrate an existing Web site

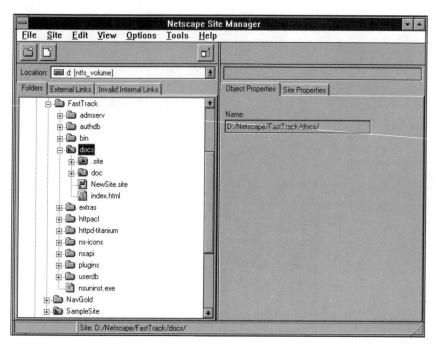

Figure 3.8 Existing Web sites can be brought under management with Site Manager.

from your HTTP server to LiveWire, copy all the files in your site to a new directory outside the HTTP server document root before bringing the site under management. Then, follow the instructions found later in this chapter to build the .WEB file and deploy the site, under its original name, using LiveWire.

Link Management

One of the most time-consuming tasks in managing a Web site is ensuring that all of your hyperlinks point to valid Web pages. As your site becomes increasingly complex, and as other sites to which your site links undergo change, it is common for internal and external links to become invalid. Detecting broken links and repairing them is critical to the quality of your Web site, but can lead to a great deal of maintenance. Site Manager simplifies link management by automatically testing all the links in your Web site and providing a simple interface that allows you to fix any problems it detects.

Viewing Links

One nice feature of the Site Manager is its ability to view all the links in each file of your application. This keeps you from having to go through all the pages by hand looking for every link. Even using Navigator Gold, you would find this chore tedious. For you to view links, your site must be under management by the Site Manager. Figure 3.9 shows the Netscape Site Manager with the **Folder** tab selected in the left window. In this window, select a folder containing an application for which you would like to view the links. Once the application is selected, choose **Site|Check External Links** from the Site Manager menu.

Once Site Manager has completed the task of checking the external links, double-click on the folder icon to expand the folder. An expanded folder displays all the files in your application as shown in Figure 3.9. Also notice that expanded folders have a minus sign [–] in the box to the left of the folder where unexpanded folders have a plus [+].

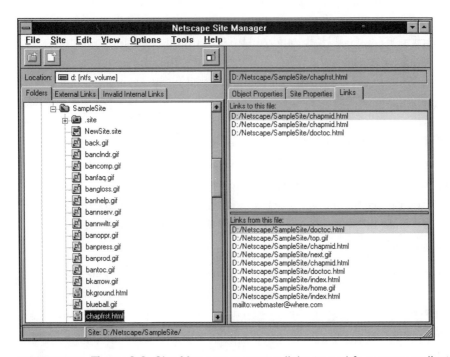

Figure 3.9 Site Manager manages links to and from your application Web source files.

Select one of the HTML files (Web source files) in your application. None of the other file types are likely to have valid links. Referring once again to Figure 3.9, notice that the two windows on the right contain link information. Make certain that the **Link** tab is selected above these windows. The upper-right window contains information about links within your application to the selected HTML file. It would be nice, but is currently not possible, to view links to your application from external sources. If possible, maintain a manual list of any external sites you know that link to your application. This list is important when you change your application in such a way that their links become invalid. You will want to notify those linking to your page that changes have been made and give them the new URL to point to. When managing many lists, you may want to use a Listserver program to maintain e-mail lists of webmasters maintaining links to your site so that you can quickly send e-mail to an entire list of webmasters simultaneously.

In the lower-right Site Manager window the links from the selected Web source file appear. This list includes links to other Web pages as well as other network protocols, such as FTP:, GOPHER:, and MAILTO:. Although it isn't possible for the Site Manager to check the validity of these links, they are still listed for completeness. You can see the MAILTO: resource listed in the example in Figure 3.9.

Fixing Invalid Links

Site Manager can do more than view and list the links in your application. As a true management tool, it offers the ability to correct links that are no longer valid. In Figure 3.9 you can see that in the left window there are three tabs. Click the **Invalid External Links** tab to display a complete list of links Site Manager found to be invalid (Figure 3.10).

Clicking on a link from the list of invalid links will bring up the **Modify Link** dialog (shown in Figure 3.10), allowing you to correct the link. Making this change here will correct all your Web source files without the use of Navigator Gold. This automatic link maintenance can save many long and frustrating hours of link management.

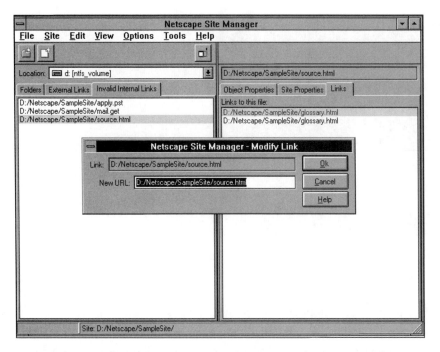

Figure 3.10 Correct invalid links quickly and easily in Site Manager.

Build WEB Utility

The LiveWire Site Manager has a feature that is sometimes referred to as the *LiveWire compiler*. This feature has an unfortunately confusing name. LiveWire "compiles" all the resources for your Web application into a special .WEB file. Programmers normally use programs known as compiles to transform their source code into an executable binary format, but this is not what the LiveWire utility does. Instead, it is the menu selection used to start the compiler application, so we will refer to the LiveWire compiler as the *Build WEB* utility.

Use the Build WEB utility when you are ready to prepare your Web application for final production release. In the Site Manager window (as shown in Figure 3.9) select a folder containing the Web application you would like prepared by the Build WEB utility, then choose **Site|Build WEB** from the LiveWire menu to start the Build WEB utility. Build WEB lets you watch its progress as it continually updates the Netscape Site Manager dialog that appears on your screen (Figure 3.11).

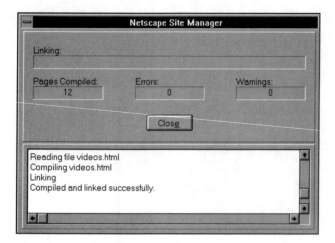

■■■■ **Figure 3.11** Build WEB utility displays its progress when preparing your Web application.

The Build WEB utility checks all the JavaScript, whether it is embedded in Web source files or saved in .JS files. Any JavaScript syntax errors are reported, and an internal link management web is created. All Web pages that link to one another in your application are validated.

Two files are created by the Build WEB utility: a .WEB file and a .SITE file. The .WEB file contains your complete application, ready for on-line production by the LiveWire Application Manager. The .SITE file is created whenever a new Web application is created in Site Manager. The .SITE file contains the internal link management information. Both .WEB and .SITE files must exist in your application's directory before your application can be brought on-line with the Application Manager.

If an error occurs while you are building your Web application, the error will be reported in the status window of the dialog shown in Figure 3.11. Scroll through all the status messages using the scroll bar on the right to view the entire build process.

Command-Line Build WEB Utility

For simple management of your Web site, nothing beats the graphic interface of the LiveWire Site Manager. However, there are times when it may be important to have access to some of these utilities from the command line. One important utility available from the command line is the Build WEB utility. Running Build WEB from the command line offers you an increased number of options, like creating batch files to create your Web applications. The video example that comes with LiveWire uses a batch file. You can find **build.bat** in the directory containing your video example. This batch file contains the command to start the command-line Build Web utility, command-line parameters, as shown later in this section, and the names of all the files in the application.

The command-line version of Build WEB performs all the same tasks as the visual interface. It assembles all your Web application resources into a single .WEB file and creates a .SITE file with the application's link management information.

Using the command-line Build WEB utility you can also create a CGI program that will allow you to run Build WEB remotely from a Web browser. You already have remote access to the LiveWire Application Manager via a Web client. Remote access to Build WEB would give you much greater control over your site remotely.

Running Build WEB from the Command Line

Before running Build WEB from the command line, you must make sure your path is correctly set to the LiveWire directory containing the LiveWire executable programs. You can find these executables in **\bin,** a subdirectory of **\livewire.** (Replace the backslash [\] with the forward slash [/] when configuring Solaris versions of LiveWire.)

```
C:\livewire\bin
```

The command-line executable program is called **lwcomp.exe.** The name is easily remembered as LiveWire compiler, but remember that the LiveWire compiler does not truly compile your application. Rather, it assembles your application resources and prepares them for production release by the LiveWire Application Manager. The following is the command-line syntax for **lwcomp.exe.**

```
lwcomp    -parameters    List of file to include
```

Customize the way the command-line Build Web utility prepares your Web application by including one or several of the parameters shown in the following list.

When adding these parameters after the **lwcomp** executable, be sure to precede them with a dash as shown.

- -o output.web (specifies the name of your Web application file)
- -v (tells the Build WEB utility to print status information as it prepares your Web application)
- -c (checks syntax, but doesn't create the .WEB file)
- -? (lwcomp help)
- -d (displays JavaScript contents)

Following the parameter list you *must* list files to include in your application. The command-line Build WEB utility is powerful, but not psychic. The list of files should include a Web source file, graphic files, and JavaScript files.

Here is an example showing the video sample's **build.bat** file. The text following the command-line example is the output of lwcomp when it is used with the -v (verbose) parameter.

Figure 3.12 shows how each of the Web source files is read and compiled into a final .WEB file. Your Web application is now ready to launch in the LiveWire Application Manager.

Figure 3.12 Output of the **lwcomp.exe** program when it is used with the verbose parameter.

```
lwcomp -v -o video.web start.html home.html address.html rentals.html
customer.html add.html remove.html videos.html rent.html client.html
status.html return.html

D:\LiveWire\samples\video>lwcomp -v -o video.web start.html home.html
address.html rentals.html customer.html add.html remove.html
videos.html rent.html client.html status.html return.html

Reading file start.html

Compiling file start.html

Reading file home.html

Compiling file home.html

Reading file address.html

Compiling file address.html

Reading file rentals.html

Compiling file rentals.html
```

```
Reading file customer.html
Compiling file customer.html
Reading file add.html
Compiling file add.html
Reading file remove.html
Compiling file remove.html
Reading file videos.html
Compiling file videos.html
Reading file rent.html
Compiling file rent.html
Reading file client.html
Compiling file client.html
Reading file status.html
Compiling file status.html
Reading file return.html
Compiling file return.html
Writing .web file
```

Application Manager

Application Manager is the tool within the LiveWire tool suite that launches and manages your Web applications. Once the Application Manager is managing your application, use this program to modify, remove, stop, restart, and run the application.

Application Manager is run within Netscape Navigator. Access the application by entering the URL of your server followed by **/appmgr/**. Accessing the Application Manager via Web browser allows you to manage your Web site remotely.

```
http://yoursite.com/appmgr/
```

In this example, replace *yoursite.com* with the actual URL of your server. Remember always to add the forward slash (/) at the end, or LiveWire will not find and start the Application Manager. When Application Manager loads into your

Web browser, all the applications currently under management appear in a table as in Figure 3.13.

Adding Applications

The hyperlink **Add New LiveWire Application**, located below the table of applications, as shown in Figure 3.13, launches the *Add Application* page when clicked (Figure 3.14).

1. Enter the URI Prefix. (URI stands for Uniform Resource Identifier.) This is the name of the directory in which your application is located. For example: **/hangman**. (Use a forward slash. If you insert a back slash, LiveWire will replace it with a forward slash.)

2. Enter the Object File Path. This is the complete path to the application's .WEB file. For example: **C:/LiveWire/samples/hangman/hangman.web**. (LiveWire uses forward slashes on both Windows and Solaris machines.)

3. Enter the Default URL. The default URL of your application is the .HTML file used to start your application. For example: **hangman.html**.

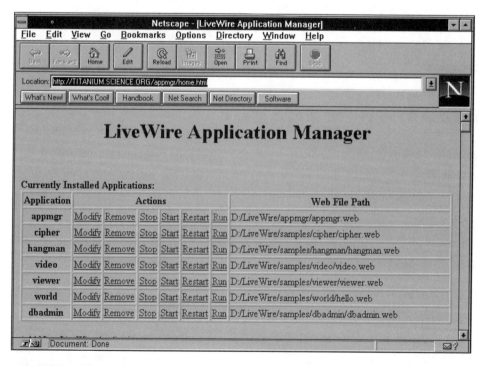

■■■■■■ **Figure 3.13** The Application Manager runs in Netscape Navigator.

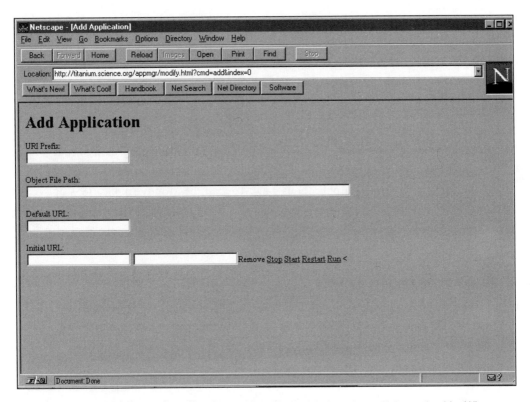

Figure 3.14 Add Application is launched from a hyperlink on the LiveWire Application Manager page.

When you have finished entering this information, click the **Start** hyperlink at the bottom of the page to start your new application. The Application Manager will send you a message letting you know if the application was successfully started.

Managing Applications

Once you have added an application to the Application Manager you are given the following options:

- Start and stop and restart an application
- Modify application parameters
- Remove an application from the Application Manager

You can start applications from either the Add Application page or the main Application Manager page. Where you start the application has no effect on how the application starts. Upon starting, your Web application will continue to run until you stop the application or the Netscape Web server is stopped. Stopping the Netscape Web server is an "ungraceful" way of stopping all your Web applications simultaneously and is not recommended. When an application has been stopped, you can choose to restart it by clicking the **Restart** link on the Application Manager page.

Modifying application parameters is similar to adding a new application. You are presented with the entry fields filled in with the information currently used to run the application. Refer to the section on adding applications for more information on the fields in the Modify Applications page. To load the Modify Applications page click the **Modify** link next to the application name listed in the first column of the table of applications (Figure 3.13). When you modify a stopped application, the Application Manager automatically restarts the application.

A Restart Shortcut

You can restart a stopped application without accessing the Application Manager page by typing the path to the application and appending **/restart**. You can restart only an application that has been stopped and is still installed in the Application Manager.

http://yourserver.yourdomain/hangman/restart

You cannot use any of the other Application Manager commands without first accessing the Application Manager Web page.

Servers

LiveWire is a dynamic tool suite. Netscape, which is known for its excellent Internet software, has built in the ability to expand the tools that make up the LiveWire tool suite. As you add new server software to your Internet or intranet site, your LiveWire system will grow in functionality. You should also consider the Netscape LiveWire system for building in-house intranet systems. When you build an intranet with Netscape Server software, your employees always have the most critical information right on their desktops—whatever their platform, wherever they're located. Netscape has developed a set of integrated servers called SuiteSpot specifically designed to work with intranets.

Netscape has included a complete set of server packages in SuiteSpot, including News, Catalog, Enterprise, Proxy, LiveWire Pro, and Mail. These servers, along with some of the Netscape servers not included in SuiteSpot, provide a powerful Internet tool suite.

FastTrack Server

Manage your Web site using Netscape's FastTrack Server Manager (Figure 3.15). Webmasters can quickly set up new applications, manage directories served over the Internet, and set up security. Here are some the features provided by FastTrack.

- Implement security and manage access to files on your Web
- Automatically forward URLs to other servers
- Serve up to 16 IP addresses with your FastTrack server
- Set up virtual servers so that one physical server can serve several domains
- Customize Web documents

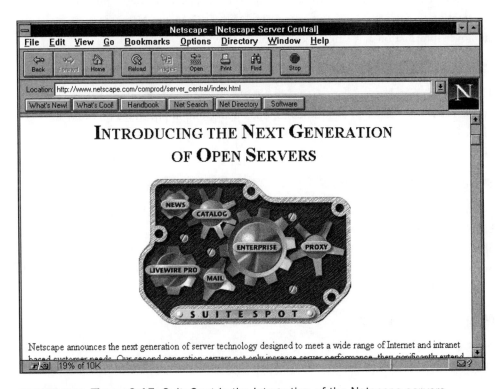

▮▮▮▮ **Figure 3.15** SuiteSpot is the integration of the Netscape servers.

FastTrack also includes a Set Up Wizard to enable people of all skill levels to get their Web sites up and running quickly and efficiently.

Commerce Server

The Commerce Server is one of the original Netscape products. This high-capacity HTTP server provides secure high-volume transaction processing over the World Wide Web.

News Server

Usenet News is still one of the top three Internet applications, and you can still reach incredible numbers of people by becoming active in the Usenet News groups. Running your own News server will allow you to control which newsgroups are carried on your local server and enable you to create new company-wide or Internetwide News groups.

Newsgroups are excellent ways to provide customer support, restricted product information to company representatives using Netscape's Secure News, and employee information at a single location or worldwide.

Catalog Server

The Netscape Catalog server presents users with a user-friendly catalog of resources on the network, such as e-mail addresses, documents, and applications that may be located on many different servers throughout an organization. This is a key component of the Netscape SuiteSpot suite of applications.

Proxy Server

Behind a firewall? The Netscape proxy server is your gateway to the Internet. The LiveWire system can be used behind a firewall for intranet applications with no fear of a security breach. For companies that have chosen to implement Internet security by installing a firewall, the Netscape proxy server will allow two-way access to the Internet without compromising Network security.

Mail Server

Netscape, in an effort to offer a complete set of solutions for both intranet and Internet communications strategy, has created the Netscape Mail server. Already,

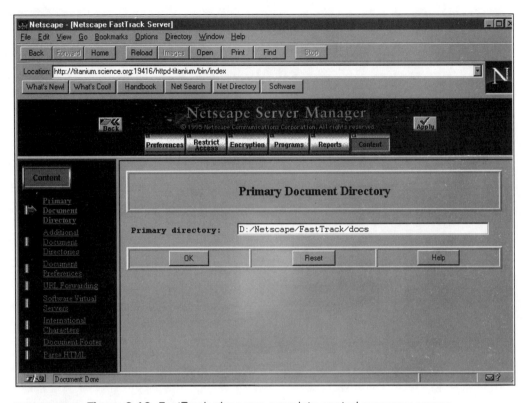

Figure 3.16 FastTrack gives you complete control over your server.

the Netscape Navigator Browser has a completely integrated, MIME-enabled e-mail client. Your company will appreciate the benefits of running its own e-mail server.

LiveWire Pro

LiveWire Pro is the LiveWire system bundled with the Informix relational database management system (RDBMS). LiveWire has database access built in as a standard feature. Using Informix, one of the highest-rated DBMS packages, you will greatly expand the capabilities of your Web site.

4

WRITING JAVASCRIPT

Anyone who has ever tried to do just a little bit more with the World Wide Web than publish a static HTML Web page has faced the confusion and inefficiency of Common Gateway Interface (CGI) programming. Before Java and Netscape's scripting language, JavaScript, all processing of any kind had to be done on the Web server. Even simple math, verification of user input, and any other information handling had to be done through CGI. Now much of the programming is done right in the Web browser. Using JavaScript, you can embed into your Web page programs that handle many of the tasks that previously had to be sent to and from the Web server, eating up time and bandwidth.

Real programming means that your Web pages can have *objects* that respond to *events*. If you aren't an experienced programmer or have never written a Windows program, these terms may seem foreign. Programming with objects, known as object-oriented programming, is easy.

■■■■■■■

In the world of object-oriented programming, everything is an object, and every object has attributes and abilities, known as *methods*. An *attribute* is what you know about an object, such as its size, position, color, and other describable features. An attribute of a person object in the real world would be eye color or height. Methods are the abilities of objects. For example, the abilities of a car object would be going forward, backing up, and stopping. Its attribute might be its color or its top speed.

When you are programming with objects, there are often objects that are already defined for you. For instance, if you're using JavaScript in the Netscape Navigator, your Web page is an object called a *document*. A few of the attributes of a document object are its title, foreground color, and background color. We've mentioned that objects can also have abilities called methods. Some of the methods of a document object are its abilities to open a new document, close the current document, clear the document, and write information onto the document.

You can refer to attributes of an object by using the *dot notation*. Begin with the name of the object, such as *document*. Follow it with the name of the attribute separated by a dot: *document.fgcolor* refers to the foreground color of the document. You can use this notation as you would any variable in a program. Set the foreground color using one of the hexadecimal numbers normally used to set colors on Web pages.

```
document.fgcolor = "#FFFFFF"
```

This example sets the foreground color of the document object to the color white (#FFFFFF). Call methods of the object use this same dot notation.

```
document.close()
```

Calling this method of the document object closes the current document.

An object can contain other objects. Consider a car once again, which consists of important component parts, like an engine, wheels, seats, and a transmission. Each of these objects also has attributes and methods. An engine attribute would be the number of cylinders (engine.cylinders = 4) or its horsepower (engine.horsepower = 150). To refer to a specific attribute of a particular car you would reference it using the same familiar dot notation.

```
car.engine.horsepower
```

If you would like to store the attribute's value in a variable, use this syntax:

```
myvariable = car.engine.horsepower
```

In the same way that a car can have objects within it, so can Netscape objects. For example, document objects can contain form objects. A form is that part of a Web document that begins and ends with the <FORM></FORM> tags. Likewise, form objects can contain objects such as text entry fields, radio buttons, and check boxes, to name a few. To refer to the value of a text entry field, begin with the document, followed by the form and then the name of the text entry field.

▬▬▬

Different parts of your application are run when an event triggers them. The end user of your application controls when various parts of the program are run by triggering events. For instance, walking into a store with an electric eye by the door triggers a chime, letting the store owner know that someone's in the store. Your Web applications work the same way. When users click on a button with their mouse, a Windows mouse event is triggered. Programs corresponding to specific events are run when the events are triggered. This process will become clearer as you begin developing Web applications that use forms. Each of the objects you have included in your form has certain events that can be triggered. For example, a button has a clicked event that is triggered whenever anyone clicks on the button with a mouse.

Some JavaScript Basics

JavaScript is a compact, object-based scripting language for developing Internet applications. Netscape Navigator 2.0 has the ability to interpret JavaScript embedded within normal HTML and use objects and events to create powerful programs that run right in the Netscape Navigator client. This reduces some of the need for powerful back-end programs, such as CGI programs. Much of the processing can be done by the Web browser before any data is ever sent to the Web server. In many cases, JavaScript will remove the requirement for any programs to run on the server.

There are some important distinctions between JavaScript and its namesake, Java. JavaScript is an interpreted language, which means that a program, like Netscape, is required to interpret each of the commands as the JavaScript program is running. Java programs are compiled and can run all on their own. In the last paragraph we mentioned that JavaScript is object based, which means that JavaScript uses built-in objects. In JavaScript you cannot create classes or use other object-orientation features such as inheritance. This doesn't mean that JavaScript isn't without some advantages. JavaScript is extremely easy to use and can be embedded right into HTML. JavaScript, like Java, is safe to use because neither language allows information to be written to the local hard drive. This safety feature keeps unwanted viruses or other destructive programs from having access to and doing damage to your hard drive.

JavaScript Variables, Operators, and Condition Statements

Writing computer applications is different from creating HTML pages. Computer applications (programs) can process information and make decisions. To process information, they store some of it in *variables*. Variables are temporary storage places with a name. Let's say we have a variable called *name*, and in the *name* variable we store "Fred." Now, whenever we refer to the *name* variable, it's the same as referring to the word "Fred."

Operators are symbols also used in processing data. Nonprogrammers might be most familiar with operators used in arithmetic. The plus sign (+), minus sign (−), and other math symbols are examples of common operators. There are many types of operators used in addition to the math operators.

If you paid attention to the title of this section, you know the next thing we talk about is condition statements. The previous sentence is a good example of a condition statement. Condition statements are used to make decisions within a program, directing the flow of the program. For example, if one thing is true, do this, or if it's not true, do something else. Once you know about variables, operators, and condition statements, you'll be well on your way to being an application developer.

Creating Variables

Variables in JavaScript are easy to create; make up a variable name and store a value in it. Unlike with other programming languages, it isn't necessary to declare a variable (make a space in memory) before using it. A variable is automatically declared the first time it's used. Variables are said to have types. You can think of types of variables as you think of types of boxes. If someone says "tissue box," you picture a particular type of box in your mind. If on the other hand someone says "hat box," you think of an entirely different box. The same is true of variables, as in the following:

- String variables store text.
- Numeric variables store numbers.
- Boolean variables store True or False.
- Object variables store objects, like forms and documents.
- Null is a special variable type that stores nothing, literally.

The datatype of the variable is determined by what you store in it. Creating string variables is as simple as storing text in a variable.

```
MyVariable = "Hello cyberspace."
```

The variable *MyVariable* is now a string variable with the value, "Hello cyberspace."

To be more correct, *MyVariable*, becomes a string object. This subject is covered in the section on programming with JavaScript objects.

When creating variable names, you must start them with a letter or an underscore. Variable names can't start with numbers. It's also important to note that JavaScript is case sensitive. Forgetting about case sensitivity can create all kinds of grief, so keep this stipulation in mind when creating variable names.

Creating Objects

You create some objects by using HTML. For example, you can create the *document* object once a Web page containing <HEAD> and <BODY> tags is loaded. In the same way, you can create *form* objects by adding a <FORM> tag and other form elements to a Web page. This chapter explains these objects in greater detail in the JavaScript Objects section.

You can create some JavaScript objects using the keyword *new*. This is sometimes known as the *new operator*. Begin creating objects, like *date* objects, by creating a variable that will hold your new date object. Follow this variable with an equals sign, the new operator, and then the type of object you are creating. The following example shows how to create a new date variable.

```
MyDateObject = new date(1997, 12, 25)
```

In JavaScript it's possible to create new custom objects by first creating a function (see Creating Functions). Then, the *new* operator is used to create a new instance of your custom object.

Arrays

An array is a special kind of variable. If a variable can be likened to a storage box, think of an array as a box with dividers inside. An array is a single variable made up of many variables, each numbered with an *index*. Each individual "storage compartment" within the array is known as an *array element*. Here is how you would store information in array elements. Notice that each element is identified with the *index* in square brackets.

```
color[1] = "brown"
color[2] = "red"
color[3] = "blue"
```

Once you have information stored in your array elements, you can refer to information stored in an individual element by the element's index number.

```
print(color[3])
```

This example prints the word "blue."

You'll find that arrays are important when you are writing JavaScript programs because Netscape keeps track of many of its objects using an array. For example, all the elements that make up a form are stored in an array and can be referred to by their index number.

Using Operators to Create Expressions

Operators are used to create JavaScript *expressions*. As a kid, you created expressions on a plastic potato by sticking the right plastic pieces into it. In JavaScript, you create expressions by adding the right programming components, variables, functions, and operators in the proper order. There are normally two sides to an expression separated by an operator. For example, 25 + 16 is an expression involving the *literals* 25 and 16. A literal is a value that is what it appears to be; 25 means the number 25. The operator in this expression is the math operator (+). In most expressions the results are either evaluated to a True or False (Boolean) value or stored in a variable. In the following example the JavaScript expression is evaluated to be either True or False.

```
MyVariable == 25
```

If the value stored in the variable *MyVariable* is 25, the expression evaluates to True. One creates JavaScript expressions using the operators found in Table 4.1. C++ programmers are very familiar with these operators. We include Table 4.1 as a handy reference for people who are not as familiar with them. The operators in this table include both *unary* and *binary* operators. Unary operators work with a single operand (x++) whereas binary operators work with two operands as in most arithmetic (x + y), string (x + y), logical (x && y), bitwise (x & y), and comparison (x >= y) expressions.

■■■■■■ **Table 4.1** JavaScript Operators

Operator Type	Operator	Description
Arithmetic	+	Addition
	–	Subtraction
	*	Multiplication
	/	Division
	%	Modulus
Unary	++	Increments numeric variable by one
	--	Decrements numeric variable by one
	-	Negation, turns a positive number into a negative number
String	+	Concatenates
	+=	Shorthand assignment, simple way to concatenate to an existing variable
Logical	&&	Logical AND, returns True if both operands are True

■■■■ **Table 4.1** Continued

Operator Type	Operator	Description
	||	Logical OR, returns True if either operand is True
	!	Logical NOT, negates an operand; True becomes False and False, True
Bitwise Logical	&	Bitwise AND, returns a 1 if both operands are 1
	|	Bitwise OR, returns a 1 if either operand is 1
	^	Bitwise XOR, returns a 1 if either but not both operands are 1
Bitwise Shift	<<	Left shift, shifts operand to the left a specified number of bits
	>>	Sign-propagating right shift, shifts operand right specified number of bits
	>>>	Zero fill right shift, shifts operand right, zeros filled from the left
Comparison	==	Equals, returns True if both operands are exactly equal
	>=	Greater than or equal to, returns True if left operand is greater than or equal to right
	>	Greater than, returns True if left operand is greater than the right operand
	<	Less than, returns True if left operand is less than the right operand
	<=	Less than or equal to, returns True if left operand is less than or equal to right
	!=	Not equal to, returns True if left operand is not equal to the right operand

■■■■

Controlling Program Flow with Condition Statements and Loops

Computer programs have the ability to evaluate expressions and choose what program statements (commonly called code) the program will execute. Programs can also loop back and repeat the same code over and over again in what is called a *loop*. Condition statements and loops are used to control the flow of the program, meaning the direction your program takes depending on choices the user and your program make.

The condition statement used in JavaScript is the *if* statement. Given a Boolean expression (one that evaluates to True or False), the program code that follows the *if* statement is either executed or not. The expression evaluated by the *if* statement is called the *condition*, which is why the *if* statement is called a condition statement. When constructing an *if* statement, begin with the *if* followed by the condition in parentheses. The program code that is to be executed if the condition evaluates to True follows the condition surrounded by braces {}. Here's what it looks like.

```
if (condition)
        { program statements
         go here
         }
```

You can also have statements execute where the condition evaluates to False. These program statements are included in an *else* statement that follows the *if* statement. It looks like this:

```
if (condition)
        { program statements
         go here
         }else
          program statement
```

Now, we'll create a real example.

```
MyWeight = 110
LunchCalories = 1000

if (LunchCalories > 1000)
        {
           MyWeight = 115
        }
if (MyWeight < 115)
```

```
{
   MyDressSize = 5
} else
   MyDressSize = 7
```

This depressing lunch example shows how decisions are made in JavaScript using variables, operators, and condition statements. Another way to direct the flow of the program is to put it into a loop. There are two basic types of loops in JavaScript:

- While loop
- For loop

Like the *if* statement, the *while* statement or *while* loop, as it's better known, has a condition statement. The *while* loop continues to execute program statements while the condition evaluates to True. Be warned that creating a loop that never evaluates to False is called an endless loop. There probably isn't a programmer alive who hasn't created at least one endless loop. It isn't really damaging, although you may have to press Ctrl-Alt-Del and end the task to stop your program from running and running and running. The *while* loop is constructed in nearly the same way as the *if* statement. Begin with the word *while*, followed by the condition within parentheses, and finally, the program statements to execute enclosed in braces.

```
while (condition)
        { program statements go here }
```

Each time the last program statement is executed, the condition statement is reevaluated. When it evaluates to False, the program continues executing on the program statement immediately after the *while* loop. The *for* loop also executes program statements more than once, employing a counter to loop a specified number of times. If you want a loop that will execute the program statements exactly five times, this is the loop you want to use. The syntax of the *for* loop is a little more involved than that for the *while* loop of the *if* statement. The *for* loop has four parts.

- Initial expression
- Condition

- Update expression
- Program statements

The *initial expression* sets your counter variable. The *condition* evaluates your counter to some expected number of loops. The *update expression* increments your counter. If your counter will be incremented by a value of one each time, the update expression is not required. When you want your counter incremented by values greater than one, or decremented (adding a negative number), you specify this in the update expression. Lastly, the *program statements* are the JavaScript code that gets executed multiple times. If you're new to *for* loops, you'll want to pay particular attention to this example.

```
for (var counter = 1; counter < 10; counter++)
    {
        program statements go here
    }
```

In the initial expression section, we created a new variable called *counter* using the *var* statement and set it equal to 1. The condition will be True while the counter is less than 10. Notice in this example we used the unary operator ++ after the variable *counter* in the update expression to increment *counter* by 1.

Creating Functions

Both stand-alone functions and methods of objects begin with the declaration *function* followed by the function name and optional parameters separated by commas enclosed in parentheses. Functions without parameters still include empty parentheses. The actual program code of a function is enclosed in braces, as in C or C++.

```
function MyFunction(myVar1, myVar2)
            {
            program code goes here
            }
```

Unlike with some other programming languages, JavaScript functions are not required to return a value.

Commenting Your JavaScript

Good programmers add comments to their code, this helps programmers working on complex programs remember what each part of the program is supposed to do. Comments also help other programmers read programs they didn't write. Commenting your programs, even small programs, is a good habit to get into.

One of the ways to add comments to your JavaScript is to precede each comment with a double slash (//).

```
// This is a JavaScript comment
```

You can also add comments to the end of a line of JavaScript code, but you can't embed comments in the middle of a line of JavaScript.

```
MyVariable = "Hello World" // This creates a string variable
```

When you use the double slash (//), each comment line must start with //. You may add lengthy comments without entering a double slash on each line by beginning these comments with /* and ending them with */.

```
/* This is a JavaScript comment
        That can run for several lines
        until it is ended with a slash star. */
```

Embedding JavaScript in HTML

The main enabling ability of JavaScript is that it can be embedded into the HTML of a Web page. JavaScript is embedded in a Web page through use of the <SCRIPT> and </SCRIPT> tags.

```
<SCRIPT>
function MyFunction(myVar1, myVar2)
                {
                program code goes here
                }
</SCRIPT>
```

The <SCRIPT> tag has been designed for the possible inclusion of other scripting languages that may be developed later on, but because JavaScript is the only script-ing language in common use today, the basic <SCRIPT> tag expects to then interpret JavaScript. To prevent ever having to go back and change any programs should other scripting languages develop, you can include the following attribute description in the first <SCRIPT> tag.

```
<SCRIPT language="JavaScript">
```

For programming convenience, and because the browser goes through and interprets the JavaScript first, it's often recommended that you place JavaScript functions within the <HEAD> and </HEAD> tags of your HTML document. Once the JavaScript functions have been interpreted and loaded into memory, they can be called from within the body of your document.

Not everyone uses the Netscape Navigator browser, and not all browsers are capable of interpreting JavaScript. To ensure that this JavaScript is not displayed within incompatible browsers, you should include the following code.

```
<script language="JavaScript">
<!- hide script from old browsers
  function ...............{
  ........................
  }
// end hiding contents ->
</script>
```

The hide contents code effectively prevents the JavaScript code from being displayed in old browsers.

JavaScript can also be placed within other HTML tags in place of attribute names or values but requires the use of a backquote (`) at the beginning and end of the script. Make sure that you use the backquote (`), not the single quote ('), which is a typical mistake. Here is an example where the JavaScript has been used as an attribute value.

```
<IMG src =`request.attributevalue`>
```

The JavaScript code that would go with this line of HTML might look like the following.

```
<HEAD>
<SCRIPT language="JavaScript">
if (user.request == "DogImage") {
        request.attributevalue = "pets/dog.gif";
        }
(user.request =="CatImage"){
        request.attributevalue = "pets/cat.gif";
        }
</SCRIPT>
```

Assuming the user.request chosen would be for the dog image, the resulting attribute value would be replaced in the HTML tag.

```
<IMG src="pets/dog.gif">
```

When JavaScript is used as an attribute value, the LiveWire system automatically places the JavaScript output within quotes, but no quotes are provided when JavaScript is used for an attribute name.

Event Programming

Once you've written your JavaScript functions, you'll want to be able to call them from within the body of your HTML document. You do so by triggering *events*. An event is a message to your program that something has occurred, like a mouse click, or that the mouse pointer is positioned over a particular object on the screen. JavaScript recognizes several basic programming events as illustrated in Table 4.2. When JavaScript functions are associated with an event, the function is run when the event occurs. Each object may or may not have certain events that it can handle. When the object does handle events, these are known as *event handlers*.

■■■■■■■■ **Table 4.2** JavaScript Programming Events and Descriptions

Programming Events	Description of Event
onLoad	The onLoad event occurs whenever a window is finished loading or all frames are within a <FRAMESET>, after which the JavaScript code would be executed.

▬▬▬▬▬ **Table 4.2** Continued

Programming Events	Description of Event
onClick	The onClick event is triggered when certain objects on a form are clicked.
onMouseOver	The onMouseOver event is triggered whenever the pointer of the mouse passes over certain objects.
onSubmit	Whenever a form is submitted, the onSubmit event is triggered.
onSelect	The onSelect event is triggered when text within a text or textarea field is selected.
onChange	The onChange event occurs whenever a select, text, or textarea object has been changed and the field loses focus.
onFocus	The onFocus event occurs whenever any field first gets input focus, which occurs any time a user selects with the mouse pointer or by tabbing to the desired input field.
onBlur	The onBlur event occurs whenever any field loses input focus.
onUnload	The onUnload event occurs when the current document is exited.

▬▬▬▬▬

To run a JavaScript function when one of these event handlers is called, include the name of the function after the event handler you want to call this function.

```
onClick="MyFunction()"
```

This statement is included within an object's definition. For example, *onClick* is an event handler for the button object, among others.

```
<INPUT TYPE="button" NAME="MyButton" VALUE="OK" onClick="MyFunction()">
```

The event programming feature enables JavaScript to perform such functions as validations, calculations, and checks of form input. Most Windows applications are written so that functions are called when event handlers are triggered. When learning about JavaScript objects in this chapter, make sure you pay attention to the object's event handlers.

Programming with JavaScript Objects

With JavaScript you may use some of the basic objects provided such as string objects and math objects. Choose to use Netscape objects like the document and form objects, or create your own objects. If you're an object-orientation guru you'll notice that JavaScript is object based and not fully object oriented. Some of the things you can do are the following:

- Use the standard object attributes and methods
- Extend the standard objects by adding your own attributes and methods
- Create entirely new objects

Of course, you won't find full object-oriented features such as inheritance in JavaScript.

The JavaScript Built-in Functions

Escape()

Escape sounds like a function we'd all like to use once in a while, but its actual use is a little less exciting than a vacation in Hawaii. CGI programmers will use this function. Certain characters in the CGI (Common Gateway Interface) are required to be *escaped*. The **escape**() function returns the hexadecimal value preceded by a percent sign of all the characters that need to be escaped. Other characters are returned by the **escape**() function unchanged.

```
escape(")")
```

This example in which we have passed a left parenthesis returns "%29."

```
escape("The escape() function is fun.")
```

This sentence passed to the **escape**() function is returned as:

```
"The %20escape%28%29%20function%20is%20fun."
```

Notice in this example that the white space is returned as %20, and the parentheses as %28 and %29.

Eval()

In the section called Using Operators to Create Expressions, you learned how to create JavaScript expressions. The **eval**() function evaluates JavaScript expressions and returns their results. Here are some examples of simple expressions and their results.

```
eval(2 + 3)                     //returns 5
eval("Smith" == "Jones")        //returns false
```

Unescape()

The **unescape**() function is used much the same as the **escape**() function, except it does just the opposite. Instead of "escaping" certain characters, it converts the %Hex values back into their normal ASCII characters.

```
unescape("The %20escape%28%29%20function%20is%20fun.")
```

This cryptic-looking example returns the value, "The **escape**() function is fun."

The JavaScript Standard Objects

JavaScript has quite a few built-in objects for you to use. Table 4.3 lists the standard objects included in the JavaScript language. To use these objects you should familiarize yourself with the following:

- *Properties*—Attributes or variables used to store information about an object
- *Methods*—Abilities or functions of an object
- *Event handlers*—The ability of an object to respond to Windows events

▮▮▮▮▮▮▮▮▮ **Table 4.3** JavaScript Standard Objects

anchor	form	math	string
button	frame	navigator	submit
checkbox	hidden	password	text
date	history	radio	textarea
document	link	reset	window
elements array	location	select	

▮▮▮▮▮▮▮

It's important to know that Netscape keeps track of many of these objects in an *array*.

Anchor

You create an *anchor object* by using the <A> tag in an HTML page. An anchor is defined as a target for a hypertext link. We'll use a simple example to make this very clear. We'll start with an anchor, and we'll include a Name property. Our example is named *LiveWire*.

```
<A NAME="LiveWire">LiveWire Documentation</A>
```

Our example anchor is in a file called **info.html**. To create a link to **info.html** that also jumps right to the anchor, *LiveWire* create a link that looks like this:

```
<A HREF="info.html#LiveWire">LiveWire Documentation</A>
```

Anchors are among the types of JavaScript objects that are stored in arrays, as we described earlier in this chapter. Even though the anchor object has no properties or methods, the *anchor array* does have the *length* property. This value tells you how many anchors there are on your Web page. You can't refer to the information stored in the array, nor can you store information in the array element. You can refer only to the named element to validate the anchor's name. It's possible that you will never use the anchor array.

The most common use of anchors is to construct a hypertext link. Anchor objects that are used to construct links can be found in the link object array as well as the anchor array (see Link object).

Button

The *button object* is the familiar pushbutton found on HTML forms. Create a button object as you would any button in a form. Remember that to use a button on a Web page, you have to include it within the <FORM> tag. You'll want to give the button a name to make it easier to refer to in your JavaScript program.

```
<INPUT TYPE="button" NAME="MyButton" VALUE="Text" [onClick="JavaScript"]>
```

You can view or change the properties of a button by referring to the property preceded by the name of the button.

```
MyButton.value = "Push Me"
```

Buttons have two properties: *name* and *value*. The *name*, is the name of the button object and the way you refer to it in your JavaScript program. The *value* is the text that appears on the face of the button. Button objects have a single method, *click*, which simulates the click of the mouse on the button. Include the click() method in your JavaScript programs when you need to simulate mouse clicks that would otherwise be performed by the end user.

Button objects have only a single event handler: *onClick*. When you click the button, any JavaScript tied to the onClick event handler will be run. Include the name of the JavaScript function you want to run when the onClick event is triggered like this:

```
<INPUT TYPE="button" NAME="MyButton" VALUE="Push Me" onClick="PushThis()">
```

Checkbox

Checkboxes are objects used for form inputs. These are the familiar little boxes that, when clicked, appear either with or without an "x." These objects are used for selection of one or more choices. Use the checkbox as a "toggle" where a choice is either selected or not.

Create a checkbox object by using normal HTML. The properties of the checkbox object include *name, value, checked,* and *defaultchecked.*

```
<INPUT TYPE="checkbox" NAME="MyCheckBox" VALUE="ReturnValue" [CHECKED]
[onClick="MyFunction()"]>
```

The *name* property is the checkbox name and the way you will refer to this object in your JavaScript program. The *value* property contains the value that is returned to the server when the form is submitted. The default for the *value* property is "on." The *checked* property is a Boolean (True or False) value that reflects the current state of the checkbox. You can use this property either to refer to or to change the state of the checkbox.

```
form.MyCheckBox.checked = TRUE
```

This example sets the state of the checkbox object to "checked" and places an "x" in the box. You will also notice that to refer to this object you must precede the name of the checkbox with either the word *form* or the actual name of the form containing the checkbox object. Checkbox objects must always be included as part of a form. The *defaultchecked* property is a Boolean value that determines whether or not a checkbox appears checked when a form is first loaded. You can refer to this value, because changing its setting has no effect.

Checkbox objects have a single method: *click*. Like the button object, click is used to simulate a mouse click on the checkbox. This is a handy method for setting the checked states of checkboxes based on other user input. The checkbox, again like the button object, has a single event handler: *onClick*.

Date

The JavaScript language handles dates much as the Java language does, with both languages keeping track of dates in terms of milliseconds since January 1, 1970. The date object has no properties yet has quite a number of methods (refer to Table 4.4).

Table 4.4 Date Object Methods

Methods	Description
getDate	Returns the day of the month
getDay	Returns the day of the week
getHours	Returns the hour
getMinutes	Returns the minute
getMonth	Returns the month
getSeconds	Returns the seconds in the current time
getTime	Returns the numeric value for the time of the date object
getTimezoneOffset	Returns the time zone offset in minutes for a current time zone
getYear	Returns the year of the date object
parse	Returns the number of milliseconds in a date string, since January 1, 1970
setDate	Sets the date of the month for the date object
setHours	Sets the hours in the current time
setMinutes	Sets the minutes in the current time
setMonth	Sets the month in the current date
setSeconds	Sets the seconds in the current time
setTime	Sets the value of the date object

■■■■■■■■ **Table 4.4** Continued

Methods	Description
setYear	Sets the year in the current date
UTC	Returns the number of milliseconds since January 1, 1970

■■■■■■■■

Date objects are created not through use of a simple HTML, but with the *new* operator. Create a date object and store its value in a variable in one of these four ways:

- dateObjectVariable = new Date()
- dateObjectVariable = new Date("month day, year hours:minutes:seconds")
- dateObjectVariable = new Date(year, month, day)
- dateObjectVariable = new Date(year, month, day, hours, minutes, seconds)

The date object is one of JavaScript's built-in objects, and these built-in objects have no event handlers. Remember that event handlers are triggered when something "happens" to an object, and nothing ever "happens" to a date object.

Document

Document objects are created with HTML. The document has two parts: a head specified with the <HEAD> tag and a body specified with the <BODY> tag. Once a Web page with these tags is opened in a Web browser, a document object is created. One of the foundational objects, the document object contains many other objects such as forms and form elements, links, and anchors. References to all the objects within a document can be found stored in the document's properties. See Table 4.5 for a complete list of the properties of the document object.

■■■■■■■■ **Table 4.5** Document Object Properties

Property	Description
anchors	An array listing all the anchors in the document
bgColor	The background color of the document
cookie	Information sent from the server
fgColor	Foreground color of text in the document

■■■■■ **Table 4.5** Continued

Property	Description
forms	An array listing all the forms in the document
lastModified	The date the document was last modified
linkColor	The color in which a link appears on a document
links	An array listing all the links in the document
location	The URL of the document
referrer	The URL of the document that called the current document
title	The title of the document
vlinkColor	The color of followed links

■■■■■

The document has five methods, as shown in Table 4.6. Use these methods when creating dynamic Web pages with JavaScript.

Elements

The *elements object* is an array of the objects that make up a form. This object is created automatically whenever there is a form on the Web page and is used to reference objects in a form without using the names of the objects.

```
MyForm.element[3].value
```

This example references the value property of the third object on the form. You can also refer to this object by name.

■■■■■ **Table 4.6** Document Object Methods

Method	Description
clear	Clears the current document
close	Closes the current document
open	Opens a new document of a specific MIME type to accept output of write and writeln
write	Writes text onto a document
writeln	Like the write method, but adds a carriage return at the end of text

■■■■■

```
MyForm.UserInput.value
```

The element array has a single property, *length,* which corresponds to the number of objects on a particular form. The element object has no methods and no event handlers.

Form

The *form object* allows you to add user interactivity into your Web pages using only HTML. Forms have been around for quite awhile now, but JavaScript is adding an entirely new dimension to forms. The form object is created with the <FORM> tag and consists of several other user entry objects. Once someone has entered values in a form, the results are *submitted* to the Web server. Normally, a program specified by the *action* property accepts and processes the values received from the Web browser.

There are two ways to refer to a form object in a Web page, by its *name* and by the *form array*. Like many of the other objects, an array keeps track of each form on a Web page. Because each form is located on a document object, when referring to a form or an object on the form, you will need to precede the name of the form with the word *document*.

```
document.MyForm
document.form[1]
document.MyForm.EntryField.value
document.form[1].EntryField.value
```

As in other objects that can be referenced in an array, one of the properties of the form array is the *length*, specifying how many forms are in the document. Table 4.7 lists the possible form object properties.

■■■■■ **Table 4.7** Form Object Properties

Property	Description
action	The action property designates what action should take place when the form is submitted.
elements	This is an array containing a reference to all the objects within the form.
encoding	This is the ENCTYPE type of the form.

length	This is the number of elements on the form.
method	This is the method of submitting the form (e.g., POST or GET).
target	This is the TARGET of the form.

■■■■■■■

The form object has a single method: *submit*. Calling this method is the same as having the user click a **Submit** button on the form. The result is that any values entered in the form will be sent to the server and processed by whatever program is specified in the *action* property.

There is a single event handler for the form object called *onSubmit*. Whenever the **Submit** button is clicked or the *submit* method is called, the onSubmit event handler will be triggered.

Frame

Frames are among the new HTML features in Netscape that allow you to divide the Netscape window into smaller individual windows. Each new window, also known as a frame, is a JavaScript object. When you are using frames, the first document that is loaded will have a <FRAMESET> tag to define the frames. Once the frames have been set, frame objects are created in HTML with the <FRAME> tag.

You'll find that there are many similarities between the *frame* and *window* objects. Because each frame is also a window, many of the properties and keywords used to reference windows are also used to reference frames.

- *self.* References the current frame
- *window.* References the current frame
- *top.* References the top frame
- *parent.* References the parent of the current frame

Because you can have multiple frames in a document, there is a frames array to keep track of each *child frame*.

For instance, if a window has four child frames, they can be referred to as parent.frames[0], parent.frames[1], parent.frames[2], and parent.frames[3]. Notice that, as in C or C++, the array index begins at 0. As with other objects with which references are stored in an array, the frames array has a *length* property that contains the number of child frames.

The only other property of a frame we haven't discussed yet is the *name* property. This property is particularly important because it is rare that you would have a single frame. Even though you can reference each frame using the frames array, it's always easiest if you can refer to a frame using its name.

The frame object has two methods: *setTimeout* and *clearTimeout*. The *setTimeout* method is a useful method for evaluating expressions, values, launch functions, and other methods after a specified period of time. *SetTimeout* has two parameters, the first of which is the expression or function you want evaluated. The second parameter is the number of milliseconds to wait until evaluating the expression in the first parameter (10000 = 10 seconds).

```
timer = setTimeout('DoSomething()', 10000)
```

The *timer* variable is used to capture the return value of *setTimeout*, which is a special timer ID. Use this ID when you need to cancel the *setTimeout* method before the first parameter is evaluated. The timer ID is passed as a parameter to the *clearTimeout* method to cancel *setTimeout*.

The frame object doesn't have any event handlers of its own. Remember that frame objects are also window objects. The onLoad and onUnload window object event handlers can be set within the <FRAMESET> tag.

Hidden

Objects are great for retrieving user input. Sometimes, though, you may need a special invisible object that only your JavaScript can interact with. The *hidden object* is a special object that can be placed on forms for just this purpose. Totally hidden from the user, but not your JavaScript programs, this object is great for performing many different types of programming tasks. Think of it as a generic object with a *name* property and a *value* property. Hidden objects don't have any built-in methods.

History

As people navigate to new pages on the World Wide Web, their Web browsers keep track of which pages they've visited. Netscape Navigator keeps track of the last 20 sites a user has visited and calls this record *History*. If you're curious about what the History looks like, select **Go** from the Netscape Navigator menu. It's a quick and easy way to return to a page you've visited during your surfing venture on the Web. This is an alternative to clicking the **Back** button over and over again.

Using the JavaScript history object, you can move to any page in the user's History. For security reasons, the JavaScript programmer does not have access to the text contained in the History. This is to keep programmers from being able to find out where people have been on their trips through the Internet. It's also to keep programmers from having access to FTP logons and passwords if they happen to be contained in the History. For this reason, you must refer to each URL in the history object by its numeric place in History. Place 1 is the current page. Place 2 is the page you were on before navigating to the current page.

The history object has only one property, *length*, which contains the number of sites contained in the history. You'll need to know this number if you're going to do any programming with the history object. You will get an error if you try to issue a direction using one of the methods of the history object (Table 4.8) that does not exist.

The *back* method is used simply to go back one page in the history. This is the same as if the end user had clicked the **Back** button.

■■■■■ **Table 4.8** The Methods of the History Object

Method	Description
back	Reloads a page the specified number of pages back in the History
forward	Reloads a page the specified number of pages forward in the History
go	Goes directly to a specified page designated by its numeric place in the History

■■■■■

```
history.back()
```

In the same way, it's possible to move forward in the History with the *forward* method. This is the same as if the user had clicked the **Forward** button in Navigator.

```
history.forward()
```

Unlike links and buttons found in Web pages now, these new methods give you the unique ability to have the user navigate to and from pages that are not found on your server. Web pages often have ways to return to the home page of the server providing the page. These links, or buttons, are most often fixed, not allowing you to return users to the page from which they came. Using the *back* and *forward* methods, you can make users feel as though your pages have been personalized for them.

There is a third method to the history object: *go*. Using this method, you can send users to a particular page in their History. This method is a little trickier to use than *forward* and *back*. First, you have to know how many pages there are in the History using the *length* property. Second, it helps to know where people have been so that you know where you're sending them. The *go* method accepts a parameter that sends someone forward (using a positive number) and back (using a negative number) the specified number of pages.

```
history.go(3)
history.go(-2)
```

The history object can be referred to as part of a window object or a frame object. Begin with the name of the window or frame followed by the word *history* and then either the property or method of the history object to which you would like to refer.

```
MyWindow.history.back()
```

This example takes you back one page in the current session of the window called *MyWindow*. To navigate using the history object's methods where there is more than one frame, begin with the keyword *parent*. Follow *parent* with either the name or the frame.

```
parent.MyFrame.history.forward()
```

Table 4.9 Link Object Properties

Property	Description
hash	Anchor name normally preceded by a hash mark (#)- (see Anchor)
host	Hostname and port designation within the URL
hostname	Domain name or IP address of a host on the Internet
href	The entire URL of the target document
pathname	Path within the URL
port	Communications port to contact on the server (WWW is normally port 80.)
protocol	Designates what protocol to use when communicating with the server
search	Query information embedded in the URL that normally begins with a question mark (?)
target	The target of the link

Link

A *link* object is also known as a *hypertext link*. Created with HTML, the *link* object can be either text or a graphic that when clicked by the user, loads a new resource specified by the *href* property. The link object has quite a number of properties, as shown in Table 4.9.

The links array, which keeps track of references to all links in the Web document, has a single property: *length*. The length of the array is equal to the number of links on the page. It should be noted that when a link is also an anchor, a reference is placed in the anchor array.

There are two event handlers for the link object. The onClick event handles mouse clicks on the link, and the onMouseOver event handler is triggered when the mouse pointer is placed above a link with no mouse buttons pressed. The onMouseOver event handler is useful when you want to update the Netscape status message at the bottom of the display.

Location

The *location object* describes the URL of the page that is currently loaded in the Web browser. The location object has exactly the same properties as a link object (refer to Link), but is different from a link object in two important ways. First, a location doesn't have a target property. Because the location is describing the current Web page, there is no need for a target. Second, there can be only one location; therefore, there is no need for a location array. Location objects have no methods or event handlers.

Math

One of JavaScript's important capabilities is performing calculations and various other mathematical operations within the client itself, eliminating the need to send data input by the user back to the server and some CGI program. The math object built into JavaScript has numerous methods to assist in performing these client-based calculations. Experienced programmers will find that the math object has the expected methods and properties associated with it that are typical of most programming languages. Table 4.10 illustrates the methods associated with the math object.

Table 4.10 Methods of the Math Object

Method	Description
abs	Returns the absolute value of the argument
acos	Returns the arc cosine of the argument (radians)
asin	Returns the arc sine of the argument (radians)
atan	Returns the arc tangent of the argument (radians)
ceil	Returns the least integer greater than or equal to its argument
cos	Returns the cosine of the argument
exp	Returns e to the power of its argument
floor	Returns the greatest integer less than or equal to its argument
log	Returns the natural logarithm (base e) of its argument
max	Returns the greater of its two arguments
min	Returns the lesser of its two arguments
pow	Returns base to the exponent power

■■■■ **Table 4.10** Continued

Method	Description
random	Returns a pseudo-random number between one and zero, but only on X-platforms
round	Returns the value of the argument rounded to the nearest integer
sin	Returns the sine of the argument (radians)
sqrt	Returns the square root of the argument
tan	Returns the tangent of the argument (radians)

■■■■

Navigator

The *navigator function* supplies information about the version of Netscape Navigator being used. JavaScript will be used in more than just Netscape Navigator. It's uncertain what effect the navigator function will have when JavaScript employing the navigator function is run in other Web browsers. Be warned, it may cause an error.

The navigator object is for informational purposes only. It has no methods or event handlers, and its properties (Table 4.11) are read only.

Password

When you need to supply a field for the user to enter a password, you can use the *password object*. It appears the same as any text object with one major difference:

■■■■ **Table 4.11** Navigator Object Properties

Property	Description
appCodeName	This is the code name of the Web browser. For Netscape Navigator this is Mozilla.
appName	This is the brand name of the Web browser. Of course, for Navigator this is Netscape.
appVersion	Application version number. For version 2.0 running on Windows 95; 2.0 (Win95; I).
userAgent	Specifies the user-agent header, such as Mozilla/2.0 (Win95; I).

■■■■

when the user enters information, all the characters appears as asterisks. Passwords are then safe from prying eyes.

The password object has three properties:

- *defaultValue.* Use this property when you want to supply a default password. This will appear as asterisks.
- *name.* This is the name of the password object.
- *value.* This is the value after the user enters a password.

The password object's three methods are focus, blur, and select. The focus method makes the password object active as though the user had clicked in the entry area of the password object. The blur method removes focus from (deselects) the password object. The select method will select any text already entered in the password object. By selecting the text, the user may begin typing a new password without erasing the old one. The selected text (asterisks in this case) will disappear as soon as the user begins typing. The password object has no event handlers.

Create password objects using HTML.

```
<INPUT TYPE="password" NAME="ThePassword" VALUE="" SIZE=30>
```

Radio Buttons

Radio button objects allow you to choose a single selection from a group of selections. They get their name from the old-style car radios where when one selector button was pushed in, any others were ejected. Only one button could be pushed in at a time. These radio button objects, sometimes called *radio* objects, are created with HTML and must be placed on a form. Radio buttons wouldn't be much good if there weren't at least two of them. Also, they must be grouped. If they weren't grouped, there would be no way that the other radio buttons would know to uncheck themselves when a new radio button is selected. Give each radio button in a single group the same *name* property (Table 4.12). This way, you can have more than one group of radio buttons on a form.

■■■■■■ **Table 4.12** Radio Button Object Properties

Property	Description
checked	This property allows you to check a radio button using JavaScript.

■■■■ **Table 4.12** Continued

Property	Description
defaultChecked	When this property has a True value, this radio button is checked by default (only one radio button in the group can have the defaultChecked property set to True).
length	This property is the number of radio buttons in the group.
name	This is the name of the radio object. This property groups the radio buttons.
value	This is the value sent to the server if the radio button is selected at submit time.

■■■■

The only method of the radio object is the click method. This is another way to click a radio button using JavaScript rather than having the end user do it with the mouse. Radio objects have a single event handler, *onClick*, that is triggered whenever the user clicks on a radio button.

Reset Button

The *reset button object* resets all the form elements when it is clicked. Each form element is either emptied or set to the default value if there is one. The **Reset** button is created with HTML and has only two properties: *name* and *value*. The *name* property is the object name of the **Reset** button. The *value* property specifies what is printed on the face of the **Reset** button.

Being a button, the reset button object has a click method and an onClick event handler. Use the click method to simulate a mouse click on the reset button.

```
<INPUT TYPE="reset" NAME="MyReset" VALUE="Clear Form">
```

Selection List

The selection list is known as the *select object,* which is also known as a listbox. This form element is created with HTML and allows the end user to select from a scrolling list of options that is created in HTML with the <OPTION> tag. Once the options have been specified, an array of these options is kept as one of the properties of the select object. (For other properties of the select object see Table 4.13.)

▬▬▬ **Table 4.13** Select Object Properties

Property	Description
length	This is the number of options selectable in a select object.
name	This is the name of the select object.
options	This is the options array containing all the selectable options.
selectedIndex	This is the number (index) of the selected (highlighted) option. This is the index of the first selected option if more than one option is selected.

▬▬▬

This array is read only, so it isn't possible to change the array elements using JavaScript.

As we mentioned, the *select* object has an array. This array is different from those of other objects that have an array. Instead of keeping track of all the select objects, this one keeps track of the options in a single object. Table 4.14 lists all the properties of the select object array, also known as the *options array*.

▬▬▬ **Table 4.14** Options Array Properties

Property	Description
defaultSelected	This property is True if this option is selected by default.
index	This is the number (index) within the options array. The first item is 0, the second is 1, etc.
length	The length of the array tells you the number of options.
name	This is the name of the select object.
selected	This property allows you to use JavaScript to select an option.
selectedIndex	This property is the number of the selected, or first selected, option.
text	This property is the text to display in the list of options.
value	When selected, whatever is stored in the value property gets sent to the server when the form is submitted.

▬▬▬

The select object has two methods, *focus* and *blur,* which allow you to use JavaScript either to give focus (*focus*) to the select object or remove focus (*blur*). There are three event handlers:

- *onBlur.* Triggered when focus is lost
- *onChange.* Triggered when a change occurs
- *onFocus.* Triggered when focus is given to the object

This is a relatively complex object. Even though this is not a text on creating HTML, we thought it would be useful to include a sample of a select object.

```
Choose your favorite ice cream toppings

<P>
<SELECT NAME="toppings" MULTIPLE>
   <OPTION> Chopped Nuts
   <OPTION> Candy Sprinkles
   <OPTION> Hot Fudge
   <OPTION> Marshmallow
</SELECT>
```

This sample creates a select object that allows multiple options to be selected. (What fun is ice cream if you can't have more than one topping?) The options array would contain five elements. The name of the object is *toppings*. To create a default selection, add the keyword SELECTED within the <OPTION> tag like this:

```
<OPTION SELECTED> Chopped Nuts
```

String

The *string object* has all the basic character string-handling capabilities you might expect in a programming language. It has only one attribute: *length*. Of course, this attribute contains the length of the string as an integer. Table 4.15 is a list of the methods of the string object. You can see that there isn't much you can't do with a string object.

■■■■■ **Table 4.15** Methods of the String Object

Method	Description
anchor	Converts string text to an anchor format
big	Formats a string with the big tags

▮▮▮▮▮ **Table 4.15** Continued

Method	Description
blink	Formats a string with the blink tags
bold	Formats a string with the bold tags
charAt	Returns the character at a particular position within a string
fixed	Formats a string with the typewriter text tags
fontColor	Formats a string with a specific font color
fontSize	Formats a string with a particular font size
indexOf	Returns the numeric position of the first occurrence of a particular character within a string
italics	Formats a string with the italics tags
lastIndexOf	Returns the numeric position of the last occurrence of a particular character within a string
link	Formats a string as a link and includes the URL
small	Formats a string with the small tags
strike	Formats a string with the strike-through tags
sub	Formats a string as a subscript
substring	Returns a specified portion of a string
sup	Formats a string as a superscript
toLowerCase	Returns the string as all lowercase characters
toUpperCase	Returns the string as all uppercase characters

▮▮▮▮▮

Any string you create is automatically a string object. Saving a string into a variable makes that variable a string object. Here's an example of creating a string object and using a method to create a new string object that contains bold tags.

```
MyString = "Hello cyberspace."
NewString = MyString.bold()
```

The value of the variable *NewString* is now "<B>Hello cyberspace.</B>" We could have formatted "Hello cyberspace." without storing it into the variable *MyString* like this:

```
NewString = "Hello cyberspace.".bold()
```

Submit Button

The **Submit** button is the only required element of a useful form. The *submit object* is created with HTML, and when clicked by the user, it submits all the form values to the Web server. As important as this object is, there isn't much to know about it. It has two properties: *name* and *value*. The *name* property is the object's name. The *value* property specifies the text that appears on the face of the button.

You can click the **Submit** button with JavaScript using the *click* method. Of course, the event handler is *onClick*, which is triggered whenever either the button is clicked with a mouse or the click method is called.

```
<INPUT TYPE="submit" NAME="MySubmit" VALUE="Submit Form">
```

Text

The *text object*, the familiar text entry box, is one of the most used of all the form elements. Text objects have three properties:

- *defaultValue*. Use this property when you want to supply default text.
- *name*. This is the name of the text object.
- *value*. This is the value entered by the end user.

The three methods associated with text object are focus, used to set the focus to the text object; blur, used to remove focus; and select, used to select the value already entered in the text object.

```
<HTML>
<HEAD>
<TITLE> Text Entry Example </TITLE>
<SCRIPT>
function testFunction(MyForm){
        //Function statements go here
        }
}
</SCRIPT>
</HEAD>
<BODY>
<h2>Text Entry Example</H2>
```

```
<FORM name="MyForm">
Enter some information:
<input type="text" name="entry" size=25 onBlur="testFunction(this.form)">
</FORM>
</BODY>
</HTML>
```

This sample program is an example of the use of the *onBlur* event handler of the text object. The event handlers for the text object are:

- *onBlur.* Triggered when focus is removed
- *onChange.* Triggered when text is added or changed
- *onFocus.* Triggered when focus is given
- *onSelect.* Triggered when text is selected

TextArea

TextArea objects, used on forms to allow users to enter large amounts of text, are sometimes known as multiline edit controls. The TextArea object is created with HTML and can be customized more than most objects. We'll include the HTML syntax for the TextArea object so that you can see the many attributes you can set using HTML.

```
<TEXTAREA
   NAME="textareaName"
   ROWS="integer"
   COLS="integer"
   WRAP="off|virtual|physical"
   [onBlur="handlerText"]
   [onChange="handlerText"]
   [onFocus="handlerText"]
   [onSelect="handlerText"]>
   textToDisplay
</TEXTAREA>
```

The TextArea object has only three properties:

- *defaultValue.* This is any text you would like to appear in the TextArea object by default.

- *name.* This is the name of the TextArea object.
- *value.* This is the text entered into the TextArea object.

The three methods of the TextArea object are *focus, blur,* and *select.* These methods allow the object to obtain and lose focus and select text within the object. The event handlers correspond almost directly with these methods. The event handlers are:

- *onBlur.* Triggered when the object loses focus
- *onChange.* Triggered when text is entered or changed in the object
- *onFocus.* Triggered when the object is given focus
- *onSelect.* Triggered when text is selected by either dragging across the text with the mouse or using the select method

Window Object

The *window object* is the parent object for all other objects in a Web document. When a Web page is loaded, a window object is automatically created. You've seen with other objects that to refer to properties and methods, it's necessary to precede the property or object with the name of the object. With window objects, it is assumed that you are referring to the current window. Therefore, it isn't necessary to precede methods and properties with the word *window* when referring to them.

The window object's status property allows you to change the message in the status bar found in the bottom left corner of the client window. The following is a sample JavaScript program that makes for a more interactive and informative window.

```
<a href="www.cnet.com" onMouseOver="window.status='Great News Site';
return true"> CNET Online</a>
```

Table 4.16 shows the object properties for window.

■■■■■■ **Table 4.16** Window Object Properties

Property	Description
defaultStatus	The default message that is displayed in the window object's status bar
frames	An array referencing all the frames in the window
length	The length of the frames array (the number of frames)
name	The name of the window object

Table 4.17 Methods of the Window Object

Method	Description
alert	Opens an alert window displaying a desired message
close	Closes the window
confirm	Opens a confirm dialog displaying a desired message
open	Opens a new Navigator window
prompt	Opens a prompt dialog displaying a desired message
setTimeout	Evaluates an expression after a specified amount of milliseconds have elapsed
clearTimeout	Stops and clears the evaluation in the *setTimeout* method

There are many ways to refer to a window object in your JavaScript programs. In other words, there are many synonyms for the word *window*. One synonym is parent, which refers to a window containing a frameset.

Self refers to the current window, and *top* refers to the top-most Navigator window. Of course, you can still use the word *window* to refer to the current Navigator window. The methods for the window object are listed in Table 4.17.

The two event handlers for the window object are placed in either the <BODY> or the <FRAMESET> tag. These event handlers are *onLoad* and *onUnload*.

Netscape Objects

When a page has been loaded into the client Navigator, four main objects are created, which prove useful for developing JavaScript applications. There is a specific object hierarchy illustrated in Figure 4.1.

Figure 4.1 Netscape object hierarchy.

```
window
  |
  +--parent, frames, self, top
  |
  +--location
```

Continued...

```
|
+--history
|
+--document
    |
    +--forms
    |  |
    |  elements (text fields, textarea, checkbox, password
    |        radio, select, button, submit, reset)
    +--links
    |
    +--anchors
```

These four main objects have the following properties associated with them.

- *window.* Top-level object that contains properties that apply to the entire window
- *location.* Contains properties of the current URL
- *history.* Contains properties on the URLs the client had visited previously
- *document.* Contains properties for Web page content, including title, and form elements such as buttons and checkboxes

Whenever the properties of any of these objects are specified, the object name and its ancestors must also be included. There are numerous object properties and values for a typical Web page.

Validate User Inputs

JavaScript has made it simple to perform validation of form data right on the client. In the past, form input would have to be sent to a server program, processed, and checked for validity, and then a response would be sent back to the client Web browser. This was, and is, a time-consuming process. Most importantly, it's no longer necessary.

Now you can build JavaScript directly in the client HTML document to prevent a user from entering the wrong data into a form. Simple JavaScript functions can

ensure that all data entered into a form can be correctly read by the server
JavaScript functions. Here is one example in which the JavaScript is designed to
ensure that a true e-mail address is entered correctly.

```
<HTML>
<HEAD>
<SCRIPT language="JavaScript">
function testEmail (MyForm){
        bFound = false
         n = MyForm.entry.value.length
        for (var i=0; i <= n; i++) {
                if (MyForm.entry.value.charAt(i)=="@" )  {
                        bFound = true
                }
        }
        if (bFound==false) {
                alert("Your entry is not a correct e-mail address.")
        }
}
</SCRIPT>
</HEAD>


<BODY>
<h2><B>Test For Proper E-mail Address JavaScript</B></H2>
<FORM name="MyForm">
<input type="text" name="entry" size=25,10 maxlength=25 onBlur="
testEmail(test)">
</FORM>
</BODY>
</HTML>
```

In this example you will see that we've put the function in the <HEAD> portion of
the Web page. This ensures that the function is loaded into memory before any
other parts of the Web page. Look at the function and you'll see that the name of
the form is passed as a parameter to the function. This is so that individual form

elements and their properties can be accessed from within the function. Within the function a new Boolean variable, *bFound,* is created when you store a False value into it. This variable will be set to True if an at sign (@) is found within an e-mail address.

Here is a good example of a for loop. This section of code will loop until all the characters entered in the text object have been checked. If no at sign is found, an alert dialog is called with the *alert* method of the window object. Because it is assumed that the current window is active, it is unnecessary to precede the window methods with the word window.

Calculations

JavaScript allows for the generation of programs on the client side that can do a variety of calculations based on the values entered into a form. Using the math object, you can perform extremely complex calculations. It's possible that all the calculations necessary for your program can be performed without contacting the server. Here's an example.

```
<HTML>
<HEAD><TITLE>Number Multiplier</TITLE>

<SCRIPT>
function compute(MathForm)
{
        xanswer = MathForm.NUM1.value * MathForm.NUM2.value
        MathForm.ANSWER.value = xanswer
        return true;
}
</SCRIPT>
</HEAD>

<H1>Multiplier</H1>
Enter two numbers to be multiplied and then hit the Compute button.
<P>
<FORM method=POST NAME="MathForm">
<INPUT TYPE=TEXT NAME=NUM1 SIZE=5> *
<INPUT TYPE=TEXT NAME=NUM2 SIZE=5> =
```

```
<INPUT TYPE=TEXT NAME=answer SIZE=9>
<P>
<INPUT TYPE="button" VALUE="Compute" onClick=compute(this.form)>
</FORM>


</BODY>
</HTML>
```

Don't Go There!

JavaScript has a set of words that can't be used as names of variables, objects, or functions. Using these *reserved words* in your program will either create an error or eventually lead to some type of programming disaster. In Table 4.18 you'll find a list of these key words that JavaScript either uses as part of its internal program or believes are programming directives, like *if* and *short*. Netscape may list these words as reserved simply so that they can be used by Navigator in the future without causing concern about whether or not they will interfere with someone's JavaScript program.

▬▬▬ **Table 4.18** Reserved Words

abstract	extends	interface	synchronized
Boolean	false	long	this
break	final	native	throw
byte	finally	new	throws
case	float	null	transient
catch	for	package	true
char	function	private	try
class	goto	protected	var
const	if	public	void
continue	implements	return	while
default	import	short	with
do	in	static	
double	instanceof	super	
else	int	switch	

Getting More Information

The Internet is an excellent source of information on JavaScript programming. The Netscape site has a full on-line guide to JavaScript programming.

http://home.netscape.com/eng/mozilla/Gold/handbook/javascript/index.html

Another great Web page for more information is the JavaScript Index:

http://www.c2.org/~andreww/javascript/

This chapter has gone a long way to introducing you to this exciting language.

5

CLIENT/SERVER

JAVASCRIPT

I n Chapter 4 we introduced JavaScript, a versatile language for writing World Wide Web client/server applications. The JavaScript covered in Chapter 4 focused only on client-side application development, but in fact the true power lies in JavaScript's ability to run on both the server (the machine running your World Wide Web server software) and the client (the computer running the Web browser). The ability to write server applications opens a whole new realm of capabilities. Client/server JavaScript also replaces current inefficient ways of creating interactive Web applications using CGI programs.

Before jumping into the numerous applications for JavaScript, it's best to review some of the steps used in the creating and deploying a typical application that utilizes client/server JavaScript.

1. JavaScript source code is written for both the client and the server, and it can be embedded in the same Web page The Navigator Gold editor can be used to place both client and server JavaScript in your Web source file along with any text, graphics, and hyperlinks required by each Web page in the application.

2. LiveWire's Site Manager is used to generate a **.site** file that lists each of the application components.

3. The Web page source files and other components in the .site file are compiled in Site Manager, and a .WEB file is created.

4. The application (in the form of its .WEB file) is added to the Application Manager of LiveWire to make it available on the Netscape server.

5. A client contacts an application's URL, which triggers server JavaScript code processing. LiveWire sends HTML and client JavaScript to the client Web browser for display and processing.

There are some significant differences between this approach and traditional Web application development. To begin with, you no longer have to concern yourself with two separate files in an application: the front-end file containing the HTML definition of your page and its associated back-end CGI script. Instead, you write client JavaScript code and HTML to define the client-side display and write server JavaScript code to define server-side processing all in the same file. We use the term *Web page source file* in this book to refer generically to any file that contains the definition of a Web page, regardless of the format of its contents.

Like a traditional CGI script, server JavaScript allows you to produce Web pages *dynamically*. When a Web page is produced dynamically using server JavaScript, the script determines what information should be displayed on the page rather than just serving a static file. Dynamic pages can even include dynamic client-side JavaScript code. You may have written CGI scripts in the past to process form input and generate a dynamic HTML response. Creating similar processing using JavaScript is much simpler, and the range of functionality available in your dynamic response is much greater.

This chapter should add to your understanding of the JavaScript language by illustrating the added capabilities of Web applications that utilize both server and client JavaScript code. There are complete descriptions of several new objects that are added by the LiveWire system to the JavaScript language, which expand your ability to write useful JavaScript applications. For those who don't write perfect code the first time, the LiveWire system also adds a debug and trace feature to assist in debugging your new application. After completing this chapter you should be well on your way to designing powerful new JavaScript applications that will add a whole new dimension to your Web applications.

JavaScript Everywhere

Before Web applications, traditional Web pages sent data to the server for processing. All Web clients could do was request Web pages and submit user-entered values via a form. Using JavaScript in an application frees you from this limitation. You can now write JavaScript that can:

- Be embedded in HTML so that it runs in a Web browser (client application)
- Be run on the server (server application)
- Access objects for complete server and application control

With the ability to write JavaScript applications that run on the client's computer, it's possible to process information that would have previously required a CGI program running on the server. Running CGI programs can eat valuable server resources. Repeated data transfer to and from CGI programs to refine queries can take a long time, especially over a slow connection. With client-side JavaScript, data validation can be done entirely on the client. In Chapter 3 we showed how JavaScript can be embedded directly in your HTML code. This ability is extended by LiveWire with the addition of four more built-in objects. These objects extend the ability of the client program to interact with the server, other applications, and other clients accessing the same application. This is what we call *client/server JavaScript*.

JavaScript can be written and stored in a separate file so that LiveWire can compile it and store the compiled version on the server. To distinguish this capability from JavaScript running on the client we call these JavaScript programs *server* programs. JavaScript server programs can be accessed with a normal URL. In fact, end users never realize that they've requested anything other than a static Web page. Additionally, LiveWire allows the server program to conduct relational database searches, returning the results to a Web client. The advanced version of LiveWire, LiveWire Pro, includes the Informix relational database.

Using the LiveWire Source Files

LiveWire applications are created from several different sources. As we mentioned, JavaScript creates Web content from more than just static Web pages.

A LiveWire JavaScript application can be created from the following types of source files:

- Web source files, sometimes known as HTML files. These will have either a .HTML or .HTM file extension.
- Web source files with embedded JavaScript. These files will also have a .HTML or .HTM file extension.
- JavaScript-only files. These files have a .JS file extension.

LiveWire creates a special .WEB file when you select the Build Web feature in the LiveWire Site Administrator. To run this Web application file, you must first install it on a Netscape server that has LiveWire installed. Users can access your application using a normal URL as though they were requesting a static Web page.

Embedding JavaScript in HTML

There are two ways to run JavaScript in LiveWire, one of which is the JavaScript-only .JS file extension (described previously). The other way is to embed JavaScript into a Web source file. Insert JavaScript directly into the HTML. To embed JavaScript that runs on the server, you must write it within <SERVER></SERVER> HTML tags. Include a single or as many JavaScript statements as you want between the <SERVER> tags. Check your release notes. When this book was written there was a special bug workaround that called for including an empty set of SERVER tags (<SERVER></SERVER>) after certain JavaScript **write**() functions. There is never a reason to embed SERVER tags inside another set of SERVER tags. This will result in an error message.

Another way to include JavaScript in an HTML Web source file is by using back-quotes (`), sometimes known as *back-ticks*. The back-ticks are used for including JavaScript within an HTML tag. Don't try to use them outside an HTML tag because they won't work. Include JavaScript within HTML tags to create attributes or attribute values based on JavaScript expressions.

Learning To Use the <SERVER> Tag

There seem to be two ways of doing just about everything in JavaScript. HTML <SERVER> tags are no exception.

- Use <SERVER> tags with the **write**() function to generate HTML.
- Execute a JavaScript statement.

The server communicates with the client programs that access it by sending HTML using the **write**() function. Web browsers can't tell the difference between HTML from the **write**() function and HTML sent from static Web pages.

```
<P>Hello there <SERVER>write(request.name)</SERVER>
```

The second way of including JavaScript is to execute a simple JavaScript statement. For example, if you wanted to change the value of request.name in the preceding example, you would include this JavaScript statement:

```
<SERVER>request.name = "Sally Jones"</SERVER>
```

Executing the first example would print **Hello there Sally Jones.**

Embedding JavaScript with Backquotes

Substitute HTML attribute names and attribute values using backquotes (`` ` ``). This may seem a little basic, but it's important that you know what we mean by a backquote. The backquote is found under the tilde (~) on most keyboards. It is *not* the single quote found beneath the double quote on the keyboard. Using JavaScript within backquotes embeds the result automatically in your HTML. Don't use the **write**() function to insert the return value of your JavaScript statement.

Netscape offers a great example of using the backquote in an HTML tag in the example program "Hangman."

```
<IMG SRC=`"images/hang"+client.num_misses+".gif"`>
```

This is another sample of what has been referred to as "quote hell." We'll take this sample apart to explain what all the quotes and plusses mean.

- First, the entire expression after IMG SRC is enclosed within backquotes.
- Second, the string "images/hang" is embedded in double quotes ("). Literal string values must always be embedded in quotes.
- Next, the "images/hang" string is added to the value stored in the server's client object property client.num_misses. (More on the server objects later in this chapter.) Adding strings is called *concatenation.*
- Once again, the string created in the previous step is added to another string: ".gif." Together, this entire string is the path and filename of the new image file that will be shown in the Web page.

You will find that there are very few places for which adding JavaScript won't extend the capabilities of your Web page.

JavaScript Server Functions

The duty of the Netscape Web server is to deliver multimedia content in the form of Web pages to a Web browser. Using LiveWire, information sent to a Web client is created dynamically by LiveWire. This section covers some of the functions LiveWire provides that allow you to perform all types of important programming tasks. Here are some of the things that LiveWire does when a browser loads an application.

- Web pages stored on the server are read and delivered unchanged to the client.
- Server JavaScript programs develop content for Web pages dynamically.
- Database queries send data to client Web browsers.

LiveWire has several functions that give your applications the ability to print information to a dynamic Web page. The server functions also allow you to redirect requests for URLs, perform property housekeeping, test an application, and lock objects in the server application. Your LiveWire application uses these functions along with the LiveWire objects, covered in the LiveWire Objects section, to construct dynamic pages.

write() Function

The **write**() function is one of the most important functions in client/server JavaScript programming. It provides the ability to send data from the server to the client Web browser in HTML format. In an interactive application, where a client Web browser sends requests to the server, this is the function the server uses to send a reply. The **write**() function accepts one parameter: the information to be printed. Remember that the parameter is placed inside the parentheses.

```
write("Any type of information goes here.")
```

The **write**() function can be used to send information to the Web browser from any of the other LiveWire objects discussed in this chapter. Because it sends information to a Web browser, the **write**() function is used to create entire Web pages *dynamically*. By dynamically, we mean that the Web page is created using information created entirely on the spot by the server. The Web page it sends to the client didn't exist before it was sent. The server constructs the page on the fly using information provided by the JavaScript program.

redirect() Function

How would you like to vary your home page depending on who requests it? You can have a different Web page sent to the client based on information contained in any of the LiveWire server objects described in "LiveWire Objects." Reroute each request to the Web page of your choice using the **redirect**() function.

```
redirect("http://url of your choice")
```

From the sample, you can see that the **redirect**() function accepts a URL as a parameter. This is the URL of the Web resource you want the client program to be sent. This can be any valid URL. For example, it can be a news:// URL that directs users to a Usenet newsgroup. The parameter can also be an FTP resource that sends the client a file when the application is accessed. As you learn about LiveWire objects, you will learn how this function can be used to create powerful business applications on the Web.

defined() Function

You learned in Chapter 3 that a variable is a temporary place to store information, and a property is a variable stored as part of an object. The **defined**() function is used to make sure a property or variable exists. Because variables and properties can be changed, created, and destroyed in LiveWire applications, this function helps control the flow of your program by checking for the existence of a variable or property. For example, before using the information stored in a variable not completely controlled by your LiveWire application (see Server Object), you should make sure the variable or property exists. Otherwise, trying to access information in a variable that does not exist will cause your program to stop running and display an error message.

```
defined(variable name)
```

The **defined**() function returns a Boolean (True or False) value depending on whether the parameter in this case, a variable or property name exists. You'll see this function used in the sample applications throughout the rest of this chapter.

debug() Function

The **debug**() function allows you to test the contents of various variables and properties during the execution of an application. **Debug**() does exactly what it says — it helps you debug your application. One of the things a programmer needs to know as a program is proceeding is what values are stored in variables and properties. The **debug**() function is used in concert with the *trace utility* built into LiveWire to display the contents of variables and object properties.

```
debug("text to display",property)
```

When the trace utility is then executed, the following values of the properties identified in the debug function are illustrated. The **debug**() function is a very convenient tool to monitor property values when you are testing a Web application. There is more about using **debug**() in the *Debugging* section at the end of this chapter.

lock() and unlock()

Some of the LiveWire objects described in the next section have the ability to be *locked*. An application locks these objects to keep other applications from changing the information stored in these objects. The **lock**() function tells any other objects trying to change the information in an object that it has to wait until the current application is through, and the **unlock**() function is issued.

Using the **lock**() function will help you avoid referring to server object variables while they are being changed. Without **lock**() it's possible to refer to object variables that may be in the process of being changed by another application.

Don't be the block, always **unlock**().

flush () Function

The **flush**() function can improve the performance of your application by managing the way data is sent from the server to the client Web browser. By using the **flush**() function, you can specify, in your JavaScript program, when data should be sent to the client Web browser. You may create very complex and powerful programs using JavaScript. When someone accesses your application and requests data, it's hard to send data to the client in "bite-sized chunks" instead of large blocks of data. A good example of when to use the **flush**() function is sending a large text file to the Web browser. Execute the **flush**() function after several readln() processes.

This way, the client can see data being transferred instead of waiting for all the data on the server to be processed before sending it to the client.

An important thing to remember when using the function is that you must make any changes to the client object before flushing the buffer. Flushing the buffer will write the cookie file to the client as part of the HTTP header.

registerC( ) Function

Even though it is undocumented as we write this book, it is possible to register functions in a .DLL or .SO (Shred Object) file so that they can be called from your server JavaScript programs. Register C functions on your server using the **registerC()** function. You must register any C functions before calling them, using the **callC()** function.

callC( ) Function

Use this function to call C functions from a .DLL or .SO file. You may call only those functions you have registered using the **registerC** function. This function is undocumented as we deliver this book.

LiveWire Objects

The LiveWire application comes with a set of four predefined objects that are used to allow JavaScript programs to access information about the server, the client, the active request, and any LiveWire applications running on the server. These four objects can be used in JavaScript programs running on either the client or the server.

Each object has a *lifetime*, which is the period of time the object sticks around after being created. Objects' lives end in one of two ways. LiveWire destroys an object whose lifetime has expired, and applications can request that an unneeded object be destroyed.

- *Server.* All the applications on the server share the server object. This object has the longest life, remaining alive as long as there are applications running.
- *Project.* This object is created whenever an application is started in the LiveWire Application Manager. The project object contains information about an application that is shared among all the clients contacting that application. This object stays alive for the duration of a single application.

- *Client.* The client object contains data specific to the client (browser) that has contacted a Netscape HTTP server. The lifetime of an object is controlled by either the JavaScript program, which can call the destroy function, or the LiveWire Application Manager, which can define a timeout for the client object.

- *Request.* The request object is a short-lived object created for each request submitted by a client. The request object has properties that describe each request.

- *Database.* This object allows connectivity to client/server databases.

Server Object

The *server object* serves as the base object in the LiveWire object framework. It is created whenever the server is started and destroyed when the server is shut down. The server object contains global data for all applications that may be running and can be used to obtain information about the server itself or allow information to be shared among different applications all running on the same server.

The server object properties when initially created are as follows:

- *hostname.* Complete machine name and port (titanium.science.org:80)

- *host.* Machine name without the port number (titanium.science.org)

- *protocol.* Specifies the type and version of HTTP protocol the server is currently using to communicate, which typically returns the value "HTTP/1.0"

- *port.* Port number only (80 is the default port for HTTP)

- *agent.* Indicates the type of server that's running, which for a Netscape Communications server would return the value "Netscape Communication server"

You may be scratching your head and wondering what you would do with these bits of information. You can use them in creating JavaScript applications or choose to print them in the client Web browser using LiveWire's **write()** function. What's more important than these two built-in server properties is your ability to create new server variables. You aren't limited to just the default properties of the server object. Additional properties can be defined for the server object that can be used in your Web applications. Remember, the server properties can be seen by all the applications running on your Web server. This is an excellent way to share information among applications. A common example of how you might use this is to have a counter on the server that prints the total number of accesses to your server, not just your application. You can also add a "thought for the day" that gets printed in all your applications. Figure 5.1 shows some examples that demonstrate using server variables across applications.

This first application is a Web source file that includes JavaScript. The first thing to notice is that all the scripts are contained within <SERVER></SERVER> tags. This is a little different from what you learned in Chapter 3, where all the JavaScript was contained in <SCRIPT></SCRIPT> tags. This is because the JavaScript we've written here is going to be run by the Web server. If you forget this and put the code in <SCRIPT></SCRIPT> tags, you'll get strange error messages when you try to compile your application.

The next thing to notice about this application is that we've created a new property of the server object simply by storing a value in a property.

```
server.MyNewVariable = "Hi there!"
```

Figure 5.1 Use the **write()** function to send information from the server to the client.

```
<HTML>
<HEAD>
<TITLE>Server Application #1</TITLE>
<SERVER>
server.MyNewVariable = "Hi there!"
</SERVER>
</HEAD>
<BODY>
<SERVER>
write(server.MyNewVariable)
</SERVER>
</BODY>
</HTML>
```

Remember from the last application that storing a value in a variable automatically creates the variable and the type of variable. In this case, the variable *MyNewVariable* is a string variable containing the value "Hi there!"

In the body of the Web page source file we have another server directive, the **write**() function. This function simply prints the value of the *server.MyNewVariable* property in the page sent to the Web browser that ran this application.

The next example (Figure 5.2) is an application that will access the server property created in the first application (Figure 5.1).

Notice in this example that the server property, *server.MyNewVariable,* was not created. That's because the property already exists and has a value stored in it. The **write**() function will print the value "Hi there!" when this second application is run by a client Web browser.

The server object has two methods: *lock()* and *unlock().* These methods are used to lock the property values while they are in use by a client to avoid network conflicts and access by another client in the middle of changing values. It would be bad if one client read the values in the properties while another client was in the middle of changing them. For this reason, when you are changing values on the server, it is important to lock() the server and then unlock() it when you are finished updating.

■■■■■ **Figure 5.2** Access server properties defined by another application.

```
<HTML>
<HEAD>
<TITLE>Server Application # 2</TITLE>
</HEAD>
<BODY>
<SERVER>
write(server.MyNewVariable)
</SERVER>
</BODY>
</HTML>
```

Project Object

The *project object* contains data about a particular Web application running on your Netscape server. Remember that to use the server objects, your application must be compiled and managed by LiveWire. The project object has a relatively long lifetime because it is created whenever an application is started and destroyed when the application is stopped. The project object isn't initialized with any property values, but typically it has property values assigned to it by an application. All clients accessing an application may access these project values. This makes the project object particularly useful when it is passing information to different clients accessing the same application.

Values stored in the project object are useful when information must be passed to each client, or some type of counter must be incremented. For example, if you have a chat application that allows only 10 simultaneous users, you can keep a counter on in the project object. Each time users log into the application, you may choose to let them know what number they are or send them onto another page while they wait their turn.

See Figure 5.3 for an example of the project object management.

▰▰▰▰▰▰ **Figure 5.3** Use the project object to manage application-specific information.

```
<HTML>
<HEAD>
<TITLE>Chatty Patti's Page</TITLE>
</HEAD>
<BODY bgcolor = "#FFFFFF">
<SERVER>
if (project.usercount > 10){
        redirect("waitingroom.html");
{
</SERVER>
<H2>Welcome to the Chatty Patti Chat Page</H2>
/* Chat application goes here */
</BODY>
</HTML>
```

The property object has two methods: *lock()* and *unlock()*. As with the server object, these methods are used to temporarily lock the values stored as properties of the object. As we mentioned, there are no default properties of this object, but lock() will protect any values stored there by applications. If you forget to use the unlock() method, LiveWire automatically unlocks the object after each request to prevent any chance of an object's being locked permanently.

Client Object

The *client object* is created by every client that contacts the server, which typically results in many different client objects existing at the same time. The client object makes it simpler to keep track of the multiple transactions that occur between the server and a particular client during a session, which is very useful because many different clients may be contacting a server at the same time.

Client Object Properties

Client objects are created only if the application requires them. Client objects don't come with predefined property values, but allow for JavaScript code to create new properties and values. If there are no application-specific properties, no client object is required or created by LiveWire. Not creating useless client objects saves system resources.

Figure 5.4 shows how you can store client information.

In this example, the information passed as part of the request object (covered later in this chapter) is stored in the client object. Client objects have a longer potential

■■■■■ **Figure 5.4** Store information about the client in the client object properties.

```
<SERVER>
client.UserName = request.user  //store user name in client
client.Password = request.pass  //store password in client
</SERVER>
```

■■■■■

lifetime than request objects. The client object is a better place to store the user information, especially if you want it to last between transactions. This is true of any information stored as properties of the request object. If you want these values to stick around, the client object is a good choice for storing them.

If you're creating Web applications for a business, the opportunities created by this function are endless. We know from Chapter 4 that it's possible to know what page the client was on before landing on your page. Let's say your company sells books. Your marketing department is very aggressive in cyberspace and has managed to get links to your home page on the NASA page, the Dilbert page, and Better Homes and Gardens page. In your application, you check the referrer property, and if client browsers came from the NASA page ,you show them a Web page that highlights books about outer space, astronauts, cosmology, and this month's special, "How to Freeze Dry Your Own Meals." Of course, if they came from the Dilbert page you'll show them all the Scott Adams books, and you'll show them the book on growing roses if they came from the Better Homes and Gardens page.

Maintaining the Client Object

There are times that you will want to save your client object information between transactions. Saving the client object information for use later is known as *saving the state of the client object*. The state information is stored in a structure called the *state structure*. You won't need to concern yourself too much with the state structure; it's created automatically by LiveWire.

There are two places you can save the client information: on the server and on the client itself. There are advantages and disadvantages to each location, which we will cover so that you can choose the best approach for your application.

Client Cookies

There are two methods that involve saving the transaction information on the client. The first method is known as: *client cookies*. A cookie is basically a token that indicates that a transaction has taken place. For example, a server may give your client a packet of information, and your client gives the server a cookie for the transaction. A real world example would be getting a receipt after paying for a meal at a restaurant.

Client cookies use the Netscape cookie protocol to transfer client information. When using client cookies, the server passes all the client object information as name/value pairs to the client.

There are some advantages and disadvantages to using client cookies.

Advantages:

- They work with server farms.
- They will continue to work even if the server must restart.

Disadvantages:

- You must use Netscape Navigator to use client cookies.
- There is only a limited amount of cookie memory.
- Using them creates a small increase in network traffic.

Client URL Encoding

The second method used for saving client object information is known as client URL encoding. This data transfer scheme works by having the server send all the client information by attaching it to server-generated URLs. The information is still sent as name/value pairs when attached to the URLs. One of the downsides to this is that if the page refers to multiple URLs, the information is sent multiple times, once for each URL.

Advantages:

- Works with all browsers.
- Works with server farms.
- Works across server restarts.

Disadvantages:

- Requires dynamically created URLs.
- Large increase in network traffic.

Examining Client Cookies on the Server

There may be occasions when you would like to have access to the contents of the client cookie from your server JavaScript program. Precede the value you would like to have access to with 'NETSCAPE_CLIENT', and it will be reconstructed on the server.

```
document.cookie="NETSCAPE_CLIENT.MyVariable=MyValue";
```

When the request is made, the client object should have a property named *MyVariable* and a value of *MyValue*.

Server Cookies

We have seen how client object information is stored on the client between transactions. It's also possible to store the client object information on the server. One of these ways is using *server cookies*. Server maintains the state, and cookie holds the handle.

IP Address on the Server

Maintaining the state of the client object on the server using the client's IP address is one of the ways in which all the IP addresses in the system are known. This is great for in-house applications that run with a single server. All the information is stored in a data structure on the server and indexed by IP number.

Advantages:

- Works with all browsers.
- No increase in network traffic.

Disadvantages:

- Requires shared memory or database.
- Does not support dynamic IP address providers, multiuser systems, or users behind a firewall.

Short Cookies

Short cookies is a way the server gives the client a temporary nickname. The client can then use this automatically generated nickname when contacting the server in the future. The server then accesses the state data structure to retrieve the client state information. The client uses the Netscape cookie protocol when contacting the server with its nickname in subsequent transactions.

Advantage:

- Little increase in network traffic.

Disadvantages:

- Requires Netscape Navigator.
- Requires shared memory or database.

Short URL Encoding

The short URL encoding technique is similar to the short cookie. An automatically generated name is sent to the client attached to server-generated URLs.

Advantages:

- Works with all browsers.
- Little increase in network traffic.

Disadvantages:

- Requires dynamically generated URLs.
- Requires shared memory or database.

Client Object Lifetime

The client object is created each time a particular client browser contacts a server. The client object stores the information during this session for all information passed between the server and a particular client, which includes any property values assigned to the client object. This client object keeps some sense of order in the client/server transactions, which could get messy because many different clients may be contacting the same server with each one creating a new client object.

When the client object is created, there are no guarantees that there will be any additional transactions, so there is a time expiration default built into the client object. How long it is before the expiration default destroys the client object depends on whether the client object is stored on the server or the client. If it is stored on the server, the client object expiration default is set at 10 minutes, but if it is stored in the client software using cookies, the expiration default is set to destroy the client object whenever the client exits the client software.

Rather than depending on the default expiration time for the client object, you can specify the desired expiration time, making it either longer or shorter than the default. This expiration time can be set using the following command.

```
client.expiration(#)
```

In this command # is the number of seconds desired before the expiration of the client object. For many applications you may not want to wait for a specified period of time before destroying the client object. The following command allows for you to instantly destroy a client object.

```
client.destroy()
```

Whether the client object is destroyed by time expiration or is destroyed directly, any existing client assigned properties are removed.

Request Object

The *request object* contains the information sent from the client sent to the server, which is some sort of a request of the server. In many cases this is simply the client requesting that different HTML document be loaded from the server. After the server responds to the request by providing the desired information, the request object is destroyed. Obviously, this practice results in the request object's being a very short-lived object, and many request objects are created and destroyed in a typical client-to-server connection. Because the request object is the most dynamic and has a significant number of tasks, such as requesting URLs for particular HTML documents or passing form information back to the server, it has a significant number of different properties and methods associated with it.

Properties

The basic predefined properties associated with the request object can enable the server to determine needed information to better respond to a particular request. Here are the definitions of the four properties and examples in which information obtained from these request properties is used to improve the application's response.

- *ip address.* This is the IP address of the client that has contacted the server, which is represented in the form of four numbers separated by a period, such as "204.94.74.209." Knowing the IP address could allow the server to determine if the user at that particular IP address has already contacted the particular application; if not, a window could be launched for the user to enter demographic information.

- *protocol.* This is the type of HTTP protocol that the client is capable of supporting. The first and still current version of the HTTP protocol is 1.0, and the value of protocol is illustrated as "HTTP/1.0."

- *method.* This is the particular HTTP request of the server, which is either GET, POST, or HEAD. It allows the server to properly reply with the desired information for a particular request.

- *agent.* This is the particular client browser used to contact the server. For the Netscape Navigator browser, this property would return the value "Mozilla/1.1N." The agent information can allow the application to be designed not to let the user contact HTML pages that might contain features such as plug-ins or Java applets that the user's agent would be incapable of viewing.

Other than these four predefined request properties, the request object generates properties for form inputs and allows the developer to pass specific values embedded in URLs.

Form Inputs Create Request Properties

Whenever a form is submitted using a form **Submit** button, a request object is automatically created on the server. Each of the form's elements becomes a property of the request object. In the example in Figure 5.5, *MathForm*, has several input elements, each with a value. These form elements and their values will become the request object's properties and property values.

On the server you can now write JavaScript that will refer to these properties of the request object. This server example in Figure 5.6 is not as elegant as the one that calculated the answer on the client as shown in Chapter 4.

Passing Values by Adding Them to URLs

You can also pass variables to the server by embedding them in a URL. To embed values in the URL begin by adding a question mark (?). This marks the beginning of the list of variables you are adding into the URL. Follow the question mark with the name of a variable then the name of the variable with an equals sign (=) and the

■■■■■■■ **Figure 5.5** Access form elements as properties of the request object.

```
<FORM method=POST NAME="MathForm">
<INPUT TYPE="TEXT" NAME="NUM1"  SIZE=5> *
<INPUT TYPE="TEXT" NAME="NUM2"  SIZE=5> =
<INPUT TYPE="TEXT" NAME="ANSWER" SIZE=9>
<P>
<INPUT TYPE="button" VALUE="Compute" onClick=compute(this.form)>
</FORM>
```

Figure 5.6 Each form property is available to the server processing the request.

```
<SERVER>
NewValue = request.NUM1 * request.NUM2;
write(NewValue);
</SERVER>
```

value for that variable. When there is more than one variable, add an ampersand between the value of one variable and the name of the next. You do not add white space between the values.

```
<A href="test.html?NUM1=12&NUM2=13">Calculate</A>
```

This operation will create a request object that is identical to one created when values are sent as part of a form input.

Database Object

The *database object* is covered in great detail in Chapter 6. Briefly, the database object allows you to connect to various client/server databases. If you purchase LiveWire Pro, your LiveWire product will include the popular Informix client/server database. People who are using the standard version of LiveWire, can easily connect to the following databases and database type:

- Oracle
- Sybase
- Informix
- Illustra
- ODBC

There are JavaScript functions that allow you to connect to the database, change and add values to the database, and delete rows from the database. The connect() method of the database object allows you to specify to which of these databases you would like to connect. If the database you own is not on the list, you should check the database documentation to see if it is ODBC compliant. Many of the popular database management systems are ODBC compliant.

One of the simple features you will read about in the next chapter is the database. SQLTable() method. This function returns the results of a database query as a pre-formatted table in your Web page.

File Object

There is a server object that allows you to manipulate text files on the server. Remember, because of security precautions, it's not possible to manipulate files on the client using JavaScript. Being able to open, read, and write files on the server allows you a great deal of flexibility.

The file object has several methods for manipulating files and data (Table 5.1). Before you can use any of the methods of the file object, you must create a file object. To do so, use the new operator and include the name of the file you want opened as a parameter.

```
MyFile = new File("MyTextFile.txt")
```

You do not open the file by creating the file object but by using the file.open() method. Files can be opened for reading, writing, or both when you specify one of the following parameters. Adding "b" to any of the parameters will open the file as a binary file.

- "r"—*open for reading*. If the file does not exist, returns False.
- "w"—*open for writing*. Creates a new, empty file. If the file exists, it will be overwritten.
- "a"—*open for appending (writing at the end of the file)*. If the file doesn't exist, one will be created.
- "r+"—*open for reading and writing*. Reading and writing start at the beginning of the file. Returns True if the file exists and False if it doesn't.
- "w+"—*open for reading and writing*. Creates a new, empty file. If the file exists, it will be overwritten.
- "a+"—*open for reading and writing*. Reading and writing start at the end of the file. A new file is created if it doesn't exist.

▰▰▰▰ **Table 5.1** File Object Methods

Method	Description
file.open(modeString)	Opens a file. The modeString determines whether the file was opened for reading, writing, or both. Returns a Boolean value.
file.close()	Closes an open file. Returns a Boolean value.
file.flush()	Flushes the file buffer.
file.setPosition(position)	Sets the file pointer to a place in the file. 0 = beginning, 1 = current position, 2 = end. Returns a Boolean value.
file.clearError()	Clears a file error from the error buffer.
file.getPosition()	Returns the position in the file in bytes.
file.getLength()	Returns the size of the file in bytes.
file.exists(filename)	Determines if a file exists. Returns a Boolean value.
file.eof()	Determines if the end of the file has been reached. Returns a Boolean value.
file.error()	Returns the number of any error that has occurred while handling the file.
file.toString()	Converts a byte value to string.
file.read(count)	Reads the number of bytes in a file set by count. Returns a string.
file.readln()	Reads an entire line from a file. Returns the line as a string.
file.readByte()	Reads bytes from a file. Returns a number.
file.write(string)	Writes string into a file.
file.writeByte(number)	Writes number to a file.
file.writeln(string)	Writes string to a file and adds a carriage return line feed.
file.byteToString(number)	Converts numbers to a string.
file.stringToByte(string)	Converts a string to a numeric datatype.

■■■■■■■ **Figure 5.7** Use the file object to manage files on the server.

```
<SERVER>


MyFile = new File("MyTextFile.txt")


Opened = MyFile.open("r");
if (Opened)
{
        write("File: " + MyFile + "<P>");        //Writes filename
to Web page


        while (!MyFile.eof())   {
                ReadLine = MyFile.readln();
                write(ReadLine + "<BR>");
        }


        if (MyFile.error() != 0)        //If there's an error
                write("<P> There was a problem reading the
file.");


        MyFile.close()                  //Close the file
}


</SERVER>
```

In the example in Figure 5.7 you can see that a new file object, *MyFile*, is created in the first line of the program. MyTextFile.txt is specified as the file opened in the second line. Notice that the file is opened in "read only" mode because the "r" is passed to the open() method. The **write()** function in this example is not the file.write() method. It's easy to confuse the two functions. The **write()** function used here writes output from the server to the Web client.

Two of the commonly used functions in file handling are **readln**() and **eof**(). **Readln**() is used to read a line from a file and return it into a variable. In this program, the information from the file is being sent directly to the Web browser, adding a break <BR> at the end of each line. The file is being read one line at a time in a *while* loop. The *while* loop will continue processing the **readln**() function until the end of file is reached. The **eof**() function returns True when the end of file is reached by either the read() or readln() method. Remember to close the file when you're finished, using the close() method. The close() method will return True if the file was closed successfully.

Error checking is important to add in any well-written program. The error() method returns True if an error occurs in any of the file-handling functions. You could test for errors using the **error**() function after each function call if you really wanted to. How often you call the error() method depends solely on how critical your application is.

Running Your Web Application

As soon as you have used the Application Manager to install and start your application, it is ready to run. To access the application, type the URL you specified in the application manager.

```
http://www.myserver.com/appname/
```

It's very important to remember to add the last forward slash when referring to your application by the directory name. Forgetting to add the slash will cause the application to be "Not Found."

You can also enter the full path and filename of your application.

```
http://www.myserver.com/appdirectory/appname.html
```

The application should run just fine. If it doesn't, you may want to debug your application using some of the trace and debug functionality explained in the next section. It's also handy to know exactly what happens when you run your application. This will help you troubleshoot any problems you may encounter.

When an application runs, LiveWire performs the following steps in processing each page request:

1. *Server authorization.* When requests fail server authorization, none of the other steps occur.

2. *Create New Request Object.* When the server creates a new request object, it also initializes the built-in properties and forms properties that may be associated with the request.

3. *Create or Restore Client Object.* If no client object exists, and one is required, LiveWire will create one.

4. *Save Client Object Properties.* Before sending data back to the client, LiveWire will save any client object properties that may exist. Remember that the client object has no *default* properties. This step occurs only if a client object exists.

5. *Send HTML to the client.* A Web page is sent to the client. This Web page may have been created dynamically by JavaScript or it may have been a static Web page.

6. *Save or Destroy the Client Object.* If a client object was created, it will either be saved or destroyed in this step.

7. *Destroy Request Object.* The request object created in step 2 is destroyed by LiveWire.

8. *Update Server Logs.* The Netscape server updates its logs as a part of its administrative tasks.

Remember, both server and project objects will already exist when the request is sent. The server object is created when the server is started, and the project object is created when the application is first started.

Debug Function and Trace Utility

For those who don't always generate perfectly working applications the first time, there are some debug and trace features to work out any bugs in your application. There are two features in LiveWire for finding problems in your program.

- Trace
- Debug

Tracing

Trace features are used to trace the activity of a program while it's running. Some trace utilities are very thorough and follow every line processed by the application. The trace feature in LiveWire isn't quite that thorough. What you can see are values of object variables and the values of properties in debug functions (explained later in this section).

To utilize the trace utility you must start a second copy of Navigator. (Two copies of Navigator will run simultaneously.) In one running copy (instance) of Navigator you will run your application. In the other instance you will run the trace utility. Start a new copy of Navigator by selecting **File|New Web Browser**.

Wait before starting either the trace utility or your application because they have to be started in a specific order. Once you have both copies of Navigator running, start the trace utility in one of them. Start trace by adding **/trace** to the end of the URL you would normally use to start your application.

```
http://titanium.science.org/video/trace
```

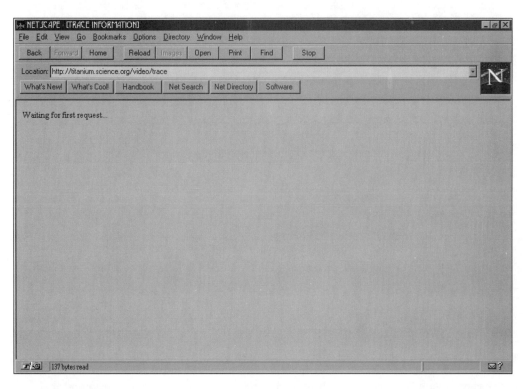

▬▬▬▬▬ **Figure 5.8** The trace utility has started and is waiting for the application to send a request.

In Figure 5.8 you see that the trace utility has started and is waiting for input. Don't get excited about the fact that your Netscape icon will continue to have a meteor shower. The trace utility page will appear to continue receiving data until the trace utility is stopped.

Switch to the other running version of Navigator and start your application. If you are using Windows 95, you can click on the Netscape icon in the lower status bar. If you are using Windows 3.1, you can press **Alt-Tab** until the Netscape program appears. Start your application as explained earlier, by typing in the correct URL to access the application. Once your application is running (Figure 5.9), switch back to the Navigator running trace, and you will see the object values displayed in the Navigator window.

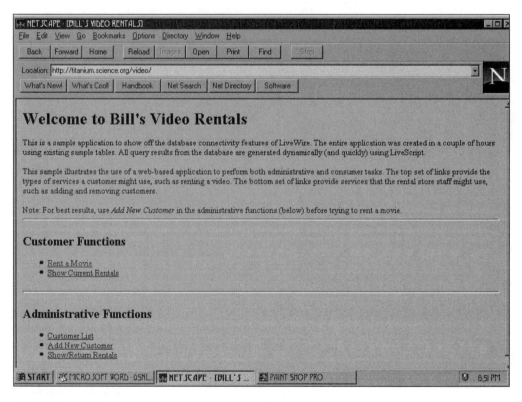

Figure 5.9 The sample video application is running in the second copy of Navigator.

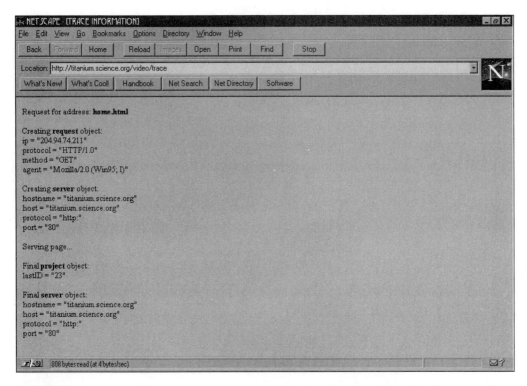

Figure 5.10 Trace displays the status of the application and values stored in object properties.

Debugging

LiveWire provides a function for displaying specific values in the trace utility while the program is running. In some application development environments these are known as "watch variables." The **debug**() function has two parameters, text and display, and a variable whose value you want to display in the trace window.

```
debug("The value I want to see is: ", client.userName)
```

Embed this function in your JavaScript program. When trace is not running, this function is ignored.

What the Future Holds

LiveWire and JavaScript are still new. As new releases come out, some of the things we can look forward to are:

- Greater access to databases
- Communication between JavaScript and Java (JavaScript Wiring)
- Greater access to C programs and legacy systems
- Interobject communications, through which objects can talk to each other using a special object request broker

If the world is your oyster object, then JavaScript is the oyster.pearl.

## CHAPTER 6

USING DATABASES
IN YOUR LIVEWIRE
APPLICATION

Introduction to Databases

A *database management system (DBMS)* is a software package with one simple function: to store data in a special file known as a *database*. Storing information in a database is a little trickier than it may sound. There are some basic technologies you will need to become familiar with to work with databases. To begin, you will need to learn how databases are designed to store information. Then, you will have to learn the Structured Query Language (SQL) to enable you to create a database, add data, change data, delete data, and most importantly, retrieve data.

This chapter is not meant to be an all-encompassing guide to databases. We offer a simple overview of database technology common to most client/server database management systems. To go beyond the information in this chapter, refer to the technical documentation of your DBMS software package.

The Database Object

In Chapter 5 we briefly mentioned that LiveWire has a special server JavaScript object called a database object. Everything you do with a database in JavaScript is done with the database object. This object allows you to perform all the tasks necessary for getting data into and out of a database.

You can think of the database object as being like a file cabinet. This object is responsible for managing and organizing information in the same way a filing cabinet is used in the physical world. The methods of the database object are used to perform all the tasks necessary to store information, change information, and retrieve information from a database.

The database object is a server-only object that is created whenever a connection to a database is established. You can't refer to the database in your client-side JavaScript. Your client-side JavaScript can take advantage of the server programs that can manipulate information in the database.

Connecting to the Database

One of the first things you must do before any dealings with the database can happen is establish a connection between your JavaScript program and the database software. To connect to a database use the database object method *connect()*.

```
database.connect(DBTYPE, servername, username, password, databaseName)
```

- *DBTYPE*. This is the type or brand of DBMS to which you are connecting.
- *servername*. This is the name of the server (machine) on which the database is located.
- *username*. Required by database security, this is the name of the user connecting to the database.
- *password*. Also required by database security, this is the password of *username*.
- *databaseName*. This is the name of the file used to store information within a DBMS.

At this time, there are several types of DBMS brands and types (DBTYPE) with which the JavaScript database object will connect: Oracle, Sybase, Informix, and Illustra. There is a standard database interface known as ODBC, and the database object will also connect to databases that support this common interface. These include database packages like Watcom, Visual dBASE, and XDB. If you have any question about whether your database management system supports ODBC, refer to the documentation or contact your DBMS vendor.

Your database does not have to reside on the same machine as the Web server, provided that the database is accessible by network. Remember that the Internet is a network, which means that as long as your database is accessible via the Net, you can talk to it from your Web server JavaScript program. A little warning, though: until network-level encryption is implemented, information sent between your JavaScript program and the database will be sent unencrypted.

Most client/server database management systems provide security at the user level. This means that to access a database, the DBMS requires a user ID and a password. You can choose to give each user his or her own password or implement a single user ID and password used by your JavaScript program. How you implement security depends entirely on the application you are building. If you are implementing public access to your database, it makes sense to have a single user ID and password in your JavaScript program.

A *database* is a file in which information is stored by a database management system. A database is organized into smaller units called *tables*. Each database management system can have many different databases. For example, one database might store a company's financial data; a different database can be used to store video clips and animations used to create exciting Web content. When you use the connect() method of the database object, you are connecting to just one of these databases.

Once you've attempted a connection to the database using database.connect(), it's good form to make sure you are actually connected. Otherwise, every other attempt to talk to the database will fail. The database object has a *connected()* method that tests the connection to the database. This method returns a True value if the connection to the database is valid and False if there is no connection.

Here is an example that uses the connected() method to test the connection. (Notice that the (!) is a Boolean operator that means *not*.)

```
<SERVER>
database.connect(SYBASE, myserver, ted, mypassword, mydatabase);
if(!database.connected())
        write("There was an error connecting to the database.");
</SERVER>
```

A Web application establishes a single connection to the database, either when the application is first loaded or when the first request is sent for information contained in the database.

Although an application is limited to one single database connection at any one time, it isn't limited to communicating with a single database. At any time, an application can establish a connection with another database. This database does not have to be contained within the same DBMS or located on the same server.

To be able to connect to another database, it's important to be able to disconnect from a database. Use the disconnect() method of the database object to sever your connection to a database. When this method is called, all connections to the database are immediately terminated. This must happen before a connection with a different database can be established.

```
<SERVER>
database.disconnect()
database.connect(INFORMIX, newserver, ted, mypassword, newdatabase);
if(!database.connected())
        write("There was an error connecting to the database.");
</SERVER>
```

There are two different approaches to establishing database connections:

- *Standard.* The application establishes a connection in an initial page. All the clients are connected to the database at the same time, and they all share the same connection.
- *Serial.* Each client connects to the database in series (one at a time).

You use the standard approach when you are offering public access to a database. All the client Web browsers that use the applications share the same connection to the database, so new connections to the database are not required for each person who wants to access the database. This is known as the standard approach because it has the greatest potential for client applications on the Internet.

Use the serial approach when you want to restrict access to your database. The serial approach requires that new clients log in to the database using their own user name and password. The example at the end of the chapter demonstrates how this approach can be used to allow users to log in to an online magazine only if they have subscribed. If you were going to expand this application, you might consider the standard approach for allowing nonsubscribed users to add themselves to a *new_subscriber* database. Once the new subscribers had been validated and given user names and passwords, they would be moved into the *subscriber* database. (See the example at the end of this chapter.)

Tables

Databases store information in tables. Just like an organized chest of drawers, a database is organized into logical divisions. You can see in Figure 6.1 that the database *MyDatabase* is organized into four tables containing video clips, animations, photos, and sounds. If this were a database that collected financial information, the tables could be organized by type of ledger.

Organizing a database into tables is the first step in designing a system that stores information. We aren't pretending to teach you everything there is to know about

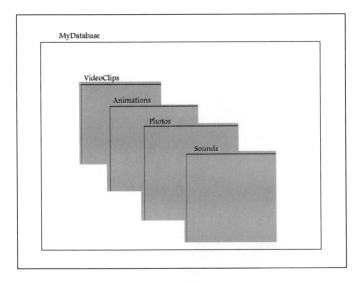

MyDatabase

VideoClips

Animations

Photos

Sounds

Figure 6.1 Databases are organized into tables.

database design in a single chapter. There are people who devote their entire lives to learning better methods of designing databases.

Columns and Rows

There are several layers of detail in creating and using databases. You have seen that the top level of detail is the DBMS. Within a DBMS you have databases, and within a database you further organize information into tables. The lowest and most important levels of detail are the columns and rows. Information stored in a table is held in a grid fashion. If you are familiar with spreadsheets, you will note some similarity to the grid fashion used to store information in cells. Tables store specific types of information, such as someone's name, address, and telephone number. Each type of information is stored within a column, so designing tables consists of determining what columns will exist within a table.

Columns in database tables are also known as *fields.*

Figure 6.2 shows the *sounds* table blown up so that you can see the detail. Four columns are defined: Description, SoundType, SoundFile, and Sound. You can also see in this figure that each of the columns has a type and length identified. Most client/server databases have other column attributes that can be defined, such as

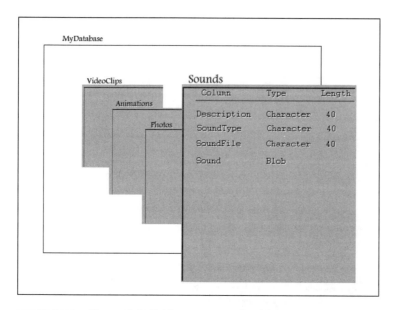

MyDatabase

VideoClips

Animations

Photos

Sounds

Column	Type	Length
Description	Character	40
SoundType	Character	40
SoundFile	Character	40
Sound	Blob	

■■■■■ **Figure 6.2** Tables are organized into columns of information.

whether or not a null value can be stored in the column being defined. Be sure to check the DBMS manual.

It's important to understand that databases are made of tables and tables are organized into columns. This is how you will put information into a database as well as retrieve it. When you add information to a database table, it is added as a row of information. For example, in the *sounds* table from Figures 6.1 and 6.2 each new sound you store in the table creates a new row of information. If a table has no information, it will have columns, but no rows.

Each column has a datatype. Only information of the datatype matching that of the column type can be stored in rows within a column. For instance, if a column is *character type,* only character (text) data can be stored in that column. If you try to store number or date data in a character column, you will receive an error message.

Relationships

You may have heard the term *relational database.* Information in a relational database is organized in tables that are related to one another (Figure 6.3). You could say that the tables were tied together by a common link. This link that ties the tables together in relationships is usually a common column in each table. Here is an example:

```
Table PersonInfo

Column          Type            Size

======================================

Name            Character       40

Address         Character       40

City            Character       20

State           Character       2

Zipcode         Character       5

SSN             Character       9


Table AccountInfo

Column          Type            Size

======================================

SSN             Character       9

AccountType     Character       15

AccountNumber   Character       15
```

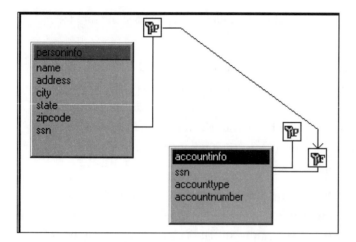

■■■■■■■ **Figure 6.3** Tables are related by key fields shown here marked with a key.

These two tables, PersonInfo and AccountInfo, are related by the SSN column. This way, information about a person does not have to be duplicated in the AccountInfo table. The PersonInfo table is the *parent* table, and the AccountInfo table is the *child* table. Tables can have multiple relationships. A parent table can also be related as a child table to another parent.

The way tables are related is most important when you are trying to retrieve information. For example, you may want to retrieve all account information stored in the AccountInfo table for an individual who has an entry in the PersonInfo table. You do this by using a special database query language called SQL.

Introduction to SQL

SQL, or Structured Query Language, is an industry-standard language used for communicating with client/server databases. Almost all DBMS software packages support the use of SQL to perform tasks such as:

- Creating new databases
- Creating tables
- Adding new rows of data to a table

- Changing or updating information stored in a database
- Deleting information stored in a database
- Retrieving information from the database

An explanation of creating databases and tables is beyond the scope of this book. A special application for LiveWire database administration called DBAdmin is designed specifically for database administrative tasks such as creating new databases and tables. Unless you are a database administrator, it's more likely that you will be building Web applications that communicate with existing databases. For that reason we will be concentrating on the ability to add, change, delete, and retrieve data. If you are a database administrator, make sure to contact Netscape for information on DBAdmin.

Executing SQL in JavaScript

As you learn how to construct powerful SQL statements, you will want to be able to execute them from your JavaScript applications. One of the ways SQL statements are sent to the database management system to be executed is using the execute() method of the database object. SQL statements are character strings that are passed as parameters in the execute() method. Make sure you place the SQL statements within quotes.

```
<SERVER>
AcctType = "Checking"
AcctNumber = "5555123456789"
database.execute("INSERT INTO AccountInfo (AccountType,AccountNumber) VALUES
(AcctType,AcctNumber)")
</SERVER>
```

This example shows how an SQL statement used to insert data into the AccountInfo table is sent to the DBMS using the execute() method. The specifics of how to create this SQL statement will be covered in greater detail later in this chapter. Another method used specifically for retrieving data from a database and displaying it in an HTML table is the SQLTable() method.

```
<SERVER>
database.SQLTable("SELECT AccountType, AccountNumber FROM PersonInfo,
AccountInfo WHERE PersonInfo.SSN == AccountInfo.SSN")
</SERVER>
```

There are other special methods of the database object used to send SQL to the database manager. Ddatabase.execute() and database.SQLTable() are the two primary methods used for manipulating and retrieving data from a database.

Data Handling

The primary job of any database application is to handle data. What is actually done with the data depends entirely on the type of application you are building. For applications known as data entry programs, the prime purpose is to allow users to enter data into a database. There are some programs that only retrieve information from a database. These programs are sometimes known as reporting or query programs. The information is usually read-only and can only be retrieved from the database. Full-featured applications allow users to add, change, and delete information as well as retrieve information. You can do all of these through your Web applications. You can allow users to enter data into a form and have it saved into a database. You can also allow them to modify information already stored in the database by first providing the existing information on a form and then letting them modify the information, saving the changes back to the database.

The most popular type of database application on the Internet today is a query-only type. These Web applications retrieve data from a database based on information entered into a form by a user. This type of querying is sometimes known as an *ad hoc* query. An ad hoc query is one that a user constructs rather than run a pre-existing (hard-coded) query. Familiar examples of this type of query are the search capabilities of popular directories such as Yahoo! and Inktomi (Figure 6.4).

Using the database.execute() Method

Database Management Systems are controlled entirely by commands issued in SQL. The name SQL is a little misleading because you might think that this language is used only for retrieving data from the database. In actuality, SQL is used for nearly every purpose from creating new databases, dropping databases, creating and dropping tables, adding data, and changing data to deleting data. Of course, SQL is also used to query the database.

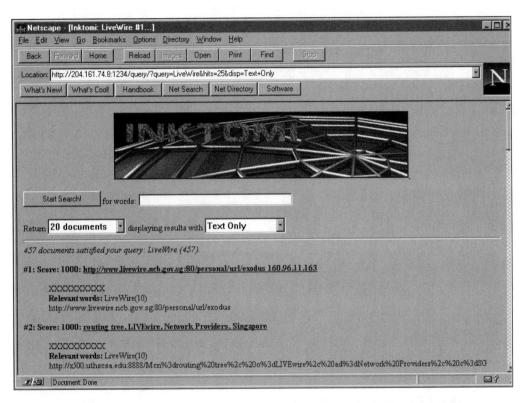

Figure 6.4 The Inktomi Internet query form queries millions of database records.

JavaScript has a special database object method called execute(). This method allows you to pass SQL statements to the DBMS program, which will interpret them and carry out whatever directives are in the statement. Building all the SQL statements into JavaScript really isn't possible because of the different implementations of SQL in each DBMS package. Most SQL statements are similar because SQL is based on an ANSI standard, but each DBMS vendor has extended SQL to add functionality and features.

If you are an advanced database programmer you will want to use the execute() method to communicate with stored procedures and database triggers.

Inserting Information into the Database

The SQL statement used for adding new rows of information into a database is INSERT. The INSERT statement needs to include:

- The name of the table to which you are adding data
- The columns in which the data will reside
- The values you would like to add

```
<SERVER>

database.execute("INSERT INTO AccountInfo (SSN, AccountType, AccountNumber)
VALUES ('888871234', 'Checking', '1233546894')")

</SERVER>
```

This INSERT statement adds a new row into the AccountInfo table. After the required INSERT INTO statement, include the name of the table into which you are inserting values. Next, list each of the three columns in the first set of parentheses. This list is followed by the SQL keyword VALUES, followed by the value to be entered in each column. The INSERT statement is simple compared to some of the other SQL statements: using INSERT INTO you add data to a single table one row at a time.

Updating the Database

Once information is stored in a database, you can change it by using the UPDATE statement.

```
<SERVER>

AcctNumber = "123234345456"

AcctType = "Checking"

AcctSSN = "888871234"

database.execute("UPDATE AccountInfo SET AccountNumber = AcctNumber

WHERE AccountType == AcctType and SSN == AcctSSN")

</SERVER>
```

The SQL statement UPDATE requires the name of the table you are updating. Follow the name of the table with the SET keyword, which specifies which columns are being updated and tells their new values. Unlike with the INSERT INTO statement, you do not use the keyword VALUES in the UPDATE statement. Notice the WHERE statement, sometimes known as the *WHERE clause*. It specifies exactly which rows you want updated. In this case, that means only the rows in which the AcctType is equal to "Checking" and the SSN number is equal to "888871234." All other rows not matching these criteria will remain unchanged.

Deleting Information from the Database

The DELETE statement is used to remove rows from the database. When deleting from a database table, you must delete entire rows. To delete information in a single column use the UPDATE statement.

```
<SERVER>
AcctType = "Checking"
AcctSSN = "888871234"
database.execute("DELETE FROM AccountInfo
WHERE SSN == AcctSSN")
</SERVER>
```

In this example all rows in which the social security number equals the value stored in AcctSSN will be deleted. After the keywords DELETE FROM, include the name of the table from which rows are to be deleted. WARNING: Not adding a WHERE clause will delete all rows from the table!

Retrieving Information from a Database

Entire books can be and probably have been written about the SQL statement SELECT, which is used to retrieve information from a database. The description below gives you the bare essentials of how to use the SELECT statement to retrieve information from a database. We will not cover many of the features, such as sorting and grouping data, and some of the more interesting subtleties of outer and inner JOINS.

The SELECT statement can retrieve information from one or several tables simultaneously and return the result of its query, which can be a single row or many rows. There are two ways to return information from a SELECT statement, as explained in the next section. Do not use the database.execute() method because it cannot return data from an SQL statement.

The execute() method will not allow values to be returned.

Returning Database Values
into a Web Page

There are two ways to display the results of a database query in a Web page. One is to format the data yourself using HTML syntax. A much simpler way to return data is using the database.SQLTable() method, which writes the result of your database query into an HTML table. There is no simpler way to display your data. You do, however, lose control of how the information is formatted. The SQLTable() method creates a simple table with column names appearing at the head of each column.

```
database.SQLTable(SQL SELECT Statement)
```

Be warned that a large database may return thousands of values. SQLTable() will return these values into a Web page that may take a great deal of time to load (Figure 6.3).

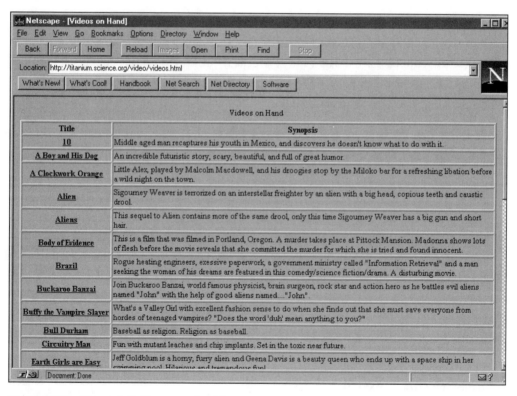

■■■■■■ **Figure 6.5** The sample video store application is a good example of how data is returned to the Web browser.

Using the SELECT statement to Query the Database

The SELECT statement has many possible clauses and keywords. Refer to your DBMS manual for a good overview of using SELECT with your database. For now, here's a simple example:

```
database.SQLTable("SELECT AccountType, AccountNumber FROM AccountInfo
WHERE PersonInfo.Name == "Smith" and PersonInfo.SSN == AccountInfo.SSN")
```

The SELECT statement has features that are similar to those in the other SQL statements. You must include the column names you would like returned from your query and the table names where the columns can be found, following the FROM keyword. In this example, we have included an optional WHERE clause to limit the results of the query.

As we mentioned, there is no way to cover the SELECT statement in all of its complexity in this short description. This is the most commonly used SQL statement, and it's worth knowing well. You should definitely find out how your DBMS implements this powerful statement.

Database Column Types

Databases store information in columns, each of which has a datatype. Databases support a wide variety of datatypes, and some even offer money as a datatype. LiveWire converts each of these datatypes to JavaScript values. You may want to check the documentation for your DBMS and match datatypes against JavaScript equivalents.

- Character datatype is converted to a JavaScript string.
- Numeric datatype is converted to a JavaScript number.
- Dates are converted to JavaScript date objects.
- Null values are converted to JavaScript null values.

Remember from Chapter 4 that working with dates is a little different in JavaScript. Dates are objects created with the *new* operator.

```
dateObject = new Date("dateString")
```

Before storing a date value in a database date column, you must make sure that your date is a valid JavaScript date object. To be a valid JavaScript date object it must have been created with the syntax we've included previously.

Database Cursors

Cursors provide a special way of handling data with SQL when you expect one or more rows to be returned from a query (SELECT statement). When you use a cursor, values (rows of information) are returned from a query and stored temporarily in your computer's memory. Using some of the special methods of the database object, you can manipulate this group of rows in memory. A row is often known as either an *answer set* or *result set*. The way you work with a cursor is by incrementing your way through the rows in the answer set. We'll begin by creating a cursor.

```
<SERVER>

UpDate = True

MyResult = database.cursor("SELECT * from PersonInfo WHERE State =
'CA'",UpDate);

</SERVER>
```

In our sample, searching on "CA" returns many rows of information. There is a second parameter to the cursor() method that tells the database object whether the database can be updated or not.

Once a cursor has been created, which means that an answer set is now residing in memory, it will remain in memory until the *cursor.close()* method is called. This removes the answer set from memory, releasing any memory space it had occupied.

A couple of limitations to using cursors are the following:

- Cursors cannot span more than one Web source file (Web page).
- Cursors must be updatable before you can use insert, update, and delete methods (described next).

Navigating Through the Data

The SELECT statement you include in your database.cursor() method will run a query against the database returning a set of rows. This set of information, the answer set, is held temporarily in your computer's memory as a *cursor object*. Therefore, you create the cursor object by storing the result of the database.cursor() method. In the example code from the previous section, the value *MyResult* is the cursor object. To use this information (cursor object) you must be able to "move" through the information.

When a cursor object is created, it points to the first row in the answer set by default. It's important to be able to navigate through the data, which means being able to refer to the different columns of information within a row and being able to move to the next row. There are two methods that will help you refer to columns in an answer set. The first method is cursor.columns(), which will return the number of columns in the answer set. The second, cursor.columnNames(), returns the names of all the columns in the answer set. You may then refer to the value in each column by referring to the column name.

You can imagine that the cursor object has a row pointer. As we mentioned earlier, this pointer will point to the first row when the cursor is first created. To be able to increment through the rows, the cursor object has a method called *cursor.next()* that moves the row pointer to the next row in the answer set. The column values will then reflect whatever is stored in the row currently pointed to by the row pointer.

```
<SERVER>
UpDate = True
MyResult = database.cursor("SELECT * from PersonInfo WHERE State =
'CA'",UpDate);

Name1 = MyResult.Name
MyResult.next()
Name2 = MyResult.Name
</SERVER>
```

In this example, the *Name1* variable is filled in with the value, stored in the *Name* column of the answer set (see Table 6.1). By default, references to the answer set will refer to the first row returned. *Name2* returns the value stored in the Name column of the second row.

■■■■■■■■ Table 6.1 The Cursor Object Consists of a Query Result

Name	Address	City	State	Zip Code	SSN
Joe Smith	123 Elm St.	Hawthorne	CA	90250	555-55-5555
Terri Jones	2345 Oak St.	Torrance	CA	92024	444-44-4444
Vivek Patel	2121 34th St.	Palo Alto	CA	92123	333-33-3333
Susan Anderson	12 Park Lane	Barstow	CA	95432	222-22-2222

You can refer to information in the answer set like this:
CursorName.NameOfColumn where *CursorName* is the name of the cursor object
and *NameOfColumn* is the name of the column in the database table.

```
MyResult.Name

MyResult.Address

MyResult.City
```

This works great if you know the names of the columns in the database. When the
column names are not available, there is still a way to refer to each column. Use the
columnName property of the cursor object like this: *CursorName*.columnName(*n*)
where *CursorName* is the name of the cursor object and *n* is the number of the column, beginning with zero. In the sample result set in this section, the *Name* column
can be referred to as MyResult.columnName(0).

```
<SERVER>

UpDate = True

MyResult = database.cursor("SELECT * from PersonInfo WHERE State =
'CA'",UpDate);


Name1 = MyResult.Name          //This returns the same value

Name1 = MyResult.columnName(0)  //as this.

</SERVER>
```

Using cursor objects, you can create and work with information returned from the
database, build reports, evaluate information, and perform ad hoc queries using the
database and cursor objects.

Inserting Rows with Cursors

Earlier in this chapter you learned how it is possible to add information to a database using the SQL statement INSERT. When working with cursors, you have a
simple way to add information to the database.

1. Begin by creating a cursor.
   ```
   MyResult = database.cursor("SELECT SSN, AccountType, AccountNumber FROM
   AccountInfo", TRUE);
   ```

2. Set new values for each column.
   ```
   MyResult.SSN = "444-44-4444";
   ```

```
MyResult.AccountType = "Savings";

MyResult.AccountNumber = "0123345343434";
```

3. Use the insertRow() method of the cursor object to add a row to the database table.

```
myResult.insertRow(AccountInfo);
```

The information set in step 2 will be added as a new row in the AccountInfo table.

Updates with Cursors

Update the information stored in a database table using cursors in a way similar to inserting information using cursors (explained in the previous section). Instead of using the *cursor.insertRow()* method, use *cursor.updateRow()*.

1. Create the cursor by first performing a query (see Inserting Rows with Cursors).

2. Set the column values.

```
MyResult.SSN = "444-44-4444";

MyResult.AccountType = "Savings";

MyResult.AccountNumber = "0123345343434";
```

3. Use the updateRow() method of the cursor object to update the table information.

```
MyResult.updateRow(AccountInfo)
```

Only the row that is currently being accessed by the cursor will be updated.

Deleting with Cursors

Deleting the information in a database table using cursors is similar to updating information. To delete information use the *cursor.deleteRow()* method of the cursor object.

1. Create the cursor by first performing a query (see Inserting Rows with Cursors).

2. Set the cursor to the row you want deleted using the next() method.

```
MyResult.next();
```

3. Use the deleteRow() method of the cursor object to delete the current row.

```
MyResult.deleteRow(AccountInfo);
```

Make certain the correct row is selected before calling the deleteRow() method.

Support for BLObs

Many client/server databases have a special datatype known as a BLOb (binary large object) that stores binary information such as sound data, audio data, and video data. Although there are many other types of digital information, these three types are important to creating multimedia Web content.

We explained earlier that each column in a database table is given a datatype. These datatypes can be character, numeric, date, Boolean, and several other types, depending on the brand of DBMS you purchase. To store binary information in a column, you must designate it as a BLOb. Because this datatype is a little unusual, the database cursor object uses special methods and functions to handle BLOb data.

Inserting BLObs into the Database

When not stored in a database, binary data is normally stored in files. For example, one type of binary file commonly used by Web developers is a .JPG graphic file. Storing this binary file in a BLOb field is a two-step process. First you must use the **blob()** function to convert the information in the JPG file to BLOb format and store the return value in the cursor field.

```
MyResult.BlobFieldName = blob("ocean.jpg")
```

The second step is to use the insertRow() method explained earlier to insert the cursor information into the database table. Here is an sample that inserts a new row into the table called *picture_table* (Figure 6.6).

Figure 6.6 A new row is inserted into the picture_table.

```
<SERVER>
MyResult = database.cursor("SELECT * FROM picture_table");
MyResult.description = "Sunset over Stone Steps Beach";
MyResult.image = blob("sunset.jpg");
MyResult.insertRow("picture_table");
</SERVER>
```

Tables can have more than one BLOb field. An example of a table with more than one column containing BLOb data is one in which a picture is associated with a sound file. You could play a .WAV file of surf crashing on the beach while displaying the graphic of the sunset.

BLObs as HTML Images

Web site developers are familiar with the HTML <IMG> tag that allows you to insert an image into a Web page. <IMG> tags have the names of the graphic files they display "hard coded" as a parameter of the tag. Using BLOb data images in your Web pages can be dynamic. The image displayed can be binary graphic data returned from a database query.

The **blobImage**() function displays binary information stored in a BLOb field as an image in a Web browser. Format the blobImage() method the same way you would an <IMG> tag. To properly format the blobImage() method, include the following parameters:

- Format type of the image
- A string to be displayed by text-only Web browsers (optional)
- A string to set left, right, or center alignment (optional)
- The ISMAP parameter is included when the image is to be used as a clickable image map (optional)

```
MyResult.BLObfieldname.blobImage(ImageFormat, ALTstring, ALIGNstring, ISMAP)
```

Linking to BLOb Fields

There are times when you won't want your BLOb data to appear directly in your Web page. In these cases you will want a link to your BLOb field so that users can take the binary data into their Web page with a click of their mouse. The blobLink() method is used to create this link. There are two parameters to the blobLink() method: mimetype and linktext. The mimetype is the string that includes the top-level MIME type and the sublevel MIME type ("audio/x-wav"). The linktext is the character string that appears in the Web page as the link.

```
Blobfieldname.blobLink(mimetype, linktext)
```

The blobLink() method keeps the binary data in memory until the user clicks on the link. The binary data is not stored indefinitely in memory; after 60 seconds the information is removed from memory.

On-Line Transaction Processing

On-Line Transaction Processing, commonly known as OLTP, supports the ability for a computer application to *roll back* changes made to the database. Undoing changes made to a database is known as *rollback*. For applications in which many changes and additions are made to the database, an ability to roll back changes is an important feature. For example, a point of sale (cash register) program is being used by a clerk selling socks. The entire order is rung up, and changes are made to the cash and inventory tables. Unfortunately, the customer has forgotten his wallet and wants the transaction voided. The rollback feature of the database is used to undo any changes made to the database.

Because you would not want to undo all changes made for the entire day, week, or year the database has been running, the concept of a *transaction* exists. As in the example of the cash register, each sale is a transaction. Changes made during that transaction only can be rolled back. Prior transactions have already been *committed* to the database. When information is committed, the database enters it into the tables in such a way that subsequent rollback commands will not affect this information.

The database object has three methods used for controlling transaction processing in a JavaScript application.

- *beginTransaction()*. Used to begin a transaction
- *commitTransaction()*. Commits data into the database and ends a transaction
- *rollbackTransaction()*. Undoes any changes to the database during a transaction and ends the current transaction

Almost all client/server databases use transactions, although it's not always required that application developers concern themselves with transactions. Transaction procession will still continue in the background with a built-in database feature known as *auto commit*. Unless you issue the beginTransaction() method, transaction processing will be set to auto commit by default. The rest of this description of OLTP will assume that the developer has chosen to have greater control over transaction processing by using the transaction processing methods of the database object.

Transactions always begin with the beginTransaction() method. Transactions can end in one of four ways:

- A commitTransaction() method is called.
- A rollbackTransaction() method is called.
- The user exits the Web page.
- The computer crashes.

We haven't really talked about the last possibility. This is another reason OLTP is so important in database applications. In the event of a power failure or other catastrophic computer failure, all changes that have been committed to the database will be safe. Any uncommitted changes will be lost.

In the event of a catastrophic computer failure, uncommitted changes to the database are lost.

Transactions can not span multiple Web pages. When a user exits a Web page, the database performs a commit automatically. This is a fail-safe action on behalf of the database. The database management system does not see exiting the Web page normally as a catastrophic event, so the DBMS determines that a normal commit should occur. If you want to override that action, issue a rollbackTransaction() in the onUnload event of your window object.

When using most of the supported database management systems, before beginning a new transaction, you must first resolve the current transaction by committing or rolling back the transaction. Nested transactions are supported only by Sybase.

To Commit or Not to Commit

Transaction processing is another one of those database topics on which entire books have been written. When to end a transaction is the topic of much debate. We will explain the question on a very superficial level and leave the choice of when to end transactions up to you.

In a Web source file you have placed three forms, each with its own **Submit** buttons. The information entered in these three forms is all related, and each form updates the database. Do you commit the data after each submit or after the last submit? Here are some of the pros and cons:

- If you commit after each submit, and you need to cancel during the other two, removing the changes from the database will be very difficult.
- If you commit only after the last submit and an error occurs during data entry of the last form, the end user will have to re-enter data in the previous two forms.

Ask yourself how much data it's safe to have uncommitted at any one time, and balance that against how difficult it might be to remove committed data from the database. To remove data that has already been committed you must have a record of what changes were made and then issue the deleteRow() method to remove the data. Basically, you don't want to delete committed data if you can help it.

Here is an example that rolls back a transaction if the INSERT to the database returns an error (Figure 6.7).

■■■■■■ **Figure 6.7** Rollback() will return database values to their prechange values.

```
<SERVER>
database.beginTransaction()      //This begins the transaction


ReturnError = database.execute('INSERT INTO PersonInfo (
Name,
Address,
City,
State,
Zipcode,
SSN )
VALUES (
"Matthew Wagner",
"2121 Elm Street",
"Cardiff by the Sea",
"CA",
"92102",
"555-55-5555")');


if (!ReturnError){
```

```
        ReturnError = database.execute('INSERT INTO AccountInfo (
        AccountType,
        AccountNumber)
        VALUES (
        "Savings",
        "342344365")');

        if (ReturnError){
                database.rollbackTransaction();
        else    //No error occurred, OK to commit
                database.commitTransaction();
}
else    //An error occurred in the attempt to save to PersonInfo
        database.rollbackTransaction();


</SERVER>
```

Database Error Handling

No one likes errors, but they happen, and it's your job is to be prepared for them.
The database object returns error codes when something goes wrong. This could
mean problems with the server, a library error, or a lost connection, or your computer could be out of memory. The database object has four additional methods for
discovering what type of error has occurred so your program can take the appropriate action.

- *database.majorErrorCode()*. This returns the major error code returned by
  the DBMS server or connectivity library.

- *database.majorErrorMessage()*. This returns the text describing the major
  error that has occurred.

- *database.minorErrorCode()*. This returns a code describing minor errors
  reported by the DBMS.

- *database.minorErrorMessage()*. This returns the text of the error message returned by the DBMS. It also returns the name of the server in case there is a server error.

To see the error messages returned by the error-handling methods, you must be using the trace utility when running your application. When you are not running trace, the error messages will not appear.

Database Status Codes

Database status codes are returned from most of the different database methods. You can use these return codes to evaluate the success or failure of your database access attempts. We have included a table of Netscape LiveWire's status code descriptions (Table 6.2). You can build an error-handling routine that will allow your JavaScript applications to return these messages.

■■■■■■■ **Table 6.2** Database Status Codes

Status Code	Description
0	No error
1	Out of memory
2	Object never initialized
3	Type conversion error
4	Database not registered
5	Error reported by server
6	Message from server
7	Error from vendor's library
8	Lost connection
9	End of fetch
10	Invalid use of object
11	Column does not exist
12	Invalid positioning within object (i.e., bounds error)
13	Unsupported feature
14	Null reference parameter
15	Database object not found
16	Required information is missing

▪▪▪▪▪▪ **Table 6.2** Continued

Status Code	Description
17	Object cannot support multiple readers
18	Object cannot support deletions
19	Object cannot support insertions
20	Object cannot support updates
21	Object cannot support updates
22	Object cannot support indices
23	Object cannot be dropped
24	Incorrect connection supplied
25	Object cannot support privileges
26	Object cannot support cursors
27	Unable to open

▪▪▪▪▪▪

Database Object Sample Application

We are including a small application to demonstrate the use of the database object and its methods.

We begin by creating *index.html*. This is the page the user will first see. In this page we use the database.connected() method to determine whether or not the database was connected before this page was loaded.

▪▪▪▪▪▪ **Figure 6.8** The index.html.

```
<HTML>
<HEAD>
<TITLE>Web Programmer's Journal</TITLE>
</HEAD>


<BODY bgcolor="#FFFFFF">
<SERVER>
```

Continued...

```
if (!database.connected())              //Check for a DB connection
{
        if (server.dbtype = "INFORMIX")
        {
                database.connect("INFORMIX", "NEPTUNE", "ted",
"webpgrm", "subscribers");
        }

</SERVER>
<CENTER>
<H1>Web Programmer's Journal</H1>
</CENTER>
<HR>
<FORM name="login" action="process.html">
<H3>Subscriber Login</H3>
Name: <input type="text" name="s_name" size=25>
Password: <input type="password" name="s_pass" size=25>
<P>
<INPUT TYPE="submit" NAME="MySubmit" VALUE="Login">
<HR>
</FORM>
</BODY>
</HTML>
```

Figure 6.9 This Web source file authenticates the user's password in the database.

```
<HTML>
<BODY>
<SERVER>
subscriber = request.s_name
password = request.s_pass
```

```
MyResult = database.cursor("SELECT name, password FROM subscribers")


while (MyResult.next())

        {

                if (MyResult.name == subscriber && MyResult.password ==
password)

                {

                        redirect("magazine.html")

                }

        }
</BODY>
</HTML>
```

▉▉▉▉▉▉

▉▉▉▉▉▉ **Figure 6.10** This is the magazine users see when their password is authenticated.

```
<HTML>
<HEAD>
<TITLE>Web Programmer's Journal</TITLE>
</HEAD>


<BODY bgcolor="#FFFFFF">
<CENTER>
<H1>Web Programmer's Journal</H1>
</CENTER>
<HR>
Welcome to the Web Programmer's Journal.
<HR>
</BODY>
</HTML>
```

Database applications make up about 90% of all business applications. These database access features of LiveWire allow you to create powerful client/server database applications that run over the World Wide Web. You can offer global access to your company data or restrict access to authorized individuals. You can create contact management programs, accounting systems, inventory control, point of sale, and hundreds of other database applications. You won't be limited to what you can do by LiveWire!

JAVA APPLETS

The Web is rapidly changing from an environment consisting of dull, static text and images into an exciting new multimedia-enhanced environment. Java applets can add this new multimedia capability to your Web site, producing everything from scrolling advertisements and news ticker tapes to Internet relay chat utilities. Amazing features and capabilities are now available for integration in your Web site in the form of Java applets.

Java applets are a subset of the Java language, which is rapidly becoming the Internet computer language. Unlike typical computer applications, Java applets are interpreted rather than compiled. When a computer program is compiled, the written source code is written into machine code. The compiled machine code can then run only on the same operating system that it was compiled on, such as Unix or Windows. A dream of programmers has been to have a computer language that can create an application that can run on every type of operating system. This need has become even more important with the development of the Internet. On the Internet users with a variety of different operating systems interact with the same Web content. Anyone who produces content on the Internet would prefer to not have to provide different content for users with different operating systems.

Java applets have emerged as the solution to these compatibility issues. The solution is based on the difference between Java applets and typical computer programs. When a Java applet class is compiled, it is converted into a generic byte code rather than an operating system-specific machine code. Because the compiled Java applet exists only in byte code, it can't run by itself, but must be run in a program that has a built-in Java interpreter. The Java interpreter reads the byte code and converts it into platform-specific API calls that allow the compiled Java applet to execute on the operating system it has been loaded onto.

Java applets have become integrated into the Internet since the Java interpreter capabilities have been built into Web browsers such as Netscape Navigator 2.0. Now a developer can provide Java applets on a Web site that will be accessible by all users who have the Netscape Navigator 2.0 browser, regardless of whether they are using an Apple or Unix computer.

This chapter demonstrates the features of a wide selection of Java applets. Many of these Java applets are available free or for a small license fee. This availability allows you to quickly add them to your Web pages to expand the appeal and functionality of your Web site.

Placing Java Applets in Web Pages

The structure of the HTML code that is used to place applets in Web source files is very similar to the HTML code required for placing images in Web source files. Rather than the <IMG> tag used for images, applets require the <APPLET> tag to indicate the presence of an applet. In the first <APPLET> tag various attributes can be added that define the characteristics of the applet that will be displayed. These characteristics include information about the name of the applet class file that will be loaded, the URL location to the applet class, and the applet's size dimensions. The list of attributes that you use to define the applet is in Table 7.1.

■■■■■ **Table 7.1** Attributes Used to Define the Operation of the Applet in a Web Source File

Attribute	Description
CODEBASE	The path to the URL location of the applet class.
CODE	The applet class that is to be executed.
NAME	The name of the appletInstanceName that is created. The default is the applet class filename.
WIDTH	The width, in number of pixels, of the applet that will appear.
HEIGHT	The height, in number of pixels, of the applet that will appear.
ALT	Specifies any text that should appear if the user's browser recognizes the <APPLET> tag, but can't run the applet.
ALIGN	The alignment of the applet. The possible entries are the same as with images and include left, right, top, bottom, texttop, middle, absmiddle, baseline, absbottom.

The following example shows the basic structure for the <APPLET> tag that is used to incorporate an applet into a Web source file. This example code also shows the required attributes for successful applet execution.

```
<APPLET CODE=test.class WIDTH= 200 HEIGHT=200>
</APPLET>
```

The other attributes defined in Table 7.1 are optional. This example uses the CODE attribute to identify the location of the applet class file and the WIDTH and HEIGHT attributes to define the dimensions of the applet.

The CODE attribute specifies the desired applet class, which is expected to be in the same location on the server as the Web source file that references it. Many Java applets that are featured in this chapter are freely available for download and integration within your Web site. In some cases an applet class is located in a different location on your local system than it is on the Web source file referencing it. The applet class may even be located on a remote server. You can still incorporate these applets within your Web source file using the CODEBASE attribute to specify the path as shown in the following example.

```
<APPLET CODEBASE="http://www.science.org/donb  CODE=cool.class
WIDTH=100HEIGHT=100>
</APPLET>
```

In this example, the cool.class applet is loaded from the http://www.science.org/donb location. The CODEBASE attribute truly characterizes the spirit of the Internet, giving you the ability to use components from a variety of locations and incorporate them seamlessly into your own Web site.

Applets also feature the ability to have parameters passed to them in the form of NAME|VALUE pairs that the developer can specify to customize an applet for a particular application. The following example code illustrates how parameters are specified with the <APPLET> tag.

```
<APPLET CODE=test.class WIDTH=200 HEIGHT=200>
<PARAMETER  NAME=speed   VALUE=5>
<PARAMETER  NAME=title     VALUE="Don's Fictitious Applet.">
<PARAMETER  NAME=color    VALUE=blue >
</APPLET>
```

In this example several different parameters are specified by the developer. Every applet class has its own parameters to which it is responsive.

■■■■■

> The <APPLET> tag and HTML code are not case sensitive. All the examples in this book show the HTML code in CAPS to differentiate them for the reader. There are some applet parameter NAME|VALUE pairs that are case sensitive, but these particular applets will be identified when they are described.

■■■■■

Some users have Web browsers that don't have a built-in Java interpreter and are unable to recognize the <APPLET> tag. When placing an applet in your Web source file, you should also include the <EM> tag that will display a text message to users who don't have a Java-compatible browser.

```
<APPLET CODE=test.class  WIDTH=100  HEIGHT=100>
<EM> This is for users who aren't using a browser that is Java compatible and
therefore can't see the applet on this Web page. </EM>
</APPLET>
```

Although the majority of Internet users have the Netscape Navigator browser, it is recommended that you include this simple tag with your applets to ensure that users who access your Web pages are aware that their browser prevents them from viewing all of the provided content. You could include in this tag a simple hyperlink to the Netscape site where the user can download a Java-compatible browser.

Using ONETAG

Whenever you place a Java applet within a Web source file, you regularly need to enter numerous parameter NAME|VALUE pairs that pass information to the applet. An example of the typical <APPLET> tag with numerous parameters is shown below.

```
<APPLET  CODE=search.class    WIDTH=250    HEIGHT=175>
<PARAM  NAME=url1    VALUE="http://www.infoseek.com"  >
<PARAM  NAME=url2    VALUE="http://yahoo.com"  >
<PARAM  NAME=sound1    VALUE=welcome.au >
<PARAM  NAME=sound2    VALUE=bye.au >
</APPLET>
```

The developers at Sun Microsystems have created the ONETAG feature to make the entry of parameter NAME|VALUE pairs much simpler for applets that require a large number of parameters. Now you can simply use the NAME=ONETAG command followed by all the different values that are listed in a long string. Here is what the previous <APPLET> tag would look like when the ONETAG feature is used.

```
<APPLET CODE=search.class    WIDTH=250    HEIGHT=175 >
<PARAM   NAME=ONETAG  VALUE="* Name=Value*Name=Value*">
</APPLET>
```

This can dramatically decrease the amount of HTML code written, but keep in mind that the ONETAG feature can be used only with Java applets that are designed to accept it. These applets must have a parsing method built in to allow the name and value entries to be parsed from the parameter code that is passed to the applet. All Java applets that use the ONETAG parameter entry should be backward compatible with the conventional method for entering NAME|VALUE pairs. For more information on the ONETAG, you can check out the following URL address.

http://www.xm.com/cafe/onetag.html

Several of the applets found at this URL location are designated as compliant with the ONETAG feature.

Functions in Applet Execution

When a user contacts a Web page that contains an applet, several stages of execution are completed before the applet can run. This list clearly illustrates the various stages as they occur.

1. An instance class of the applet's controlling class is created.
2. The applet is loaded onto the user's computer.
3. The applet is initialized.
4. The applet starts to run.

As you experiment with applets, you will notice that the status of the loading, initialization, and running stages is displayed in the bottom left side of the Netscape Navigator window, giving the user some visual feedback on what the computer is processing. This visual feedback is useful for you to check to see if an applet is running on your computer even though it may not be visible.

When you advance to another page (or minimize the Web browser with an applet loaded), the applet stops, but it can restart itself if the user returns to the same Web page. Before an applet is unloaded, it is stopped and performs a cleanup procedure, freeing any resources it was using as part of the final destroy process.

Applet Security Features

Java applets can present a major security problem, because a user browsing the Web could unknowingly contact a Web page where a mischievous applet resides. This applet could be downloaded to the user's computer, and while the user is checking stock quotes, the applet could be destroying files that reside on the user's computer. Java applets were therefore designed with several security features built into the run-time environment to limit what they are capable of doing.

The most important security feature prevents Java applets from being able to access files on the computer on which they are being run. A Java applet can neither read nor write to files on a computer system where they reside.

Another security feature prevents Java applets from being able to establish a socket connection to a server other than the server from which the applet was downloaded.

The following is an example of what could happen if Java applets had the ability to establish socket connections to remote servers. A user could contact a particular Web site that has a Java applet residing on it that displayed some animation, such as steam rising from a cup of coffee. While the user admires this cute applet, another part of the applet could contact the Pentagon, and hack its way into the tactical command computer system. Any information that the applet downloaded would be sent to a server in Russia. The user would not realize that any of this information transfer occurred until the CIA shows up, since they would have traced the connection to the computer at the Pentagon from the user's computer. Netscape Navigator prevents scenarios like this by not allowing an applet to contact remote servers.

Java Developer's Kit

The Java Developer's Kit (JDK) is the tool developed and freely distributed by Sun Microsystems that developers can use to create Java applications and Java applets. The JDK has several functions that allow developers to compile classes, run applets, and debug applications. It can be downloaded from Sun Microsystems at the following URL.

http://java.sun.com

After you download the JDK you should make the necessary changes to the autoexec.bat file as directed by the readme file. In this chapter, the JDK serves both as a resource for numerous applets ready for immediate integration into your Web site and as the tool that allows you to convert existing source code into compiled applet classes.

Viewing and Debugging Applets

The JDK is a valuable resource for Java applets because it comes with numerous Java applet classes that you can use. After you have installed the JDK, see a list of the Java applet classes it contains by going to the demo directory.

```
C:\Java\demo
```

Several of these applet classes can add useful multimedia capabilities to your Web site, but of course you first need to see them for yourself. There are two ways for you to view the way these applets look and function. The first way is to simply use your Netscape Navigator browser, but rather than opening a file at a particular location, choose the **File|Open File** selection. This selection allows you to open a local file in the browser window. Then simply choose the desired example HTML file found in each of the demo applet class directories. This should load the applet and execute it in the Netscape Navigator, giving you a chance to evaluate its performance.

The other technique to test and evaluate a particular applet involves using the appletviewer command that is built into the JDK. After finding the appropriate applet, simply type the **appletviewer** command followed by the HTML filename as shown in the following example.

```
C:\Java\demo\ScrollingImages> appletviewer  example1.html
```

The appletviewer feature requires that the indicated applet class be in the same directory as the HTML filename that references it, unless the CODEBASE attribute is used to specify the path to the applet class. Once the command is entered, the appletviewer will be launched as shown in Figure 7.1, and you will be able to see the applet execute.

When the appletviewer is executed, you will see not only the applet execute, but also run-time information displayed in the DOS window as illustrated in Figure 7.2. The run-time information includes information such as if the referenced applet class was found and when various streams are opened. The appletviewer in combination with the information that is displayed in the DOS viewer is a very useful tool to debug your applets.

Another debugging tool that you have at your disposal is the Java console window you can display by choosing the **Options|Show Java Console** selection in the Netscape Navigator browser. This results in Netscape Navigator launching a pop-up window that displays information if some problem occurs when the applet is running.

Figure 7.1 The **appletviewer** window displays the applet and any errors that may occur with it.

▆▆▆▆▆▆▆▆ **Figure 7.2** Applet run-time information is displayed in the DOS window to assist in debugging.

Figure 7.3 shows the Java console window containing information when an applet didn't successfully run. The problem with this particular applet was that it tried to contact a remote location that would violate its security restrictions.

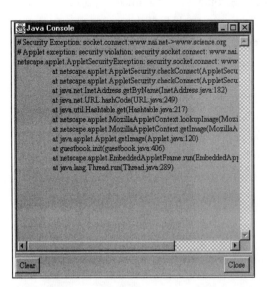

▆▆▆▆▆▆▆▆ **Figure 7.3** The Java console gives you information about why a particular applet doesn't successfully run.

The appletviewer in the JDK and the capabilities of the Netscape Navigator give you the ability to view, evaluate, and debug applets that you plan to incorporate into your Web site.

Demo Applets

In the demo directory of the JDK you will find numerous applets that you can immediately incorporate within your Web site. Of course, some of these applets are more impressive than others. Many of the existing Java applets that have been developed produce graphical animations, which ideally should produce interesting nonstatic Web pages. The problem is many of the graphical animation Java applets that have been created might appear just fine on a Cray supercomputer, but on the typical Internet user's system, these Java applet animations run painfully slow. It is important for you to evaluate an applet's performance on the same type of machine the majority of your users will be viewing it on before you incorporate it into your Web site. Keeping this in mind, we have included a description of several of the demo applets that we found to be quite impressive.

When you incorporate any of these applets from the JDK into your Web site, you will find relatively little documentation on the various attributes and parameters that must be included with the <APPLET> tag. You can best obtain this parameter information simply by viewing the HTML source code of the example HTML file included with every applet. You will still need to do some experimentation, replacing various values for the required parameters to customize the applet to meet your specifications.

ScrollingImages

The ScrollingImages applet allows you to produce an applet that scrolls various images across a Web page from right to left. This is an impressive multimedia-enabling applet that runs quite efficiently. When you run the ScrollingImages applet in the example1.html file, you should see pictures of the Java Developer Team at Sun Microsystems scroll across the Web page.

■■■■

> You may even recognize a couple of famous—or infamous—faces when you run the ScrollingImages applet.

■■■■

Using this applet, you can have any images you like scroll across the Web page. The following example illustrates some of the parameters used in conjunction with the ImageTape.class applet that must be included in the <APPLET> tag.

```
<APPLET CODE="ImageTape.class"  WIDTH=550  HEIGHT=50>
<PARAM NAME=speed    VALUE="4">
<PARAM NAME=img    VALUE="images/team">
<PARAM NAME=dir   VALUE="4">
<PARAM NAME=nimgs   VALUE="15">
</APPLET>
```

These parameters are relatively straightforward, with the *img* parameter indicating the path to the images that are to be displayed and *nimgs* indicating the number of images that will be displayed. You can also see that all of the images are located in the "images/team" subdirectory of the JDK demo directory, and these images are named in sequential order.

ImageMap

The ImageMap applet is also an impressive applet that allows an image to be placed on a Web page while enabling various user interactivity to be linked to specified areas of the image. When you run the example1.html file in the "demo/ImageMap" directory, you should see the image illustrated in Figure 7.4.

Moving your pointer over the man's mouth in the image will result in a sound file playing, and the text "Hi" will appear in the bottom left corner of the viewer. As you can see, this applet allows you to trigger a variety of events.

- Specific text can appear in the browser window when you use the "NameArea" value.
- Sound files can play when you use the "SoundArea" value.
- A hyperlink to a desired URL can be produced when you use either the "HrefButtonArea" or "RoundHrefButtonArea" values.

The following sample code illustrates the sample <APPLET> tag used in the *example1.html* file. Different mapped areas of the image are defined with the *area#* parameter, while the desired effect is defined as the value of the parameter.

Figure 7.4 When you move your mouse pointer over specific areas of the image, various messages will appear or sound files will play.

```
<APPLET CODE=ImageMap.class WIDTH=522 HEIGHT=486>
<PARAM NAME=img  VALUE="jim.graham.gif">
<PARAM NAME=highlight value="brighter30">
<PARAM NAME=area1 VALUE="SoundArea,260,180,120,60,audio/hi.au">
<PARAM NAME=area2 VALUE="Namerea,260,180,120,60,Hi!">
<PARAM NAME=area3 VALUE="NameArea,265,125,45,20,That is my right eye">
<PARAM NAME=area4 VALUE="NameArea,335,130,45,20,That is my left eye">
<PARAM NAME=area5 VALUE="HrefButtonArea,200,7,210,300,/~flar/">
<PARAM NAME=area6 VALUE="RoundHrefButtonArea,60,0,100,120,duke.wave.html">
<PARAM NAME=area7 VALUE="SoundArea,425,98,27,27,audio/chirp1.au">
<PARAM NAME=area8 VALUE="NameArea,425,98,27,27,Chirp!">
<PARAM NAME=area9 VALUE="ClickArea,0,0,522,486">
</APPLET>
```

This applet even allows you to have multiple events occur within a mapped area or to have mapped areas overlap. The ImageMap applet is an impressive and useful applet that can introduce a truly exciting and interesting multimedia capability into your Web pages.

Modifying Applets

Not only are there numerous compiled applet classes in the demo directory of the JDK, but the uncompiled source code for the various applets is also provided as .JAVA files. The availability of the uncompiled source code gives you the option of further modifying a particular applet to meet your needs. You can begin by loading the .JAVA source code file into a text editor and make the desired modifications. After you have edited the source code, you need to compile the .JAVA file to create the compiled applet .CLASS file. You can execute the Java compiler by typing the javac command in combination with the .java source code file as shown in the following example.

```
C:\java\demo\ImageTest>javac  ImageTest.java
```

When this command is executed, the ImageTest.java source code is compiled to create the ImageTest.class applet class, in addition to creating other classes such as the ImageCanvas.class and ImagePanel.class. All of the classes created are needed for the applet to execute, but only the ImageTest.class file needs to be referenced by the CODE attribute in the <APPLET> tag.

Various Java Applets

The realm of possible applications of Java applets is only beginning to be explored, but many Java applets are available for you to use on the Internet. The applications of these applets include graphical animations, chat utilities, and even poetry generators. Many of these applets have features and abilities that can add substantially to the content and presentation of your Web site. Of course, why should you waste the time building something that someone has already built? The Java applets featured in this chapter are available in a variety of forms for you to incorporate into your own Web site. Some of the applets are available as compiled applet classes that you can download and immediately place on your server. For other applets the source code has been made available that you can compile with the JDK compiler and then place the applet class file on your server. There are even some applets featured in this chapter that, although neither the compiled applet class nor the source code is readily available, you can still integrate into your Web site using the CODE-BASE attribute.

IRC Utility

One of the most interesting Java applet applications allows for the incorporation of an IRC (Internet Relay Chat) utility in a Web page. Not only does this application illustrate the exciting potential for you to embed Java applets that can communicate on different Internet protocols within a typical Web page, but it is also a useful application that allows your users to communicate with each other while enjoying your Web site.

Cafe

Now your users can contact your Web site and instantly be able to converse with each other over the quality of your products. Of course you hope that they will be saying good things, but the point is that you can now add this exciting capability to your Web site using the Cafe Java applet. First check out this Java applet by going to the following URL.

http://www.dimensionx.com/chat/index.html

When you contact this URL, you will find that the Navigator window is divided into a top and bottom window. The bottom window contains the IRC applet as illustrated in Figure 7.5.

After typing your name in the chat window, you can immediately begin to converse with any other individuals who are currently "in the room." This Java applet works very well as an IRC utility, and we were impressed with the speed of response of this utility compared with that for conventional IRC applications.

This applet has several useful features, which include a hyperlink capability and control panel feature. When conversing with other individuals in this applet, users can type out various URLs that actually become active hyperlinks. If another user clicks on the hyperlink, the top window of the Navigator browser advances to the designated URL, while the chat utility remains completely functional. The IRC Java applet also features a control panel to allow for private conversations when more than two individuals are communicating. This feature is a Java pop-up window that is launched when the More button is clicked on the Java chat utility illustrated in Figure 7.6.

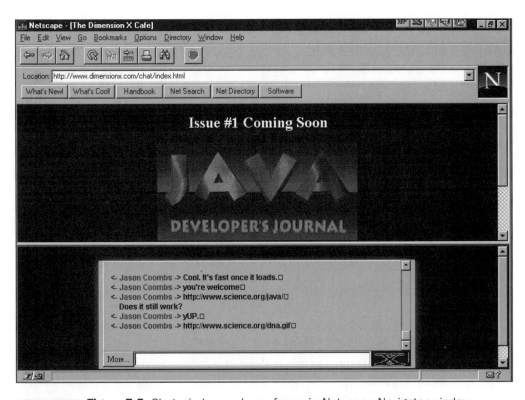

Figure 7.5 Chat window as lower frame in Netscape Navigator window.

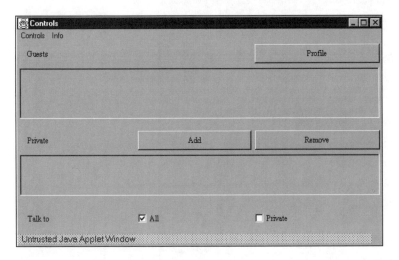

Figure 7.6 Control info window allows users to specify individuals with whom they want to converse within the IRC applet.

The control panel window still has some slight bugs associated with it; for instance, it is often difficult to close the control panel window when you are done using it. The best way to close the control panel window is to choose the **Controls|Close Window** command selection. The control panel also features the ability to lift the Cafe Java applet out of the Web page within which it is integrated, while it remains completely functional. After you select the **Controls|Lift Cafe out of browser** command, the Cafe applet actually creates its own window as shown Figure 7.7.

This feature allows you to view other URLs in a full-size browser window and still be able to converse in the Cafe chat utility.

■■■■■■

As you can see in Figure 7.7, the full-size chat window does have a slight design problem with it, the text entry line is cut off on the bottom.

■■■■■■

Deploying Cafe—IRC Java Applet

After experiencing the potential of this applet, you will be more than happy to know that you don't have to go out and create your own IRC Java applet, but in

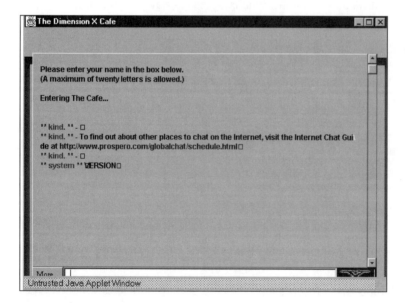

■■■■■■■■■■ **Figure 7.7** Cafe chat Java applet lifted from out of the Web page.

fact you can download it and integrate it within your Web site. The files for the Cafe applet can be downloaded from the following URL.

http://www.dimensionx.com/chat/index.html

To provide the Cafe applet on your Web site you must be running an HTTP server and an IRC server on the same host server. The two servers must be on the same host server because of the security limitations of Java applets that operate in the Netscape Navigator browser.

The Cafe applet is compatible with any IRC server, and if you don't already have an IRC server, you can find several that are available for free evaluation. Global Stage chat has several versions of its IRC server that you can use; you can find them at the following URL.

http://www2.prospero.com/globalstage/

After you have successfully installed the IRC server and the Cafe applet, you must include the proper <APPLET> tag to include the applet in your Web source file. As with all Java applets, there are several parameter NAME|VALUE pairs that must be passed to the applet for it to function when integrated in a Web site (Table 7.2).

Here is an example of the <APPLET> tag used to include the Cafe in a Web source file.

■■■■ **Table 7.2** Attributes for Cafe Java Applet

Name	Description
server	Specifies the IRC server
channel	Specifies the IRC channel to which Cafe will connect
chanac	Specify a password if required for channels to be created
cafe_name	The title of the Cafe window that is created if the **Lift Cafe out of Browser** option is selected
private_sound	Sound file (*.au) that is played when a private message is received (optional)
enter_sound	Sound file (*.au) that is played when a message is entered (optional)

```
<APPLET CODE=Talk.class    WIDTH=525    HEIGHT=180>
<PARAM NAME=server   VALUE=www.science.org>
<PARAM NAME=channel   VALUE=#dnxtalk>
<PARAM NAME="enter_sound"   VALUE="Welcome.au">
<PARAM NAME="private_sound"   VALUE="SeeYa.au">
</APPLET>
```

Now you should be able to provide this useful chat utility applet in your Web site, giving it a truly interactive feel.

Gamelan Chat Applet

Incorporating a chat applet into your Web page can add interesting content while giving you the ability to gauge users' responses to your Web site or company's products. In the previous chat example, you needed to run your own IRC server, but the Gamelan chat applet can be integrated into your Web site without an IRC server. You simply use the CODEBASE attribute to specify the applet class on the Gamelan server. This allows you to have your own chat capability in your Web pages within a couple of minutes and not have to worry about the various IRC server requirements. Before you add the Gamelan chat applet to your Web page, you can take a look at how it works and looks by selecting chat at the following UR.

http://www.gamelan.com/

You can integrate the Gamelan chat applet within your own Web page using the proper <APPLET> tag as illustrated in the following example.

```
<APPLET CODEBASE="http://www.gamelan.com/chat" CODE=chat.class WIDTH=500
HEIGHT=300>
<PARAM NAME="port" VALUE="5011">
<PARAM NAME="boot" VALUE="http:startchat.cgi?5011">
<PARAM NAME="title" VALUE="Don's Great Chat Room">
</APPLET>
```

You should keep all of the attributes and parameters the same as illustrated in the example code, but you can make modifications to the title that appears in the pop-up window. Once you have included the above code in your Web page, anyone visiting your Web site will be able to run the chat applet. When the Web page is first loaded with the Gamelan chat utility, it should produce a window as illustrated in Figure 7.8.

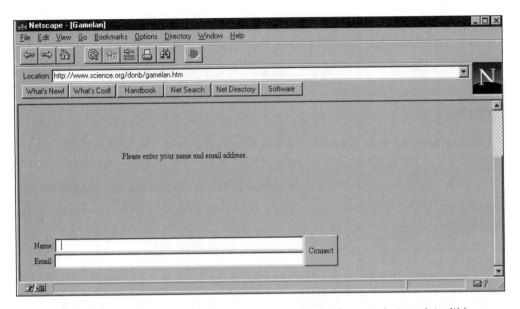

Figure 7.8 Entry window that will initialize and run a chat applet within your Web page.

Users then simply need to enter their name and e-mail address, then click on the connect button to activate the chat applet. The chat applet will then appear on the Web page, allowing users to type in messages that will be posted to the window that other users will all be able to respond to. You can even launch the chat applet

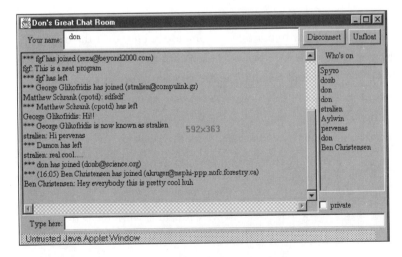

Figure 7.9 Chat applet pop-up window.

into a separate Java pop-up window by clicking on the Float button. Once launched, the chat applet window should appear as illustrated in Figure 7.9.

This is an impressive Java applet that can now exist on your own Web pages. The only disadvantage to using the CODEBASE attribute with this chat applet is that your users will also be interacting with chat users on the Gamelan Web page.

Impressive and Useful Java Applets

There is already a wide variety of applications for Java applets, with new ones being developed every day. These applications include the ability to incorporate sounds into your Web pages or even create an on-line TourGuide that users visiting your Web site can employ. The applets featured in this section are those that are truly useful and do not run so slowly as to be encumbering.

ButtonPLUS2

Creating a Web site with more movement and animation can add significant entertainment value and information that will cause users to visit your site more often. The ButtonPLUS2 Java applet allows you to create buttons on your Web pages that can change instantly to display additional information whenever a user initiates an event, such as positioning the mouse pointer over the button. An example of the ButtonPLUS2 applet working can be found at the following URL.

http://www.xm.com/cafe/ButtonPLUS/button.html

When you first load this Web page, you will find that the text on the two buttons at the top of the page changes when you position your mouse pointer over the buttons. You can use this applet on your Web pages by downloading the ButtonPLUS2 applet from the following FTP site and placing it in the same directory as the Web source file that references it. The <APPLET> tag with the desired parameter NAME|VALUE pairs then needs to be included in the Web source file. Table 7.3 indicates the different parameters that are associated with this applet.

Table 7.3 Parameters for ButtonPLUS2 Applet

Name	Value	Description
URL	path	URL destination when the button is clicked by the user.

■■■■■ **Table 7.3** Continued

Name	Value	Description
FONT	string, such as courier	The font of the text that appears on the button; the default is courier.
FONTSIZE	number	The size of the text that appears on the button; the default is 12 point.
TEXT	"string|string|string"	Text that is displayed when button is first loaded, when a mouseover event occurs, and when the user clicks the button.
BGCOLOR	number,number, number or random	Three numbers should be entered for the Red, Blue, and Green values of the color of the text to be displayed. The numbers should range inclusively from 0 to 255. The default color is gray (192,192,192).
TEXTCOLOR	number,number, number	Three numbers should be entered for the Red, Blue, and Green values of the color of the text to be displayed. The numbers should range inclusively from 0 to 255. The default color is white (255,255,255).
IMAGE	"path|path|path"	The first path is to the image file that is displayed when the button is initially displayed, the second path is to the image file that appears when the pointer enters the applet, and the third path is to the image file that is displayed when the user clicks the button.
SOUND	"path|path"	The first path is to the sound file that plays when the mouse pointer enters the applet, and the second path is to the sound file that plays when the button is clicked.

■■■■■ **Table 7.3** Continued

Name	Value	Description
HIGHLIGHT	number	When a value greater than 0 is chosen, the background color of the button will change its shade of color when clicked to make it appear to be depressed.
TEXTALIGN	left, right, or center	How the text should be justified; the default is center.
VTEXTALIGN	top, bottom, or center	Where the text should be vertically aligned; the default is center.

■■■■■

It is important that you capitalize all of the parameter names as they are illustrated in Table 7.3 because this applet does have parameter case-sensitivity. As you can see in Table 7.3, the parameters such as TEXT, IMAGE, and SOUND involve several values separated by the symbol | acting as the delimiter. It is important that when you use these parameter names, you always include the | symbol even if you don't want anything to appear for a particular event. The following example illustrates the <APPLET> tag that would be needed to have the TEXT parameter produce a message that appears on the button when the Web page is first loaded, then a different message on the button when it is clicked. In this particular case, no message should appear on the button when the applet is first entered by the mouse pointer.

```
<PARAM NAME=TEXT VALUE="Try this | | Now you've done it">
```

As you can see in this example, two of the | symbols are used with no message placed between them. When you use the parameters TEXT, IMAGE, and SOUND, you must include the indicated number of | symbols even if you don't want the text, image, or sound to execute for a particular event. The following is an example of the <APPLET> tag used to place this applet within a Web source file.

```
<APPLET CODE=ButtonPLUS2.class  WIDTH=125  HEIGHT=40>
<PARAM NAME=HIGHLIGHT  VALUE=4>
<PARAM NAME=URL  VALUE=www.science.org/>
<PARAM NAME=FONTSIZE  VALUE=14>
<PARAM NAME=TEXT  VALUE="Click this button!||Now you're on the way.">
```

```
<PARAM NAME=BGCOLOR   VALUE=100,100,50>
<PARAM NAME=TEXTCOLOR   VALUE=0,200,0>
</APPLET>
```

When you don't include the particular parameter NAME|VALUE in the <APPLET> tag, the default value is used for that parameter name if one exists. In this particular example, the FONT parameter was left out, and the default font type Courier was then used.

This applet can add information and create dynamic changes on buttons to make your Web pages more interesting and informative; it doesn't take very long for it to initialize and run.

TourGuide Applet

Let's say your company has an extensive range of different products, including everything from computers to medical devices. Not only is your Web site quite large, but it doesn't seem very cohesive.

The TourGuide applet may be the answer to your problems. Using the TourGuide applet you can have tours through your Web site with one tour designed for users who are interested in your company's computer products and another for users interested in the medical products. You can see how the TourGuide applet works by accessing the following URL.

http://www.xm.com/cafe/TourGuide/index.html

After you click on the Start Tour button, the TourGuide applet begins by creating a pop-up window as illustrated in Figure 7.10. Once the TourGuide applet appears, it begins by loading all the various URLs that the user will visit, while another Netscape Navigator window is opened with the first URL of the applet TourGuide.

■■■■■■■■■ **Figure 7.10** TourGuide pop-up window that gives the user control of the tour.

The user can then sit back and watch as the TourGuide applet contacts the specified URLs that make up the tour and displays them for a specified delay period. The TourGuide pop-up window also allows the user to fast forward or go back to a particular URL.

For you to integrate the TourGuide applet into your Web site requires that you have the following six classes located in the same location as the Web source file that references the TourGuide applet.

- TourGuide.class
- MyCanvas.class
- MyPanel.class
- MyWindow.class
- delMgr.class
- gratAn.class

These six classes can be downloaded from the TourGuide directory found at the following FTP site.

ftp://xm.com/pub/incoming/cafe/

After you have downloaded these classes, you need to include the proper <APPLET> tag in your Web source file. As with all applets, there are various parameters that must be used to pass information to the TourGuide applet. For the TourGuide applet this parameter information includes the various URLs that will make up the tour and the delay period for displaying the URL in the browser window. These parameters are fully described in Table 7.4.

■■■■■■■ **Table 7.4** Parameters for TourGuide Applet

Name	Value	Description
url#	"http://...."	URLs of the various destination of the TourGuide applet
name#	"string"	Names of the destinations corresponding to the different sites
delay#	seconds	Amount of time the TourGuide applet will spend at each of the sites
sound#	sound file	The name of the sound file to be played with a particular URL

The # symbol at the end of the various parameter names illustrated in Table 7.4 corresponds to the designated number of the different sites that will be visited, beginning with (1), then (2), and so on. This numerical ordering of the sites as part of the parameter names is clearly illustrated in the following example that shows the proper <APPLET> tag needed for the TourGuide applet to successfully execute.

```
<APPLET ALIGN=middle CODE=TourGuide.class WIDTH=128 HEIGHT=32>
<PARAM NAME=url1 VALUE=http://www.science.org>
<PARAM NAME=url2 VALUE=http://www.cnet.com>
<PARAM NAME=url3 VALUE=http://www.cnn.com>
<PARAM NAME=name1 VALUE="SCIENCE.ORG's Home Page">
<PARAM NAME=name2 VALUE="Internet and Computer News">
<PARAM NAME=name3 VALUE="World News">
<PARAM NAME=delay1 VALUE=10>
<PARAM NAME=delay2 VALUE=5>
<PARAM NAME=delay3 VALUE=1>
<PARAM NAME=sound1  VALUE=hello.au>
<PARAM NAME=sound3 VALUE=bye.au>
</APPLET>
```

This <APPLET> tag example indicates that three different URLs will make up this particular tour. When each of the URLs is being loaded by the TourGuide applet, the value of the name# parameter will be displayed in the TourGuide pop-up window. For example, when the CNN home page is being loaded, the "World News" text will be displayed in the TourGuide pop-up window. This example code also demonstrates that you can insert various sound files (*.au) to play during the TourGuide's execution. This applet goes a long way in demonstrating the wide range of functionality and uses of applets.

Guestbook Applet

Wouldn't it be nice if users who contact your Web page could send you a quick message giving you their opinion? The Guestbook applet allows you to place this message capability within your own Web site. Although most developers place e-mail contact information on the bottom of their Web pages already, this applet serves to illustrate the potential of applets to easily use a variety of Internet protocols. It actually establishes a connection on Port 25 using the TCP/SMTP specifications and then sends the user's message. You can see how this applet works by visiting the following URL where you should see the applet as illustrated in Figure 7.11.

http://www.nai.net/~rvdi/home.htm#Guestbook

◼◼◼◼◼◼◼ **Figure 7.11** Clicking on the button will open the message pop-up window.

◼◼◼◼◼◼◼ **Figure 7.12** Source code for Guestbook applet.

```
/ * guestbook.java - 10 Feb 1996 - Version 1.04a
 *

 *

 * Copyright 1996 by William Giel, L.S.

 *

 * E-mail: rvdi@usa.nai.net

 * WWW: http://www.nai.net/~rvdi/home.htm

 *

 * Version 1.04a - Replaced Helvetica font with System font (19 Feb
 * 1996)

 *

 * Version 1.03a corrects code so that when the dialog is reopened after
 * canceling, window does not grow! Replaced 'disposed()' with 'hide()'
 * in guestbookWindow.action(...) and guestbookWindow.handleEvent(...)
 * methods (10 Feb 1996)

 *

 * NOTE: TO RECEIVE GUEST BOOK ENTRIES, YOU MUST SPECIFY YOUR E-MAIL

 *          ADDRESS AS THE 'RECEIVER' PARAMETER IN THE APPLETS HTML TAG.

 * YOUR LOCAL HOST MUST SUPPORT SMTP MESSAGES ON PORT 25
```

```
*
*
* ADDENDUM TO DOCUMENTATION (7 Feb 1996) - Some of you have been
* unable to get your guestbook applets to work on your own home
* pages, while others have been successful.
*
* If you have a chance to study the code of the mailMessage method
* of  the 'send' class, you'll see that guestbook first establishes
* a socket with the 'mailhost' at port 25, in accordance with
* TCP/SMTP specs (see RFC 821).
*
* Then, guestbook waits for the 220 'service ready' message
* transmission

* over the socket. After successfully receiving 220, it then obtains
* the 'helohost' domain name from the server and transmits the HELO
* <domain> command over the socket. If accepted, the receiver-SMTP
* returns a 250

* (OK) reply.
*
* Following that, guestbook sends MAIL FROM: <sender>, then  RECPT TO:

* <receiver>, expecting 250 replies after each. Note that in guestbook,
* the sender and receiver addresses are the same.
*
* It then sends the DATA command, and expects 354 intermediate reply
* from the SMTP server. All that follows DATA is the standard text
* message in the format defined in RFC 822, with a standard 'Subject:'
* field, followed by a blank line. What follows the blank line is the
* actual text (your guest's optional name, optional email address and
* comments or suggestions.)
*
* After the message is transmitted, guestbook transmits a single '\r\n
* \r\n',

* signifying end of message, waits for a 250 (OK) reply, then
* transmits a final QUIT command, and anticipates receipt of 221,
* indicating the server is closing the SMTP channel.
*
* The mailMessage method then closes the socket before returning true,
* only if all of the above were successful. mailMessage returns false
```

Continued ...

```
 * on any errors, or if the receiver parameter is null.
 *

 * Guestbook should work just fine on your homepage, so long as your
 * www host supports the above SMTP protocol. You may otherwise have
 * to experiment to get guestbook to work with custom settings. That
 * could actually be fun... but since guestbook works as-is on my www
 * server, I have no need to mess with it :-(
 *

 * Please let me know if you manage to get guestbook working by
 * revising it for conditions other than those it is designed for.
 *

 * I hope this additional information is helpful.
 * -----------------------------------------------------------------------
 * Send class built up from code demonstrated in sendmail.java
 * by Godmar Back, University of Utah, Computer Systems Lab, 1996
 * (a simple applet that sends you mail when your page is accessed)
 * -----------------------------------------------------------------------
 * Permission to use, copy, modify, and distribute this software and its
 * documentation without fee for NON-COMMERCIAL purposes is hereby
   granted,
 * provided that any use properly credits the author, i.e. "Guestbook
   applet
 * courtesy of <A HREF="mailto:rvdi@usa.nai.net">Bill Giel</A>.
 * -----------------------------------------------------------------------
 */
import java.awt.*;
import java.applet.*;
import java.lang.*;
import java.io.*;
import java.net.*;
import java.util.*;
class Send
{
    String              result = "";
    String              lastline;
```

```
short               port = 25;
DataInputStream     in;
String mailhost, receiver,  sender;
public Send( String host,String recvr)
{
            mailhost=host;
            receiver=recvr;
            sender=recvr;
}


    void expect(String expected, String msg) throws Exception
{
            lastline = in.readLine();
    if (!lastline.startsWith(expected))throw new Exception(msg +
    ":" + lastline);
            while (lastline.startsWith(expected + "-"))lastline =
            in.readLine();
}
public boolean mailMessage(String subject,String message)
{
            /////////////////////////////////////////
            //Will not send mail without a receiver!
    /////////////////////////////////////////
            if(null==receiver)return false;

            Socket s = null;
    try {
            String res;
            s = new Socket(mailhost, port);
            PrintStream p = new PrintStream(s.getOutputStream());
            in = new DataInputStream(s.getInputStream());
            expect("220", "no greeting");
```

Continued ...

```
                  String helohost = InetAddress.getLocalHost()
                  .toString();

                  p.print("HELO " + helohost + "\r\n");

                  expect("250", "helo");

                  int pos;

                  String hello = "Hello ";

                  if ((pos = lastline.indexOf(hello)) != -1) {

                                    helohost = lastline.substring(pos +
                                    hello.length());

                                    helohost = helohost.substring(0,
                                    helohost.indexOf(' '));

                          }


                      p.print("MAIL FROM: " + sender + "\r\n");

                      expect("250", "mail from");


                  p.print("RCPT TO: " + receiver + "\r\n");

                      expect("250", "rcpt to");


                      p.print("DATA\r\n");

                  expect("354", "data");

                      p.print("Subject: " + subject);

                          p.print(" (" + helohost + ")");


                  p.print("\r\n\r\n");

                              //Use two CRLF's above because we need a null
                                line following

                  //standard fields to indicate following DATA is
                    message body.


                  DataInputStream is =

                              new DataInputStream(new
                              StringBufferInputStream(message));

                      while (is.available() > 0) {
```

```
                        String ln = is.readLine();
                        if (ln.equals("."))
                ln = "..";
            p.println(ln);


    }

        String days="SunMonTueWedThuFriSat";
        String months="JanFebMarAprMayJunJul
        AugSepOctNovDec";
    Date date=new Date();
    p.print("(Accessed at " +
        Integer.toString(date.getHours()) + ":" +
        Integer.toString(date.getMinutes()) + " on "
+
        days.substring(date.getDay()*3,
        date.getDay()*3+3) + ", " +
        Integer.toString(date.getDate()) + " " +
        months.substring(date.getMonth()*3,
        date.getMonth()*3+3) + " " +
        Integer.toString(date.getYear()+1900) + ")");


    p.print("\r\n.\r\n");
expect("250", "end of data");
p.print("QUIT\r\n");
    expect("221", "quit");
} catch(Exception e)
        {
        result = e.getMessage();
        return false;
        }finally
                {
                try {
                            if (s !=
                            null)s.close();
```

Continued ...

```
                                        } catch(Exception e)

                                              result = e.getMessage();

                                        }

                        return true;

        }


}
class guestbookWindow extends Frame
{

        static final int FONTHEIGHT=12;

        static final String FONTSTRING="System";


    TextArea txt3=null;

    TextField txt1=null;

    TextField txt2=null;

    Send send=null;

    AppletContext appletContext;


    public guestbookWindow(AppletContext app, String mailhost,String
    receiver)
    {

        send= new Send(mailhost,receiver);

        appletContext=app;


                Label lbl1,lbl2,lbl3;

        Button butt1, butt2;


        GridBagLayout gridbag=new GridBagLayout();

        GridBagConstraints c=new GridBagConstraints();


        setFont(new Font(FONTSTRING,Font.BOLD,FONTHEIGHT));

        setLayout(gridbag);
```

```
setBackground(Color.lightGray);
c.fill=GridBagConstraints.NONE;
c.weightx=1.0;c.weighty=1.0;
c.ipadx=4;c.ipady=4;
c.insets=new Insets(5,5,5,5);

lbl1 = new Label("Your Name (Optional):");
gridbag.setConstraints(lbl1,c);
add(lbl1);
c.anchor=GridBagConstraints.WEST;
        txt1 = new TextField("", 20);
gridbag.setConstraints(txt1,c);
add(txt1);


        c.anchor=GridBagConstraints.CENTER;
        butt1 = new Button("Send");
gridbag.setConstraints(butt1,c);
add(butt1);


c.gridwidth=GridBagConstraints.REMAINDER;
        butt2 = new Button("Cancel");
gridbag.setConstraints(butt2,c);
add(butt2);
c.gridwidth=1;
c.weightx=1.0;c.weighty=1.0;
lbl2 = new Label("Your EMail(Optional):");
gridbag.setConstraints(lbl2,c);
add(lbl2);

c.gridwidth=GridBagConstraints.REMAINDER;
c.anchor=GridBagConstraints.WEST;
```

Continued ...

```java
        txt2 = new TextField("", 20);
            gridbag.setConstraints(txt2,c);
        add(txt2);
        c.gridwidth=GridBagConstraints.REMAINDER;
        c.fill=GridBagConstraints.BOTH;
        lbl3=new Label("Any comments or suggestions?");
        gridbag.setConstraints(lbl3,c);
        add(lbl3);
        c.gridwidth=GridBagConstraints.REMAINDER;
            c.fill=GridBagConstraints.BOTH;
                txt3 = new TextArea(5,66);
        gridbag.setConstraints(txt3,c);
        add(txt3);
        }
public boolean action(Event evt, Object arg)
{
            if(arg.equals("Cancel"))
    {
            hide();
        return true;
    }
    else if(arg.equals("Send")){
            if(txt1.getText().length()>0 ||
                txt2.getText().length()>0 ||
                txt3.getText().length()>0){
                            String message="Guest: " +
                            txt1.getText() + "\n" +

                                    "Address: " +
                                    txt2.getText() +
                                    "\n\n" +

                            txt3.getText() ;


                            if(true==send.mailMessage("Guestbook
                            Entry!",message))
```

```
appletContext.showStatus("Entry logged into guest book!");
                                   else

appletContext.showStatus("Entry NOT logged.");
                }
                else appletContext.showStatus("Nothing to send!");
                hide();
                return true;
        }
        return false;
        }
        public synchronized boolean handleEvent(Event e)
        {
                if (e.id == Event.WINDOW_ICONIFY ||e.id == Event.WIN-
DOW_DESTROY) {
                hide();
                return true;
                }
                return super.handleEvent(e);
        }
        public void show()
        {
                txt1.setText("");
                txt2.setText("");
                txt3.setText("");
                super.show();

        }
}
public class guestbook extends Applet
{
        static final int FONTHEIGHT=12;
        static final String FONTSTRING="System";
```

```
        final String BUTTON = "Guest Book";

        final String VERSION = "GUESTBOOK.JAVA - v1.04a - 19 Feb
        1996";


        guestbookWindow window=null;

        Image image=null;

        Button button;

        int width, height;

    MediaTracker  tracker = new MediaTracker(this);

        //////////////////////////////////////////////////

        //Applet parameters - pretty much self-explanatory

        //////////////////////////////////////////////////

    public String[][] getParameterInfo()

    {

                String[][] info = {

            {"width",         "int",         "width of the applet, in
            pixels"},

            {"height",        "int",         "height of the applet, in
pixels"},

            {"receiver",        "string",       "SMTP 'RCPT TO:'
parameter <null>"},

            {"imageurl",        "string",       "name of icon to
            display <null>"},

            {"title",           "string",       "title for popup
            dialog <Guest Book>"},

        };

        return info;

    }

        /////////////////////////////////////

        //Applet name, author and info lines

        /////////////////////////////////////

    public String getAppletInfo()

    {

        return (          VERSION + " - simulates a guest log\n" +

                                 "by E-mailing guest data to page
```

```
owner, by Bill Giel\n" +
                                    "http://www.nai.net/~rvdi/home.htm
or  rvdi@usa.nai.net\n" +
                                    "Copyright 1996 by William Giel.");

    }


        public void init()
        {
                String receiver, szImage, szTitle;
                URL imageURL=null;
                receiver = getParameter("receiver");
            if(null == receiver)
                        showStatus("No RECEIVER parameter - applet
will not log entry!");
                    if(null==(szTitle=getParameter("title")))
                        szTitle="Guest Book";


        szImage=getParameter("IMAGEURL");


                window=new
guestbookWindow(getAppletContext(),getCodeBase().getHost(),receiver);
                window.setTitle(szTitle);
                window.pack();
        setFont(new Font(FONTSTRING,Font.BOLD,FONTHEIGHT));
                add (button = new Button(BUTTON));
                width=size().width; height=size().height;
                if(null != szImage){
                try{
                        imageURL=new URL(getDocumentBase(),szImage);
                } catch (MalformedURLException e)
                  {
                        imageURL=null;
                        image=null;
```

Continued ...

```
                }
            }

        if(imageURL != null){
                image=getImage(imageURL);
                if(image != null)
                    tracker.addImage(image,0);
            }
        button.move((width-button.size().width)/2,
                                            (width-
                                            button.size().width
                                            )/2);

        }
        public void paint(Graphics g)
        {
                Color color=g.getColor();
                g.setColor(Color.lightGray);
                g.fill3DRect(0,0,size().width,size().height,true);
                g.setColor(color);
                if(image != null){
                        try{
                tracker.waitForID(0);
            }catch (InterruptedException e)
                {
                        return;
                }

                        g.drawImage(image,(width-image.getWidth
                        (this))/2,button.size().height
                            +2*(height-image.getHeight(this)
                            -button.size().height)/3,this);
                }
            }
        public boolean action(Event evt, Object arg)
```

```
    {
                    if(arg.equals(BUTTON) && !window.isShowing())
        {
                        window.show();
                        return true;
        }

                else return false;

    }

}
```

When the button on the applet is clicked, a Java pop-up window is launched where the message, name, and e-mail address of the sender can be entered. After this information is entered, you can send the message by simply clicking on the **Send** button on the pop-up window.

This applet is useful and worth placing within your Web site, and it is fortunate that the author has made the source code available to the public for noncommercial use. The source code for this applet has been included in Figure 7.12, which you can copy, or you can contact the URL where the source code is also available.

You must complete several procedures to convert the source code into the appropriate applet classes that can be added to your Web site.

1. Copy the source code into an appropriate text editor, such as Notepad.
2. Save the text file with the name of the applet that will be created and the .JAVA extension. For this applet example you should save the text file as guestbook.java.
3. Make sure that you have the JDK (Java Developer's Kit) version 1.0 from Sun Microsystems and that it's properly installed on your computer system.

4. Use the javac command on the guestbook.java file you create, which should then compile three different classes: guestbook.class, Send.class, and guestbookWindow.class. These three classes are all needed for you to make this applet available on your Web site.

5. Copy all three classes into the directory on your server where the Web source file that references the applet is located.

After you successfully create the three classes that constitute this applet, you must add the <APPLET> tag to the Web source file. Here is an example of the <APPLET> tag that is used to incorporate this applet within your Web site.

```
<APPLET CODE="guestbook.class"  WIDTH=125  HEIGHT=100>
<PARAM NAME=IMAGEURL VALUE="icons155.gif">
<PARAM NAME=RECEIVER VALUE="rvdi@usa.nai.net">
<PARAM NAME=TITLE VALUE="Rocco V. D'Andrea, Inc. - Guest Book">
</APPLET>
```

Although the source code creates three different classes, only the guestbook class is an extension of the Applet class. The guestbook class is therefore the only class that needs to be referenced by the CODE attribute to successfully launch the applet. There are also three parameters associated with this particular applet for which you need to replace the values when you deploy this applet.

- *RECEIVER*. The value of this parameter should be the e-mail address to which you want the messages sent. This parameter is required for the applet to work.

- *IMAGEURL*. The value of this parameter should be a path to an image file that will be displayed on the initial applet window. This parameter is optional.

- *TITLE*. The value of this parameter should be the title you want to give to the pop-up window that is created. This parameter is optional.

This is a very useful applet that demonstrates the extensive abilities of Java applets, because it actually sends a message using the SMTP Internet protocol.

Java Sound Applet

The word multimedia implies sound capabilities in addition to visual stimulation. The AudioItem Java applet allows the integration of sound files into a Web site. The AudioItem applet developed by Sun Microsystems can now be integrated into your Web pages to play various sound files when a user contacts the Web page. You can hear a demonstration of this sound applet by going to the following URL.

http://java.sun.com/applets/applets/AudioItem/index.html

When the Web page is first loaded, you should hear the sound file play, and then if you click on the speaker image, a different sound file will play. The Java applet doesn't produce the best sound or have the fastest play time that you might find with some audio inline plug-ins. The advantage of this Java applet is that anyone using a browser with a built-in Java interpreter will be able to hear whatever sounds you place on your Web site.

Like the guestbook applet previously described, the AudioItem.class isn't available as a compiled class, but the source code has been made available and is displayed in Figure 7.13.

The procedure to create the AudioItem.class is the same as the procedure you used to create the guestbook.class.

1. Copy the source code into an appropriate text editor, such as Notepad.
2. Save the text file with the name of the applet that will be created and the .JAVA extension. For this applet example, you should save the text file as AudioItem.java.
3. Make sure that you have the JDK (Java Developer's Kit) version 1.0 from Sun Microsystems and that it's properly installed on your computer system.
4. Use the javac command on the AudioItem.java file, which should create the AudioItem.class file.
5. Copy the AudioItem.class file into the directory on your server where the Web source file that references the applet is located.

After you successfully create the AudioItem.class file, you then need to place the proper <APPLET> tag in the Web source file. This sound-playing applet has very simple applet code parameters to incorporate it into a Web source file as illustrated in the code on page 224.

```
/*
 * @(#)AudioItem.java    1.26f 95/03/22 James Gosling
 *
 * Copyright (c) 1994 Sun Microsystems, Inc. All Rights Reserved.
 *
 * Permission to use, copy, modify, and distribute this software
 * and its documentation for NON-COMMERCIAL purposes and without
 * fee is hereby granted provided that this copyright notice
 * appears in all copies. Please refer to the file "copyright.html"
 * for further important copyright and licensing information.
 *
 * SUN MAKES NO REPRESENTATIONS OR WARRANTIES ABOUT THE SUITABILITY OF
 * THE SOFTWARE, EITHER EXPRESS OR IMPLIED, INCLUDING BUT NOT LIMITED
 * TO THE IMPLIED WARRANTIES OF MERCHANTABILITY, FITNESS FOR A
 * PARTICULAR PURPOSE, OR NON-INFRINGEMENT. SUN SHALL NOT BE LIABLE FOR
 * ANY DAMAGES SUFFERED BY LICENSEE AS A RESULT OF USING, MODIFYING OR
 * DISTRIBUTING THIS SOFTWARE OR ITS DERIVATIVES.
 */
import java.io.InputStream;
import java.util.Hashtable;
import java.util.Enumeration;
import java.util.StringTokenizer;
import java.awt.*;
import java.net.*;
import java.applet.AudioClip;
/**
 * A simple Item class to play an audio clip.
 * @author James Gosling
 */
```

```java
public class AudioItem extends java.applet.Applet {
    /**
     * The sounds to be played.
     */
    private String sounds;
    /**
     * The index of the next sound in the sounds strings.
     */
    private int index;
    /**
     * The currently playing audio stream, or null
     * when no audio is playing.
     */
    private AudioClip audio;
    /**
     * Play the next sound. The sound URLs are obtained
     * from the "snd" attribute. You can specify a list
     * of them by separating the sounds by '|'s.<p>
     * Note that the URL is constructed relative to the
     * getDocumentBase(), that is because the URL is obtained
     * from within the document
     */
    public void next() {
        try {
            if (audio != null) {
                audio.stop();
                audio = null;
            }

            String url = sounds;
            if (sounds.indexOf('|') >= 0) {
```

Continued ...

```
                    int start = index;
                    if ((index = sounds.indexOf('|', index)) < 0) {
                        url = sounds.substring(start);
                        index = start;
                    } else {
                        url = sounds.substring(start, index++);
                    }
                }
                if (url.length() > 0) {
                    audio = getAudioClip(new URL(getDocumentBase(), url));
                    audio.play();
                }
            } catch(Exception e) {
            }
        }
        /**
         * Initialize the applet. First resize it, then get the
         * "snd" attribute.
         */
        public void init() {
            resize(10, 12);
            sounds = getParameter("snd");
            if (sounds == null) {
                sounds = "doc:/demo/audio/ding.au";
            }
        }
        /**
         * When the applet is started play the next sound.
         */
        public void start() {
            next();
```

```
    }
    /**
     * When the applet is stopped, stop playing the current sound.
     */
    public void stop() {
        if (audio != null) {
            audio.stop();
            audio = null;
        }
    }
    /**
     * When the user clicks in the applet, play the next sound.
     */
    public boolean mouseUp(java.awt.Event evt, int x, int y) {
        next();
        return true;
    }
    /**
     * Paint an audio icon.
     */
    public void paint(Graphics g) {
        double f = ((double)(size().height - 1)) / ((size().width - 1)
        * 2);
        int offset = size().height / 2;
        for (int i = size().width - 1; i >= 0; i -= 3) {
            int h = (int)(i * f);
            g.drawLine(i, offset - h, i, offset + h);
        }
    }
}
```

```
<APPLET CODE=AudioItem.class   WIDTH=15   HEIGHT=15>
<PARAM NAME=snd VALUE="Hello.au|Bye.au">
</APPLET>
```

As you can see in this example, different sound files are separated with the | symbol. In this example, the Hello.au file would play when the Web source file is first loaded, and the Bye.au file would play whenever the user clicks on the speaker image. When using this applet, you could use just one sound file without the | symbol, which would result in the specified sound file playing both when the Web source file is first loaded and whenever the user clicks on the speaker icon. This is a simple applet that can now allow you to integrate sounds into your Web site, making it truly an interesting multimedia experience.

Just Gotta Scroll

Java applets have been continually used for creating scrolling images or text messages. This is a very useful application of Java applets that can give your Web pages a true multimedia feel, while also providing useful information to your users.

Scrolling Advertisements on your Web Site

Now that you are well on your way to having a Web site that gets numerous hits a day, you are probably planning to have companies pay you large sums of money to post ads on your Web site. The adSpace applet can allow you to place these ad images on your Web site in the form of a scrolling advertisement. Why place a boring ad on a Web page when you can have several different ads scroll on the page, giving the advertisements a more eye-catching appearance? To get some idea of what this scrolling advertisement would look like, check out the following URL.

http://www.virtual-inn.co.uk/orbital/beta/adSpace/

Not only does the applet display the image, but it also allows for the advertisement image to be a hyperlink to a URL address. The applet can also allow for a sound file to play when the image is being displayed. Whether this applet is actually used for advertising or some other purpose, it is an impressive applet that can easily be added to your Web site.

▬▬▬▬ **Table 7.5** Attributes for AdSpace Java Applet

Name	Value	Description
adlist	filename	Specifies the file that contains the list of URLs for the image files, hyperlinks, and sound files
pause	milliseconds	Number of milliseconds pause between image displays
scrollpause	milliseconds	Number of milliseconds to pause between scrolling animation frames
numFrames	number	Number of frames for each image
deltaY	number	The amount to scroll in the animation
aniaudio	filename	An audio file to play at the beginning of each animation

To incorporate this applet in your Web application, begin by downloading the ad.tar.Z file that contains the adSpace.class, Advert.class, and the adList.txt. These three files need to be placed in the same directory as the Web source file that will integrate the applet within it. There are also several parameters that are specifically associated with this applet's integration in a Web source file. These parameters are fully described in Table 7.5.

The following example code illustrates the proper <APPLET> tag needed to place the adSpace applet in a Web document.

```
<APPLET CODE="adSpace.class"   WIDTH=750   HEIGHT=250>
<PARAM NAME=adList   VALUE="adlist.txt">
<PARAM NAME=pause   VALUE=100>
<PARAM NAME=deltaY   VALUE=1>
<PARAM NAME=scrollPause   VALUE=40>
</APPLET>
```

This example code clearly shows that not every parameter to which the adSpace applet is capable of responding needs to be included in the <APPLET> tag for it to be executed, but each parameter does gives you the option to utilize other features and capabilities of the applet. The numerical values entered for some of the various parameter values are somewhat arbitrary and are best determined by your own preferences.

One of the most important parameters associated with this applet is the adList parameter. The value for this parameter is the name of the file that contains the URLs for the image files, hyperlinks, and sound files for each advertisement. An example of the adList.txt file and the information it should contain is illustrated in Figure 7.14.

When you incorporate the adSpace applet within your Web document, it is very important that the URLs you specify for the image and sound files in the text file be located on your local server. The security features associated with applets prevent a Java applet from establishing a socket connection to a remote server.

With this applet you are well on your way to making millions of dollars in advertising revenue featuring this scrolling image advertising applet on your Web site. Even if you are based in reality and don't expect to earn significant advertising revenues by selling ad space on your Internet site, this applet can still add exciting multimedia content on your Web site.

Ticker Mania

Numerous Java applets have been created to display a ticker tape on a Web page, including everything from the hottest news stories to stock quotes and even sports scores. The Sports Ticker Java applet is an impressive display of how multimedia animation can be added to a Web page in the form of useful information. You can appreciate how the Sports Ticker applet works by going to the following URL.

http://www.sportsnetwork.com/java.html

You can activate the Sports Ticker applet by choosing one of the desired sports buttons such as the NFL demo or NHL. Once selected, the Sports Ticker applet is launched as a pop-up window. Figure 7.15 illustrates the NFL demo Sports Ticker applet when it is launched.

Because the Sports Ticker is launched as a pop-up window, it can run whether you remain on the URL from which you originally launched it or go to another URL location. When you are tired of the particular applet, you can simply close the applet window in the same fashion that you would close any other application window.

This is an impressive applet, which you can very simply incorporate within your own Web page. Most of the other Java applets that have been featured in this

Figure 7.14 Form of information that should be in the adList.txt file.

```
# Format is:
#
#        {
#                    URL to image
#                    URL this image should link to
#                    URL to an audio file
#        }
{
         http://www.virtual-inn.co.uk/orbital/beta/adSpace/home.gif
         http://www.science.org/
}
{

         http://www.virtual-inn.co.uk/orbital/beta/adSpace/new.gif
         http://www.economist.com/
}
{

         http://www.virtual-inn.co.uk/orbital/beta/adSpace/banner.gif
         http://home.netscape.com/
}
{

         http://www.virtual-inn.co.uk/images/sun_ad.gif
         http://www.sun.com/
}
```

Figure 7.15 Sports Ticker applet pop-up window.

chapter typically require that you download the appropriate applet class or compile the applet class from the source code and place the applet class in the same directory as the Web source file that references it. You then include the name of the applet class with the CODE attribute, as illustrated in the following example.

```
<APPLET   CODE="NeatApplet.class" WIDTH=200 HEIGHT=200>
<PARAM NAME=title VALUE="Check this out.">
</APPLET>
```

Rather than downloading the applet class for the Sports Ticker, you can use the CODEBASE attribute to integrate the Sports Ticker applet within your own Web page by simply designating that the tsnHighlightTickerApp.class be accessed at the appropriate URL. You can integrate a NHL version of the Sports Ticker within your own Web page using the following example <APPLET> tag in your Web source file.

```
<APPLET CODEBASE="http://backstage.wais.com:2420/java/"
CODE="tsnHighlightTickerApp.class" WIDTH=150 HEIGHT=25>
<PARAM NAME=createBtnTitle VALUE="Cool Sports Ticker For NHL!">
<PARAM NAME=tickerGreeting VALUE="Watch here for live NHL scoring updates!">
<PARAM NAME=tickerTitle VALUE="Live NHL Sportswire">
<PARAM NAME=tickerUrl VALUE="http://www.sportsnetwork.com/">
<PARAM NAME=tickerIdleText VALUE="Check out SCIENCE.ORG --
http://www.science.org/">
<PARAM NAME=rcvrDirURL VALUE="http://backstage.wais.com:2420/nhl/hticker">
<PARAM NAME=rcvrLatestURL
VALUE="http://backstage.wais.com:2420/nhl/hticker/latest">
</APPLET>
```

When users first contact your Web page containing the Sports Ticker applet, they will see a button, and when they click on the button, it will launch the pop-up window for the Sports Ticker applet. You can also customize the Sports Ticker applet for your Web site by changing some of the parameter values indicated in Table 7.6.

As you saw on the Sports Ticker home page, there are applets available for NFL, NBA, and NHL sports. You can change the type of Sports Ticker that is displayed on your Web page by changing the pro sport syntax for the rcvrDirURL and rcvrLatestURL. For example, the code in the previous example created a NHL

▬▬▬ **Table 7.6** Sports Ticker Parameters

Name	Value	Description
createBtnTitle	"string"	The text that appears on the button on your Web page that activates the Sports Ticker applet
tickerGreeting	"string"	The text that you want to appear in the Sports Ticker applet window when it is first loaded
tickerIdleText	"string"	The text that you want to appear in the Sports Ticker applet window when it is not receiving any values

▬▬▬

Sports Ticker, whereas you could make the NBA Sports Ticker applet appear by making the following changes to the previous example.

```
<PARAM NAME=rcvrDirURL VALUE="http://backstage.wais.com:2420/nba/hticker">

<PARAM NAME=rcvrLatestURL
VALUE="http://backstage.wais.com:2420/nba/hticker/latest">
```

This example is not only an impressive applet, but an excellent example of how you can incorporate very exciting and interesting applets in your Web pages even if you can't download the particular applet class. You can simply use the CODEBASE attribute in your <APPLET> tag to specify the URL location of the desired class along with checking the HTML source code for the applet to ensure that you use the correct parameter NAME|VALUE pairs in your own Web source file.

Just Plain Fun Applets

We have included a couple of unique Java applets that are as fun as a Java applet could ever expect to be. You may not want to incorporate these particular Java applets into your Web site, but they are worth checking out.

Poetry CreatOR2 Applet

Some students at Stanford have created a Java applet that can create a poem with either random subject material or the user's own subject material, although either way it isn't exactly Pulitzer Prize material. The applet can be found at the following URL.

http://www-cs-students.stanford.edu/~esincoff/poetry/jpoetry.html

After you contact this URL, you should see the Java applet in the middle on the Web page. When you click on the Properties button, a Java pop-up window titled Poetry Variables appears that allows you enter some characteristics of the poem that will be created. When the Poetry Variables pop-up window first appears, you need to enlarge the window to see the buttons at the bottom. The Poetry CreatOR2 applet and the Poetry Variables pop-up window are illustrated in Figure 7.16.

To create the poem, you need to enter the desired variables in the Poetry Variables pop-up window, select the OK button, and then select the Generate button. This is a fun and interesting applet that illustrates the endless number of different applications of Java applets that are being continually developed.

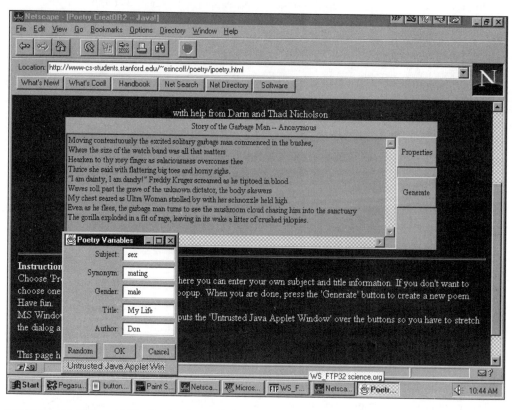

Figure 7.16 Poetry CreatOR2 applet and Poetry Variables pop-up window.

Space Invaders Java Applet

Java applets are even being used to create games. The Java applet found at the following URL reproduces a game similar to the age-old space invaders game that was popular many years ago.

http://www.magnastar.com/games/space/

When you contact this URL, you should see the game as shown in Figure 7.17, where you can move the bottom ship to shoot down the space invaders.

You will find the game doesn't have the same technological flare you might get with the Sony Playstation game player, but this Java applet game does give some idea of things to come. Java applets and Java applications are being used to create the next generation of games that will play across the Internet, and you should see much higher-quality Java applet games develop in the very near future. Who knows? Someone might even be able to reproduce "Pong" one day.

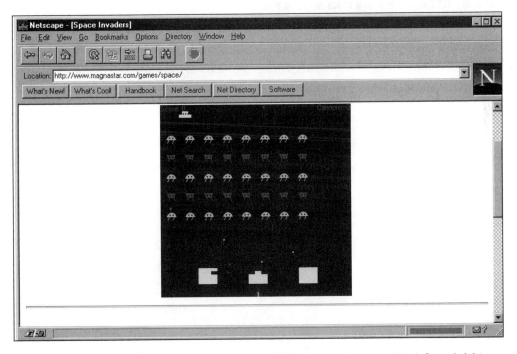

Figure 7.17 Use the "J" key and "K" key to move your ship left and right and fire by pressing the space bar.

Valuable Java Applet Sites

The wealth of Java-related information that exists on the Internet is growing rapidly every day. There are some very important sites that you should check out to keep informed about any new Java developments and have access to new freely distributed applets.

Sun Microsystems

It should be more than obvious that the company that created the Java language would have the most interest in making important developer information and resources readily available. The following URL is for Sun Microsystems's Java-related information.

http://java.sun.com

At this site you can download not only the JDK, but also a variety of freely distributed applets. It is a good idea to periodically check this site for new Java developments and for new compiled applet classes that Sun has created and made freely available.

Sun Microsystems Cafe

In the deepest, darkest recesses of the Sun Microsystems' labs employees have been continually creating and freely distributing new applets that aren't immediately distributed on Sun's main Java Web site. These very useful applets can be found at the following URL location, otherwise known as Cafe Del Sol.

http://www.xm.com/cafe/

This site proves to have very many useful Java applets, more so than Sun Microsystems' main Java page. If you find an applet that interests you, you can download it from Sun's FTP site at the following location.

ftp://xm.com/pub/incoming/cafe/

Several of the compiled applets available on this FTP site, such as the TourGuide and ButtonPLUS applets, were even featured in this chapter. We encourage you to check out this URL for some of the useful cutting-edge applets from the people who created the Java language.

Gamelan

By far the most complete guide to Java-related information on the Internet is at the Gamelan Web site, which can be found at the following URL.

http://www.gamelan.com

The information available at this site includes Java applications, Java applets, and JavaScript, which are all grouped together. When you do choose a topic in the Gamelan Directory, such as Special Effects or Multimedia, you'll find the numerous entries are briefly described, evaluated, and labeled as applets or JavaScripts. This site is the largest and most comprehensive culmination of Java-related information on the Internet, and it should be your starting place when you are looking for help, documentation, working examples, or news updates.

When to Use Java Applets

Marathon runners call it "the wall" — the point in the race past which the runner must go on pure force of will. In relation to the subject of this chapter, "the wall" can best be described as the point at which your computer tries to do anything else while a Java applet is running on it. Java applets represent an impressive and useful multimedia capability that you can integrate into your Web site, but we urge you to use them cautiously. Java applications and Java applets may be the future of the Internet, but the fact is that the future isn't here yet. Many developers create Java applets that run great on a Pentium processor with 64MB RAM, but they forget that most Internet users have only a 486 processor with 8MB RAM. This oversight has resulted in many Web pages running pathetically slow graphical Java applets that do relatively nothing. Here are several guidelines to keep in mind when deciding to place a particular Java applet on your Web site.

- **Use only useful Java applets.** For example, don't place a bouncing ball Java applet across your Web page just to show users that you can do it, but use applets that add functionality to the Web site.

- **Don't put Java applets on the main page of your Web site.** Most users who first visit a Web site have been sent there from some hyperlink, and they typically want to quickly evaluate your Web site for their particular interest. If you place a Java applet on the first Web page users contact, they will often find it very frustrating to wait a relatively significant amount of time for the applet to download, initialize, and begin running. You should place your Java applets on other Web pages on your Web site, and you can even indicate on your home page that exciting Java applets exist on these pages. Any users who knowingly view these pages will then not be frustrated by any slow applet execution.

- **Don't put more than one Java applet on a Web page.** Although you can place more than one Java applet on a particular Web page, we advise that you don't. An example of a poor Web page design that has more than one Java applet running on it can be found at the following URL: http://www.uib.no/isf/javatest.htm. On a typical Internet user's computer this Web page runs poorly.

The Java applets featured in this chapter follow these basic guidelines and proved impressive in both capability and processing speed when evaluated with a 486/66MHz processor with 8MB RAM and running the Windows 95 operating system.

Conclusion

Java applets are not the answer to creating every type of multimedia experience, but they do have several key capabilities that can significantly add to the multimedia appearance and functionality of a Web site. Because Java applets are interpreted on the fly, they run more slowly than typical compiled computer applications. In many cases this lack of running speed contributes to a lackluster performance, so a Web developer must first ensure that the Java applet runs efficiently before choosing to employ it on a Web site. The Java applets that have been featured in this chapter are those that we believe do significantly add to a Web site, and they do not run so slow that they would detract from the Web site.

In this book, Java applets represent just one of the alternative technologies that you can incorporate in your Web sites to truly revolutionize them. When you incorporate specific capabilities or entertaining multimedia content in your Web site, you must decide which of these technologies is capable of achieving the desired objectives and which is the easiest to implement. It is important to recognize the one distinct advantage Java applets have over inline plug-ins, which is that all a user needs to execute a Java applet is a Web browser with a built-in Java interpreter. No additional programs need to be installed with the browser for the content to be viewed by the user.

Even a user who does not have any idea what a Java applet is will still be able to see it execute on your Web page without any knowledge other than how to use a

Web browser. This simplicity of user execution becomes more important as increasing numbers of less computer-literate users get on the Internet.

Java is here to stay, and it is one of the technologies now available for you to use to create the next generation of multimedia-enhanced Web sites.

8

JAVA APPLET

CREATION TOOLS

T he ability to exploit the potential of Java applets until now has been limited to those individuals who have both programming experience and a lot of time on their hands. Programmers who have written Java code using Sun's Java Development Kit (JDK) have been looking forward to visual development tools that will simplify Java applet creation. Today's programmers are accustomed to using visual development tools such as PowerBuilder and Visual C++. A programmer using one of these tools can add basic objects such as buttons and text input fields to a computer application in seconds. Then the development tools generate the actual source code for the objects that have been placed in the application. Now tools with this capability are available for Java. This chapter describes several visual development tools used to create Java applet animations and basic Java applications.

Just-in-Time Compiler

People who have had exposure to Java applets will notice how slowly they often run. The slow execution speed is because Java applets are run as interpreted byte code rather than run as precompiled programs. This method can result in certain Java applet applications, such as graphical animations, having an undesirable slow motion or disjointed effect when they are run on a Web page. Several solutions are emerging to improve the run-time speed of Java applets.

The simplest solution is to require that everyone have a 200MHz Pentium processor with 16MB RAM to run a Java applet. Being realistic, we can assume that the estimated 120 million existing computers aren't going to be upgraded overnight, no matter how much Intel wishes that they would.

This leaves only the possibility of a software solution to improve the run-time performance of Java applets. The emerging software solution known as a Just-In-Time (JIT) compiler can produce amazing results in increased run-time performance. Borland is one of the first companies to develop a Java JIT compiler, known as the AppAccelerator, that can increase the performance of Java applets 5 to 10 times. The JIT compiler works by reading the byte code of a Java applet and then compiling the Java byte code into machine code. Then the Java applet is executed as a compiled program. Because it is run as a compiled program, it runs significantly faster.

The limitation is that the Java JIT compiler must be resident on the user's computer. The JIT compiler can be integrated into either the browser or the operating system itself. When JIT compilers are integrated in this fashion, users will be able to appreciate a high-performance run time for the Java applets they download from the Web. Then there will be relatively few performance limitations on the Java applets you can create and place in your Web applications.

Java Applet Animation

Java applet animations are an impressive way for you to "spice up" your Web applications. Why display your company's logo motionless on a Web page when you can animate it? You can use Java applet animations in an endless number of creative ways to enhance the entertainment or informative capability of your Web pages.

When you begin to create Java applet animations, don't bother tackling the intricacies of Java programming. There are already several tools available that allow you to create Java applet animations without ever writing a line of code. Select the image you want, indicate its path in your animation with simple point-and-click utilities, and export the animation to HTML. In a couple of minutes you can create a Java applet animation that you can embed in your Web pages. The development tools provide the Java applet classes and produce the HTML source code. All you have to do is create dynamic Web content.

The Easy Animator

The Easy Animator (TEA) is a visual Java applet animation creation tool developed by Dimension X. To create animations with this tool you don't have to know anything about the Java language—you need to know only how to use TEA's visual tool capabilities. The TEA program described in this chapter is available as a free version known as FreeTEA. TEA Lite and TEA PRO are two other versions available that offer additional features, but they are not available free. Before you can install the FreeTEA program, Sun's JDK must be installed on your computer system. You can download Sun's JDK from the following URL.

http://java.sun.com

Once you have the JDK installed, you can download FreeTEA from Dimension X at the following URL location.

http://www.dimensionx.com/

After you download FreeTEA, you must unzip and properly install it. When this program is unzipped, you will notice that it was actually written in Java with the JACK (Java Animation Construction Kit) API. Because FreeTEA was written in Java, it contains numerous Java.CLASS files.

FreeTEA has several directories that must be placed in specific locations within the Java directory where the JDK is installed. The readme.txt file that is included with FreeTEA gives detailed instructions on the proper location for the various directories and the changes that need to be made to the class path when the JDK was installed. Once you have successfully installed FreeTEA, you can execute it by running the TEA.BAT file.

■■■■■■

When you unzip this file, it is important that you use a decompression utility that maintains the entire file extension of the compressed files. The FreeTEA file contains several Java .CLASS files, which can't be shortened to .CLA files for the program to run. Many compression and decompression utilities modify long file extensions such as these. Use a decompression utility that doesn't shorten long file extensions.

Earlier versions of the popular Winzip program made this undesirable modification to files that it decompressed. To ensure there are no problems when using Winzip, you need to download the most current Winzip program or use at least version 6.1 to avoid file extension problems. Stroud's Consummate Winsock Web site is a superb site from which to obtain useful freeware and shareware software. You can find this Web site at the following URL.

http://cws.wilmington.net/

■■■■■

1. Start the DOS command window.
2. Switch to the C:\java\dnx directory.
3. Type TEA on the DOS prompt command line. To edit an existing scene JCK file, type the TEA command along with the path to the desired JCK file.

When you first run FreeTEA, two windows will appear: the Root Scene Properties window and the Scene Editor window. The Root Scene Properties window allows you to designate the properties of the animation such as looping and scene name. The Root Scene Properties window appears only when you don't designate a JCK file to open when you run FreeTEA (Figure 8.1).

The first time you run FreeTEA, input the desired Scene Name and then close the Root Scene Properties window. The Scene Editor window is the main creation window that will remain open. It allows you to integrate various images, add behaviors or movement, and preview the animation that you are creating (Figure 8.2).

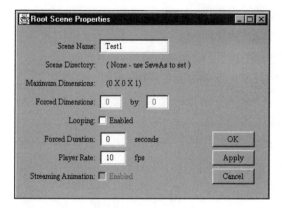

████████ **Figure 8.1** Name the scene you want to create and close the Root Scene Properties window.

The Scene editor has a tool bar at the bottom of the window that gives you the ability to preview the animation in a variety of modes. These are standard animation viewing buttons that allow you to play the animation, fast forward through the animation, and even reverse the playback of the animation.

When you create a new animation, you must first save the file for the scene. Choose the **Scene|Save As** menu selection and enter the desired filename of the JCK file and the directory you want to save it in. When you add images and audio files to the scene, file FreeTEA will automatically create an image and audio subdirectory where it will place the added files.

████████ **Figure 8.2** Use the Scene Editor window to run and evaluate Java applet animations.

The Content window is important in creating animations. The Content Manager window allows you to import and organize an animation's image and sound files. When you create an animation, the first image you load in the Content Manager should be the background image. Open the Content Manager window by choosing the **Element|Add Image** menu selection (Figure 8.3).

The Content Manager window allows you to add either one image or a sequence of images from a file or even a URL. When you add a sequence of images, enter only the first image file of the sequence. As with most animation sequences, the files have the same file name with an increasing numerical order. For example, an animation sequence could consist of four files named T1.tif, T2.tif, T3.tif, and T4.tif. After you choose the first file of the image sequence, you need to indicate the number of frames. The number of frames will be the number of different image files that make up the animation sequence.

When you create an animation, the first image that you add in the Content Manager window is the background image. After you have loaded the background image, you can add other images or image animation sequences. You can even add audio files to your animation, depending on what version of TEA you are using.

Your animation wouldn't be all that interesting if the images were limited to a stationary location. FreeTEA provides the ability to add motion to an animation.

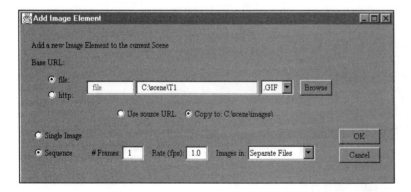

■■■■■■■ **Figure 8.3** Use the Content Manager window to add images to your animation.

First, select the image to which you want to add motion, and then choose the **Behavior|Motion Behavior** menu selection. Here is a list of the several different behaviors you can add to your image, although most of them are not available in the FreeTEA version.

- DrawnPath
- Gravity
- Jump
- Pinball
- Shapes
- Spline
- Wander

Figure 8.4 displays the Edit DrawnPath Behavior window that appears when you select the **DrawnPath** menu selection in FreeTEA.

Leave this window open and hold down the left mouse button as you designate the path for the image. The designated path will appear as white dots. When you have chosen the desired path, click **OK** in the Edit DrawnPath Behavior window. Then click on the **Play** button to see the image move along the path you just created.

Now that you are familiar with the basic tools of FreeTEA, here is a list of the basic procedures to create your own Java applet animations.

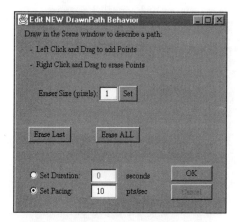

▰▰▰▰ **Figure 8.4** Leave this window open while you create the motion path for the highlighted image.

1. Run FreeTEA and enter the name of the scene in the Root Scene Properties window.

2. Save the new JCK file for the animation that you will create by choosing the **Scene|Save As** menu selection.

3. Load the first image that will serve as the background image for the animation by choosing the **Element|Add Image** menu selection.

4. Choose the **Element|Properties** menu selection and enable the Position Lock option so that you don't accidentally move the background image.

5. Add more images or sequences of images by choosing the **Element|Add Image** menu selection.

6. Add motion behavior to an image by selecting it in the Scene Editor window and then choosing the **Behavior|Motion Behavior** menu selection. Trace the desired path of the image by holding down the left mouse button. Then click on the **OK** button in the motion behavior window when you have created the desired motion.

7. Choose the **Scene|Export HTML** menu selection to create the HTML file that would contain the JCK file you have created.

8. Run the TEACOPY.BAT file to copy the PlayerApplet classes into the directory that contains the animations JCK file.

9. Load the HTML document in a Web browser and watch the Java applet animation play.

Export HTML

After the animation is created, you can incorporate it in your Web site. When you choose the **Scene|Export HTML** menu selection, TEA generates the necessary HTML source code. Here is an example of the HTML source code generated when the **Scene|Export HTML** menu selection is chosen.

```
<HTML>
<HEAD>
<TITLE>TEA Scene: Try</TITLE>
<!-- Created by {You Are Here} -->
</HEAD>
<BODY BGCOLOR="#000000">
<APPLET CODE="dnx.jack.PlayerApplet.class" CODEBASE="./" WIDTH=200 HEIGHT=200>
<PARAM NAME=scene VALUE="try.jck">
```

```
<PARAM NAME=playerBkgd VALUE="000000">
<PARAM NAME=playerRate VALUE="10">
</APPLET>
</BODY>
</HTML>
```

TEA doesn't actually generate a new applet for each animation, but instead creates the JCK file. The JCK file serves as a scripting file that is read by the Java applet classes that TEA uses to display the animation. Figure 8.5 is an example of a JCK file that was created for an animation. This example produced an animation sequence of 15 different image files that moved around on a background image.

■■■■■■■■■ **Figure 8.5** Contents of JCK file created by FreeTEA for a Java applet animation.

```
//JACK V1.00 scene description, by TEA 0.1
{
dnx.jack.Scene {
  name "Try"
  position { x 0 y 0 z 0 }
  loops 0
  locked 0
  forcedDur 0
  comment ""
  viewCube { x 0 y 0 z 0 w 200 h 200 d 2147483647 }
  behaviors 0
  elements 2
    dnx.jack.SceneElement {
      tyTiming 0
      offset 0
      sequence dnx.jack.ImageSequence {
        name "images/BACK"
        position { x -1 y 1 z 0 }
        loops 0
```

Continued...

```
      locked 0
      forcedDur 0
      comment "null"
      nFrames 1
      useURLBase 0
      seqType 0
      fps 1
      base "file:C:/scene/" source "images/BACK"
      extension ".gif"
      behaviors 0
      }
  }
dnx.jack.SceneElement {
  tyTiming 0
  offset 0
  sequence dnx.jack.ImageSequence {
    name "images/team/T1"
    position { x 35 y 25 z 0 }
    loops 0
    locked 0
    forcedDur 0
    comment "null"
    nFrames 15
    useURLBase 0
    seqType 0
    fps 1
    base "file:C:/scene/" source "images/team/T"
    extension ".gif"
    behaviors 1
      dnx.jack.behaviors.DrawnPath {
        name "DrawnPath"
      durBased 0
      duration 22300
```

```
    period 100
    positions 223
        { x 35 y 25 z 0 }   { x 36 y 25 z 0 }   { x 37 y 25 z 0 }
{ x 37 y 26 z 0 }   { x 38 y 27 z 0 }

        { x 39 y 28 z 0 }   { x 39 y 29 z 0 }   { x 39 y 30 z 0 }
{ x 39 y 31 z 0 }   { x 40 y 31 z 0 }

        { x 40 y 32 z 0 }   { x 41 y 33 z 0 }   { x 42 y 33 z 0 }
{ x 43 y 34 z 0 }   { x 44 y 37 z 0 }

        { x 46 y 39 z 0 }   { x 47 y 41 z 0 }   { x 47 y 43 z 0 }
{ x 48 y 43 z 0 }   { x 49 y 44 z 0 }

        { x 49 y 45 z 0 }   { x 50 y 45 z 0 }   { x 51 y 45 z 0 }
{ x 51 y 46 z 0 }   { x 51 y 47 z 0 }

        { x 51 y 48 z 0 }   { x 51 y 49 z 0 }   { x 53 y 49 z 0 }
{ x 53 y 50 z 0 }   { x 55 y 52 z 0 }

        { x 55 y 53 z 0 }   { x 57 y 56 z 0 }   { x 58 y 57 z 0 }
{ x 59 y 57 z 0 }   { x 59 y 58 z 0 }

        { x 59 y 59 z 0 }   { x 60 y 60 z 0 }   { x 61 y 61 z 0 }
{ x 63 y 62 z 0 }   { x 63 y 64 z 0 }

        { x 64 y 65 z 0 }   { x 65 y 66 z 0 }   { x 67 y 67 z 0 }
{ x 67 y 69 z 0 }   { x 69 y 69 z 0 }

        { x 71 y 71 z 0 }   { x 72 y 73 z 0 }   { x 73 y 73 z 0 }
{ x 73 y 74 z 0 }   { x 74 y 74 z 0 }

        { x 74 y 75 z 0 }   { x 75 y 76 z 0 }   { x 78 y 78 z 0 }
{ x 79 y 79 z 0 }   { x 81 y 80 z 0 }

        { x 82 y 81 z 0 }   { x 84 y 82 z 0 }   { x 85 y 83 z 0 }
{ x 87 y 84 z 0 }   { x 88 y 85 z 0 }

        { x 94 y 87 z 0 }   { x 95 y 88 z 0 }   { x 97 y 88 z 0 }
{ x 107 y 89 z 0 }   { x 115 y 88 z 0 }

        { x 117 y 88 z 0 }   { x 119 y 88 z 0 }   { x 119 y 87 z 0 }
{ x 121 y 87 z 0 }   { x 124 y 85 z 0 }

        { x 125 y 84 z 0 }   { x 126 y 83 z 0 }   { x 127 y 82 z 0 }
{ x 128 y 81 z 0 }   { x 129 y 80 z 0 }

        { x 130 y 79 z 0 }   { x 131 y 77 z 0 }   { x 133 y 76 z 0 }
{ x 134 y 75 z 0 }   { x 135 y 73 z 0 }

        { x 135 y 72 z 0 }   { x 136 y 71 z 0 }   { x 137 y 70 z 0 }
{ x 138 y 69 z 0 }   { x 139 y 68 z 0 }

        { x 139 y 67 z 0 }   { x 139 y 65 z 0 }   { x 140 y 65 z 0 }
{ x 141 y 63 z 0 }   { x 143 y 61 z 0 }

        { x 143 y 60 z 0 }   { x 143 y 59 z 0 }   { x 143 y 58 z 0 }
{ x 144 y 57 z 0 }   { x 144 y 56 z 0 }
```

Continued...

```
      { x 145 y 54 z 0 }  { x 147 y 53 z 0 }  { x 147 y 52 z 0 }
{ x 147 y 53 z 0 }  { x 146 y 53 z 0 }

      { x 146 y 52 z 0 }  { x 145 y 51 z 0 }  { x 144 y 50 z 0 }
{ x 143 y 49 z 0 }  { x 143 y 48 z 0 }

      { x 142 y 47 z 0 }  { x 141 y 47 z 0 }  { x 141 y 46 z 0 }
{ x 139 y 45 z 0 }  { x 139 y 43 z 0 }

      { x 138 y 43 z 0 }  { x 137 y 42 z 0 }  { x 135 y 41 z 0 }
{ x 134 y 41 z 0 }  { x 131 y 39 z 0 }

      { x 127 y 38 z 0 }  { x 120 y 37 z 0 }  { x 119 y 36 z 0 }
{ x 117 y 36 z 0 }  { x 103 y 35 z 0 }

      { x 101 y 35 z 0 }  { x 97 y 37 z 0 }  { x 92 y 39 z 0 }
{ x 91 y 40 z 0 }  { x 87 y 41 z 0 }

      { x 86 y 42 z 0 }  { x 83 y 43 z 0 }  { x 80 y 45 z 0 }
{ x 77 y 47 z 0 }  { x 74 y 49 z 0 }

      { x 71 y 50 z 0 }  { x 70 y 51 z 0 }  { x 68 y 52 z 0 }
{ x 67 y 53 z 0 }  { x 65 y 55 z 0 }

      { x 63 y 57 z 0 }  { x 60 y 59 z 0 }  { x 58 y 63 z 0 }
{ x 57 y 64 z 0 }  { x 57 y 65 z 0 }

      { x 57 y 66 z 0 }  { x 57 y 67 z 0 }  { x 57 y 68 z 0 }
{ x 59 y 69 z 0 }  { x 59 y 70 z 0 }

      { x 59 y 74 z 0 }  { x 62 y 78 z 0 }  { x 63 y 79 z 0 }
{ x 63 y 80 z 0 }  { x 64 y 81 z 0 }

      { x 64 y 82 z 0 }  { x 67 y 84 z 0 }  { x 68 y 86 z 0 }
{ x 69 y 87 z 0 }  { x 71 y 89 z 0 }

      { x 72 y 91 z 0 }  { x 74 y 93 z 0 }  { x 75 y 94 z 0 }
{ x 77 y 96 z 0 }  { x 79 y 98 z 0 }

      { x 79 y 100 z 0 }  { x 81 y 101 z 0 }  { x 82 y 103 z 0 }
{ x 85 y 111 z 0 }  { x 85 y 112 z 0 }

      { x 85 y 113 z 0 }  { x 86 y 115 z 0 }  { x 87 y 117 z 0 }
{ x 87 y 119 z 0 }  { x 87 y 120 z 0 }

      { x 87 y 123 z 0 }  { x 87 y 124 z 0 }  { x 87 y 125 z 0 }
{ x 87 y 126 z 0 }  { x 87 y 127 z 0 }

      { x 87 y 128 z 0 }  { x 87 y 129 z 0 }  { x 87 y 131 z 0 }
{ x 87 y 133 z 0 }  { x 87 y 134 z 0 }

      { x 87 y 135 z 0 }  { x 87 y 136 z 0 }  { x 86 y 137 z 0 }
{ x 86 y 139 z 0 }  { x 86 y 141 z 0 }

      { x 87 y 143 z 0 }  { x 87 y 144 z 0 }  { x 88 y 144 z 0 }
{ x 92 y 145 z 0 }  { x 96 y 146 z 0 }

      { x 103 y 147 z 0 }  { x 127 y 147 z 0 }  { x 129 y 147 z 0 }
{ x 135 y 148 z 0 }
```

```
{ x 140 y 148 z 0 }
        { x 140 y 147 z 0 }  { x 140 y 146 z 0 }  { x 140 y 144 z 0 }
{ x 141 y 137 z 0 }
{ x 141 y 135 z 0 }
        { x 142 y 130 z 0 }  { x 143 y 129 z 0 }  { x 143 y 126 z 0 }
{ x 143 y 119 z 0 }
{ x 143 y 117 z 0 }
        { x 143 y 116 z 0 }  { x 143 y 111 z 0 }  { x 143 y 108 z 0 }
{ x 143 y 107 z 0 }
{ x 143 y 106 z 0 }
        { x 143 y 105 z 0 }  { x 143 y 104 z 0 }  { x 143 y 103 z 0 }
{ x 143 y 101 z 0 }
{ x 143 y 100 z 0 }
        { x 138 y 101 z 0 }  { x 116 y 100 z 0 }  { x 92 y 99 z 0 }
{ x 88 y 98 z 0 }  { x 85 y 97 z 0 }
        { x 84 y 97 z 0 }  { x 84 y 98 z 0 }  { x 84 y 98 z 0 }
    }
   }
  }
 }
}
```

▬▬▬▬

The JCK file is an editable file that advanced programmers can modify. You can contact Dimension X to obtain documentation on how to modify JCK files.

To run a Java applet animation created by TEA in your Web site, you need to copy the following files onto your server.

- JCK file for animation
- HTML file generated when the **Scene|Export HTML** menu selection was chosen
- PlayerApplet classes and Behavior classes created when you run TEACOPY.BAT

TEA is an impressive and easy-to-use tool for Java applet animation creation. Using TEA, you can have your Web sites full of exciting Java applet animations within minutes.

Corel WEB.MOVE

Get ready to be amazed. Corel WEB.MOVE is a tool that you can now use to easily create eye-catching applet animations. Produce applet animations using prebuilt actors and props and the simple editing tools that make up Corel WEB.MOVE. Once you have created your animation, choose the **File|Author to Java** menu selection. Corel WEB.MOVE then creates the HTML source code for the animation. Creating Java applet animations for your Web pages this way is easy and fun. Here is a list of just some of the activities possible with Corel WEB.MOVE.

- Use numerous built-in actors or props to quickly create animations
- Easily create motion paths for actors in the animation with point-and-click ease
- Use simple timeline and cel entry tools to modify animations
- Add sound to your animation
- Add cues to allow for user interactivity
- Use VCR controls to preview animations for frame-by-frame analysis

Unlike with other animation creation programs, you don't have to learn an entire scripting language. Corel WEB.MOVE features a simple creation window with the animation scene under development placed in the center and the toolbars located on the bottom and left side of the window. A sample animation loaded in Corel WEB.MOVE is shown in Figure 8.6.

Creating animations with Corel WEB.MOVE is simple because you use only four basic components to construct all animations.

- Prop objects are images in the animation that are used for background images and typically aren't animated.
- Actor objects are dynamic images that can have their own animation sequence and can move along a customized path in the animation scene.
- Sound files can play in various sequences of the animation.
- Cue objects can be placed in an animation to allow interactivity with the viewer and can be made to pause or accelerate the frame rate of an animation.

With Corel WEB.MOVE you're in the director's chair. Of course you need the same tools and resources to make your animation that directors like Steven Spielberg

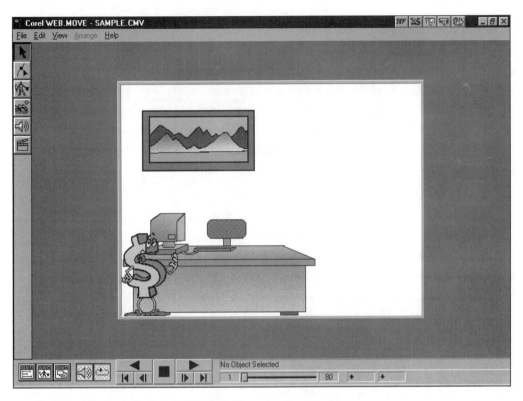

Figure 8.6 Corel WEB.MOVE application window.

need for their movies. Props, actors, and your director cues are all components available to you to create your animations.

No respectable director would ever make a movie without using props ranging from background scenery to a picture on a wall. When you create animations with Corel WEB.MOVE, you can use prebuilt prop images or create your own. As you create your animation, use these prop images for the background or inanimate objects within the animation.

A movie without actors probably wouldn't be a box office smash, nor would the animation you create be interesting without actors. The actors you add to your animation can be either single-cel or multiple-cel actors. A multiple-cel actor is a sequence of still images of the same basic image that when run together produce an animated movement. For example, in Corel WEB.MOVE a bear actor has 10 cels that make it appear to walk. Corel WEB.MOVE allows you to add actor images to your animation and even provides hundreds of prebuilt multiple-cel actors.

The movie Star Wars probably wouldn't have been a blockbuster if it had been a silent film. The undeniable fact is that sound is an important element to any multimedia presentation. Corel WEB.MOVE recognizes this and allows you to add .AU or .WAV files to the animations you create. Not only can you add existing sound, but Corel WEB.MOVE lets you record your own sounds. Some of the prebuilt multiple-cel actors even have sounds associated with them.

Cues are the controls that you can place in an animation to direct it. Corel WEB.MOVE allows you to enter cues to pause the animation at a desired frame, accelerate the frame display of the animation, or even require user interactivity for the animation to play. For example, you could have the animation pause until the user clicks on a specific object in the animation scene. Cues are a useful way to integrate user involvement in the execution of an applet animation.

Opening Animation File

Corel WEB.MOVE provides several sample animations that you can open to explore its potential. Choose the **File|Open** menu selection to open the Open Animation File window shown in Figure 8.7.

The two types of files you can open are .CMV animation files created by Corel WEB.MOVE and Promotion .MWF files. When you select the desired animation file, a preview of it is shown in the Open Animation File window before it is opened.

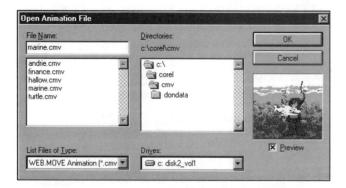

■■■■■■■ **Figure 8.7** Select the desired animation file to be opened.

Figure 8.7 displays the preview that appeared when the sample marine.cmv animation file was selected.

Toolbars

Corel WEB.MOVE provides you with simple functions that allow you to easily add objects to an animation, control their movement, and preview them. All the capabilities you need are found on the Toolbox and Control Panel toolbars. When you first run Corel WEB.MOVE, the Toolbox toolbar is located in the left side of the application window. Figure 8.8 illustrates the Toolbox toolbar that consists of six buttons.

The pick tool that features the pointer icon is found at the top of the Toolbox toolbar. This tool is used to select objects in the animation scene. You can select an object in the animation scene and move it around the animation scene. When you double-click on an object in the animation scene, an information window for that object appears. The actor information window that appeared when an actor object was double-clicked is shown in Figure 8.9.

Figure 8.8 Select the desired button to add or modify objects in an animation.

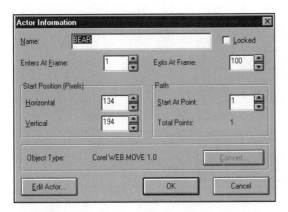

Figure 8.9 Vary the frame number in which the actor enters or exits the animation.

Using the spinner controls, you can vary the frame number in which the selected actor enters or exits the animation. Click on the **Edit Actor** button to edit the appearance of an actor. When this button is clicked, the selected actor appears in an edit window. A drawing tools window also appears so that you can modify one or more of the actor's cels to achieve the desired animation effect.

The multiple-cel actors may produce an animated movement, but it probably wouldn't be much of an animation if they were limited to the same location. The **Path** button is used to define a path for the actor's movement in the animation scene. After you click on the **Path** button, you then select an actor. Click your mouse button in the animation scene to produce the points in the path through which you want the actor to move.

The remaining buttons on the Toolbox toolbar allow you to add the four basic components to your animation. Figure 8.10 shows an example of the New Actor window that appears when the **Actor** button is clicked.

The actor you add to the animation can be one you create or one that already exists. When you select the **Create New** radio button, you can create an actor using the drawing tools in Corel WEB.MOVE or other Corel programs. When you select the Create from **File** radio button, you can choose an existing actor file or even an actor that exists in another Corel WEB.MOVE .CMV animation file to add to the animation. When you click on either the Prop or Sound button, a window similar to the New Actor window appears, allowing you to add new props or sounds.

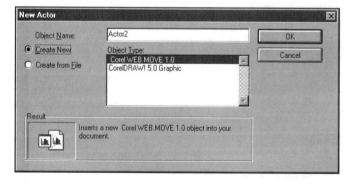

■■■■■ **Figure 8.10** Create your own actor object or choose one from an existing file.

Cues allow you to add interactivity to the animations you create. When you click on the **Cue** button, the Cue Information window appears (Figure 8.11).

Use cues to direct the animation. The example shown in Figure 8.11 illustrates the different Conditions and Actions you can set for your animation. This example shows one cue that would pause the animation until the user clicked on the specified actor. In addition to various conditions for restarting the animation, you can vary the action that takes place when the condition is satisfied. Here is a list of the different actions that take place in this example when certain conditions are satisfied.

- Continue
- Change frame rate to: 18
- Pause until above condition occurs again
- Goto frame: 33

Interactivity is the key to creating interesting multimedia Web content. Cues give you the ability to make your Java applet animations truly interactive with the user.

The Control Panel toolbar at the bottom of the Corel WEB.MOVE window has several utilities that you will continually use to develop your animations (Figure 8.12).

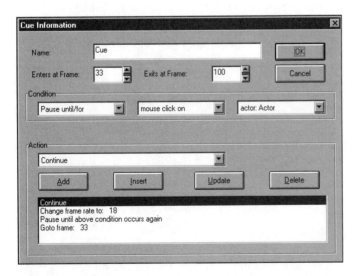

Figure 8.11 Add interactivity to your animation with cues.

Figure 8.12 Use the three buttons on the right side of the toolbar for animation design modifications.

The three main buttons you use most often in animation creation can be found on the Control Panel toolbar.

- *Timeline button.* Shows all the prop, actor, and sound objects that constitute the animation along with the frame that they enter and exit
- *Library button.* Allows you to enter one of the many multiple-cel actors found in the CorelMOVE library
- *Cel Sequencer button.* Allows you to modify the size of any actor in your animation in a specific frame

When you click on the **Timeline** button, the Timeline window is opened. The Timeline window is the tool you will use most often when you create and modify animations. The Timeline window displays all of the prop, actor, sound, and cue objects that exist in your animation. Figure 8.13 shows an example of the Timeline window that would appear for a typical animation.

The top part of the Timeline window has four buttons representing the four main animation components: actor, prop, sound, and cue. You can choose to display or not to display these different objects in the Timeline window by clicking on the appropriate button. You can temporarily remove an object from the animation

Figure 8.13 Double-click on an object in the Timeline window to modify the selected object.

scene by clicking on the check mark next to the object. When there is no check mark next to an object, it won't appear when you run the animation. You can see in this example that when the PRE-HISTORIC prop object was selected, there were also several numbers displayed in the bottom of the Timeline window. These numbers indicate the following information for the selected object.

- The number next to the UP arrow indicates the frame number in which the object enters the animation.
- The number next to the DOWN arrow indicates the frame number in which the object exits the animation.
- The number in the far right is the frame number of the animation you are currently viewing.

You may decide that you want a particular object to enter the animation a little sooner. Double-click on the object in the Timeline window to open the information window for the desired object. In Figure 8.14 the PRE-HISTORIC prop object was chosen.

Click on the spin controls to vary the frame number in which the object enters or exits the animation. You can even vary the horizontal or vertical position of the object in the animation scene. When you are done making the desired changes, click **OK**.

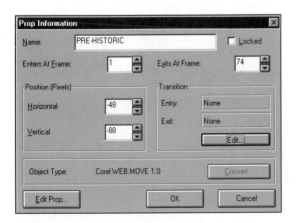

■■■■■ **Figure 8.14** Change the frame number in which the object enters and exits the animation.

Click on the **Library** button to add props or multiple-cel actors to your animation. The Open Library window appears, displaying numerous .MLB files you can choose. These .MLB files contain hundreds of prebuilt multiple-cel actors. When you select a .MLB file, a window appears, displaying the desired file. Figure 8.15 illustrates the window that appears when the animals.mlb file is selected.

The window containing the .MLB file allows you to observe the animated movement of the multiple-cel actors. Move the scroll bar to view other multiple-cel actors that are contained in the .MLB file selected. You will find that there are even sound objects in some .MLB files. When you find an actor or sound object you like, just click the **Place** button. The object will automatically be placed in the particular frame of the animation you are currently viewing.

The **Cel Sequencer** button allows you to vary the size or the sequence of cels displayed for a chosen actor. Select an actor in your animation and then click on the **Cel Sequencer** button to open the Cel Sequencer window (Figure 8.16).

In the example shown in Figure 8.16 all the frames were selected for the Size% option. Then the arrow next to this row was clicked, opening a pop-up window. In this pop-up window there are various selections that can be chosen to vary the size of the image that is displayed in the selected frames. For example, if you want to make the image appear to be running away, you would select the Large to Small option. The Size% of the image would be automatically changed, and when the animation is played, the actor object would decrease in size as the frame number displayed increases.

Figure 8.15 Move the scroll bar to view other actor objects in the desired MLB.

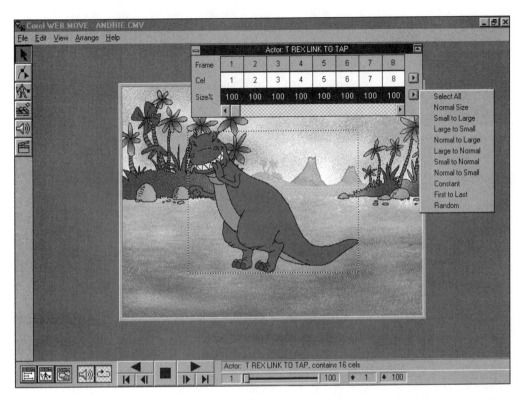

Figure 8.16 Choose the desired frames in either the Cel or Size% row, and then choose the desired modification.

The capabilities of the other buttons present on the Control Panel are quite simple. The **Speaker** button when clicked activates the sound, while the **Loop** button when clicked makes the animation run in a continual loop. Next to these buttons are the various VCR buttons that allow you to play the animation forward and backward or even pause it. Whenever you select an object in the animation scene, the object's name appears above the frame indicator. The frame indicator displays the frame number of the animation you are currently viewing and provides a slider control to vary that animation.

Creating an animation is a touch-and-feel exercise requiring you to add and modify objects in the animation and then view their performance. Because of the need for this constant variation, Corel WEB.MOVE is conveniently designed so that the

Timeline and Cel Sequence windows are integrated with the Control Panel display. For example, if you select an actor object in the Timeline window, its respective cel size information will be displayed in the Cel Sequence window, and the selected object will be also be displayed in the Control Panel window.

Create Your Own Animation

Now that you are familiar with the tools and capabilities of Corel WEB.MOVE, you can create your own animation. First set the desired characteristics of the new animation file using the Preferences window. Choose the **File|Preferences** menu selection to open the Preferences window shown in Figure 8.17.

Figure 8.17 shows the Preferences window with the **New Image** tab selected. In this window you can vary the defaults settings for the size of new animations scenes you create. You can also vary the basic frame rate of the animation that will play and designate the frame length of the animation. After the appropriate Preferences have been set, you can create a new animation file. Choose the **File|New** menu selection and enter the name and location for the animation you will create. Then combine your creativity with the capabilities you've learned about Corel WEB.MOVE to produce the most riveting Java applet animations.

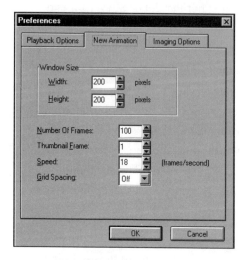

Figure 8.17 Select the **New Image** tab and modify default settings as desired.

Tips

There are several design hints to keep in mind when developing your Java applet animations. The basic goal is to keep the animation file as small as possible for quick download.

- Don't use extraneous objects that add little to the animation.
- Use a reasonably sized animation scene.
- Use sound files sparingly. Try to use .AU sounds files instead of .WAV sound files because .AU sound files are not as wide.
- Use a photo background image to give the animation a real-life effect.

Author to Java...

Once you have created your animation, place it in a Web page. Corel WEB.MOVE features the ability to generate an HTML file containing the Java applet animation. Create the HTML source code by choosing the **File|Author to Java** menu selection. Figure 8.18 displays the typical HTML source code generated by Corel WEB.MOVE for a Java applet animation.

▬▬▬▬ **Figure 8.18** Example HTML source code generated when you select the **File|Author to Java** menu selection.

```
<HTML>
<HEAD>
<TITLE> An Animator Demo Program </TITLE>
</HEAD>
<BODY>
<APPLET CODE="Anim.class" WIDTH=480 HEIGHT=360>
<param name=HEADER value="CorelJAVA Animator 1.0 Data">
<param name=USERPAUSE value="false">
<param name=DATASOURCE value="ANDRDATA">
<param name=REPEAT value="true">
<param name=TOTALFRAMES value=100>
<param name=TOTALACTORS value=4>
<param name=TOTALPROPS value=3>
<param name=TOTALSOUNDS value=0>
```

Continued...

```
<param name=FPS value=18>

<param name=ACTOR0 value="A0|CJA|1|8|4@123,1|-5@118,2|
-3@116,3|4@112,4|4@114,5|5@115,6|5@113,7|5@122,8|4@123,1|-5@118,2|
-3@116,3|4@112,4|4@114,5|5@115,6|5@113,7|5@122,8|4@123,1|-5@118,2|
-3@116,3|4@112,4|4@114,5|5@115,6|5@113,7|5@122,8|4@123,1|-1@-1,-1|
-1@-1,-1|-1@-1,-1|-1@-1,-1|-1@-1,-1|-1@-1,-1|-1@-1,-1|-1@-1,-1|
-1@-1,-1|-1@-1,-1|-1@-1,-1|-1@-1,-1|-1@-1,-1|-1@-1,-1|-1@-1,-1|
-1@-1,-1|-1@-1,-1|-1@-1,-1|-1@-1,-1|-1@-1,-1|-1@-1,-1|-1@-1,-1|
-1@-1,-1|-1@-1,-1|-1@-1,-1|-1@-1,-1|-1@-1,-1|-1@-1,-1|-1@-1,-1|
-1@-1,-1|-1@-1,-1|-1@-1,-1|-1@-1,-1|-1@-1,-1|-1@-1,-1|-1@-1,-1|
-1@-1,-1|-1@-1,-1|-1@-1,-1|-1@-1,-1|-1@-1,-1|-1@-1,-1|-1@-1,-1|
-1@-1,-1|-1@-1,-1|-1@-1,-1|-1@-1,-1|-1@-1,-1|-1@-1,-1|-1@-1,-1|
-1@-1,-1|-1@-1,-1|-1@-1,-1|-1@-1,-1|-1@-1,-1|-1@-1,-1|-1@-1,-1|
-1@-1,-1|-1@-1,-1|-1@-1,-1|-1@-1,-1|-1@-1,-1|-1@-1,-1|-1@-1,-1|
-1@-1,-1|-1@-1,-1|-1@-1,-1|-1@-1,-1|-1@-1,-1|-1@-1,-1|-1@-1,-1|
-1@-1,-1|-1@-1,-1|-1@-1,-1|-1@-1,-1|-1@-1,-1|-1@-1,-1|-1@-1,-1|
-1@-1,-1|-1@-1,-1|-1@-1,-1|-1@-1,-1|-1@-1,-1|-1@-1,-1|-1@-1,-1|
-1@-1,-1|-1@-1,-1|-1@-1,-1|-1@-1,-1">

<param name=ACTOR1 value="A1|CJA|1|12|-1@-1,-1|-1@-1,-1|-1@-1,-1|
-1@-1,-1|-1@-1,-1|-1@-1,-1|-1@-1,-1|-1@-1,-1|-1@-1,-1|-1@-1,-1|
-1@-1,-1|-1@-1,-1|-1@-1,-1|-1@-1,-1|-1@-1,-1|-1@-1,-1|-1@-1,-1|
-1@-1,-1|-1@-1,-1|-1@-1,-1|-1@-1,-1|-1@-1,-1|-1@-1,-1|-1@-1,-1|
-1@-1,-1|11@117,1|19@104,2|19@92,3|32@83,4|44@77,5|49@74,6|59@68,7|
71@55,8|79@53,9|93@43,10|106@37,11|114@35,12|121@34,1|114@46,2|96@51,3|
84@57,4|73@69,5|65@83,6|64@98,7|69@101,8|81@96,9|97@85,10|116@77,11|
126@73,12|123@71,1|123@71,2|114@73,3|120@77,4|127@82,5|124@84,6|
127@85,7|127@82,8|127@82,9|127@77,10|128@73,11|126@73,12|123@71,1|
-1@-1,-1|-1@-1,-1|-1@-1,-1|-1@-1,-1|-1@-1,-1|-1@-1,-1|-1@-1,-1|
-1@-1,-1|-1@-1,-1|-1@-1,-1|-1@-1,-1|-1@-1,-1|-1@-1,-1|-1@-1,-1|
-1@-1,-1|-1@-1,-1|-1@-1,-1|-1@-1,-1|-1@-1,-1|-1@-1,-1|-1@-1,-1|
-1@-1,-1|-1@-1,-1|-1@-1,-1|-1@-1,-1|-1@-1,-1|-1@-1,-1|-1@-1,-1|
-1@-1,-1|-1@-1,-1|-1@-1,-1|-1@-1,-1|-1@-1,-1|-1@-1,-1|-1@-1,-1|
-1@-1,-1|-1@-1,-1|-1@-1,-1">

<param name=ACTOR2 value="A2|CJA|1|13|-1@-1,-1|-1@-1,-1|-1@-1,-1|
-1@-1,-1|-1@-1,-1|-1@-1,-1|-1@-1,-1|-1@-1,-1|-1@-1,-1|-1@-1,-1|
-1@-1,-1|-1@-1,-1|-1@-1,-1|-1@-1,-1|-1@-1,-1|-1@-1,-1|-1@-1,-1|
-1@-1,-1|-1@-1,-1|-1@-1,-1|-1@-1,-1|-1@-1,-1|-1@-1,-1|-1@-1,-1|
-1@-1,-1|-1@-1,-1|-1@-1,-1|-1@-1,-1|-1@-1,-1|-1@-1,-1|-1@-1,-1|
-1@-1,-1|-1@-1,-1|-1@-1,-1|-1@-1,-1|-1@-1,-1|-1@-1,-1|-1@-1,-1|
-1@-1,-1|-1@-1,-1|-1@-1,-1|-1@-1,-1|-1@-1,-1|-1@-1,-1|-1@-1,-1|
-1@-1,-1|-1@-1,-1|-1@-1,-1|-1@-1,-1|-1@-1,-1|-1@-1,-1|-1@-1,-1|
-1@-1,-1|-1@-1,-1|-1@-1,-1|-1@-1,-1|-1@-1,-1|-1@-1,-1|-1@-1,-1|
-1@-1,-1|-1@-1,-1|-1@-1,-1|95@112,1|95@112,2|95@111,3|96@103,4|
99@98,5|97@100,6|94@105,7|70@105,8|51@91,9|-24@28,10|-49@6,11|
-81@-25,12|96@37,13|-1@-1,-1|-1@-1,-1|-1@-1,-1|-1@-1,-1|-1@-1,-1|
-1@-1,-1|-1@-1,-1|-1@-1,-1|-1@-1,-1|-1@-1,-1|-1@-1,-1|-1@-1,-1|
-1@-1,-1|-1@-1,-1|-1@-1,-1|-1@-1,-1|-1@-1,-1|-1@-1,-1|-1@-1,-1|
-1@-1,-1|-1@-1,-1|-1@-1,-1|-1@-1,-1|-1@-1,-1|-1@-1,-1">

<param name=ACTOR3 value="A3|CJA|1|8|-1@-1,-1|-1@-1,-1|-1@-1,-1|
-1@-1,-1|-1@-1,-1|-1@-1,-1|-1@-1,-1|-1@-1,-1|-1@-1,-1|-1@-1,-1|
-1@-1,-1|-1@-1,-1|-1@-1,-1|-1@-1,-1|-1@-1,-1|-1@-1,-1|-1@-1,-1|
```

```
-1@-1,-1| -1@-1,-1|  -1@-1,-1| -1@-1,-1| -1@-1,-1| -1@-1,-1| -1@-1,-1|
-1@-1,-1| -1@-1,-1| -1@-1,-1| -1@-1,-1| -1@-1,-1| -1@-1,-1| -1@-1,-1|
-1@-1,-1| -1@-1,-1| -1@-1,-1| -1@-1,-1| -1@-1,-1| -1@-1,-1| -1@-1,-1|
-1@-1,-1| -1@-1,-1| -1@-1,-1| -1@-1,-1| -1@-1,-1| -1@-1,-1| -1@-1,-1|
-1@-1,-1| -1@-1,-1| -1@-1,-1| -1@-1,-1| -1@-1,-1| -1@-1,-1| -1@-1,-1|
-1@-1,-1| -1@-1,-1| -1@-1,-1| -1@-1,-1| -1@-1,-1| -1@-1,-1| -1@-1,-1|
-1@-1,-1| -1@-1,-1| -1@-1,-1| -1@-1,-1| -1@-1,-1| -1@-1,-1| -1@-1,-1|
-1@-1,-1| -1@-1,-1| -1@-1,-1| -1@-1,-1| -1@-1,-1| -1@-1,-1| -1@-1,-1|
-1@-1,-1|94@38,1|92@30,2|94@27,3|93@27,4|95@36,5|94@40,6|95@36,7|
93@30,8|94@38,1|92@30,2|94@27,3|93@27,4|95@36,5|94@40,6|95@36,7|
93@30,8|94@38,1|92@30,2|94@27,3|93@27,4|95@36,5|94@40,6|95@36,7|
93@30,8|94@38,1|92@30,2">

<param name=PROP0 value="P0|CJA|0|1|420|280|0|1|420|280|-27@-15|-1|-1|
-1|-1|-1|-1|-1|-1|-1|-1|-1|-1|-1|-1|-1|-1|-1|-1|-1|-1|-1|-1|-1|
-1|-1|-1|-1|-1|-1|-1|-1|-1|-1|-1|-1|-1|-1|-1|-1|-1|-1|-1|-1|-1|
-1|-1|-1|-1|-1|-1|-1|-1|-1|-1|-1|-1|-1|-1|-1|-1|-1|-1|-1|-1|-1|
-1|-1|-1|1|1|1|1|1|1|1|1|1|1|1|1|1|1|1|1|1|1|1|1|1|1|1|1|1|1|1">

<param name=PROP1 value="P1|CJA|0|1|420|280|0|1|420|280|-48@-
88|1|1|1|1|1|1|1|1|1|1|1|1|1|1|1|1|1|1|1|1|1|1|1|1|1|1|1|1|1|1|
1|1|1|1|1|1|1|1|1|1|1|1|1|1|1|1|1|1|1|1|1|1|1|1|1|1|1|1|1|1|1|1|
1|1|1|1|-1|-1|-1|-1|-1|-1|-1|-1|-1|-1|-1|-1|-1|-1|-1|-1|-1|-1|-1|
-1|-1|-1|-1|-1">

<param name=PROP2
value="P2|CJA|0|1|420|280|0|1|420|280|151@7|1|1|1|1|1|1|1|1|1|1|1|
1|1|1|1|1|1|1|1|1|1|1|1|1|1|1|1|1|1|1|1|1|1|1|1|1|1|1|1|1|1|1|1|
1|1|1|1|1|1|1|1|1|1|1|1|1|1|1|1|1|1|1|1|1|1|1|1|1|1|1|1|1|1|1|1|
1|1|1|1|1|1|1|1|1|1|1|1|1">

</APPLET>

</BODY>

</HTML>
```

As you can see in this example, the majority of the HTML source code that is generated by Corel WEB.MOVE is parameter values that are passed to the Anim.CLASS Java applet.

Now it's time to integrate the Java applet animations you've created into your own Web applications. You can either use the Web page generated by Corel WEB.MOVE or copy the HTML source code into your existing Web pages. Place the Java classes in a location accessible by the Web page on which they will be displayed. Corel WEB.MOVE has several Java classes that you must first copy onto your server before the applet animation can be successfully deployed. Here is a list of the classes that you must copy to your server before you can provide the applet animation on your Web site.

- Actor.class
- Anim.class
- Bitio.class
- Effect.class
- LZW.class
- LZWFile.class
- Prop.class
- Sound.class
- Thumbnail.class

Corel WEB.MOVE provides the Java applet classes; the animation you create generates the necessary parameter values that are passed to these applet classes. The result is a simple-to-create Java applet animation capability that you can integrate into your Web applications.

Java Visual Development Tools

Java is much more than a tool to create cool animations for Web pages. It has an endless number of potential applications, ranging from IRC applets to applets that your refrigerator may use one day to call for service when it breaks. The Java visual development tools give programmers a convenient and unrestricted capability for creating Java applications for any use desired.

JFactory

JFactory is a Java visual rapid application development tool created by Rogue Software. JFactory got its name from the idea that a factory is where components are assembled into finished products. JFactory provides several tools you'll need to create Java applets, Java applications, and Java Applications with menus.

Getting Started with JFactory

The JFactory toolbar (Figure 8.19) floats on the desktop. Select **FilelNew** from the JFactory menu. A new project dialog will appear on the screen (Figure 8.20). To

■■■■■■■ **Figure 8.19** The JFactory toolbar can be found floating on the desktop.

start creating a new Java application or Java applet you must begin by creating a new project. Give your project a name and choose what type of application you will build by selecting from the application icon types.

Once you've saved your new project, the project dialog closes, and both the Object Manager (Figure 8.21) and Project Manager (Figure 8.22) dialogs appear on the screen. According to the JFactory documentation, congratulations are in order—you've just created your first application!

Testing Your First Application

In the Project Manager dialog (Figure 8.20) click on the project name (designated by the cube icon) with your right mouse button. Your new Java application will begin running (Figure 8.23). Try all the menu choices.

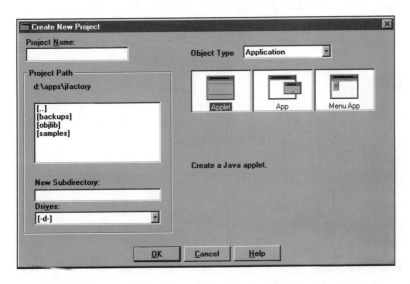

■■■■■■■ **Figure 8.20** Before you start creating a Java application, you'll need a new project.

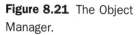

■■■■ **Figure 8.21** The Object Manager.

■■■■ **Figure 8.22** The Project Manager.

Compiling and Making Your Application

Once you've tested your application and everything seems OK, you'll want to compile and make your new Java program. Select **Project|Generate & Make** from the JFactory menu on the floating toolbar. A DOS box will open while JFactory is compiling, and it will let you know as soon as it's done. We've included the code generated by the JFactory programs because it is an excellent example of a good Java applet (Figure 8.25). You can view the source of your application by selecting **Project|Edit Source...** from the JFactory menu.

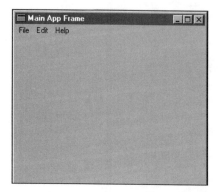

■■■■ **Figure 8.23** Your new Java applet is running in the test environment.

Adding Controls

In the Application Manager double-click the Main window icon. The window editor
will appear on the screen, allowing you to add controls. A small controls toolbox will
also appear on the screen. Choose a control from the control toolbox and then click
on the Main window. A new control will be placed on the window (Figure 8.24).

Modify each of the controls using the Object manager. Change the properties using
the **Properties** tab in the Object Manager. To add functionality to a control you will
have to add functionality to a control event. Click the **Event** tab and select the
event for which you would like to add functionality. JFactory provides some built-
in functionality, such as a save and open dialog. You can also choose to add your
own Java code to one of these events.

The About window is a standard part of the Help system. When you have finished
adding controls to the Main window, you will want to add text that describes your
application on the About window. Select it in the same manner you selected the Main
window. Add text from the control toolbar. It's not normal to add controls to the
About window beyond the **OK** and **Cancel** buttons that come default on this window.

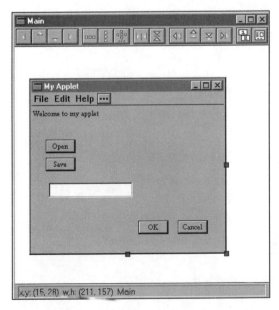

▬▬▬▬▬ **Figure 8.24** Add controls to the Main window.

Java Applet Sample Code

■■■■■■■■ **Figure 8.25** The JFactory Java applet code.

```java
// myproj.java -
// Version - 1.0
// 3/14/96 - 7:41:22pm
//
//
// zpb_begin Revisions
// zpb_end

import java.awt.*;
import java.util.*;
import java.applet.Applet;
import LogFontLayout; // Fixed position layout based on font size

// zpb_begin UserImports
// zpb_end

// zpb_begin AppSecurityManager
// Override SecurityManager so getImage() will work
import java.io.FileDescriptor;
class EmptySecurityManager extends SecurityManager {
        public void checkCreateClassLoader() {}
        public void checkAccess(Thread g) {}
        public void checkAccess(ThreadGroup g) {}
        public void checkExit(int status) {}
        public void checkExec(String cmd) {}
        public void checkLink(String lib) {}
        public void checkRead(FileDescriptor fd) {}
        public void checkRead(String file) {}
```

```
        public void checkRead(String file, Object context) {}
        public void checkWrite(FileDescriptor fd) {}
        public void checkWrite(String file) {}
        public void checkDelete(String file) {}
        public void checkConnect(String host, int port) {}
        public void checkConnect(String host, int port, Object context)
{}
        public void checkListen(int port) {}
        public void checkAccept(String host, int port) {}
        public void checkPropertiesAccess() {}
        public void checkPropertyAccess(String key) {}
        public void checkPropertyAccess(String key, String def) {}
        public boolean checkTopLevelWindow(Object window) {return true;}
        public void checkPackageAccess(String pkg) {}
        public void checkPackageDefinition(String pkg) {}
        public void checkSetFactory() {}

}
// zpb_end


public
class myproj extends Frame {

        private static Applet applet;

        Dimension initialSize;
        Point initialLocation;
        // zpb_begin MainUserVars
        // zpb_end

        public
```

Continued...

```
myproj(Applet app, String title) {
        super(title);
        applet = app;

        // zpb_begin MainConstructor_1
        // zpb_end

        setBackground(Color.lightGray);
        LogFontLayout lfLayout = new LogFontLayout(this);
        setLayout(lfLayout);

        MenuBar mbMenu1 = new MenuBar();
        MenuItem mi;
        Menu mFile = new Menu("File");
        mFile.add(mi=new MenuItem("New"));
        mFile.add(mi=new MenuItem("Open..."));
        mFile.add(mi=new MenuItem("Save"));
        mFile.add(mi=new MenuItem("Save as..."));
        mFile.add(new MenuItem("-"));
        mFile.add(mi=new MenuItem("Exit"));
        mbMenu1.add(mFile);
        Menu mEdit = new Menu("Edit");
        mEdit.add(mi=new MenuItem("Cut"));
        mEdit.add(mi=new MenuItem("Copy"));
        mEdit.add(mi=new MenuItem("Paste"));
        mbMenu1.add(mEdit);
        Menu mHelp = new Menu("Help");
        mHelp.add(mi=new MenuItem("Contents"));
        mHelp.add(new MenuItem("-"));
        mHelp.add(mi=new MenuItem("About"));
        mbMenu1.add(mHelp);
        this.setMenuBar(mbMenu1);
```

```
            // zpb_begin MainConstructor_2
            // zpb_end


            // Size and Position in logical units
            initialSize = new Dimension(211, 157);
            initialLocation = lfLayout.du(15, 28);


            pack();
            move(initialLocation.x, initialLocation.y);


            // zpb_begin MainConstructor_3
            // zpb_end
    }


public Dimension minimumSize() {


            // zpb_begin MainMinimumSize
            // zpb_end


            return initialSize; // Let layout manager size Window
            using logical units
    }


public boolean handleEvent(Event e) {
            if (e.id == Event.WINDOW_DESTROY) {
                    // zpb_begin MainDestroy
                    // zpb_end
                    System.exit(0);
                    return true;
            }


            // zpb_begin MainHandleEvent
            // zpb_end
```

Continued...

```
        return super.handleEvent(e);
}

public boolean action(Event evt, Object obj) {
        if (evt.target instanceof MenuItem) {
                String label = (String)obj;
                if (label.equals("New")) {
                        // zpb_begin MainFileNewSelection
                        // zpb_end
                }
                else if (label.equals("Open...")) {
                        FileDialog fd = new FileDialog(this,
                        "File Open Dialog");
                        // zpb_begin MainFileOpenSelection
                        // zpb_end
                        fd.show();
                        // zpb_begin MainFileOpenSelection2
                        // zpb_end
                }
                else if (label.equals("Save")) {
                        // zpb_begin MainFileSaveSelection
                        // zpb_end
                }
                else if (label.equals("Save as...")) {
                        // zpb_begin MainFileSaveasSelection
                        // zpb_end
                }
                else if (label.equals("Exit")) {
                        // zpb_begin MainFileExitSelection
                        // zpb_end
                        System.exit(0);
                }
```

```
                  else if (label.equals("Cut")) {
                          // zpb_begin MainEditCutSelection
                          // zpb_end
                  }
                  else if (label.equals("Copy")) {
                          // zpb_begin MainEditCopySelection
                          // zpb_end
                  }
                  else if (label.equals("Paste")) {
                          // zpb_begin MainEditPasteSelection
                          // zpb_end
                  }
                  else if (label.equals("Contents")) {
                          // zpb_begin MainHelpContentsSelection
                          // zpb_end
                  }
                  else if (label.equals("About")) {
                          about dAbout= new about(applet, this,
                          "About", true);
                          // zpb_begin MainHelpAboutSelectionShow
                          // zpb_end
                          dAbout.show();
                          // zpb_begin MainHelpAboutSelection
                          // zpb_end
                  }

          return true;
}

// zpb_begin MainAction
// zpb_end

return true;
```

Continued...

```
        }

        public static void main(String args[]) {

                // zpb_begin AppMain
                // zpb_end

                // zpb_begin AppSecurityManager_2
                // Override SecurityManager so getImage() will work
                System.setSecurityManager(new EmptySecurityManager());
                // zpb_end

                myproj f = new myproj(null, "Main App Frame");
                f.show();

                // zpb_begin AppMain_2
                // zpb_end
        }

        // zpb_begin MainUserMethods
        // zpb_end
}

class about extends Dialog {

        private static Applet applet;
        Button pOK;

        Dimension initialSize;
        Point initialLocation;
        // zpb_begin AboutUserVars
        // zpb_end
```

```
about(Applet app, Frame parent, String title, boolean modal) {
        super(parent, title, modal);
        applet = app;
        setResizable(false);

        // zpb_begin AboutConstructor_1
        // zpb_end

        LogFontLayout lfLayout = new LogFontLayout(this);
        setLayout(lfLayout);

        pOK = new Button("OK");
        add("83 110 35 17", pOK);
        // zpb_begin AboutConstructor_2
        // zpb_end

        // Size and Position in logical units
        initialSize = new Dimension(201, 140);
        initialLocation = lfLayout.du(15, 28);

        pack();
        move(initialLocation.x, initialLocation.y);

        // zpb_begin AboutConstructor_3
        // zpb_end
}

public Dimension minimumSize() {

        // zpb_begin AboutMinimumSize
        // zpb_end
```

Continued...

```
                return initialSize; // Let layout manager size Window
                using logical units
    }


public boolean handleEvent(Event e) {
        if (e.id == Event.WINDOW_DESTROY) {
                // zpb_begin AboutDestroy
                // zpb_end
                dispose();
                return true;
        }


        // zpb_begin AboutHandleEvent
        // zpb_end


        return super.handleEvent(e);
    }


public boolean action(Event evt, Object obj) {
        if (evt.target == pOK) {
                // zpb_begin AboutOKClicked
                // zpb_end
                dispose();
                return true;
        }


        // zpb_begin AboutAction
        // zpb_end


        return true;
    }
```

```
        // zpb_begin AboutUserMethods
        // zpb_end
}


// zpb_begin UserClasses
// zpb_end
```

▬▬▬▬

Add Windows, Dialogs, and Menus

Most applications use more than one window or dialog. To create new windows, dialogs, or menus select **Setup|Object Library...** from the JFactory menu. You will be able to select the type of window, dialog, or menu you would like to create by clicking on the icon that corresponds to the type of object.

You can contact Rogue Software at the following URL for information about Jfactory.

http://www.roguewave.com/

Other Java Visual Development Tools

Here is a list of several URLs to companies with other Java visual development tools.

Check out Powersoft's Optima++ product:

http://www.powersoft.com/

Check out Borland's Latte product:

http://www.borland.com

Check out Symantec's Cafe product:

http://www.symantec.com

INLINE PLUG-INS

An inline plug-in is a program run within your Netscape browser, extending its capabilities. With it, you can add new and powerful abilities to your World Wide Web pages and dazzle visitors to your Web page with multimedia sound and graphics. Put the power of client/server databases into your Internet site or create games and virtual worlds. Provide music, headline news, and a stock ticker right on your home page. People will flock to your Web pages because they're exciting and useful when you provide content accessed through inline plug-ins.

One of the most exciting HTML extensions is the one that allows for inline plug-ins. An inline plug-in is an executable program that runs within the Netscape browser environment. Even though it's a separate program, it appears to be part of Navigator. Plug-ins replace the old helper application feature that existed in earlier versions of Netscape Navigator. In the past, helper applications, external programs designed to handle various types of MIME content, were launched outside the Navigator window.

The inline plug-in feature extends the ability of Netscape Navigator to display all types of MIME content directly on the Navigator window. Extending Navigator's capabilities with plug-ins allows for an unlimited range of multimedia and business applications to be run right in a Web browser.

Installing Plug-ins

Inline plug-ins are typically large, application-specific programs that have been adapted for integration into the Netscape Navigator environment. Netscape Navigator 2.0 does not currently ship with any inline plug-ins installed because doing so would make the download time for Navigator unreasonably long. Navigator users can pick and choose which plug-ins they would like installed. This arrangement gives users a great deal of flexibility and allows them to add new plug-ins as they are created.

To assist in this process Netscape has introduced a step in the Navigator installation process in which users can choose which plug-ins they would like to install. During this installation step, users are given the option of connecting to the Netscape inline plug-in Web page. The plug-in Web page lists some of the more popular plug-ins available and includes a short description of each plug-in. Clicking the hyperlink next to the description allows you to download the plug-in. It's a good idea to check this Web page once in a while, because new plug-ins are being created all the time. Netscape's plug-in Web page is one of the best sources of information about inline plug-ins on the Internet. You can contact Netscape's Plugin Registry page at the following URL.

http://www.netscape.com/comprod/products/navigator/version_2.0/plugins/index.html

If you are already familiar with installing software on your computer, you will find that plug-in installation is basically the same as the installation process for any other computer program.

Unlike in other program installations, plug-ins have a DLL file that must be copied to the PLUGINS subdirectory of the Netscape Navigator Program directory to complete the installation. The directory structure normally looks like this:

```
netscape
    |
    +--program
            |
            +--plugins
```

When you first download and install the Netscape Navigator, you may find that the PLUGINS subdirectory does not exist. The first time you install an inline plug-in, the installation process will create the PLUGINS subdirectory and save the necessary DLL files in it. Any future inline plug-ins that you install must copy their associated DLL files into the existing PLUGINS subdirectory. Notice when you install an inline plug-in that one of the procedures of the InstallShield Wizard queries you for the proper location of the Netscape Navigator directory. InstallShield assumes the default directory (C:\Netscape) because there is currently no way for the installation process to actually identify where the Netscape Navigator program exists on your computer system. If you have saved your Netscape Navigator program in a directory other than this default directory you *must* indicate the proper directory during the inline plug-in installation.

If you install future versions of the Netscape Navigator browser into a different directory, follow these steps:

1. Create a PLUGINS directory within the new PROGRAM directory.
2. Copy the DLL files from the old PLUGINS directory into the new PLUGINS directory.

Following these two simple steps will save you the trouble of reinstalling plug-ins.

It is important to be aware of the various security issues concerning inline plug-ins. Inline plug-ins have no limitations to file access on your computer, which means that files can be copied to your local hard drive. Unrestricted file access creates the possibility that your computer can become infected by computer viruses. It's important to be vigilant when downloading software from the Internet, especially if you have never heard of the company or individual that has created it. Install a good virus checker and try to download software from only reputable companies.

Challenges with Plug-in Installation

Inline plug-ins are relatively new in the Web environment, and there are always bugs associated with any new type of computer program. Several basic problems can occur to prevent an inline plug-in from working properly. The first is that the InstallShield Wizard fails to find the PLUGINS subdirectory and installs a new PLUGINS subdirectory in the wrong location. It is very easy for you to check to see if the inline plug-in installation successfully copied the DLL file into the proper PLUGINS subdirectory. The Netscape Navigator browser can recognize the MIME file type only for inline plug-ins that have their DLL file in the proper PLUGINS subdirectory. To see if the Netscape Navigator browser recognizes the MIME file type of the inline plug-in you recently installed, simply choose the **Help|About Plug-ins** menu selection, or type **about:plugins** in the URL entry field. The browser window will show a list of the different MIME file types that the Netscape Navigator browser is capable of first recognizing and then launching the proper inline plug-in.

Figure 9.1 illustrates a particular Netscape Navigator browser that is capable of recognizing the following MIME types and their associated inline plug-ins.

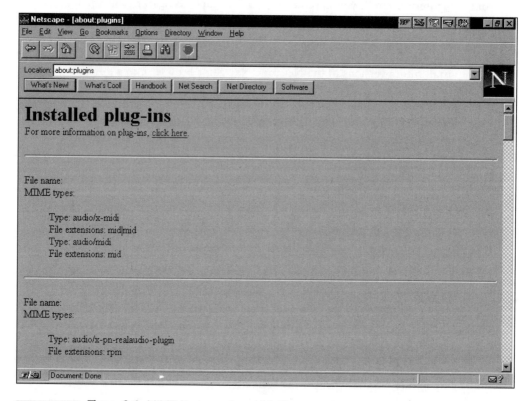

■■■■■■■ **Figure 9.1** MIME file types for which Netscape Navigator has the plug-in necessary to view.

- audio/midi (Crescendo Plug-in)
- audio/x-pn-realaudio-plugin (RealAudio Plug-in)

If the Netscape Navigator browser can recognize the MIME file type of a particular inline plug-in, but the inline plug-in doesn't work properly, the problem may be bugs within the inline plug-in itself. Inline plug-ins are still a relatively new feature, and are just plain "buggy." You may find some Web pages that contain an embedded inline plug-in that won't load in the Navigator window. If the Netscape Navigator browser doesn't crash while trying to load the plug-in, try to reload the Web page containing the inline plug-in. Keep in mind that in many cases the MIME file you are waiting to view may be extremely large and may require several minutes to download. Although occasionally bugs are associated with inline plug-ins, they are generally reliable and can only get more reliable once the programmers who build them read Chapter 10.

Deploying Inline Plug-ins

By the time you reach the end of this chapter, you'll have a good idea which plug-ins you'd like to integrate into your own Web site. To embed an inline plug-in within a Web source file, you must use the <EMBED> tag, as illustrated in the following example.

```
<EMBED SRC=URL WIDTH=width in pixels HEIGHT=height in pixels>
```

In addition to the <EMBED> tag, there are several basic attributes used to define the standard display of an inline plug-in on a Web page. The SRC attribute indicates the URL location of the inline plug-in MIME file that will be displayed on the Web page. The WIDTH and HEIGHT attributes in the <EMBED> tag specify the rectangular dimensions of the inline plug-in that will be displayed in your Web page. There are also three different display modes of an inline plug-in that you can set by adding the MODE attribute to the <EMBED> tag.

- *Embed.* The plug-in is displayed as a rectangle within the browser window on the Web page. This is the most common method for plug-in display.
- *Hidden.* The plug-in isn't visible on the Web page, but still executes. A plug-in type that uses this display mode is an audio plug-in that plays background music.
- *Full-screen.* The plug-in, when displayed, fills up the entire browser window. The plug-in takes up the entire Web page.

In the sample <EMBED> tag no MODE attribute was defined. If no MODE value is specified, the inline plug-in display defaults to the Embed mode. Whenever an inline plug-in is displayed in the Embed mode, either by MODE specification or default, the WIDTH and HEIGHT attributes must also be specified.

In addition to some of these basic attributes needed to display an inline plug-in, there are usually other attributes specific to a particular inline plug-in that must be included. For example, when using the Real Audio plug-in, you can specify the following attribute and value within the <EMBED> tag.

```
CONTROL = VolumeSlider
```

This attribute results in only the **VolumeSlider** control option being displayed on the Web page when the Real Audio inline plug-in is launched. The various application-specific attributes are described for each of the inline plug-ins featured in this chapter.

Configuring Server for MIME Files

Before you can make a particular MIME file available on your Web site using the inline plug-in feature, you must also configure your server to recognize the desired MIME file type. In your server directory there should be a configuration directory that contains a file called MIME.TYPES. In the Netscape Communication server the MIME.TYPES file can be found in the following directory.

```
C:\netscape\ns-home\httpd-80\config\
```

When the MIME.TYPES file is opened, you should see its contents as illustrated in Figure 9.2.

Several MIME file types are already recognized by the Netscape server as illustrated in Figure 9.1, but many of the inline plug-ins that have been developed are quite new, so you should always ensure that the desired MIME file type is included in this file. Three elements define each MIME file type in the MIME.TYPES file: *MIME type, Sub type,* and *File extension.* The following example illustrates the values to add the Quicktime movie MIME type.

- MIME type: video
- Sub type: quicktime
- File extension: qt,mov

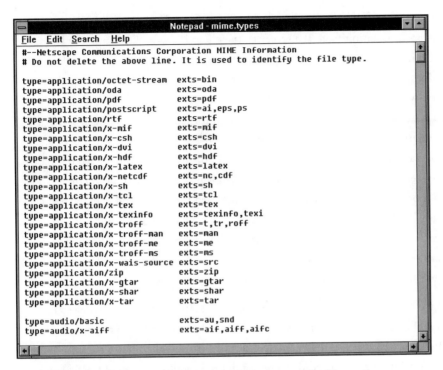

Figure 9.2 Add the new MIME type to this file.

To add the Quicktime movie MIME file type to the MIME.TYPES file, use a text editor and add the following line.

```
type=video/quicktime          exts=qt,mov
```

Once the appropriate line has been added and the MIME.TYPES file has been saved, the server will be able to serve the MIME files for the inline plug-in you want to incorporate in your Web page.

UDP and Firewalls

Firewall machines are proclaimed to be the answer to network security for those connecting to the Internet. A firewall machine is one that serves as a gateway, protecting an intranet system from the big, bad Internet and its various insecurities. The importance of firewalls is an issue worthy of debate, but at this point we are concerned mainly with the compatibility of firewalls with inline plug-ins.

It ends up that some of the plug-ins featured here use UDP (User Datagram Protocol) to transfer information from the server to the client browser. UDP transfer is known as a connectionless protocol that does not require a connection, but at the same time doesn't guarantee delivery of the information. Since UDP doesn't have to concern itself with information about the connection between the server and client, such as the state of the connection or status of the information that has been transferred, information can be transferred at higher rates. This means that when people use UDP, they are just sending out information and not really checking to see if someone is receiving it. UDP differs from TCP (Transmission Control Protocol), which does monitor the established connection between the server and client. The problem with UDP transmission is that it usually can't pass through a firewall. If you are located behind a firewall, you will need to have your network administrator configure your packet filtering router to allow inbound traffic for a UDP port to be able to use those plug-ins that transfer information in this way.

The VDOLive video plug-in is one that transfers information using the UDP system. To use this inline plug-in successfully, you must have the network administrator make the following changes to the characteristics of the firewall you are behind. First, the packet-filtering router needs to be configured to allow inbound traffic for the UDP of your choice and in-bound and outbound traffic for the proper TCP port. For the VDOLive system the TCP port is 700. After the proper firewall has been correctly configured, you should be able to view VDOLive inline plug-in content from behind a firewall.

It is important to keep in mind that many users may not be able to view content placed in your Web application when it requires an inline plug-in that transmits using the UDP protocol.

VIPs (Very Important Plug-ins)

The number of available inline plug-ins is growing every day. Many software companies believe that transforming their current software into a plug-in is the key to a successful Internet strategy. Remember that plug-ins are used on the client side (in the Netscape Navigator browser window) to allow a particular MIME file type to be viewed or played. To provide MIME files, you will normally need special software to create them. For example, to provide animations through the Shockwave plug-in, you need to use the Macromedia Director software to generate the animation and the Macromedia Afterburner software to compress the animation file. Only then can it be provided by your server. Other types of plug-ins such as Real Audio or VDOLive actually require specific server software to provide the desired MIME files to users who access your Web site.

The inline plug-ins featured in this chapter are those that add useful features and capabilities to your Web site. In addition to presenting a complete description of the inline plug-ins, where necessary, we also describe the software you will need to create the MIME files used by these plug-ins. In many cases, the plug-ins are given away free so that you will purchase the software to create the MIME files.

Several categories of inline plug-ins are emerging, and in each category there are often competing inline plug-ins that use slightly different technologies to produce the same results. Some of these categories include:

- video streaming
- audio streaming
- graphical animation
- document viewing and presentation
- image enhancement
- VRML (Virtual Reality Modeling Language) viewing
- Active X controls (formerly known as OLE controls)

Video Inline Plug-Ins

Video inline plug-ins will truly change the face of the Web. Using one of the inline plug-ins featured in this section, you can include both video and audio presentations such as one by the president of your company welcoming users to your company's Web site. Multimedia presentations can also include product demonstrations and on-line manuals for user support or simply for entertainment. It's an undeniable fact that video and TV have become the cornerstone of the world in which we live. Now, with video inline plug-ins, that world exists on the Internet.

The struggle for a successful inline plug-in that offers these video and audio capabilities is causing some concern about bandwidth limitations that are still present on the Internet. Another major concern is that the majority of users on the Internet still use either 14.4Kbps or 28.8Kbps modems. This personal bandwidth restriction will exist for some time. The highly publicized cable modems or other affordable solutions are not expected to be available for significant consumer use until early 1997. Considering the low bandwidth capability currently available to most people on the Internet, the viability of the various video related plug-ins depends on achieving the highest compression of the video and audio information.

The *streaming* capabilities are really what sets the different inline plug-ins apart. Streaming is a feature in video inline plug-ins that allows you to see the video play while you are still receiving the information. This is extremely desirable for large files because the typical user would like to see the video play after choosing to view it rather than wait for it to first be downloaded and then viewed.

These video inline plug-ins will even offer the ability in the near future to be used for videoconferencing and one-on-one video communications. We have only begun to see the potential for this integration of video inline plug-ins with the Web.

VDOLive

VDOLive is a video inline plug-in recently developed by VDOnet as one of the first video and audio streaming inline plug-ins available. Once you install the VDOLive inline plug-in, your Netscape Navigator browser can recognize the video/vdo MIME file type. VDOnet uses sophisticated compression algorithms to compress both the video and audio content so that it can be transmitted over the Internet, even to very low-bandwidth connections. Obviously, the quality of the received content, in number of frames per second, depends greatly on the Internet connection as illustrated below.

- 14.4Kbps modem: can result in up to 2 frames per second
- 28.8Kbps modem: can result in up to 10 frames per second
- ISDN line: can achieve up to 20 frames per second

To get a firsthand idea of the quality and exciting potential for this streaming video inline plug-in, download the inline plug-in from the following URL.

http://www.vdolive.com/

Once you have successfully installed this inline plug-in, you can go to several sites to see its capabilities. The first place that you should check out is VDOnet's site at the following URL. Here you can choose to view a variety of different sites that are providing exciting VDO content.

http://www.vdolive.com/newsite/watch/

If the plug-in has been successfully installed, you should initially see a window similar to that shown in Figure 9.3 appear on the top of the Web page when the VDO-Live inline plug-in is executed.

The VDOLive plug-in begins receiving the audio and video transmission after you left-click your mouse, while the pointer is over the window. For several seconds the plug-in receives information to fill up the buffer, and then the requested information is displayed, as shown in Figure 9.4.

Figure 9.3 Click on this window with your mouse to begin receiving the video.

Figure 9.4 Right-click your mouse on the VDOLive image again to stop the playing.

Once the video and audio begin playing, the VDOLive window graphically illustrates the length of time the file has been playing and the quality of the reception that you are receiving. When you decide that you have seen enough, simply right-click on the VDOLive window, which should open the pop-up menu with the Play and Stop menu. Another site that you should check out is the CBS Up-to-the-Minute report that can be found at the following URL.

http://uttm.com/

As with anything that is so new, there are some bugs with the VDOLive inline plug-in. Sometimes when you contact a Web page that has VDOLive content, the user-controlled window will not appear. If this occurs, simply try to reload the Web page; the user control window will then usually appear.

VDOLive Server Software

Now that you can appreciate the new content the VDOLive inline plug-in can produce, you need to find out the requirements for integrating this content into your own Web site. Providing streaming video that can be viewed with the VDOLive inline plug-in requires the use of a VDOLive server. The VDOLive server allows you to capture, compress, and store the video and audio information that you then provide on the Internet.

> The VDOnet compression technology converts video content into the unique VDO file format that is also compatible with the AVI video file format standard for the Microsoft Windows environment. VDOLive claims 10 to 50 times better compression ratio than the MPEG (standard video compression method developed by the Motion Pictures Experts Group) video file format with a typical minute of video requiring 200KB to 900KB in VDO file format compared with around 9MB for a comparable MPEG file.

One of the limitations of the VDOLive server software is that a server can handle a limited number of streams ranging from 5 to 100. Servers that can handle more streams obviously cost more. For server pricing information, check out VDOLive's home page URL given earlier in this section.

VDOnet has released a free personal server software package that allows VDOLive content to be provided on one to two streams. This is a good tool for you to get familiar with the VDOLive server without purchasing any software. The free personal server allows you to incorporate up to two minutes of video and audio content in your Web application. This server can be downloaded from the following URL.

http://www1.vdolive.com/

The server can be set up on a computer running the Windows 95, Windows NT, or Unix operating system, with the detailed documentation found in the PERSSERV.DOC file that is part of the executable file you download.

It is very simple to add the server as a service on the Windows NT operating system. After you have unzipped the executable file that was downloaded, run the VDOSERV.EXE file to install the personal video server on the Windows NT operating system. If you open the **Main|Control Panel** application, you should see an icon for the VDOServer that was installed. Clicking on this icon will open a window as illustrated in Figure 9.5.

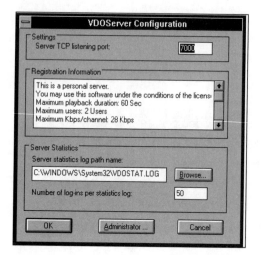

Figure 9.5 Characteristics of VDOLive Server.

Figure 9.5 illustrates the basic characteristics of the VDOServer that was installed, which include the port number it communicates on and the limitation on the number of users it can serve at any time. Other servers can be purchased that allow for more simultaneous user connections. The VDOServer is controlled in the **Control Panel|Services** application where you can choose to either start or stop the VDOServer.

After you install the VDOLive Personal Server on your particular operating system you need to modify the MIME.TYPES file on the server so that it can provide the video/vdo MIME file type.

Now all you need to do is create the content you want to provide. When the VDO-Live Personal Server software is downloaded and unzipped, you will find that it also includes the PVDOTOOL.EXE file that, when executed, installs the VDOLive Personal Tools used to capture and compress video. The VDOLive Personal Tools software can be installed *only* in the Windows 95 operating system environment. When you install the VDOLive Personal Tools software, it creates two applications: the VDO Capture Personal and the VDO Clip Personal that you can use to create the VDO video content to provide on your Web site.

▰▰▰▰ **Table 9.1** Attributes of VDOLive Inline Plug-in

Attribute	Description
autostart	This attribute specifies if the video should start on its own or manually. The values for this attribute are True and False.
loop	This attribute specifies if the video should continually loop. The values for this attribute are True and False.

▰▰▰▰

There are inline plug-in attributes (see Table 9.1) that you can use to specify the operation and display of the VDOLive inline plug-in. These attributes can be included in the <EMBED> tag.

You should now be on your way to bringing video and audio streaming to your Web site with the VDOLive inline plug-in.

PreVU Video Plug-in

The VDOLive plug-in impressively illustrates video streaming capabilities that allow the user to select a video that would begin to play shortly after it was selected. In some cases video streaming is undesirable because the video is never saved on the user's computer for viewing in the future. On the other hand, there are other software applications that allow for a video to be first downloaded and then played. The PreVU plug-in developed by InterVU not only gives a streaming video display, but it downloads and saves the selected video. This capability gives you the best of both worlds: streaming and the ability to save the video file. The PreVU plug-in can be downloaded from the following URL.

http://www.intervu.com/prevu.html

Once you have successfully downloaded and installed the inline plug-in, your Netscape Navigator browser should be capable of viewing MPEG videos because it will now recognize the video/mpeg MIME file type. The PreVU plug-in works by temporarily saving the data for a particular video in the *cached* memory of the Netscape Navigator browser. Cached means that the recently accessed information is held in fast memory for easy subsequent access. Before you download any videos from the Internet to be viewed with this plug-in, you must first ensure that the cache memory limits of your Navigator browser are sufficient. Choose the **Options|Network Preferences** selection, and then ensure that the amount in both the memory and disk inputs in the cache folder is set at 1000 Kilobytes.

You can see a sample of the PreVU inline plug-in video display by looking at the DEMO.MPG file in the HELP.HTM file that comes preinstalled with the PreVU inline plug-in. When you click on the **Run** button, which has a green triangular icon, the MPEG video begins to play. This **Run** button will turn into a **Stop** button, with a red square icon while a video is being played. Figure 9.6 illustrates a sample frame from a video that is run with the PreVU inline plug-in and shows how the inline plug-in appears on a Web page.

This DEMO.MPG example is not a true picture of how the PreVU inline plug-in will appear when you access MPEG videos across the Internet. When you actually choose a MPEG file to be displayed with the PreVU inline plug-in on the Internet, there is a period of time required for the file to download onto your computer. As the file is downloaded, the time necessary to complete the download is displayed in the bottom left side of the Netscape Navigator window. As the file is downloaded,

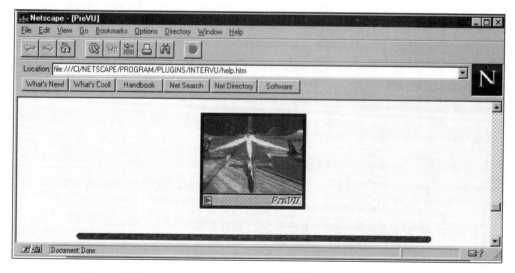

■■■■■■■ **Figure 9.6** A demo video example of the PreVU inline plug-in.

the PreVU inline plug-in will show various frames of the video in an attempt to produce a streaming video display. After the desired MPEG file is downloaded to your computer and stored in the cache memory of your Netscape Navigator browser, you can click on the **Run** button to display the MPEG video. The DEMO.MPG is a good example of how the videos will appear after they have been downloaded into the cache memory.

You can check out the true performance of the PreVU inline plug-in with MPEG video content downloaded from the Internet by going to the following URL.

http://www.vol.it/MIRROR4/EN/www.eeb.ele.tue.nl/mpeg/

When you view an MPEG video on the Internet, you will also notice that a black diskette icon will appear next to the **Run** button at the bottom of the PreVU inline plug-in window. You can save the MPEG video from the cache memory onto your hard drive when you click on the black diskette icon.

After you view these examples you may agree with our analysis that the PreVU inline plug-in streaming capability doesn't compare in quality with VDOLive streaming. The PreVU inline plug-in system is really designed to give the user some visual feedback when the file is actually being downloaded, and the quality video is displayed after the MPEG file has been downloaded and is replayed.

The first definite advantages of the PreVU plug-in is that there are no server constraints to provide video content to users visiting your Web pages, other than your existing bandwidth capabilities. This makes it cheaper for you to incorporate the PreVU video inline plug-in technology in your Web site because you don't have to incur any expensive server costs. There are also no encoder constraints because any MPEG encoder can produce content viewable with the PreVU inline plug-in. You should also not have to make any modifications to your MIME.TYPES file on your server because it should already recognize the video/mpeg MIME file type.

The PreVU inline plug-in has several additional attributes that you can place in the <EMBED> tag when you choose to feature a MPEG video in a Web source file (Table 9.2).

■■■■■ **Table 9.2** Specific Optional Attributes of PreVU Inline Plug-in

Attribute	Description
autostart	When the value <yes> is used, the MPEG file will start to play when the Web page is first loaded. The default value is <no>.
loop	The number of times you want the MPEG file to loop.
doublesize	When the value is <yes>, the file plays at double the encoded size.
halfsize	When the value is <yes>, the file plays at half the encoded size.
framerate	The frame rate (number between 1 and 20) of the video display, with smaller numbers producing a slower frame rate.
conbar	Disable the control bar by choosing the <no> value.

■■■■■

The following is an example of the <EMBED> tag used to place an MPEG video file in a Web source file. When you indicate the WIDTH and HEIGHT attributes, you need to add 10 pixels to the WIDTH value of the MPEG file to display the frame, and you need to add 29 pixels to the HEIGHT value of the MPEG file to display the frame and controls for this inline plug-in.

```
<EMBED SRC=http://www.vol.it/MIRROR4/EN/www.eeb.ele.tue.nl/mpeg/models
/erikaa.mpg WIDTH=172 HEIGHT=152 AUTOPLAY=YES>
```

You can see in this example that rather than displaying an MPEG video that is located on the local drive, the SRC attribute specifies a different URL location for the MPEG video.

If you want good video streaming, use the VDOLive plug-in technology, but if you want convenience and low cost, we recommend the PreVU plug-in technology.

Audio Plug-ins

Wouldn't it be great to have an icon on your Web site that users could click on to activate a sound message telling them about your company's newest products? This and many more audio capabilities can easily be integrated in your Web site with audio plug-ins. The obvious demand and desire for such a feature has resulted in the availability of several different audio plug-ins. The main differences are the technique used for compression of the sound files and the software required to serve the particular audio MIME files to users.

Although not faced with having to pass as much information to the user as the video/audio systems previously featured, the current limitations on Internet bandwidth prevent high-quality sound from being transmitted in real time. Because of this bandwidth limitation, the quality of audio plug-ins can vary based on the technique and algorithm used for compressing the audio information.

Another difference among the different audio plug-ins is their capability for streaming information. Streaming, with regard to audio data transmission, is a feature that allows for a small, initial amount of data to be received, creating a buffer. After this buffer is created, the sound file starts to play as additional data continues to be received. This streaming feature is very desirable for playing audio over the Internet because a user typically wants to hear the sound immediately rather than wait for an entire sound file to be downloaded before it can be played.

RealAudio

The RealAudio system, developed by Progressive Networks, has emerged as one of the premier streaming audio inline plug-ins. RealAudio began by offering the first successful streaming audio helper application. Helper applications were the precursors to inline plug-ins, but they did not operate within the Netscape Navigator browser window. Instead, they launched the application outside the browser window. The RealAudio inline plug-in can be found at the following URL.

http://www.realaudio.com/

After the RealAudio plug-in has been installed, your Netscape Navigator browser will be able to recognize the audio/x-pn-realaudio MIME file type. You can get some idea of this inline plug-in's audio quality by checking out this URL. When the RealAudio inline plug-in runs, it should produce a user interface, similar to that shown in Figure 9.7, on the Web page.

http://www.realaudio.com/2.0release/20plug_ins1.html

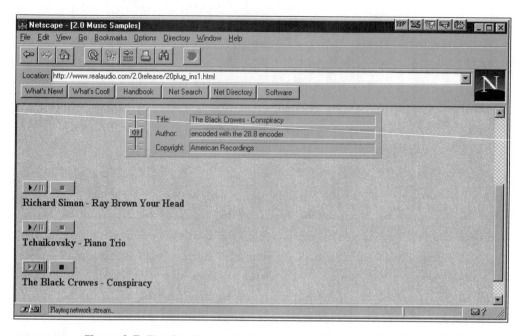

Figure 9.7 The RealAudio plug-in user interface can allow for the audio file to be played, stopped, paused, or forwarded.

After you choose the play selection for any one of the three different selections, it will begin to play, and the title and author will appear in the information box in the center of the Web page. You can see in this example that the various controls have been separated. This feature utilizes the advanced CONSOLE attribute that developers can use when placing RealAudio content in their Web pages. Before your selection begins to play, there is a delay of several seconds as the inline plug-in begins receiving the audio information and filling the buffer before the streaming audio begins to play. The RealAudio inline plug-in not only produces very good sound quality over low bandwidth connections, but also gives several desirable user interface features. You can play, pause, or stop the sound by clicking on the appropriate buttons on the user interface, which appear similar to those found on typical cassette players. The RealAudio inline plug-in also allows for any part of the audio file to be played back when you click on the slider and move it to the beginning, middle, or end of the audio file.

You may have just downloaded the RealAudio inline plug-in, and you are ready to hear some cool streaming audio over the Internet, and then nothing. One possible cause of this problem could be that your computer system is behind a firewall that is blocking the RealAudio transmission. The RealAudio system uses the UDP protocol for information transmission, and the firewall must be configured to allow this content to be passed through to your computer system. Your system administrator must configure the firewall to enable traffic on the following ports.

- *TCP port 7070.* Used to initiate communication with the RealAudio server, authenticate the player, and pass control messages back to the server
- *UDP ports 6970–7170* (inclusive). For receiving the incoming audio information only

Deploying RealAudio Inline Plug-in Content

You can create and provide RealAudio files using the RealAudio Encoder and the RealAudio Server. The RealAudio Encoder is used to convert audio files into the proper format that the RealAudio Server can then provide to multiple users. You can create your own RealAudio sound files by first downloading the encoder and the server software. This software can be found at the same URL location as the RealAudio plug-in given earlier.

The RealAudio Encoder is used to compress desired audio files, which produce an output file with the RA file extension that can be read by the RealAudio plug-in. When you first run the RealAudio Encoder, you should see an empty window. The RealAudio Encoder isn't the prettiest application you'll ever see, but it does efficiently do what it was designed for. Simply select **File|Encode**, which should allow you to choose a WAV file you want compressed and converted into a RealAudio file. When you choose the appropriate WAV file, it is compressed, and the RA file that is created is placed in the same directory as the original WAV file.

For a file to be recognized by the RealAudio plug-in, it must have an RPM file extension. RealAudio used to use the RAM file extension. There is no difference between an RPM and a RAM file other than the file extension.

The RealAudio Server is then required to provide the desired audio files to anyone using the RealAudio plug-in. RealAudio does offers a free RealAudio Personal server that you can use to provide RealAudio content to a small number of users.

If you want to provide content to more users, you can purchase one of the servers that are available.

The RealAudio inline plug-in system gives you much more versatility when you place content in your Web site than most other inline plug-ins do. Typically, when you use other inline plug-ins in your Web site, their user interface is already pre-designed for you, and you simply need to place the <EMBED> tag with the basic attributes in the Web source file. The RealAudio system gives you several additional attributes that allow you to choose exactly what that user interface will look like and what features it will have. As with nearly every plug-in, you must provide a desired width and height of the inline plug-in that will appear on the Web page. If you omit the WIDTH and HEIGHT attributes when deploying the RealAudio inline plug-in, an icon-sized user interface is all that will appear, which is usually not suitable. The RealAudio inline plug-in features a CONTROL attribute that can be placed in the <EMBED> tag. The following is a list of the various control options and the resulting inline plug-in appearance.

- CONTROL = All   Displays the entire plug-in with the Info VolumePanel, ControlPanel, and StatusBar. This is the default if the CONTROL attribute is not specified.
- CONTROL = ControlPanel   Displays only the Play, Pause, and Stop buttons along with the slider position locator.
- CONTROL = Info VolumePanel   Displays only the volume control along with the title, author, and copyright.
- CONTROL = PlayButton Displays only the Play/Pause button.
- CONTROL = InfoPanel   Shows only title, author, and copyright information with no user controls.
- CONTROL = StatusBar   Displays current playback position and audio file length.

The additional values for the CONTROL listed below result in the display of very specific components of the RealAudio inline plug-in user interface.

- CONTROL = Playbutton
- CONTROL = Stopbutton
- CONTROL = VolumeSlider
- CONTROL = PositionSlider

- CONTROL = PositionField
- CONTROL = StatusField
- When you would like a RealAudio file to play as soon as the Web page is visited, you can use the AUTOSTART attribute.

    ```
    AUTOSTART = TRUE
    ```

If you include more than one RealAudio inline plug-in on a single Web page and use the AUTOSTART attribute, only the last audio file that is loaded will be played.

The RealAudio system gives you the most flexibility of any of the inline plug-ins covered in this chapter for customizing the capabilities of the inline plug-in you feature in your Web pages.

ToolVox Inline Plug-in

We've saved the best plug-in for last. Voxware now offers a new audio plug-in known as the ToolVox player. Like the RealAudio inline plug-in, the ToolVox plug-in allows you to incorporate real-time audio streaming in your Web site. The ToolVox player can be downloaded from the following URL.

http://www.voxware.com/

Once you have installed the ToolVox player as an inline plug-in, your Netscape Navigator will be able to recognize the audio/voxware MIME file type. You can hear the impressive quality of sound that can be produced with this inline plug-in by checking out some of the demos at the following URL.

http://www.voxware.com/voxintro.htm

When you first log in to this page, you should see the Voxware player as illustrated in Figure 9.8, and when you click on the play bar, the ToolVox plug-in will start to receive the desired audio file.

▬▬▬▬▬ **Figure 9.8** Press the play bar on the ToolVox plug-in to start it.

Once the audio file begins to be received, there will be several seconds as the buffer is filled before the actual audio is played. The bar on the left gives the user visual feedback on the receipt of data, and the time that appears in the window on the right indicates how long the current audio file has been playing. You can stop the audio file when you click on the **Play** button. One of the impressive features of the ToolVox plug-in involves the slider on the very bottom of the inline plug-in window, which allows you to play the audio file back either faster or slower with no change of pitch. You can therefore play back an audio file much faster, but the sound won't remind you of Alvin of the Chipmunks. The convenience of this feature is that a user can scan through an audio file to quickly find important information, or the playback can be slowed for easier comprehension by users not fluent in the language being played. You can check out the performance of the ToolVox audio system at the succeeding URL.

http://www.allons.com/page1.htm

In this particular example, rather than requiring that you activate the inline plug-in, the Web developer placed the inline plug-in in autostart mode.

Incorporating ToolVox into Web Site

ToolVox provides the cheapest and simplest way for you to incorporate streaming audio into your Web site. Unlike the RealAudio inline plug-in that was previously featured, the ToolVox system doesn't require you to purchase any additional server software. The ToolVox Web Player (inline plug-in) is available free so that any user can listen to the VOX audio MIME file type. In addition, the ToolVox Web Encoder is available free so that you can generate the VOX files.

The ToolVox Web Encoder allows you to take one of your existing WAV audio files and compress it down to create the VOX file. Using the compression algorithms developed by Voxware, the WAV file is compressed at a typical compression ratio of 53:1 to create a very small VOX file in comparison. In the file compression there is some loss of sound quality because a typical WAV file with an 11kHz or 16kHz sampling rate is sampled down into a mono 8kHz VOX file. The ToolVox Web Encoder is available at the following URL.

http://www.voxware.com/download.htm

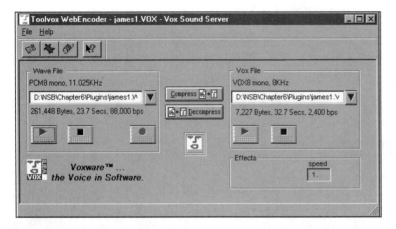

Figure 9.9 You can use the ToolVox Web Encoder to compress and decompress audio files.

When you run the ToolVox Web Encoder, it should appear as illustrated in Figure 9.9.

The ToolVox encoder works quite easily. First you need to select the WAV audio file that you are interested in compressing into a VOX file. You can either choose the **File|Open Wave File** selection or click on the triangle at the end of the input field on the Wave File side of the ToolVox Web Encoder. Once the WAV file is retrieved, the name of the corresponding VOX file that will be created is automatically added in the input field, but no actual VOX file is created until you click on the **Compress** button. The other buttons below the input fields allow you to play either the original WAV file or the newly created VOX file when you click on the button with the green triangle icon, or you can stop the audio playback when you click the **Stop** button that has a black square icon.

The ToolVox encoder has several other useful features. When converting a WAV file to a VOX file, you can also select the button with the rabbit icon or the button with the turtle icon that will change the playback speed of the VOX file. The number at the bottom right corner of the encoder window changes when you select to either speed up or slow down the playback. The ToolVox Web Encoder can even allow you to convert a compressed VOX file into a decompressed WAV file when you select the **Decompression** button.

The Voxware technology recognizes and eliminates the redundant speech waveform information that results in much higher compression rates than for typical audio compression tools while it still produces compressed audio files with very good voice quality. Because the compression capability is speech based, this technology doesn't work as well when you attempt to compress audio files such as music or sounds.

After you create the desired VOX file, you must configure your HTTP server to accept the new VOX MIME file type before these files can be made available on the Internet. You need to modify the MIME.TYPES file on the server to recognize the following VOX audio files.

```
audio/voxware vox
```

This is all you have to do to provide VOX files on the server end. You also must include the proper <EMBED> tag in your Web source file and specify the desired PLAYMODE and VISUALMODE attributes for the ToolVox inline plug-in you want to display on your Web page. The options for the PLAYMODE attribute are listed below:

- *User.* Before the sound begins to play, the user must click on either the **Start** button on the player's window or the Voxware icon.
- *Auto.* The sound begins to play as soon as the Web page is displayed in the browser.
- *Cache.* The sound file is downloaded for the user to play back later.

The options for the VISUALMODE attribute are listed below.

- *Icon.* A Voxware face icon appears on the Web page, and when the sound is playing, the icon turns red. The user can also turn the sound off or on.
- *Background.* The user has no control over the playing of the sound and has no way to stop it.
- *Embed.* The ToolVox player appears in the Web page, allowing the user to play or stop the sound, speed it up or slow it down, and see a graphical display of the gain and time of playback as the sound file is playing.
- *Float.* The ToolVox player appears as a window that the user can minimize or close.

The following HTML illustrates the typical <EMBED> tag used to incorporate a VOX file in a Web source file.

```
<embed src=http:allons.vox playmode=auto visualmode=embed>
```

ToolVox is a nifty inline plug-in that allows you to place streaming audio content in your Web site with very little difficulty and at no expense. A clear endorsement of this inline plug-in lies in the fact that Netscape has purchased Voxware.

Crescendo MIDI Inline Plug-in

Music is of undeniable importance in much of the entertainment that we enjoy. Not many people currently enjoy watching silent movies; most of us enjoy movies and television shows that use background music to enhance the experience. In the new age of the multimedia-enhanced Web, the impressive graphical images and text are still quite silent. Background music is one of the key missing elements that will truly make content on the Web interesting and entertaining.

The current limited bandwidth on the Internet serves as a major obstacle to placing impressive high-quality background sound on Web site. The limitation is a problem, since the amount of information required to duplicate a particular sound is quite large. What if, instead of transmitting information about the sound, you could simply transmit information on how to reproduce it. For example, rather than actually duplicating the sound for Beethoven's Fifth Symphony what if you could simply send information on the violin notes that need to be played to reproduce it. This is the basis of MIDI (Musical Instrument Digital Interface) devices that are capable of producing a wide variety of sounds ranging from a piano concerto to a car crash.

When you use the Crescendo inline plug-in to transfer MIDI files to users' computers, you are also requiring that their computer systems have MIDI sound-generation capabilities. The MIDI sound-generation capabilities are becoming more of a standard as illustrated with most new computers being sold as "Multimedia computers." Most new computers feature advanced sound cards that have all the MIDI sound-generation capabilities that would be required to place MIDI files on your Web site.

> The standard for sound cards was established by Creative Labs with its SoundBlaster series. The MIDI files received by the Crescendo inline plug-in were evaluated with the AWE32 SoundBlaster sound card system, and the performance was quite impressive.

You can begin to appreciate the quality of sound that can be produced with this inline plug-in by downloading it from the following URL and checking out some of the samples that can also be found there.

http://www.liveupdate.com/midi.html

Before you can provide MIDI files on your Web site, you must configure your server to recognize the audio/midi MIME file type. After you modify your server to be able to recognize the MIDI files, you then need to include the proper <EMBED> tag in the Web source file. You will see that this tag does feature the AUTOSTART attribute that is usable with the Crescendo inline plug-in.

```
<EMBED SRC="http://www.liveupdate.com/midi/liveup3.mid" WIDTH=196 HEIGHT=49
AUTOSTART=true>
```

The <EMBED> tag does limit the inline plug-in to playing only when a user has the Netscape Navigator. If you want the MIDI file to play for users with either the Netscape Navigator or Microsoft Explorer, you can use the following tag in the Web source file.

```
<BGSOUND SRC="yourmidfile.mid" LOOP=infinite>
```

The Crescendo inline plug-in is an ideal way to incorporate background music on your Web site, without downloading significantly large sound files.

Animation Inline Plug-ins

Computer animation is becoming the new standard for entertainment with movies like Toy Story being created solely with computer-generated animation. Now computer-generated animations can be displayed on the Internet with animation inline plug-ins. Animation inline plug-ins allow you to add a range of multimedia content to your Web site. The other feature of animation inline plug-ins is that many of the software programs used to generate animation content are not extremely costly, and they are easy to use.

Shockwave Inline Plug-in

One of the most powerful of these animation inline plug-ins is known as Shockwave. The Shockwave inline plug-in allows animations created with Macromedia's Director software to be viewed within a Web site. The Shockwave inline plug-in can be downloaded from the following URL.

http://www.macromedia.com/

After you install the Shockwave inline plug-in, the Netscape Navigator will be capable of recognizing the application/director MIME file type. Before you attempt to view any animations with the Shockwave inline plug-in, you must choose the **Network|Preferences** selection in the Netscape Navigator client and raise the disk cache to at least 500KB. An endless number of different "Shocked" sites can be found at the following URL.

http://www.macromedia.com/Gallery/index.html

When you first attempt to view a Web page that has a Shockwave animation in it, the window will appear with numerous gray and white Macromedia logos, while in the bottom left side of the Netscape Navigator window the time for download will be displayed.

The Shockwave animations not only are amazing in their content, but they also allow users to interact with them by clicking on specific areas of the animation. As a developer you can also integrate other inline plug-ins with the Shockwave inline plug-in such as the Live3D inline plug-in used for viewing VRML worlds.

This inline plug-in is such an enabling inline plug-in that it is featured in Chapter 11 where the Macromedia Director software is fully described, along with the procedure for deploying a Shockwave animation in your Web site.

Sizzler Inline Plug-in

You've already seen streaming video and audio on the Web. The Sizzler plug-in brings this streaming capability to animation. It is based on the same technology in the Netscape Navigator environment where an image begins to appear immediately, while more detail is added until the graphic is completely loaded. The Sizzler inline plug-in does this same progressive display of pixels for an animation with the obvious difference that the pixels are moving as they get finer and finer detail. The Sizzler inline plug-in is developed by Totally Hip Software for the viewing of interactive animation that allows for the application/x-sprites MIME file type to be displayed. The Sizzler inline plug-in can be downloaded from the following URL.

http://www.totallyhip.com/

The installation process for this inline plug-in isn't as simple as that for previous plug-ins. After you run the downloaded file, it will unzip, creating several files: npsr32.dll, default.dll, and wing32.dll. The wing32.dll file needs to be placed in your windows/system subdirectory; the other two files need to be placed in the PLUGINS subdirectory. When you have correctly installed these files, you can test some of the Sizzler animations found at the following URL.

http://www.totallyhip.com/hipstuff

After you view some of these samples, you should immediately recognize the streaming animation feature of the Sizzler inline plug-in that gives it some advantages over other animation inline plug-ins such as Shockwave. The animation begins to be displayed as soon as it starts downloading, and the detail of the animation continues to improve until the download is complete. This is a very desirable feature because users often want to see things happen immediately after they request them, rather then wait several seconds or minutes before anything happens.

Deploying Sizzler Animations

There are advantages to providing animation content on your Web page with the Sizzler system. The main advantage is that you are not limited in the development environment you can use. The Shockwave inline plug-in, for example, is limited to viewing only animations that are generated by Macromedia's Director software. This is fine if you have the appropriate development software, but what if you don't?

The Sizzler package that you downloaded was more than a plug-in; it also included the Sizzler conversion utility that allows you to convert animation content that is produced by several other types of programs into the sprite files that can be viewed by the Sizzler inline plug-in. The Sizzler conversion utility can now convert a PIC

(Apple-based multimedia file) into the sprite MIME file type. The obvious advantage is that the Sizzler conversion utility is available free and allows you to use a variety of animation generation software that you may already have or are familiar with.

After you have generated the animation content in the appropriate file type and then converted it into a sprite MIME file, you can simply configure your server to handle the MIME file type with no expensive or added server software. *Nice.*

Document Viewing

In many cases a company will want to provide an on-line resource such as a report or help manual. Often these documents can be extremely large or contain numerous graphics. There is no way you would want to convert a 100-page help manual into the HTML files necessary to provide the document on the Web.

The simple answer to this problem is inline plug-ins that allow document display. These inline plug-ins allow a variety of documents that were generated with standard document-generating software to instantly be made available on a Web site without any document conversion. For example, you may have a large help manual that was created with Adobe Acrobat software that you can now instantly make available to any user who has Adobe Amber inline plug-in installed. Some of the document viewing inline plug-ins featured in this section allow for Adobe Acrobat documents, spreadsheets, and slide show presentations to be viewed within a Web site. These document viewing inline plug-ins can significantly improve the quality of information available on the Web and in your own Web sites.

Adobe Amber Inline Plug-in

The Adobe Acrobat software products generate visually rich documents that can be created, displayed, electronically transmitted, and printed. The Adobe Acrobat software operates by generating Portable Document Format (PDF) files, which have the added feature of being cross-platform compatible because they are generated in postscript format. The Amber inline plug-in allows for PDF files to be viewed in the Netscape Navigator 2.0 environment. The Adobe Amber inline plug-in can found at the following URL.

http://www.adobe.com/Amber/

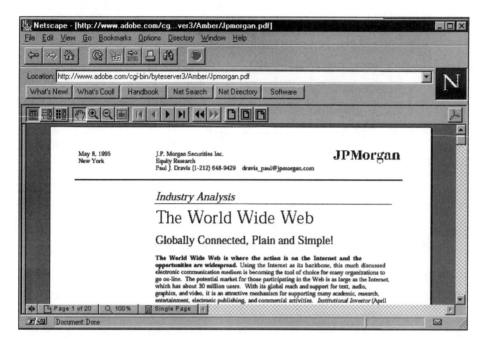

After you install the Amber inline plug-in, your Netscape Navigator browser will be capable of viewing the application/pdf MIME file type, thereby allowing you to see various PDF documents. Figure 9.10 illustrates the PDF document's appearance when it is viewed with the Amber plug-in.

This inline plug-in has several features for viewing documents. These include the ability to zoom in or out on a particular area of a document, the hand utility that allows the user to simply hold down the mouse button to move the particular page up or down for easier reading, and page-by-page document viewing. In addition, the Amber inline plug-in has three Internet-related capabilities for displaying PDF documents.

- Weblinks to other HTML or PDF documents
- "ByteServe" capability allowing Web servers to serve a page at a time of a PDF file
- Progressive display and maximum file compression of PDF files

Use the Amber inline plug-in when you want to provide large documents such as newspapers and reports that are often graphically enriched. An endless list of samples of Web pages with Adobe PDF files embedded in them can be found at the following URL where you can judge the performance of this inline plug-in.

http://www.adobe.com/Acrobat/PDFsites.html

To provide these files on your server you need to configure your server to be able to provide the application/pdf MIME file type. The <EMBED> tag required is typical of basic inline plug-ins.

ASAP WebShow

The importance of slides in presenting ideas and new concepts is well understood in the business world and recognized by Software Publishing Corporation (SPC), which has developed the ASAP WebShow inline plug-in. The ASAP WebShow inline plug-in allows you to create graphical slide shows with SPC's WordPower software that can be incorporated into your Web site. This inline plug-in allows for an impressive slide show presentation, and we highly recommend that you use it. The ASAP WebShow inline plug-in can be found at the following URL.

http://www.spco.com/

After you install this inline plug-in, your Netscape Navigator browser will be able to view the application/x-asap MIME file type that is generated by SPC's Word-Power software. You can view a sample file from the ASAP WebShow Gallery at the following URL. First you should select the SPC example that gives an overview of the ASAP WebShow technology.

http://www.spco.com/asap/asapgall.htm

Once the file has been loaded in the Netscape Navigator browser, it should appear as shown in Figure 9.11.

The ASAP WebShow inline plug-in provides a toolbar at the bottom of the plug-in window that you can use to control the presentation of the slides. When you click on the center button that has a white square icon with three dots, there should be a display of all the slides that make up this particular presentation. You can then select any one of the slides, and you will advance to that particular slide. When you

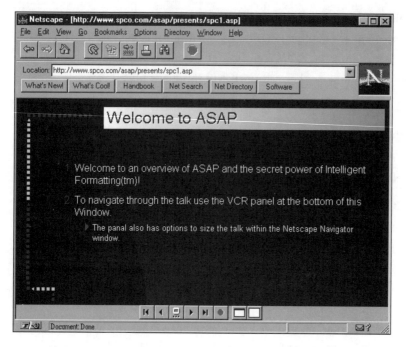

■■■■■■■ **Figure 9.11** ASAP WebShow inline plug-in example.

click on the button to the direct right of the center button, the slide presentation should advance to the next slide. The toolbar also allows you to select the size of the ASAP presentation when you click on the two screen buttons on the far right side of the window. When you click on the far right button, with the white square icon, the slide presentation window should expand to fill the entire computer screen without displaying the Netscape Navigator window environment.

The PC World online example found at the same URL as the previous example illustrates a feature of the ASAP WebShow in which the slide presentation can advance automatically. In this mode it does allow the user to click on the button with the green circle icon to stop the presentation at a particular slide.

The ASAP WebShow examples also demonstrate that the time for file download is quite short. This is a desirable feature for any Internet application or inline plug-in. The SPC system uses an "Intelligent Formatting" engine to produce such small file sizes that contain an extensive amount of material.

Deploying ASAP WebShow Content

When you decide to incorporate a slide presentation into a Web site that will use the ASAP WebShow inline plug-in, you will need to acquire SPC's WordPower Version 1.95 to produce the proper MIME file type. The WordPower slide presentation software is currently available in a free beta version and can be downloaded from the SPC home page that you previously contacted for the plug-in.

http://www.spco.com/

When you first run the WordPower software, you should see a window appear as illustrated in Figure 9.12.

WordPower is designed to allow very quick and easy generation of slide material with predesigned templates for backgrounds, color palettes, and text layout. These three types of templates are shown as file tabs on the right side of the WordPower window shown in Figure 9.12. When you click on one of the file tabs, an assortment of pre-made templates should appear, and when you select a template, the slide material should instantly transform to match the chosen template. This template capability is a very handy feature that should allow anyone experienced with

Figure 9.12 WordPower software used to generate impressive slide materials.

slide presentation software, such as PowerPoint, to master quickly and begin generating slide material content in less than five minutes. The three file tabs in the middle of the WordPower window are indicated as Outline, Preview, and Present. In Figure 9.12, Preview, which has been selected, produces a preview of how the slide material will look in its final presentation. When Outline is chosen, only the text on each slide will be illustrated, and when Present is chosen, a full screen presentation of the slides created will be launched.

WordPower is also capable of importing documents such as Word, WordPerfect, and basic text. Its very advanced import capability allows OLE objects to be inserted within the slide material when the **Insert|Object** selection is chosen. Some of the OLE objects that can be inserted include Adobe Acrobat, Excel, Paint Shop Pro, Quicktime Movies, PowerPoint presentations, and HTML documents (referred to as Netscape hypertext documents).

Once you have created the desired slide materials with the WordPower software, they must be placed into the Web source file with the proper <EMBED> tag. In addition to the basic <EMBED> tag including the SRC, WIDTH, and HEIGHT attributes, there are several other ASAP WebShow attributes that can be included to maximize the presentation capabilities of the software (Table 9.3).

■■■■■ **Table 9.3** Attributes of ASAP WebShow

Attribute	Default Value	Possible Values	Description
navbar	on	on/off	Indicates if the control bar is displayed.
autoplay	false	True/False	Determines whether the slide presentation is displayed automatically (True) or manually (False).
delaytime	10	any positive number	Number of seconds paused to present each slide when autoplay is enabled.
loopback	false	True/False	If autoplay is enabled, the loopback attribute indicates whether at the end of the presentation it is begun again (True) or not (False).

■■■■■ **Table 9.3** Continued

Attribute	Default Value	Possible Values	Description
effects	on/off	on	Controls whether slide transition effects are displayed or not.
fwd_effect	none	fade	When the effects attribute is on, the type of slide transition that is presented when the slides presentation moves forward or in reverse.
rev_effect		wipe_left	
		wipe_right	
		wipe_up	
		wipe_down	
		scroll_left	
		scroll_right	
		scroll_up	
		scroll_down	
		iris_in	
		iris_out	
		open	
		close	
orientation	landscape	landscape portrait N:M freeform	When landscape or portrait is selected, this attribute maintains the aspect ratio of the slide by letterboxing the contents. You can specify a custom aspect ratio by using the N:M selection, where N and M represent the desired proportion between the width and height. Freeform is selected when no aspect correction is desired.

■■■■ **Table 9.3** Continued

Attribute	Default Value	Possible Values	Description
background	ASAP Web-Show default	#rrggbb	When an orientation attribute value is selected that results in letter boxing, the background attribute specifies the color to backfill the areas inbetween. The number that is used is the hexadecimal digit for the desired intensity of the red (rr), green (gg), and blue(bb) that make up the desired background color.
border	window	window slide shadow none	If window is selected, the border is displayed in a nondraggable window border. Selecting slide results in the display of a 35mm slide jacket border, and selecting shadow produces a thin border with a drop shadow.slide
save_as	enabled	enabled/ disabled	When enabled is on, the user can save the document to a local file.
printing	enabled	enabled/ disabled	When enabled is on, the user can print the document.

■■■■

After you choose the desired inline plug-in attributes and place the proper <EMBED> tag in the Web source file, you then need only modify your server's MIME.TYPES file to recognize the application/x-asap MIME file type.

Formula One/NET Plug-in

Spreadsheets are a widely used and very important document type for most businesses. The Formula One/Net plug-in developed by Visual Components allows tables and spreadsheets to be viewed in Web page, while also allowing the user to input information. The Formula One/NET inline plug-in can be downloaded from Visual Components home page found at the following URL.

http://www.visualcomp.com/

After you install the inline plug-in, you can take a look at several samples at the following URL.

http://www.visualcomp.com/f1net/live.htm

In addition to allowing the user to replace information in the spreadsheet, the Formula One/NET plug-in allows the user to place URL links in the spreadsheets or create charts that can change based on the user's input into worksheet information.

Once installed, your Formula One/NET plug-in allows the MIME file type workbook/formula one to be executed. Incorporating spreadsheet files in a Web site to be viewed with the Formula One/NET inline plug-in does require that you produce the material with the Formula One software that must be purchased from Visual Components. This spreadsheet content is then produced as a VTS file type that can be viewed by the Formular One/NET plug-in. The most desirable feature of the Formula One software is that it is Microsoft Excel compatible, so that if you have already generated content with Excel, it can simply be imported.

There are no significant attributes that need to be defined to display material with this plug-in other than those basic attributes common to all plug-ins.

Image Enhancement

One of the most powerful ways to provide exciting and interesting content on the Internet involves the use of graphical images. The importance of graphical images is best illustrated (no pun intended)= by the current fervor over Internet that began when the Mosiac browser was created. This was the first browser to support graphical images. The Netscape Navigator browser natively already supports some image capabilities, including allowing the following image file types to be displayed.

- JPEG—Joint Photographic Experts Group
- GIF—Graphics Interchange Format
- TIFF— Tagged Image File Format
- RAS—Row Address Strobe

The Netscape Navigator browser 2.0 also features the ability to display images in a dithering mode, as interlaced GIFs, and as a progressive image display for JPEG files. When an image is displayed as an interlaced GIF file, the image initially appears and then slowly achieves greater detail until it is completely loaded. Progressive JPEG image display also produces the initial image, and more detail is added to the picture until it is completely downloaded. The advantage is that JPEG image files are much smaller than comparable GIF image files.

Although Netscape Navigator 2.0 has extensive capabilities for displaying images, the inline plug-ins that have been developed greatly increase the possible image display capabilities now available on the Web. These capabilities range from being able to zoom in and out on a particular area of an image, or the ability to generate even further compressed images than JPEG files, allowing even faster downloads and image display.

FIGleaf

The FIGleaf inline plug-in supports CGMs (Computer Graphic Metafiles), which are becoming the standard for displaying very complex and detailed drawings. Unlike conventional computer images, the CGM graphics are displayed as line art rather than bitmaps. The FIGleaf inline plug-in allows these drawings to be viewed within the Netscape browser environment and also allows the user to zoom in or out of the particular image being viewed. This sounds nice, but seeing is believing. First you need to install the FIGleaf inline plug-in from the following URL.

http://www.ct.ebt.com/figinline/download.html

After the plug-in has been installed, check out the following URLs to appreciate the images that can be produced and viewed with this software.

http://www.ct.ebt.com/proof/shuttle.cgm

http://www.ct.ebt.com/images.html

■■■■■■ **Table 9.4** Graphical Image/File MIME File Types FIGleaf Inline
Plug-in Allows To Be Viewed

Graphic File Type	File Extension
Computer Graphics Metafile	(CGM)
Tagged Image File Format	(TIFF)
Encapsulated PostScript	(EPSI/EPSF)
CCITT Group 4 Type I	(G4)
CCITT Group 4 Type II	(TG4)
Computer Graphics Metafile	(CGM)
Microsoft Windows Bitmap	(BMP)
Microsoft Windows Metafile	(WMF)
Portable Pixmap	(PPM)
Portable Greymap	(PGM)
Portable Bitmap	(PBM)
Sun Raster files	(SUN)
Graphics Interchange Format	(GIF)
Joint Photographic Experts Group	(JPEG)

Once you install the FIGleaf inline plug-in, your Netscape Navigator will be able to view numerous additional graphical images. Table 9.4 indicates all of the file types that are added image/file MIME files that your browser is now capable of viewing.

One of the very desirable features of this inline plug-in lies in its ability to zoom in or out of a specific area of an image. To zoom in, hold down the CONTROL key and create a rectangle by dragging your mouse over the area on which you want to zoom in. You can zoom in repeatedly, viewing more and more detail of the particular image. When you want to zoom out, hold down both the SHIFT key and the CONTROL key and left click on the picture. You can also choose from a variety of different viewing characteristics by right clicking your mouse on the image.

Carberry Conversion Machine

When you provide images to be viewed with the FIGleaf plug-in, you can choose to have them displayed in an embedded or full display MODE, as described earlier in the basic <EMBED> tag description used to include inline plug-ins in a Web application. Currently, Carberry doesn't provide the tools to convert graphic files into the CGM file format, but you can send your image files to Carberry, which will convert the files and return them to you.

Lightning Strike Inline Plug-in

There you are on the Playboy home page, you click on an interesting *umm.. article*, but then you have to wait an endless amount of time for the picture to display. Well maybe you don't ever visit the Playboy Web site, but a common problem no matter where you go on the Web is that although images can add a great deal to the content and quality of a Web site, a good-quality image often requires a substantial amount of time to download to the user's computer. The longer users have to wait to get information from your Web site, the lower the opinion they will have of it.

The solution to this problem is to compress your images so that they can be downloaded much faster. There are currently several methods for compressing images. One of the most popular and common techniques is known as JPEG 6.0, based on the DCT (discrete cosine transform) algorithm. Infinet Op has developed another image compression technique, based on wavelet compression, called Lightning Strike. The wavelet compression technique results in compression ratios similar to those for the JPEG 6.0 system, ranging from 70 to 150, but the image quality is much better.

The Lightning Strike system consists of a compression utility and a Lightning Strike plug-in that allows the viewing of these compressed images within the Navigator browser environment. To appreciate the quality of the images and the speed at which these compressed images can be delivered, download and install the Lightning Strike plug-in located at the following URL.

http://www.infinop.com/index.html

After you have downloaded and installed the Lightning Strike plug-in, your browser will be enabled to view image files of the image/cis-cod MIME file type. Before you begin viewing any figures that are generated with the Lightning Strike codec (compression and decompression code), you need to first make a slight modification to your Netscape Navigator 2.0 browser. Under the **Options|Network Preferences** raise the Disk Cache from 0KB to a recommended 1MB, which will be needed to view the very high-compression images. With your browser environment configured correctly, you need to check out some of Lighting Strike images found in the comparison table at the bottom of the following URL.

http://www.infinop.com/html/comptable.html

You should find images that have amazing quality and extremely fast downloads.

Lightning Strike Compression Utility

Now that you are thoroughly impressed with the quality of the images that are producible with the Lightning Strike codec, you can compress images and make them available on your Web site. After you have the desired image that needs to be compressed, you need to get the Lighting Strike compression utility. The compression utility for creating Lightning Strike images isn't free, but must be purchased from Infinet Op, which can be contacted at the URL above. It is well worth the investment to produce Web content containing high-quality compressed images.

The Lightning Strike Image Compressor basically converts BMP(Microsoft Windows Bitmap) files into COD files that can be displayed with the Lightning Strike inline plug-in. The operation of the compression utility is very simple. After you load the desired BMP file, all that you need to do to compress the image is to select the **File|Compress** selection, and the COD file is created. The compression utility also offers several display features that allow the image that is displayed to be varied in size or stretched in a particular direction. In addition, the compression utility offers both an easy and a master setup control that allows some degree of control on the compression algorithm that is used. For example, when you choose the **Options|Easy Setup** selection, you can vary the tradeoffs in quality of the created COD image file. The obvious tradeoff is that the higher-quality COD compression image file is desired the larger file size it will have compared to a lower-quality image. The Lightning Strike Image Compressor is an easy-to-use and convenient tool to create COD image files that can be placed on a Web site and viewed with the Lightning Strike plug-in.

Now that you have successfully compressed the image, you simply have to configure your server so that it can accept the image/cis-cod MIME file type.

Autocad Viewer by SoftSource

You just finished the engineering drawing for your company's most important product that is going into production within minutes, but your boss on the other side of the country needs to see it first, and all he has is a connection to the Internet. Wouldn't it be great if you could simply place the drawing file on the company's Web site, and your boss could view it? This sounds like an implausible example, but it does introduce the Autocad viewer inline plug-in that exists. This is an important image viewing inline plug-in because of Autocad's predominance as the standard for engineering drawings generated by computers. You can download this inline plug-in from the following URL location.

http://www.softsource.com/softsource/plugins/plugins.html

Once it is installed, you can view the standard Autocad inline plug-in viewer, and your Netscape Navigator browser will be capable of displaying standard Autocad file formats DXF and DWG. Figure 9.13 displays an architectural drawing viewed with this inline plug-in.

When you right-click on the picture, you can choose from a variety of different viewing modes, allowing you to zoom in or zoom out of particular areas of the image.

After you create the desired Autocad images, simply modify the MIME.TYPES file on the server for the image/x-dxf and image/x-dwg MIME file types and include the <EMBED> tag in the Web source file.

OLE/OCX Controls

The Netscape Navigator browser truly becomes its own operating system on the Web with the development of inline plug-ins that can support OLE/OCX controls. OLE (Object Linking and Embedding) is a distributed object system and protocol developed by Microsoft. It allows objects of one particular application to be placed within other applications that support OLE controls. Microsoft Word uses OLE every time you embed graphics in a document. It's also possible to embed Excel spreadsheets in a Word document. Once the graphic or spreadsheet (known as an object—the O in OLE) is linked (the L in OLE) or embedded (the E in OLE), you can start the program that created the object by double-clicking on the object.

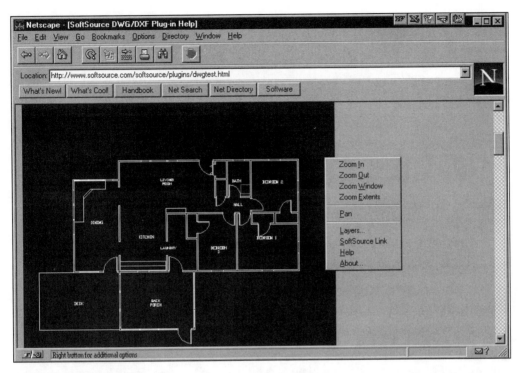

Figure 9.13 Viewing menu selection appears when you right-click on the image.

What this has done is extend the capabilities of programs like Microsoft Word by allowing other technologies to be combined with it.

There is a mad rush by software companies to implement OCX controls. (OCX controls were formerly known as VBX controls.) Very soon, powerful database access, spreadsheets, word processors, and many other types of software will be implemented in an OCX control. This means you will be able to offer these technologies right in a Web page by adding a control. OCX controls are components with which you can "build" your own software by simply adding all the components you need. Creating software by adding components is making application development incredibly simple. Add to this simplicity the power of the Internet, and you have an awesome combination. Your Web pages can contain complete and powerful software applications.

Openscape

The Openscape system allows you to create reusable, customized OLE controls that can be displayed in the inline plug-in system. When you download the inline plug-in from the following URL, you will also be downloading a visual OLE control development environment.

http://www.opower.com/

Once this inline plug-in is installed, it will enable your Netscape Navigator client to recognize the x-form/x-opnscape MIME file type that is created with the Openscape development tool. This URL site features several demos that demonstrate OLE control applications, such as the Optzee game illustrated in Figure 9.14.

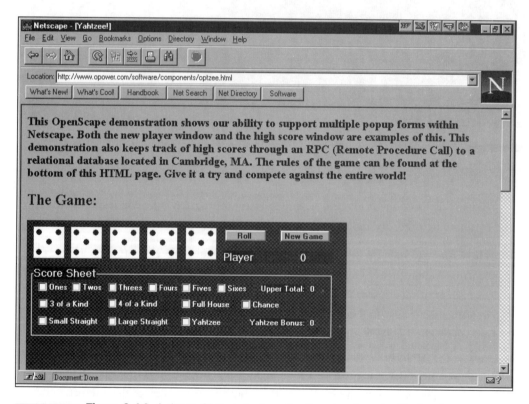

■■■■■■ **Figure 9.14** A demo OLE control application developed with the Openscape environment.

After you create your own application with the Openscape development environment, you can include it on your Web site after you modify the MIME.TYPES file on your server and include the basic <EMBED> tag in the Web source file.

Virtual Reality Worlds

The world of Virtual Reality Modeling Language (VRML) promises to create a whole new realm of entertaining, potentially informative, and interesting environments. The VRML language allows for 3D graphical environments to be created that allow the user to navigate through, view, and interact with objects in the environment.

There are several VRML viewers currently available, including Live3D owned by Netscape, WIRL by VREAM, VREALM by Integrated Data Systems, and VR Scout by Chaco Communications. Once any one of these VRML browsers is downloaded, it enables the Netscape Navigator browser to view x-world/x-vrml applications. If you install one VRML plug-in and then install another VRML plug-in that views the same type of VRML MIME file type, then when you contact a particular VRML file, the first inline plug-in that is loaded by the browser will be the one that is run. There is no way to specify which inline plug-in is loaded first.

Currently, the most popular VRML browser is the Live3D inline plug-in, and because of the prominence of its owner and its similarity to the other VRML inline plug-ins, it is the only one covered in this section.

Live3D

The Live3D inline plug-in now brings VRML viewing capabilities to your Netscape Navigator client. It was one of the first inline plug-ins created, although previously known as WebFX. Using the Live3D inline plug-in, you can now contact Web sites and navigate through informative and visually stimulating environments, not to mention gain the potential for entertainment and games. The Live3D inline plug-in offers a range of features for operating in a VRML world: collision detection, gravity, and different viewpoints are just a few. The only way you can appreciate this inline plug-in is to download and install it from the following URL.

http://www.netscape.com/

As you can see, the Live3D system is now owned by Netscape Communication—not a bad endorsement of the future success and potential of this inline plug-in. After you install the Live3D inline plug-in, the Netscape Navigator browser will be capable of viewing the x-world/x-vrml MIME file type. You can check out a couple of VRML worlds at the following URLs.

http://www.netscape.com/comprod/products/navigator/live3d/examples/live3d.wrl

When you first load one of these VRML worlds, you should see the Live3D inline plug-in window appear as shown in Figure 9.15, where various objects are spinning around the Live3D logo that is also moving.

Several options found on the bottom of the Live3D window allow you to select the method to use as you travel through the virtual world. These methods include walk, fly, and point.

- *walk*. Click the mouse button to move in the direction of the pointer or use arrow keys moving left, right, forward, and backward. Use keys A and Z to look upward or downward.

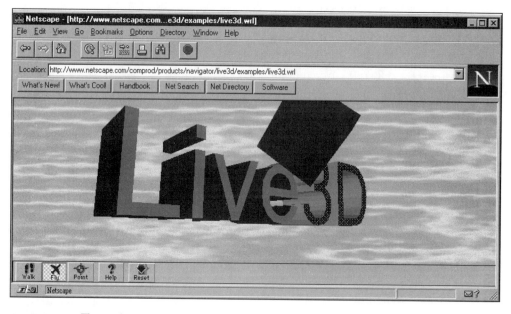

Figure 9.15 Click on the desired mode for movement through the VRML world.

- *fly*. Click the mouse button to move in the direction of the pointer at a faster speed than when you are in the walk mode, or use the arrow keys to move left and right or look upward or downward. Keys A and Z move you either forward or backward.
- *point*. Click your mouse button at a particular point in the VRML world, and you will be moved to that point.

When you right-click your mouse on the Live3D window, it should open a menu selection that gives you the ability to customize your movement through the virtual environment, such as activating the navigation lights or banking when flying. Figure 9.16 illustrates the navigation menu that appears.

Live3D also supports many of the new extensions that will exist in the VRML 2.0 standard, often referred to as Moving Worlds. The Moving Worlds standard adds movement, animation, and Java interoperability among many other improvements and features. These modifications change the VRML language as significantly as Java applets and inline plug-ins have improved the multimedia capabilities of the HTML language of the Web. Several of these new extensions are already built into the current Live3D inline plug-in that allows you to incorporate them in the VRML worlds you design.

The Spin extension allows the VRML developer to enable objects to spin rather than appear as static unmoving objects in a VRML world. The example VRML found at the following URL produces the spinning of the helicopter rotors.

http://www.netscape.com/comprod/products/navigator/live3d/examples/helicopter/helicopter.wrl.gz

Figure 9.16 Choose the desired navigation selection from this menu.

The Animation extension enables a series of animations to be programmed for a series of different objects, with which you can then interact as you view them in VRML world. The Live3D inline plug-in even as an extension for Java support is illustrated in this fighter game.

http://www.netscape.com/comprod/products/navigator/live3d/examples/fighter
/fghtentr.html

Deploying VRML Content for Live3D Viewing

If you want to place a 3D VRML world on your Web site, numerous tools are available to help you build the world of your dreams. A wealth of VRML information can be found at the VRML Repository where you can download tools to convert images and shapes created with software you may be familiar with into a VRML acceptable world. Some of these conversion tools can be found at the following URL.

http://www.sdsc.edu/SDSC/Partners/vrml/software/geom_trans.html

At the following URL you can also find numerous tools that allow you to author your own VRML world.

http://www.sdsc.edu/SDSC/Partners/vrml/software/modelers.html

An actual description on how to create VRML worlds extends beyond the scope of this book, but you should find suitable information at the URLs above or those located at the Live3D site. When you begin to create your VRML world, you can incorporate the new Live3D extensions by examining the existing Live3D API.

By using these tools you can add to your web site an entire new entertaining or informative dimension with which users will be able to interact using the Live3D inline plug-in.

Combination of Plug-ins

Although we recommended against using more than one Java applet on the same Web page, it is possible to place several inline plug-ins on the same Web page. Inline plug-ins are compiled programs that run significantly faster than Java applets that are interpreted as byte code.

Not only can more than one inline plug-in be placed on the same Web page, but in some cases inline plug-ins can be intimately combined to improve the display of a particular application. For example, you may want to combine an audio inline plug-in to provide a speaker describing various images that may be displayed with one of the image inline plug-ins. The following URL illustrates the combination of the Live3D and Shockwave inline plug-ins.

http://www.virtualtoys.com/

This is an impressive URL that gives some indication of what you can do with the inline plug-ins featured in this chapter.

Plug-ins with Java Applets

Inline plug-ins help you solve one of the restrictions of Java applets. An alternative to having multiple Java applets running on a Web page is including an inline plug-in. Plug-ins and Java applets can be safely run simultaneously on a Web page. The following URL illustrates a sample that runs a Java applet game in combination with the Crescendo inline plug-in to provide background music.

http://www.zoop.com/vnm/zoop/java-game/

This example clearly shows that Java applets and inline plug-ins can be successfully combined on the same Web page to make truly multimedia-enabled Web sites.

What If the User Doesn't Have the Plug-in?

No one likes to throw a party and have no guests show up. What if you spend an incredible amount of time and investment creating a Web site using inline plug-ins that most users visiting your site don't have installed? This is an obvious concern, but one that has been addressed. Netscape Navigator browser launches a window informing users that a required inline plug-in must be loaded, as shown in Figure 9.17. In this particular example the pop-up window was launched before all the information was downloaded.

After receiving a warning like the one in Figure 9.17, if the user clicks the **Cancel** button, the Web page will be loaded, but none of the inline plug-ins will execute. When the user clicks on the button to "Get the plug-in," the Netscape Navigator

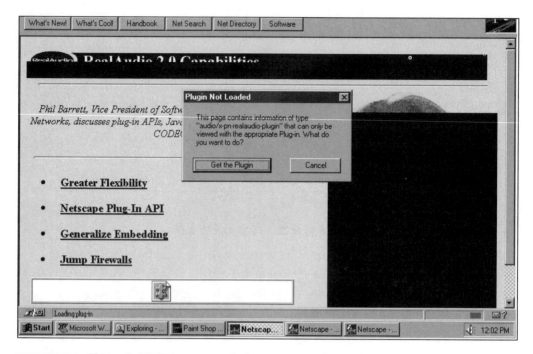

■■■■■ **Figure 9.17** This pop-up window appears when a Web page contains an unrecognized inline plug-in MIME file type.

browser advances to the Web page (see Figure 9.18) provided by Netscape, featuring a hyperlink to the Plug-ins Registry. Here the user can download the appropriate inline plug-in.

An unsophisticated user may still not retrieve the proper inline plug-in from the Plug-in Registry page. It's also possible that the inline plug-in necessary is not be present on this Web page. To avoid this problem, you can use the PLUGINSPACE attribute. The value to use for this attribute should be a URL to a CGI file where the MIME file type can be accepted as input.

```
<EMBED SRC="Demo.mpg" HEIGHT=100 WIDTH=100
PLUGINSPAGE="http://www.coolsite.com/test.cgi ">
```

You can see that the URL location illustrated in Figure 9.18 shows the CGI file that the Netscape Navigator was sent to along with the MIME file type that was passed when the "Get the plug-in" button was clicked.

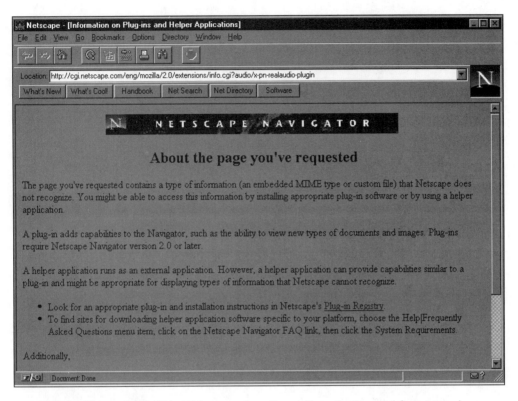

Figure 9.18 This Web page describes inline plug-ins and features a hyper-link to the Plug-ins Registry.

http://cgi.netscape.com/eng/mozilla/2.0/extensions/info.cgi?audio
/x-pn-realaudio-plugin

The PLUGINSPACE attribute is ignored if the inline plug-in has already been installed and the MIME file type is recognized.

When you design content for your Web site using inline plug-ins, it's always possi-ble that the end user may not be very comfortable with downloading and installing plug-ins. This plug-in installation feature will serve as an added reassurance that the content you provide through plug-ins will be accessible to a majority of the people visiting your Web site.

When the person is using a Web browser that doesn't support inline plug-ins, you can add a <NOEMBED> tag below the <EMBED> tag that specifies an inline plug-in. This will display a text message rather than attempt to load the plug-in.

```
<EMBED  SRC=http://www.science.org/don.mpg  WIDTH=250  HEIGHT=125>

<NOEMBED> HTML Text displayed to a user that doesn't have plug-in enabled
browser.  </NOEMBED>
```

Adding these modifications to your Web source file will ensure that users can get the needed inline plug-in to view the content on your Web site or see text telling them what they're missing.

Now It's Your Turn

This chapter demonstrates some of the most impressive inline plug-ins now available. The plug-ins provide everything from improved image compression rates to streaming audio content. The content you can now place on your Web site with this new HTML extension is limited only by your imagination. Embed full applications right in your Web pages using:

- Active X controls (formerly known as OLE controls)
- Inline plug-ins
- Java applets

Tie all these together with HTML and JavaScript to create Web content that is exciting, dynamic, and powerful. Your Web pages can have broadcast sound, 3D graphics, animations, movie clips, and even the world of virtual reality. Whether your Web creation needs are creative or strictly business, there are components available that will allow you to create whatever you need.

UNDERSTANDING THE

NETSCAPE INLINE

PLUG-IN ARCHITECTURE

Netscape inline plug-ins play a very important role in the overall LiveWire development strategy. They are ideal solutions for anything that isn't possible or doesn't execute fast enough as a Java applet or JavaScript application. Like JavaScript and Java applets, inline plug-ins are independent of LiveWire and the Netscape Communications server. Any HTTP server can be used to provide content compatible with plug-ins just as any server can provide Java applets or JavaScript to Java-enabled or JavaScript-enabled browsers. In this chapter we introduce you to the fundamentals of the Netscape plug-in architecture and its platform-independent API. The next chapter will then show you how to create your own plug-in. A custom plug-in allows you to take advantage of the power and flexibility that a plug-in provides as a client interface to the content of your Web site.

Plug-ins extend the functionality of Netscape Navigator. In effect, a plug-in embeds a separate compiled program inside the Navigator display area. There are no limits to what a plug-in can do because a plug-in is a truly compiled program executed by Netscape Navigator. The unlimited nature of plug-ins is both a reason to build them and a reason to worry about them. Nothing will stop a plug-in from erasing files, formatting disks, implanting viruses, or even reading sensitive files and sending them over the Internet to someone else. The only protection available to a user of plug-ins is provided by the user's operating system. In the case of multiuser operating systems like Unix or Microsoft Windows NT, the operating system is able to protect itself, to a certain extent, from malicious plug-ins. No existing operating system provides an ideal architecture that solves all the potential security problems associated with Internet computing. If you decide to create your own plug-in to extend the functionality of Netscape Navigator for users of your Web site, be aware that you're asking those Internet users to trust that your plug-in won't compromise their system security.

Extending the Web with MIME

MIME, or *Multipurpose Internet Mail Extensions*, is an Internet standard with which you may already be familiar through work with CGI scripts or HTTP server software. An understanding of MIME is essential if you intend to build your own Netscape plug-ins. Though simple in concept, the role of MIME in Web technology can be confusing, so a quick and simple review of MIME is worthwhile.

One of the most important things to understand about MIME is that it has a really, really unfortunate name. Before MIME was developed, STD 11 (also known as RFC 822) was the standard that defined the structure of electronic mail messages on the Internet. However, STD 11 dealt only with the structure of mail headers such as From: or To: but assumed that the content, or body, of the e-mail would contain only text. The purpose for creating the MIME standard was to extend, rather than replace, STD 11 so that the body of an e-mail message could include much more than text without changing the well-known standard for e-mail headers defined by STD 11.

■■■■■

> RFC 1521 dated September 1993 details the Multipurpose Internet Mail Extensions (MIME) standard.

■■■■■

When all was said and done, the MIME standard turned out to be a simple and powerful mechanism for representing complex, compound, or multipart document types and for accurately identifying content types in general. Thus, it was an obvious solution for any Internet software that needed to identify and process diverse data types; there was no reason to limit the use of MIME to enabling multipurpose e-mail extensions. The incorporation of MIME into the World Wide Web was a good technical decision that is emerging as a key element of advanced Web technology. Netscape is the first company to truly capitalize on the MIME architecture by enabling the development and widespread deployment of brand-new MIME content types and plug-in extensions for handling such content on the Web, in electronic mail, and in usenet news.

The heart of the MIME architecture is a simple **content-type/subtype** pair that identifies both the *top-level* content type and the content subtype. Top-level content types, listed in Table 10.1, are well-defined content categories. New MIME types are expected to use one of the official top-level content types listed in Table 10.1 followed by a subtype designator. New MIME types are created by introducing new content subtypes, not new top-level content types.

The Internet Assigned Numbers Authority (IANA) administers the assignment of MIME types. To prevent MIME type conflicts, it's important to contact IANA concerning the official assignment of your new MIME type as soon as you've determined the top-level content type and new subtype that you wish to use. IANA also provides a current list of registered (and unregistered but "known") MIME types that will help guide your new type selection.

■■■■■

> IANA can be contacted via e-mail (iana@isi.edu) or on the Web (http://www.iana.org/iana/).
>
> RFC 1590 describes in detail the procedure to register a new MIME type as an Internet standard.

■■■■■

When deciding upon a new MIME type for your plug-in and its associated content, follow these guidelines:

- Use one of the official top-level types listed in Table 10.1.
- If no existing top-level type meets your needs, use a prefix of "X-" as part of your top-level type.

- If you don't intend to register your new MIME type with IANA, use "**X-**" as a prefix to the subtype.

An example of a time that you might not register a new MIME type with IANA is when your company decides to use Netscape technology for local, company-oriented network software (sometimes called an intranet). If the MIME type is for local use only, there is no real need to establish your new MIME type as an Internet-recognized registered type. Even in this circumstance, it's important to use the X- prefix on either or both of the parts of the MIME type to further distinguish your company-only MIME type from Internet-wide types.

One question that comes up frequently as developers consider building plug-ins is what to do when the plug-in that you have in mind doesn't need a content type. Any application that you simply want to run within the Netscape Navigator window fits this description. Applications like this don't need to process and display a type of data, such as an image or HTML; they need to display only their fixed user interface. A good example would be an FTP client or other data transfer utility in the form of a plug-in or even a network-enabled word processor that allows you to

■■■■■■ **Table 10.1** Official Top-Level MIME Content Types

Top-Level Content Type	Description
text	Textual information; represented in almost any character set and including text formatting languages such as HTML
multipart	Combines several different body parts, possibly of different MIME types
application	Used for application data or generic binary data
message	Encapsulation of an e-mail message
image	Graphic image data including GIF, TIFF, JPEG, and other graphic data formats
audio	Audio or voice data including AU, WAV, and other audio data formats
video	Video or other moving image data including composite audio-video data formats

retrieve and edit files on the network. Even though applications of this sort don't rely on actual content to function, they still must have a MIME type in order to work as plug-ins. In instances like these, the MIME type is used only to trigger the display of the plug-in. Once the plug-in is displayed, its user interface takes over to provide functionality to the end user.

Netscape discourages plug-ins that don't enable new MIME content types, though. Plug-ins are meant only to enable new Web content in the form of multimedia data formats, interactive media such as virtual worlds, and static page layout languages other than HTML. The plug-in API was not designed to be an ideal object-technology component architecture for distributed network computing in which the Netscape Navigator becomes a standard platform for client/server software. Any intentions that Netscape has to build a standard Internet operating system are most definitely *not* based on the current plug-in API. The World Wide Web may represent, to some people, the Internet "operating system," but plug-ins should not be thought of as a way to build client/server applications for the Web. If your plug-in doesn't need a MIME type, maybe it shouldn't be a plug-in. This is a judgment call that you will have to make based on an assessment of the other options available and of your particular needs. The authors of this book have personally created plug-ins that don't enable new MIME types because at the time there was no better way to create and deploy a high-visibility Internet application that even novice Web users could understand and use effectively. We do not endorse the creation of plug-ins for anything other than the implementation of new MIME types on the Web. However, in the absence of a better solution for getting your Internet software in the hands of as many people as possible, a plug-in may be your only realistic option.

The purpose behind creating your own plug-in, therefore, is to establish a new MIME type that provides the kind of Web content that your site requires. Clearly, if someone else has already created a MIME type (and a plug-in that supports the type) that will meet the needs of your site, there's no need to create a new one. If, on the other hand, your site requires functionality that is unique or innovative, you'll definitely want to consider creating your own plug-in to provide exactly the content and interactive capabilities that you desire. And if your application must have the easy-deployment and novice-friendly features of a plug-in but doesn't fit the ideal plug-in model based on MIME, it's okay to bend the rules and push the envelope a bit.

Understanding the Plug-in API

Plug-in code is written so that it conforms to the platform-specific plug-in API provided by Netscape Navigator. Although the plug-in API is different between platforms, such as the use of DLLs only in the Microsoft Windows version, the core of the API is consistent regardless of platform. This consistency is reflected in the plug-in SDK provided by Netscape that is covered in the next section. This means that the process of building your own plug-in, although varied depending on the platform, is almost identical at the API level. With a solid grasp of the API and an understanding of the intentions behind Netscape plug-in architecture, creating a plug-in can be easy.

The Netscape plug-in architecture defines five distinct requirements for a plug-in. The first is a platform-specific *plug-in module* to provide the actual plug-in logic. A plug-in module is a file containing compiled plug-in code; for example, in Microsoft Windows the module is a DLL whose name must begin with the letters *NP*, as in *npavi32.dll*. The second requirement is that the plug-in module have version information accessible to Netscape Navigator without requiring that the module actually be loaded into memory before the version information can be read. The module's version information must include a list of MIME types supported by the plug-in. An example of plug-in version information for *npavi32.dll* is shown in Figure 10.1. As you'll see in the next chapter on building a plug-in with the SDK, you create version information using the resource editor included with your development tool.

The third requirement is that the plug-in module must contain certain functions that can be called by Netscape Navigator when the plug-in is used. Plug-in functions act as the primary interface between Navigator and its plug-in modules. Plug-in functions triggered by Navigator include **NPP_New,** which initializes a new instance of a plug-in MIME type, and **NPP_NewStream,** which gives the plug-in access to any data associated with the MIME instance. Each of the plug-in functions is covered in detail in the next section.

The fourth requirement is that the plug-in call Navigator functions to provide common functionality including accessing URLs, modifying the Navigator microhelp status bar, and safely allocating memory owned by the Navigator process. Netscape Navigator provides functions for these common operations both to simplify plug-in

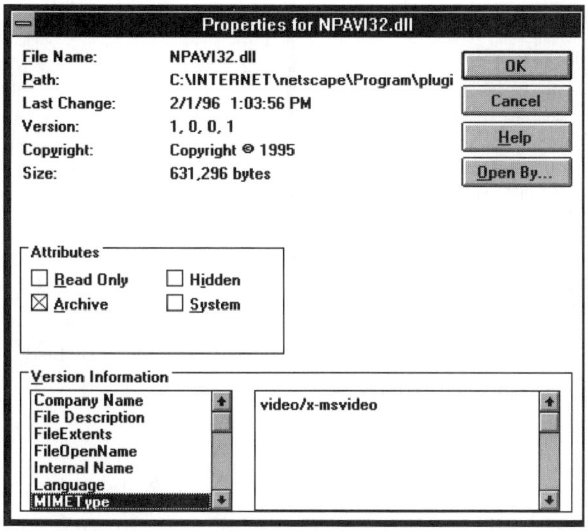

Figure 10.1 Plug-in module version information tells Navigator which MIME types are supported by the plug-in.

development and to protect the integrity of its own process—including memory management.

Finally, the plug-in is expected to "draw" on a platform-specific window handle provided to the plug-in by Navigator. In this context, the word *draw* means simply that instead of creating its own window as a typical application does, the plug-in application uses the window provided by Navigator for its display and interaction with the user. Plug-ins can create new windows if they wish, as in the case of a pop-up dialog box or even the creation and display of a brand-new application frame window residing outside Navigator. Most plug-ins, however, will restrict their user interface to the Navigator-embedded window so that the plug-in appears to exist as an integrated part of Navigator itself. Seamless integration into the Navigator display area is one of the most compelling reasons to build a plug-in in the first place.

To help illustrate the location of the Navigator-supplied plug-in window relative to other Navigator objects, we used the Spy utility provided with Symtantec C++ to investigate the list of windows present in Navigator. Figure 10.2 shows a portion of the list of windows, with the plug-in window selected. In the information box on

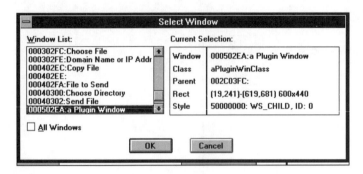

Figure 10.2 Investigate the windows present in Netscape Navigator and spy on event messages using a Spy utility.

the right side of the Spy window are details of the plug-in window. Notice that the parent window is defined as 002C03FC and that window 000502EA (the plug-in window) includes the style WS_CHILD. Like each of the other controls on the Navigator window (such as buttons and edit fields), the plug-in window is a child of the main Navigator display area. In this example, the parent window 002C03FC represents the entire Navigator display area, which includes the horizontal rule and the word *Test* shown in Figure 10.2. The Navigator display area is in turn a child of the top-level Netscape Navigator window on which are found all of the Navigator toolbars, the Location: edit field, and the other user interface controls.

Because Navigator creates and owns the plug-in window, your plug-in code doesn't really have control over things such as the type of window created by Navigator. Some operations, such as drag-and-drop in Microsoft Windows, may require that certain window styles be applied to the target window for certain features to be enabled. The plug-in window created by Navigator has only the WS_CHILD window style, so there may be built-in limitations as to what your plug-in code is able to do with its plug-in window. One way to overcome these limitations is to add a new child window to the plug-in window so that your code has control over the styles and settings defined.

A Spy utility like the one shown in Figure 10.2 enables you to learn a lot about the way the Netscape plug-in API behaves. You can monitor event messages between Navigator and your plug-in window and track down the source of problems or confusing event sequences. We strongly recommend that you become familiar with your Spy utility to simplify the process of debugging the plug-ins that you build.

Demystifying Key Plug-in API Concepts

The most important thing to realize about the Netscape plug-in API is that a single plug-in module must be able to handle multiple simultaneous instances of the MIME type supported by the plug-in. In other words, the plug-in module will be loaded into memory only once to handle a Web page that contains 16 occurrences of the same MIME type. The plug-in module must be capable of handling the display and management of all 16 such MIME instances. To add to this complexity, a single plug-in module can support multiple MIME types, in which case the plug-in code must be prepared to handle multiple instances of multiple MIME types. Keep this in mind as you learn about the API, and the API functions will make more sense to you.

▬▬

> Key concept: A plug-in must be able to handle multiple simultaneous instances of each MIME type it supports.

▬▬

Because a plug-in module draws on a Navigator-owned window instead of creating its own window, writing plug-in code is a little different from writing a normal application. Plug-in execution is entirely event-driven with two possible event sources:

- Plug-in API functions triggered by Navigator
- Plug-in window events via Navigator's platform-dependent "message pump"

Plug-in API functions, such as **NPP_New, NPP_Write,** and **NPP_SetWindow,** are triggered when Navigator expects the plug-in to perform work related to being a "Navigator extension." The plug-in should perform any processing required for the API call and return as soon as possible so that Navigator can continue with other operations. This is important even in a multithreaded operating system because the plug-in API is not designed to be multithreaded. Your plug-in can create new threads if it needs to, but it shouldn't assume that Navigator has done so prior to triggering an API function.

Plug-in window events are triggered by the operating system in the normal fashion for the operating system. When a window event occurs, the plug-in has the opportunity to do work related to being a Microsoft Windows, Macintosh, or X Windows application. This includes responding to mouse or keyboard events, painting, and any other event that your plug-in is prepared to handle. The plug-in may optionally make calls to Navigator functions to provide common plug-in functionality or allocate Navigator-owned memory space. Window event messaging is handled by a plug-in differently depending on the operating system.

■■■■■■

> Key concept: Navigator plug-in work is done in response to API function calls, while platform-specific work is done in response to platform-specific event notification delivered in the standard way for the platform in question.

■■■■■■

This chapter covers the details of only one of the two possible event sources for a plug-in, the plug-in API portion. Writing code that will respond to platform-dependent window event messages and provide the logic for the plug-in is your job as the programmer, but you'll have to learn this part somewhere else if you're not already an experienced programmer or don't have the time to struggle through it on your own. Although detailed instructions on writing event-driven, window-based applications are outside the scope of this book, there are a number of things that you should know about the relationship of your plug-in with its parent window and parent process (Netscape Navigator), and the operating system. The next section describes this important concept.

Window Event Messaging and Plug-Ins

In an event-driven, window-based user interface such as Microsoft Windows, X Windows, or the Macintosh OS, window event notification is delivered to application code in some standard way. The details of the event delivery process are different depending on the operating system, but the basic concepts are consistent. In Windows, for example, every window has an associated window procedure that processes all event messages delivered to the window. When an event occurs about which an application needs to be notified, Microsoft Windows adds a message to the systemwide message queue. The application retrieves the message from the queue, and it in turn executes the correct window procedure so that the right window gets the opportunity to process the event that has occurred, be it a mouse-click or a repaint notification or some other event.

All window-based applications are required to repeatedly (typically in a compact loop) check the systemwide message queue and handle events intended for their processes, threads, windows, or user interface controls. Application code that repeatedly checks the message queue is known as the application's *message loop*, and the process of dispatching messages to application window procedures or otherwise notifying components of the application that they should respond to an event message is known as the application's *message pump*. Most often your application development tool or the class libraries (such as the Microsoft Foundation Classes) that you use to create software will handle the low-level message loop and message pump for you. As a programmer, you simply need to think about how your application will respond to the messages. When building a plug-in, however, you must think about the message loop and the message pump in a little more detail because your code depends directly on the Netscape Navigator message pump for all of its event notification.

▬▬▬▬

> Key concept: Your plug-in depends on the Netscape Navigator message
> pump to receive window event messages.

▬▬▬▬

In a Macintosh plug-in, the API function **NPP_HandleEvent (NPP instance, void* event)** is called by Navigator to deliver window event notification to the plug-in instance. Macintosh plug-ins are the only ones that use the **NPP_HandleEvent** API function. The structure of a typical Macintosh application has a message pump architecture that requires Netscape Navigator to deliver event notification "by hand" through an explicit API function call. In contrast, Microsoft Windows' application structure and the technical design of a typical message pump using Microsoft Windows SDK functions make possible a more elegant solution to receive window event messages in your plug-in. Instead of calling the **NPP_HandleEvent** API function to deliver event notification to the plug-in window, Navigator's message pump just keeps pumping. The Navigator message pump triggers the plug-in window's window procedure—the code that handles event processing for the window—whenever the Microsoft Windows message queue provides such an event.

When a plug-in window is first created by Navigator, its window procedure is owned by Navigator itself, and the procedure is designed to do essentially nothing, because empty plug-in windows don't provide any functionality. The first task that your plug-in module must handle when it receives notification from Netscape Navigator of a new plug-in instance is to replace the Navigator-owned window procedure with a custom window procedure owned by your plug-in module. This process is known as *subclassing* the Navigator-supplied plug-in window and is the heart of plug-in technology in Microsoft Windows. By subclassing the Navigator window, your plug-in takes control of all event processing for the window without affecting the operation of Netscape Navigator in any way. Navigator's message pump keeps pumping out event notification by calling the window's window procedure, only now the window procedure being called is owned by your plug-in instead. As far as Navigator is concerned, the new window procedure works just as well as the original.

When the plug-in instance is destroyed, your plug-in module must return control of the window event processing to Navigator's original window procedure through a process known as *unsubclassing*. Unsubclassing the plug-in window ensures that Navigator can continue to function normally once the plug-in module is unloaded. The techniques of subclassing and unsubclassing and the special considerations of message loop/message pump plug-in architecture are discussed in more depth in the next chapter when we delve into programming with the Netscape plug-in SDK.

Plug-ins and the Microsoft Foundation Classes

Many plug-in developers, especially those building Microsoft Windows plug-ins, want to simplify the process as much as possible, and using the Microsoft Foundation Classes is one of the first solutions that comes to mind. MFC provides a number of class methods that greatly reduce the complexity of plug-in code, including a handy window class function called SubclassWindow that does what its name implies. However, using MFC for anything other than plug-in window subclassing and window event processing opens up a large can of worms. This section explains the problems with using MFC to build Netscape plug-ins and provides enough instruction that you should have little trouble using most of the functionality of MFC classes in writing your plug-in.

When you build a plug-in DLL using MFC, it is very important that the DLL contain a global CWinApp-derived object just like a normal MFC application. The MFC DLL requires a global CWinApp object in order for the MFC classes to work correctly. This is a basic requirement of all MFC DLLs, and its importance to your plug-in DLL can't be overemphasized. Without a global CWinApp object, your MFC DLL will not function properly.

The trick to building a successful plug-in using MFC is to completely understand the reason that problems arise in the first place. To review briefly, MFC is nothing more than a collection of classes that encapsulate the entire Microsoft Windows programming API. Instead of calling functions like **CreateWindowEx** directly in your source code, the MFC class CWnd (and any class derived from CWnd) provides a simpler **Create** function that makes the call to **CreateWindowEx** for you. Figure 10.3 shows an example of MFC source code pertaining to CWnd creation. Notice the use of ASSERT lines in the MFC source code. These ASSERTs identify assumptions that the code is making or dependencies that aren't immediately obvious but that will affect the function of MFC.

It is the ASSERT lines in the MFC source code (although not these particular ASSERT lines, as you'll find out next) that will give you the most trouble as you attempt to use MFC to build your plug-in. All of the problems you will encounter, except those that you cause yourself, have a common source: the Netscape plug-in architecture itself. Although MFC works well as a tool for building plug-ins, the

▬▬▬▬▬ **Figure 10.3** Sample MFC source code for CWnd object creation.

```
/////////////////////////////////////////////////////////////////////
//////////
// CWnd creation

BOOL CWnd::CreateEx(DWORD dwExStyle, LPCTSTR lpszClassName,
        LPCTSTR lpszWindowName, DWORD dwStyle,
        int x, int y, int nWidth, int nHeight,
        HWND hWndParent, HMENU nIDorHMenu, LPVOID lpParam)
```

Continued ...

```
{
        // allow modification of several common create parameters
        CREATESTRUCT cs;
        cs.dwExStyle = dwExStyle;
        cs.lpszClass = lpszClassName;
        cs.lpszName = lpszWindowName;
        cs.style = dwStyle;
        cs.x = x;
        cs.y = y;
        cs.cx = nWidth;
        cs.cy = nHeight;
        cs.hwndParent = hWndParent;
        cs.hMenu = nIDorHMenu;
        cs.hInstance = AfxGetInstanceHandle();
        cs.lpCreateParams = lpParam;

        if (!PreCreateWindow(cs))
        {
                PostNcDestroy();
                return FALSE;
        }

        AfxHookWindowCreate(this);
        HWND hWnd = ::CreateWindowEx(cs.dwExStyle, cs.lpszClass,
                        cs.lpszName, cs.style, cs.x, cs.y, cs.cx, cs.cy,
                        cs.hwndParent, cs.hMenu, cs.hInstance,
                        cs.lpCreateParams);
        if (!AfxUnhookWindowCreate())
                PostNcDestroy();            // cleanup if CreateWindowEx
                                            // fails too soon

        if (hWnd == NULL)
                return FALSE;
        ASSERT(hWnd == m_hWnd); // should have been set in send
                                // msg hook
```

```
        return TRUE;

}


// for child windows
BOOL CWnd::PreCreateWindow(CREATESTRUCT& cs)
{
        if (cs.lpszClass == NULL)
        {
                // no WNDCLASS provided - use child window default
                ASSERT(cs.style & WS_CHILD);
                cs.lpszClass = _afxWnd;
        }
        return TRUE;

}


BOOL CWnd::Create(LPCTSTR lpszClassName,
        LPCTSTR lpszWindowName, DWORD dwStyle,
        const RECT& rect,
        CWnd* pParentWnd, UINT nID,
        CCreateContext* pContext)
{
        // can't use for desktop or pop-up windows (use CreateEx
        // instead)
        ASSERT(pParentWnd != NULL);
        ASSERT((dwStyle & WS_POPUP) == 0);

        return CreateEx(0, lpszClassName, lpszWindowName,
                dwStyle | WS_CHILD,
                rect.left, rect.top,
                rect.right - rect.left, rect.bottom - rect.top,
                pParentWnd->GetSafeHwnd(), (HMENU)nID,
                (LPVOID)pContext);

}
```

fact is that the MFC application model is basically incompatible with the plug-in application model. MFC applications make all sorts of assumptions that are just not valid for plug-ins. It is the assumptions made by MFC that are identified by ASSERT lines, and to some extent by the rest of the MFC source code, that cause all the trouble.

To understand this point further, recall that instead of creating a new window as a typical application would do, your plug-in application must subclass the Navigator window. This means that the MFC code shown in Figure 10.3 is not executed when your plug-in window is created. Bypassing the normal CWnd creation process for the main window of your plug-in is the source of a lot of MFC plug-in grief. Many MFC classes assume that window creation has occurred normally and use ASSERT lines accordingly. When one of the ASSERTs fails as a result, you have a problem. Unfortunately, there's no simple solution to this problem; you must learn to create workaround code that either prevents MFC from executing the code that contains the ASSERT or sets up the condition required by MFC so that the ASSERT does not fail.

■■■■■

> Key concept: To build a plug-in using the Microsoft Foundation Classes (MFC) you must resolve any ASSERT failures that occur by reading the MFC source code and establishing conditions that prevent the ASSERT failure.

■■■■■

One of the best examples of the MFC ASSERT situation involves plug-in window unsubclassing. Typically, your plug-in MFC application will use the **SubclassWindow** function in the CWnd class to subclass the plug-in window supplied by Navigator. The following code snippet illustrates the key points of subclassing the plug-in window using a CWnd-derived class.

```
CMainWnd cwndTmp;         // example CWnd-derived class for the plug-in main
                          // window

HWND hwndPluginWindow;    // contains Navigator-supplied plug-in window handle


if (!(cwndTmp.SubclassWindow(hwndPluginWindow)))
{
```

```
        MessageBox(NULL,"SubclassWindow Failed","Error",MB_OK);
}
```

Once subclassing is complete, the plug-in code can proceed with whatever window setup needs to occur, such as adding controls or rendering display of the content type on the plug-in window. When the time comes to unload the plug-in module and destroy each of the plug-in instances, the application must unsubclass the Navigator window. Typically, the Microsoft Windows API function **SetWindowLong** will be called in a CWnd-derived class method named UnSubclassWindow (the unsubclass method can be named anything, though) like the following:

```
void CMainWnd::UnSubclassWindow()
{
        // Restore original Netscape WNDPROC
        WNDPROC*    lplpfn = GetSuperWndProcAddr();
        if ( !*lplpfn )
        {
                ASSERT(0);
                return;
        }
        // Set the original window procedure using Windows API function
        (WNDPROC)::SetWindowLong( m_hWnd, GWL_WNDPROC, (LONG) *lplpfn );
}
```

With such a simple example, very little can go wrong, and it's likely that the plug-in will work just fine while it's loaded. However, when the plug-in is unloaded and the Navigator plug-in window unsubclassed, a problem occurs. As the plug-in module is removed from memory and final cleanup is performed by MFC, the ASSERT failure shown in Figure 10.4 appears.

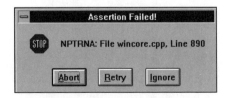

████████ **Figure 10.4** When MFC attempts to clean up during plug-in unloading, an ASSERT failure occurs.

The offending section of wincore.cpp is shown in Figure 10.5. By reading this source code and examining the line on which the ASSERT failed, you can track down the source of the problem and decide what the best workaround solution is. Lines 889 and 890 in wincore.cpp contain the following:

```
// Should have been detached by OnNcDestroy
ASSERT(!pMap->LookupPermanent(hWndOrig, p));
```

Notice that the first couple of lines in Figure 10.5 check to see if m_hWnd is equal to NULL. If it is NULL, the **DestroyWindow** function is exited immediately. The fact that a subsequent line in this function gets executed means that m_hWnd is not equal to NULL when the **DestroyWindow** function is called. It turns out that the normal CWnd destruction process calls the **Detach** function to remove the relationship between the MFC CWnd object and the Microsoft Windows HWND window handle. CWnd Detach'ing is bypassed entirely when the plug-in window is unsubclassed because the normal CWnd destruction process does not occur.

■■■■■■ **Figure 10.5** An ASSERT failure occurs in this section of **wincore.cpp** during plug-in shutdown.

```
BOOL CWnd::DestroyWindow()
{
        if (m_hWnd == NULL)
                return FALSE;


        CObject* p;
        CHandleMap* pMap = afxMapHWND();
        ASSERT(pMap != NULL);
        BOOL bInPermanentMap = pMap->LookupPermanent(m_hWnd, p);
#ifdef _DEBUG
        HWND hWndOrig = m_hWnd;
#endif
        BOOL bRet = ::DestroyWindow(m_hWnd);
        // Note that 'this' may have been deleted at this point.
```

```
        if (bInPermanentMap)
        {
                // Should have been detached by OnNcDestroy
                ASSERT(!pMap->LookupPermanent(hWndOrig, p));
        }
        else
        {
                ASSERT(m_hWnd == hWndOrig);
                // Detach after DestroyWindow called just in
                // case
                Detach();
        }
        return bRet;
}
```

The solution is to set m_hWnd = NULL following unsubclassing to prevent subsequent MFC operations from trying to do things with the HWND during cleanup. With m_hWnd set equal to NULL, MFC notices (in the **DestroyWindow** function) that there is no HWND attached to the CWnd-derived class and doesn't try to do additional Detach'ing or other CWnd-shutdown related activities. The following code snippet shows a modified **UnSubclassWindow** function that performs this extra step:

```
void CMainWnd::UnSubclassWindow()
{
        // Restore original Netscape WNDPROC
        WNDPROC*    lplpfn = GetSuperWndProcAddr();
        if ( !*lplpfn )
        {
                ASSERT(0);
```

```
            return;
        }
        // Set the original window procedure using Windows API function
        (WNDPROC)::SetWindowLong( m_hWnd, GWL_WNDPROC, (LONG) *lplpfn );
        m_hWnd = NULL;
    }
```

Another possible solution is demonstrated by the sample AVI plug-in provided with Netscape's Microsoft Windows plug-in SDK. In the AVI sample, a function named **KillAviWindow** executes the **Detach** function immediately following the unsubclassing. The **Detach** function has the same effect as setting m_hWnd equal to NULL in this context. The **KillAviWindow** function is shown in the following code snippet:

```
static void KillAviWindow(MyData *data)
{
    if (data->cAvi) {
        data->cAvi->Close();
        delete data->cAvi;
        data->cAvi = NULL;
    }
    UnSubclass(data);
    if (data->pWindow) {
        data->pWindow->Detach();
        delete data->pWindow;
        data->pWindow = NULL;
    }
}
```

Whether your code calls the **Detach** function or sets m_hWnd equal to NULL, this is an important step in the cleanup process of your plug-in. Like other problems associated with MFC as a plug-in development tool, the solution is to find out why the MFC source code is complaining and build an acceptable workaround. Because MFC is nothing more than a wrapper around the Microsoft Windows API, a workaround should be possible for almost any problem you encounter, though some will take more effort than others.

Handling Plug-in API Function Calls

Netscape Navigator triggers plug-in API functions to notify the plug-in that it needs to do processing related to being a Navigator extension. The Navigator-triggered plug-in API functions are listed in Table 10.2. These functions define the plug-in interface and allow a plug-in to function in conjunction with Navigator. Note that the plug-in API functions shown are provided by the Netscape plug-in SDK. You must use the SDK in order for these functions to work; you cannot just build a DLL from scratch and include your own version of these functions. The reason is that the plug-in SDK provided by Netscape maps each of the plug-in API functions to an internal SDK function and then builds a function table used by Navigator to access plug-in entry points through several plug-in SDK functions about which you need not be concerned.

████████ **Table 10.2** Plug-in Functions Triggered by Netscape Navigator

Function	Triggered When
NPError NPP_Initialize(void)	The plug-in DLL is loaded.
void NPP_Shutdown(void)	The plug-in DLL is unloaded.
NPError NP_LOADDS NPP _New(NPMIMEType plugin Type, NPP instance, uint16 mode, int16 argc, char* argn[], char* argv[], NPSavedData* saved)	Netscape Navigator creates a new instance of a MIME type handled by the plug-in and passes control for display to the plug-in.
NPError NP_LOADDS NPP _Destroy(NPP instance, NPSavedData** save)	An existing plug-in instance is removed from the Navigator window as in the case of the user switching to a new Web page.
NPError NP_LOADDS NPP _SetWindow(NPP instance, NPWindow* window)	A change occurs to the window of a plug-in instance, including creation and re-sizing.
NPError NP_LOADDS NPP _NewStream(NPP instance, NPMIMEType type, NPStream* stream, NPBool seekable, uint16* stype)	A new data stream (NPStream *stream) becomes available for a plug-in instance specified by the NPP instance parameter.

■■■■ **Table 10.2** Continued

Function	Triggered When
void NP_LOADDS NPP _StreamAsFile(NPP instance, NPStream* stream, const char* fname)	Navigator reads a file, either from cache or from a local file, and sends the contents to a plug-in instance in the form of a stream.
NPError NP_LOADDS NPP _DestroyStream(NPP instance, NPStream* stream, NPError reason)	A previously open stream is closed and deleted for some reason (NPError reason).
int32 NP_LOADDS NPP_ WriteReady(NPP instance, NPStream* stream)	Navigator is preparing to call NPP_Write to send data over a stream to a plug-in instance, and it needs to know how many bytes of data the instance is prepared to receive in response to the NPP_Write call.
int32 NP_LOADDS NPP _Write(NPP instance, NPStream* stream, int32 offset, int32 len, void* buffer)	Navigator sends data over a stream to a plug-in instance (NPP instance) after determining how many bytes to send through NPP_WriteReady.
void NP_LOADDS NPP _Print(NPP instance, NPPrint* platformPrint)	A plug-in instance needs to be printed, as in response to a File|Print menu selection.
int16 NPP_HandleEvent(NPP instance, void* event)	Navigator has received a window event for a Macintosh-plug-in window, and it needs to pass the event notification along to the Macintosh plug-in module for processing (NPP_HandleEvent is Macintosh only).

■■■■■

This section describes each plug-in API function in more detail and shows sample source code for each. Bear in mind that what your plug-in code does in response to these plug-in API function calls depends primarily on your programming technique. There are no hard and fast rules about what your plug-in code should do in these functions or how it should do it. Remember that even the plug-in SDK file **npshell.cpp** provided by Netscape provides only one possible strategy for coding a plug-in module. In the next chapter on programming with the SDK, we elaborate on a plug-in module design strategy that we find particularly useful for building Microsoft Windows plug-ins using MFC, and you'll find portions of this strategy outlined here as well.

NPError NPP_Initialize(void)

The **NPP_Initialize** function is triggered once when the plug-in module is loaded by Navigator.

Write code in a plug-in module's **NPP_Initialize** function to provide global initialization for the plug-in module. **NPP_Initialize** returns an error value indicating which error, if any, occurred during initialization. The possible return values are:

- NPERR_NO_ERROR. Initialization was successful.
- NPERR_GENERIC_ERROR. An error occurred during initialization.
- NPERR_OUT_OF_MEMORY_ERROR. An out-of-memory error occurred.

A typical **NPP_Initialize** function will either do nothing and return NPERR_NO_ERROR, as in the following code snippet, or attempt to perform one-time initialization for the plug-in module and return any of the three return values. Initialization could include loading dynamic libraries required by the module, allocating memory for use by the module, or even executing an external application that will assist in plug-in functionality in some way.

```
NPError NPP_Initialize(void)
{
        return NPERR_NO_ERROR;
}
```

void NPP_Shutdown(void)

The **NPP_Shutdown** function is triggered once when the plug-in module is unloaded by Navigator.

Code in the **NPP_Shutdown** function should handle any cleanup required for the plug-in module. If memory was allocated for the plug-in module, it should be freed in **NPP_Shutdown**. If dynamic libraries were loaded, they can be unloaded in **NPP_Shutdown**. If external applications were started when the plug-in module was initialized, they can be instructed to terminate themselves. There is no return value for this function.

```
void NPP_Shutdown(void)

{

}
```

NPError NP_LOADDS NPP_New(NPMIMEType pluginType, NPP instance, uint16 mode, int16 argc, char* argn[], char* argv[], NPSavedData* saved)

The **NPP_New** function is called to inform the plug-in module of a new plug-in instance. It is called before Navigator calls **NPP_SetWindow** for the plug-in instance. The **NPP_New** function parameters are:

- *NPMIMEType pluginType.* Contains the MIME type (**content-type/subtype** pair) of the new plug-in instance.
- *NPP instance.* Identifies the plug-in instance. This NPP structure is considered a *handle* to the plug-in instance.
- *uint16 mode.* Indicates the mode of the plug-in instance: NP_EMBED, NP_FULL, or NP_BACKGROUND.
- *int16 argc.* The number of <EMBED> tag parameters supplied. Determines the length of each parameter array.
- *char* argn[].* An array, *argc* items in length, that contains the names of any <EMBED> tag parameters.
- *char* argv[].* An array, *argc* items in length, that contains the values of any <EMBED> tag parameters.
- *NPSavedData* saved.* Contains any saved data associated with the URL of this plug-in instance. See **NPP_Destroy.**

The MIME type of the new instance (in the form of a char *) and any parameters provided by the <EMBED> tag are provided to the plug-in module through this function call. If you saved data for the previous instance of this plug-in, Navigator provides the saved data to your plug-in module through the NPSavedData *saved parameter. The NPSavedData structure has the following format:

```
typedef struct _NPSavedData

{

        int32   len;

        void*   buf;

} NPSavedData;
```

Also provided is an NPP instance handle that the plug-in module should save for later reference. Several of the Netscape Navigator functions accept an NPP instance handle to uniquely identify the plug-in instance. For example, the **NPN_GetURL** function accepts the NPP instance handle of the plug-in instance making the **NPN_GetURL** request. We can't emphasize enough how important it is that your **NPP_New** function preserve the NPP instance handle for the new plug-in instance. The NPP structure has the following format:

```
typedef struct _NPP
{
        void*   pdata;              /* plug-in private data */
        void*   ndata;              /* netscape private data */
} NPP_t;


typedef NPP_t*  NPP;
```

The sample code listed in Figure 10.6 shows how a plug-in module will normally handle the **NPP_New** function call. Notice that the NPP instance handle for the new plug-in instance is saved in *nppInstance*, a CMainDialog instance variable. Later, when the instance needs to make Navigator **NPN_*** function calls, the plug-in instance can provide the correct NPP instance handle. Also, note the way this sample code supports multiple simultaneous plug-in instances using a dynamic CPtrArray named *instanceArray*. The sample code shown is just one possible way to handle the requirements of code for the **NPP_New API** function.

▬▬▬▬▬ **Figure 10.6** Sample code for the **NPP_New API** function.

```
NPError NP_LOADDS NPP_New(NPMIMEType pluginType, NPP instance, uint16
mode, int16 argc,
                char* argn[], char* argv[], NPSavedData* saved)
{
        int iArraySize, a;
        CMainDialog *cmdlgTmp;


        if (instance == NULL)
                return NPERR_INVALID_INSTANCE_ERROR;
```

Continued ...

```
instance->pdata = NPN_MemAlloc(sizeof(PluginInstance));
PluginInstance* This = (PluginInstance*) instance->pdata;


if (This == NULL)
        return NPERR_OUT_OF_MEMORY_ERROR;


// The PluginInstance structure in this example contains two
// members:
//      NPWindow*        fWindow;
//      int       iArrayIndex;


This->fWindow = NULL;


// Add one element to the CWinApp object's CPtrArray
// instanceArray
iArraySize = theApp.instanceArray.GetSize();
This->iArrayIndex = iArraySize;
iArraySize = iArraySize + 1;
theApp.instanceArray.SetSize(iArraySize,1);


// Create a new CMainDialog object and add a pointer to it to
// the CPtrArray instanceArray
cmdlgTmp = new CMainDialog(NULL);
theApp.instanceArray.SetAt(iArrayIndex,cmdlgTmp);


// set instance variables of CMainDialog class
cmdlgTmp->m_hWnd = (HWND)NULL;
cmdlgTmp->nppInstance = instance;
cmdlgTmp->csNameArray.SetSize(argc,1);
cmdlgTmp->csValueArray.SetSize(argc,1);
for(a=0;a < argc;a++)   // store all parameters passed to this
                        // plug-in instance
{
```

```
            cmdlgTmp->csNameArray[a] = ppParamStruct.argn[a];

            cmdlgTmp->csValueArray[a] = ppParamStruct.argv[a];

      }


      return NPERR_NO_ERROR;

}
```

The possible return values for **NPP_New** are:

- NPERR_NO_ERROR - NPP_. New API function call completed success-fully.
- NPERR_GENERIC_ERROR. A generic error occurred.
- NPERR_INVALID_INSTANCE_ERROR. An invalid instance handle was provided.
- NPERR_OUT_OF_MEMORY_ERROR. An out-of-memory error occurred.

The key points to remember about the **NPP_New** function are:

- Some mechanism must be designed to enable multiple simultaneous plug-in instances.
- The NPP instance handle must be saved for each plug-in instance if your plug-in code intends to use any of the **NPN_*** Navigator functions.
- Your code won't get another chance to store the parameters passed in the <EMBED> tag, so the entire set of parameters needs to be saved in the plug-in instance or acted upon immediately.
- If data was saved by the plug-in module for the previous occurrence of the plug-in instance (unique occurrences are determined by the URL used to access the plug-in data type), it will be returned to the plug-in through the NPSavedData *saved parameter.

Finally, you should realize that Navigator has not yet provided a window handle to the plug-in instance. Since nowhere in the plug-in API specification does it say that **NPP_SetWindow** will always occur immediately following **NPP_New**, your code in **NPP_SetWindow** must have a way to reconcile the plug-in instance created in

NPP_New with the window handle provided at some later time by Navigator's call to NPP_SetWindow. In Figure 10.6 you see that the PluginInstance structure and NPP instance are used to store the array index of the new plug-in instance. When NPP_SetWindow occurs later, the NPP instance handle will include the array index, and the window handle provided for the plug-in instance can be applied to the correct element of the CPtrArray instanceArray. This type of reconciliation between plug-in instance and Navigator window handle is essential if multiple instances of your plug-in MIME type are ever used simultaneously on a single Web page. It is particularly important if different <EMBED> tag parameters are passed to each of the multiple instances because the <EMBED> tag parameters will typically instruct the plug-in instance to behave in a certain way. If your plug-in module is not able to reconcile plug-in instance with Navigator-supplied plug-in window handle, there is no telling which plug-in instance will be associated with which set of <EMBED> tag parameters.

NPError NP_LOADDS NPP_Destroy(NPP instance, NPSavedData** save)

The NPP_Destroy function is called to inform the plug-in module that a plug-in instance is being removed from the Navigator. It is usually called only when Navigator shuts down or when the user leaves the current page that contains one or more plug-in instances and goes to another page. Parameters to the NPP_Destroy function are:

- *NPP instance.* Identifies the plug-in instance. This NPP structure is considered a *handle* to the plug-in instance.
- *NPSavedData** save.* A reference to the pointer in which the plug-in can save data for use when the URL is reactivated.

The plug-in code for NPP_Destroy should be certain to free any memory previously allocated by the plug-in. NPP_Destroy should also be used to unsubclass the plug-in window so that Navigator is able to regain control over its display area after the plug-in module is fully unloaded. Although the NPP_Destroy function pertains only to the plug-in instance referenced by NPP instance, it will almost always occur for every plug-in instance on the Navigator window if it occurs for one. Note, however, that all of the plug-in instances can be destroyed without encountering an

NPP_Shutdown, as in the case of a reload of the current Web page by the user, which first destroys every plug-in instance and then triggers **NPP_New** to re-create them.

In addition to informing the plug-in module of the need to destroy the plug-in instance and unsubclass the plug-in window, the **NPP_Destroy** function gives the instance the option of saving data for use in subsequent accesses to the URL that activated the plug-in instance. In other words, Navigator considers the URL of a plug-in instance to represent a unique instance of the plug-in MIME type. If the user visits a single URL multiple times without quitting Navigator, each subsequent visit after the first one can be considered reactivating the plug-in instance instead of activating a completely new instance each time. If the plug-in code is designed to save data in **NPP_Destroy**, each subsequent reactivation can retrieve the saved data when Navigator calls **NPP_New**. The saved data technique enables your plug-in to maintain a consistent state between reactivations rather than presenting a fresh version of the plug-in every time. One of the best examples of a way saved data can be used is the case of a video- or animation-oriented plug-in that needs to continue from where it left off if the user leaves the page and returns later. Figure 10.7 shows an example of a **NPP_Destroy** function, including the saving of data for use in reactivations of the plug-in's URL.

▬▬▬▬ **Figure 10.7** Sample code for the **NPP_Destroy** API function.

```
NPError NP_LOADDS
NPP_Destroy(NPP instance, NPSavedData** save)
{
        CMainDialog *cmdlgTmp;
        if (instance == NULL)
                return NPERR_INVALID_INSTANCE_ERROR;


        PluginInstance* This = (PluginInstance*) instance->pdata;


        // The PluginInstance structure in this example contains two
        // members:
        //      NPWindow*       fWindow;
```

Continued ...

```
//       int      iArrayIndex;
if (This != NULL)
{

        cmdlgTmp = (CMainDialog *)
        theApp.instanceArray.GetAt(This->iArrayIndex);

        ASSERT(cmdlgTmp != (void *)NULL);


        cmdlgTmp->UnSubclassWindow();

        delete cmdlgTmp;


        theApp.instanceArray.SetAt(This->iArrayIndex,
        (void *)NULL);


        // Save data for the plug-in instance so that next time
        // the same URL is accessed, Navigator will provide

        // this data (in *saved) during NPP_New

        NPSavedData* savedData = (NPSavedData*) NPN_MemAlloc
        (sizeof(NPSavedData));

        char* myData = (char*) NPN_MemAlloc(15);

        strcpy(myData, "Here it is.\n");


        savedData->len = 15;

        savedData->buf = (void*) myData;


        *save = savedData;


        NPN_MemFree(instance->pdata);

        instance->pdata = NULL;
}

return NPERR_NO_ERROR;

}
```

Interesting to note on the subject of URLs representing unique MIME instances is that Navigator will call **NPP_New** only for a single occurrence of a given URL on a single Web page. This means that if your Web page needs multiple instances of the same exact file, you must make a copy of the file and give it a different name so that it has a different URL. Then, Navigator will trigger **NPP_New** for each occurrence because it considers them to be different MIME instances, each one of which deserves its own space on the Navigator window.

NPError NP_LOADDS NPP_SetWindow(NPP instance, NPWindow window)*

The **NPP_SetWindow** function is called after the **NPP_New** function in order for Navigator to supply the plug-in with the platform-dependent Navigator window handle for the plug-in instance. **NPP_SetWindow** is called both the first time that a plug-in instance is created and any time that the instance is resized. Parameters to the **NPP_SetWindow** function are:

- *NPP instance.* Identifies the plug-in instance. This NPP structure is considered a *handle* to the plug-in instance.
- *NPWindow* window.* Provides the plug-in with the platform-dependent window handle for the plug-in instance.

This function is called only if the plug-in instance is of the type **NP_EMBED** or **NP_FULL**. **NP_BACKGROUND** plug-in instances do not receive an **NPP_SetWindow** call. Subsequent calls to **NPP_SetWindow** for a single instance indicate that the window has been resized. Plug-in code can choose to ignore the resize notification if it so desires, or it can alter its behavior or its display to account for the change in size, as in the case of an image-display plug-in that desires to maintain aspect ratio of the image displayed. The window parameter, or its platform-specific window member value, can be NULL. This value indicates that the plug-in should no longer use the specified window and must free any resources associated with it. However, in our experience the **NPP_Destroy** function is always triggered when Navigator needs the plug-in instance to relinquish use of the window handle, so you can count on the cleanup process already coded for your **NPP_Destroy** function in this circumstance.

The **NPP_SetWindow** return value can be any of the following:

- NPERR_NO_ERROR. The **NPP_SetWindow** function completed successfully.
- NPERR_GENERIC_ERROR. A generic error occurred in **NPP_SetWindow**.
- NPERR_OUT_OF_MEMORY_ERROR. An out-of-memory error occurred.

Figure 10.8 shows sample source code for the **NPP_SetWindow** function. The sample code shown doesn't bother to check for the resize occurrence mentioned previously, but your code might want to do so. The sample code also makes what we believe to be a valid assumption that if the window parameter is NULL but the instance parameter is valid, the Navigator window went away, and cleanup and subclassing will occur upon a subsequent call to the **NPP_Destroy** function. If Netscape changes the behavior of this API function in newer versions of the plug-in API, this assumption may no longer be valid, and you'll need to be sure that your **NPP_SetWindow** code handles cleanup and unsubclassing explicitly in response to such a condition.

■■■■■■■■ **Figure 10.8** Sample code for the **NPP_SetWindow** API function.

```
NPError NP_LOADDS
NPP_SetWindow(NPP instance, NPWindow* window)
{
        if (instance == NULL)
                return NPERR_INVALID_INSTANCE_ERROR;


        PluginInstance* This = (PluginInstance*) instance->pdata;

        if (!window)
                return NPERR_GENERIC_ERROR;

        if (!instance)
                return  NPERR_INVALID_INSTANCE_ERROR;
        if (!This)
```

```
        return NPERR_GENERIC_ERROR;


    if (!window->window && !This->fWindow) // spurious entry
        return NPERR_NO_ERROR;


    if (!window->window && This->fWindow)
    {   // window went away
        return NPERR_NO_ERROR;
    }


    if (!This->fWindow && window->window)
    {   // First time in--no window created by plugin yet
        This->fWindow = window;


        CMainDialog *cmdlgTmp;
        cmdlgTmp = (CMainDialog *)
theApp.instanceArray.GetAt(This->iArrayIndex);


        if (!(cmdlgTmp->SubclassWindow((HWND)window->window)))
        {
            MessageBox(NULL,"SubclassWindow
Failed","Error",MB_OK);
        }
        else
        {
            cmdlgTmp->Invalidate(TRUE);
            cmdlgTmp->UpdateWindow();
        }
    }


    return NPERR_NO_ERROR;
}
```

Remember that your **NPP_SetWindow** code must handle reconciliation of the plug-in window with the correct plug-in instance. In the code shown in Figure 10.8 we use a simple method for reconciliation that reads the iArrayIndex variable from the PluginInstance structure provided as part of NPP instance. Recall that iArrayIndex was set in the **NPP_New** function so that any time that Navigator supplies an NPP instance handle, our code can simply read iArrayIndex and reference the corresponding array element in our plug-in module's array of plug-in instances. Although we use the MFC class CPtrArray to manage the array of plug-in instances, you could use any other array management technique to accomplish the same thing. In the plug-in SDK provided by Netscape you'll find that a linked list is used and that several functions are provided for traversing the list to locate the correct plug-in instance. The linked-list approach works, but we prefer the simpler array-index method featured in this chapter and in the next.

NPError NP_LOADDS NPP_NewStream(NPP instance, NPMIMEType type, NPStream* stream, NPBool seekable, uint16* stype)

The **NPP_NewStream** function is called when a new data stream (NPStream *stream) intended for the plug-in instance is created by Navigator. Parameters supplied to the **NPP_NewStream** function are:

- *NPP instance.* Identifies the plug-in instance. This NPP structure is considered a *handle* to the plug-in instance.
- *NPMIMEType type.* Contains the MIME type (**content-type/subtype** pair) of the new stream.
- *NPStream* stream.* Identifies the stream instance. This NPStream structure is considered a *handle* to the stream.
- *NPBool seekable.* Specifies whether or not the stream is seekable. TRUE = seekable FALSE = not seekable.
- *uint16* stype.* Allows the plug-in to request a stream mode other than NP_NORMAL. (NP_SEEK or NP_ASFILE).

Streams in the plug-in API represent the data retrieved when Navigator accesses a particular URL. The plug-in API makes it possible for plug-ins to handle data from the network through streams so that Navigator can manage the complexity involved in network communications and protocols, while the plug-in code needs to know only how to work with Navigator data streams. There can be more than one stream active for each plug-in instance, and Navigator identifies both the NPP instance and the NPStream *stream handles as parameters to the **NPP_NewStream** function. This makes it possible to distinguish between streams owned by the same instance and determine which instance owns the stream. The NPStream structure has the following format:

```
typedef struct _NPStream
{
    void*       pdata;               /* plug-in private data */
    void*       ndata;               /* netscape private data */
    const char* url;
    uint32      end;
    uint32      lastmodified;
} NPStream;
```

The void *pdata element is a pointer to plug-in private data, similar to the pdata element of the NPP structure. The uint32 lastmodifed element is a timestamp that Navigator uses to determine whether to get the stream from the server or from the cache. The void *ndata element is Netscape private data. The const char *url element is a string identifying the URL of the stream. The uint32 end element is used by Navigator to locate the end of the stream.

When a new plug-in instance is first created, Navigator calls the **NPP_NewStream** function to provide to the plug-in module the content of the URL used to activate the plug-in instance. The plug-in module should make use of the stream-related API functions to receive and process MIME-type content for the plug-in. Many plug-ins will use only API stream functions to receive data for the original file, but it is also possible for a plug-in instance to create additional streams by calling Navigator functions like **NPN_GetURL** or **NPN_PostURL**.

When a new stream is created, it is initially in *push mode*, wherein the stream data is provided one chunk at a time as it becomes available to Navigator. If a plug-in so chooses, it can switch to *pull mode*, in which data is provided over the stream only when the plug-in calls the Navigator function **NPN_RequestRead**. Depending on the technical design of the plug-in, pull mode may be an option for stream handling. However, push mode is the recommended strategy for almost all stream data transfer in a plug-in module.

Additionally, the plug-in instance can request that Navigator save the stream to a temporary file instead of providing it as a stream to the plug-in. To convert the stream to a temporary file, the uint16 *stype pointer passed in to the **NPP_NewStream** function is used to pass the value NP_ASFILE back to Navigator. The following line of code demonstrates how this is done:

```
  *stype = NP_ASFILE;
```

The use of temporary files for the storage of stream data is strongly discouraged. It is much better to have your plug-in code deal with the stream as a stream rather than use NP_ASFILE. When you use NP_ASFILE, don't expect to receive NPP_WriteReady or NPP_Write calls for the stream. Instead, your plug-in code should expect an **NPP_StreamAsFile** function call that informs it of the filename

■■■■■■■ **Figure 10.9** Sample code for the **NPP_NewStream** API function.

```
NPError NP_LOADDS

NPP_NewStream(NPP instance, NPMIMEType type, NPStream *stream, NPBool
seekable,

                    uint16 *stype)
{

     if (instance == NULL)
            return NPERR_INVALID_INSTANCE_ERROR;
     PluginInstance* This = (PluginInstance*) instance->pdata;


     *stype = NP_NORMAL;


     // code should store the NPStream *stream handle for future
     // reference and prepare

     // to do something with the stream data--but it doesn't because
     // this is just a sample
```

```
        return NPERR_NO_ERROR;

}
```

used for the temporary file. The following code shows a sample **NPP_NewStream** function that uses NP_NORMAL mode to receive the stream:

The possible return values of **NPP_NewStream** are:

- NPERR_NO_ERROR—The **NPP_NewStream** function completed successfully.
- NPERR_GENERIC_ERROR—A generic error occurred.
- NPERR_OUT_OF_MEMORY_ERROR—An out-of-memory error occurred.

void NP_LOADDS NPP_StreamAsFile (NPP instance, NPStream stream, const char* fname)*

The **NPP_StreamAsFile** function is triggered by Navigator following a call to **NPP_NewStream** in which the uint16 *stype value is set to NP_ASFILE. Parameters supplied to **NPP_StreamAsFile** are:

- *NPP instance*. Identifies the plug-in instance. This NPP structure is considered a *handle* to the plug-in instance.
- *NPStream* stream*. Identifies the stream instance. This NPStream structure is considered a *handle* to the stream.
- *const char* fname*. Contains the filename of the temporary file created by Navigator. NULL if an error occurred.

If your plug-in converts a stream to a temporary file using NP_ASFILE, the **NPP_StreamAsFile** function enables the plug-in to discover the file's name. Figure 10.10 shows a sample **NPP_StreamAsFile** function.

```
void NP_LOADDS
NPP_StreamAsFile(NPP instance, NPStream *stream, const char* fname)
{
        CString csFileName;
        if (instance == NULL)
                return;

        PluginInstance* This = (PluginInstance*) instance->pdata;
        csFileName = fname;
        // csFileName should now be saved for use later (after
        // Navigator finishes writing data to the file)
}
```

If an error occurs in Navigator's attempt to convert the stream to a file, the parameter fname is NULL. **NPP_StreamAsFile** has no return value.

NPError NP_LOADDS
NPP_DestroyStream(NPP instance,
NPStream* stream, NPError reason)

The **NPP_DestroyStream** function is triggered when a Navigator stream is destroyed. Parameters are:

- *NPP instance.* Identifies the plug-in instance. This NPP structure is considered a *handle* to the plug-in instance.
- *NPStream* stream.* Identifies the stream instance. This NPStream structure is considered a *handle* to the stream.
- *NPError reason.* Contains a value that represents the reason for destroying the stream.

Figure 10.11 shows a sample **NPP_DestroyStream** function. Plug-in code for the **NPP_DestroyStream** function will most likely need to wrap up whatever activity was occurring with the stream. There are two situations in which a stream will be

■■■■■ **Figure 10.11** Sample code for the NPP_DestroyStream API
function.

```
NPError NP_LOADDS
NPP_DestroyStream(NPP instance, NPStream *stream, NPError reason)
{
        if (instance == NULL)
                return NPERR_INVALID_INSTANCE_ERROR;
        PluginInstance* This = (PluginInstance*) instance->pdata;


        if(reason == NPRES_NETWORK_ERR || reason == NPRES_USER_BREAK)
        {
                // Stream was terminated prematurely. Perform cleanup
                // accordingly.
        }
        else
        {
                // Stream completed successfully (NPRES_DONE).
        }


        return NPERR_NO_ERROR;
}
```

destroyed: either Navigator finished with the stream normally or the stream was terminated abnormally, and Navigator could not finish with the stream. These two situations are reflected by the three possible values for the NPError reason parameter.

The parameter reason contains one of the following values to specify the reason
that the stream is destroyed:

- NPRES_NETWORK_ERR. A network error occurred, closing the stream.
- NPRES_USER_BREAK. The user requested that the stream be closed.
- NPRES_DONE. Navigator finished with the stream.

```
int32 NP_LOADDS NPP_WriteReady(NPP instance, NPStream* stream)
```

The **NPP_WriteReady** function is called when Navigator is preparing to call the **NPP_Write** function. The parameters to **NPP_WriteReady** are:

- *NPP instance.* Identifies the plug-in instance. This NPP structure is considered a *handle* to the plug-in instance.
- *NPStream* stream.* Identifies the stream instance. This NPStream structure is considered a *handle* to the stream.

NPP_WriteReady should be thought of as "Navigator is getting ready to write data to the stream so that the plug-in can receive it," but Navigator first wants to know how much data the plug-in would like to receive at this time. The name of **NPP_WriteReady** and its related **NPP_Write** function can be very confusing. Just remember that Navigator triggers the plug-in API functions **NPP_***; they aren't called by your plug-in code. Therefore, the term *write* refers to what Navigator is trying to do by triggering the function, not to anything that your plug-in is going to do to write data over the stream. The return value of **NPP_WriteReady** tells Navigator how many bytes it should send to the plug-in during the next call to the **NPP_Write** function. Figure 10.12 shows a sample **NPP_WriteReady** function.

If the plug-in instance wants zero bytes because it isn't prepared to accept any data for the stream just yet, return 0. Navigator will continue triggering the

■■■■■■ **Figure 10.12** Sample code for the **NPP_WriteReady** API function.

```
int32 STREAMBUFSIZE = 0X0FFFFFFF;


int32 NP_LOADDS
NPP_WriteReady(NPP instance, NPStream *stream)
{
        if (instance != NULL)
                PluginInstance* This = (PluginInstance*) instance-
                >pdata;

        return STREAMBUFSIZE;    // Number of bytes the plug-in is ready
                                 // to accept in NPP_Write()

}
```

NPP_WriteReady function until it receives a return value greater than zero. If the plug-in doesn't want the stream data at all and would like to discard its contents, return some large number from **NPP_WriteReady**() and ignore the data provided over the stream in the next call to **NPP_Write**(). Note that the return value of **NPP_WriteReady** does not guarantee a minimum number of bytes in **NPP_Write**; it determines the maximum number of bytes Navigator will provide in **NPP_Write**.

int32 NP_LOADDS NPP_Write(NPP instance, NPStream stream, int32 offset, int32 len, void* buffer)*

NPP_Write is triggered by Navigator in order to provide data to a plug-in instance over an existing stream. Parameters to **NPP_Write** are:

- *NPP instance.* Identifies the plug-in instance. This NPP structure is considered a *handle* to the plug-in instance.
- *NPStream* stream.* Identifies the stream instance. This NPStream structure is considered a *handle* to the stream.
- *int32 offset.* The logical position of the contents of void *buffer in the entire stream.
- *int32 len.* Indicates the number of bytes of data provided in void *buffer.
- *void* buffer.* Contains data for the stream instance. The size of buffer is indicated by the len parameter.

Remember that Navigator triggers the plug-in API functions **NPP_***; they aren't called by your plug-in code. Therefore, the term *write* refers to what Navigator is trying to do by triggering the function, not to anything that your plug-in is going to do to write data over the stream. Figure 10.13 shows a sample **NPP_Write** function.

■■■■ **Figure 10.13** Sample code for the **NPP_Write** API function.

```
int32 NP_LOADDS

NPP_Write(NPP instance, NPStream *stream, int32 offset, int32 len, void
*buffer)

{

        if (instance != NULL)
```

Continued ...

```
        PluginInstance* This = (PluginInstance*) instance-
        >pdata;


    // code should do something with the data in void *buffer


    return len;

}
```

▄▄▄▄▄▄▄

The **NPP_Write** function returns the number of bytes consumed by the plug-in. Note that a plug-in must consume at least as many bytes as indicated by the preceding **NPP_WriteReady** call (or the entire buffer if the buffer is smaller than the size indicated by **NPP_WriteReady**); otherwise, data will be lost. A negative return value causes an error on the stream, which is subsequently destroyed with a call to **NPP_DestroyStream**.

void NP_LOADDS NPP_Print(NPP instance, NPPrint printInfo)*

The **NPP_Print** function is called when the user chooses to print the current Navigator window, including any plug-in instances that are active. Parameters to **NPP_Print** are:

- *NPP instance.* Identifies the plug-in instance. This NPP structure is considered a *handle* to the plug-in instance.
- *NPPrint* printInfo.* Supplies platform-specific print information such as printer port number or a printing device context.

There are two different modes for a printable plug-in instance: NP_FULL and NP_EMBED. When a plug-in is in NP_FULL mode, its display represents the entire Web page; an NP_EMBED plug-in instance can have more information displayed on the Web page, including HTML and even other plug-in instances. The NPPrint structure is a union of two other structures: one for NP_FULL plug-in mode and the other for NP_EMBED. The NPPrint structure has the following format:

```
typedef struct _NPPrint
{
```

```
    uint16              mode;          /* NP_FULL or NP_EMBED */
    union
    {
        NPFullPrint     fullPrint;  /* if mode is NP_FULL */
        NPEmbedPrint    embedPrint; /* if mode is NP_EMBED */
    } print;
} NPPrint;


typedef struct _NPFullPrint
{
    NPBool      pluginPrinted;      /* Set TRUE if plugin handled fullscreen
                                       printing */

    NPBool      printOne;           /* TRUE if plugin should print one copy
                                       to default printer */

    void*       platformPrint;      /* Platform-specific printing info */
} NPFullPrint;


typedef struct _NPEmbedPrint
{
    NPWindow    window;
    void*       platformPrint;      /* Platform-specific printing info */
} NPEmbedPrint;
```

If your plug-in would like to take over printing completely when it is in full-screen mode, use the following line of code to indicate this to Navigator and then handle printing as required by your plug-in:

```
printInfo->pluginPrinted = TRUE;
```

To allow Netscape to handle printing for your plug-in in the normal Navigator fashion of printing the entire Web page, use the following line of code to indicate this to Navigator, and then do no printing in **NPP_Print**:

```
printInfo->pluginPrinted = FALSE;
```

Note that printOne is equal to TRUE if the **Print** button was clicked as opposed to the print menu selected. Figure 10.14 shows a sample **NPP_Print** function.

■■■■■ **Figure 10.14** Sample code for the **NPP_Print** API function.

```
void NP_LOADDS
NPP_Print(NPP instance, NPPrint* printInfo)
{
        if(printInfo == NULL)
                return;


        if (instance != NULL)
        {
                PluginInstance* This =
(PluginInstance*) instance->pdata;

                if (printInfo->mode == NP_FULL)
                {
                        void* platformPrint =
printInfo->print.fullPrint.platformPrint;
                        NPBool printOne =
printInfo->print.fullPrint.printOne;


                        printInfo->print.fullPrint.pluginPrinted =
                        FALSE;
                        // NPP_Print will be called a second time with
                        // printInfo->mode = NP_EMBED

                        // as a result of setting pluginPrinted = FALSE
                        // for an NP_FULL mode plug-in

                }
                else
                {
                        NPWindow* printWindow =
&(printInfo->print.embedPrint.window);
                        void* platformPrint =
printInfo->print.embedPrint.platformPrint;


                        HPEN hPen, hPenOld;
                        #ifdef WIN32
```

```
                              LOGBRUSH lb;

                              lb.lbStyle = BS_SOLID;

                              lb.lbColor = RGB(128, 128, 128);

                              lb.lbHatch = 0;


                              hPen = ExtCreatePen(PS_COSMETIC |
PS_SOLID, 1, &lb, 0, NULL);
                    #else

                              COLORREF cref = RGB(128, 128, 128);

                              hPen = CreatePen(PS_SOLID, 32, cref);
                    #endif
                    HDC hDC = (HDC)(DWORD)platformPrint;
                    hPenOld = (HPEN)SelectObject(hDC, hPen);


                    BOOL result = Rectangle(hDC,
                    (int)(printWindow->x),
                    (int)(printWindow->y),
                    (int)(printWindow->x + printWindow->width),
                    (int)(printWindow->y + printWindow->height));
                    SelectObject(hDC, hPenOld);
                    DeleteObject(hPen);
               }

          }

     }
```

On the Macintosh, one of the following structure elements contains the printer port:

- printInfo->print.embedPrint.platformPrint (for NP_EMBED mode)
- printInfo->print.fullPrint.platformPrint (for NP_FULL mode)

On Microsoft Windows, one of the structure elements (which one depends on the plug-in mode) contains a handle to the device context for printing. Your plug-in instance should use the handle to the device context supplied when generating its printout. Notice how the value of platformPrint is type-cast to HDC (a device context handle) in the sample code shown in Figure 10.14.

int16 NPP_HandleEvent(NPP instance, void event)*

Navigator has received a window event for a Macintosh-plug-in window, and it needs to pass the event notification along to the Macintosh plug-in module for processing (**NPP_HandleEvent** is Macintosh only). The parameters are:

- *NPP instance.* Identifies the plug-in instance. This NPP structure is considered a *handle* to the plug-in instance.
- void *event. A pointer to a Macintosh EventRecord.

Figure 10.15 shows a sample **NPP_HandleEvent** function.

The void *event passed as a parameter to **NPP_HandleEvent** is a Macintosh EventRecord*. Its value can be:

- *Any of the normal Macintosh event types.* Handle these events normally and return TRUE if handled.

Figure 10.15 Sample code for the **NPP_HandleEvent** API function.

```
int16 NPP_HandleEvent(NPP instance, void* event)
{
        NPBool eventHandled = FALSE;
        if (instance == NULL)
                return eventHandled;


        PluginInstance* This = (PluginInstance*) instance->pdata;


        return eventHandled;
}
```

- *getFocusEvent.* Informs the plug-in that it can become the recipient of key events by returning TRUE.
- *loseFocusEvent.* Informs the plug-in that it is no longer the recipient of key events.
- *adjustCursorEvent.* Indicates the mouse is over the plug-in. Return FALSE to leave the cursor unchanged.

Calling Navigator Functions from a Plug-in

Netscape Navigator makes a number of functions available to plug-ins that provide common plug-in functionality or enable Navigator memory- and stream-management. Navigator functions begin with NPN_ to distinguish them from the plug-in API functions (which begin with NPP_). Of the Navigator functions, the ones used most commonly in any plug-in are the memory- and stream-management functions. If a plug-in wants to access other URLs, either to receive the data streams directly or to provide a hyperlink-like feature, the two functions **NPN_GetURL** and **NPN_PostURL** make this possible. Table 10.3 shows the Navigator **NPN_*** functions.

▰▰▰▰ **Table 10.3** Navigator Functions Available to Plug-ins

Navigator Plug-in Function	Description
void NPN_Version(int* plugin_major, int* plugin_minor, int* netscape_major, int* netscape_minor)	Returns the plug-in API version number supported by the Netscape Navigator being used, as well as the version number of Navigator.
const char* NPN_UserAgent (NPP instance)	Returns a string containing the Navigator's "user agent" field, which identifies the browser in HTTP requests.
void NPN_Status(NPP instance, const char* message)	Displays a status message (const char *message) for the plug-in instance in the Navigator microhelp status bar.
NPError NPN_GetURL(NPP instance, const char* url, const char* window)	Requests that Navigator create a new stream for the contents of the URL (const char *url). The stream can be handled automatically by Navigator or can be provided to the plug-in through NPP_NewStream and NPP_Write plug-in functions.

■■■■■ **Table 10.3** Navigator Functions Available to Plug-ins

Navigator Plug-in Function	Description
NPError NPN_PostURL(NPP instance, const char* url, const char* window, uint32 len, const char* buf, NPBool file)	Performs an HTTP POST operation using the specified URL (const char *url) and creates a new stream to handle the response from the HTTP server.
NPError NPN_NewStream (NPP instance, NPMIMEType type, NPStream* stream)	Creates a new stream of the specified MIME type. The stream is handled by Netscape and is displayed using the current window.
NPError NPN_DestroyStream (NPP instance, NPStream* stream, NPError reason)	Closes and deletes the stream identified by NPStream *stream for the plug-in instance identified by the NPP instance.
NPError NPN_RequestRead (NPStream* stream, NPByte Range* rangeList)	Requests that a range of bytes be read on a seekable stream.
int32 NPN_Write(NPP instance, NPStream* stream, int32 len, void* buffer)	Allows a plug-in to write to a stream, typically one created by a call to NPN_NewStream.
void* NPN_MemAlloc(uint 32 size)	Allocates memory from the Navigator's memory space.
void NPN_MemFree(void* ptr)	Deallocates memory from the Navigator's memory space.
uint32 NPN_MemFlush (uint32 size)	Macintosh-specific function. Requests that Navigator free a specific amount of memory, and returns the amount freed.

■■■■■

Each Navigator function is described in more detail in the following sections. To use any of the Navigator functions in your plug-in code, you must include the **npapi.h** plug-in SDK file. Programming with the plug-in SDK is covered in the next chapter.

void NPN_Version(int plugin_major, int* plugin_minor, int* netscape_major, int* netscape_minor)*

Call NPN_Version to determine version numbers (in two-part *major.minor* version number format *e.g., 2.0*) of both Netscape Navigator and the plug-in API being used. Version numbers are returned to the calling routine by pointers passed to the following integer parameters:

- *int* plugin_major*. A pointer to an integer that will accept the major version number of the plug-in API supported.
- *int* plugin_minor*. A pointer to an integer that will accept the minor version number of the plug-in API supported.
- *int* netscape_major*. A pointer to an integer that will accept the major version number of Navigator.
- *int* netscape_minor*. A pointer to an integer that will accept the minor version number of Navigator.

The **NPN_Version** Navigator function enables a plug-in module to verify that the version of Navigator being used with the plug-in contains a version of the plug-in API that is compatible with the module. The sample code shown in Figure 10.16 demonstrates one way that **NPN_Version** might be used in the **NPP_Initialize** plug-in API function to determine whether or not the plug-in module is compatible with the version of Navigator being used.

▬▬▬▬ **Figure 10.16** Sample code that uses the NPN_Version Navigator function.

```
NPError NPP_Initialize(void)
{
        BOOL bPrepared = FALSE;
        int iPIMajor, iPIMinor, iNMajor, iNMinor;


        NPN_Version(&iPIMajor, &iPIMinor, &iNMajor, &iNMinor);


        // The plug-in API in Navigator 2.0 is version 0.6
        if(iPIMinor < 6 && iPIMajor == 0)
        {
                MessageBox(NULL,"Error: Plug-in requires Netscape
Navigator 2.0 or greater",
                        "Error initializing plug-in",MB_OK);
```

Continued ...

```
        }
        else
        {
                // Minimum plug-in API and Navigator versions present
                // so plug-in can be used.
                bPrepared = TRUE;
        }


        if(bPrepared)
                return NPERR_NO_ERROR;
        else
                return NPERR_GENERIC_ERROR;
}
```

Note that the plug-in API version number in Netscape Navigator 2.0 is version 0.6.
Subsequent releases of Navigator may or may not increment the plug-in API version
number accordingly, depending on whether or not changes have been made to the
plug-in API. There is no real correlation between Navigator version number and
plug-in API version number.

const char* NPN_UserAgent(NPP instance)

Call **NPN_UserAgent** to find out the name of the program used to activate the
plug-in. The single parameter is:

- *NPP instance.* Identifies the plug-in instance. This NPP structure is considered a *handle* to the plug-in instance.

Figure 10.17 shows a somewhat serious way that your plug-in can use
NPN_UserAgent. It is clear that the Netscape plug-in API will soon be supported
by many other Web browsers and possibly by other types of applications that can
benefit from the use of the plug-in standard. The **NPN_UserAgent** function makes
it possible for your plug-in to determine the program in which it is operating.

▬▬▬▬▬ **Figure 10.17** Sample code that uses the **NPN_UserAgent** Navigator function.

```
NPError NP_LOADDS NPP_New(NPMIMEType pluginType, NPP instance, uint16
mode, int16 argc,

             char* argn[], char* argv[], NPSavedData* saved)
{

      if (instance == NULL)
             return NPERR_INVALID_INSTANCE_ERROR;


      instance->pdata = NPN_MemAlloc(sizeof(PluginInstance));

      PluginInstance* This = (PluginInstance*) instance->pdata;


      if (This == NULL)
             return NPERR_OUT_OF_MEMORY_ERROR;


      CString csUserAgent;

      csUserAgent = NPN_UserAgent(instance);

      if(csUserAgent.Find("Mozilla") == -1)
             MessageBox(NULL,"This plug-in works better with
             Netscape Navigator",

                    "Warning",MB_OK);


      return NPERR_NO_ERROR;

}
```

Although the example shown in Figure 10.17 may be a bit controversial (especially if you're a Microsoft employee working on including Netscape plug-in support into Internet Explorer), it serves to illustrate one way that a plug-in might make decisions or alter behavior based on knowledge of its activating program. Interesting to note is that the value returned by **NPN_UserAgent** corresponds to the value of the User-Agent header line that is submitted as part of a typical HTTP request.

void NPN_Status(NPP instance, const char message)*

Call **NPN_Status** to display a custom message in the Navigator MDI microhelp status bar located at the bottom of the Navigator window. Parameters to the function are:

- *NPP instance.* Identifies the plug-in instance. This NPP structure is considered a *handle* to the plug-in instance.
- *const char* message.* Indicates the message to display in the Navigator status bar.

In Figure 10.18 you see an imaginary **OnClicked** event function for a button control on the plug-in window. The idea behind using **NPN_Status** is that your plug-in code will display informative messages related to its temporary processing or instructions to guide the user in selecting the next action. Some applications use the Navigator status bar to do nifty text-scrolling and other status-bar manipulation for special-effects purposes. Even though it looks good, we discourage such use of **NPN_Status** because it defeats the purpose of having a status bar and it often interferes with the normal display of important status messages.

Remember that Navigator itself uses the status bar to display messages. The existing status message is always replaced with the new status message, so the very last status

■■■■■ **Figure 10.18** Sample code that uses the **NPN_Status** Navigator function.

```
void CMainDialog::OnClickedSomeButton()
{
        NPN_Status(nppInstance,"Please wait...");
        // Do some processing, then display a new status message.
        NPN_Status(nppInstance,"Processing complete. You may con-
tinue.");
}
```

message update is the one that will remain visible until the next status message update. The early bird may get the worm, but it doesn't get control of the status bar.

NPError NPN_GetURL(NPP instance, const char url, const char* window)*

Call **NPN_GetURL** to get the contents of a URL as a new Navigator stream and either allow Navigator to display the contents of the URL as it normally would or receive the stream directly in your plug-in. Parameters are:

- *NPP instance.* Identifies the plug-in instance. This NPP structure is considered a *handle* to the plug-in instance.
- *const char* url.* Indicates the URL for Navigator to retrieve.
- *const char* window.* Determines the way in which Navigator (or the plug-in) will handle the stream.

The window parameter specifies the target to which the new Navigator stream should be directed. It can contain either the name of an existing frame, to direct display of the URL to a particular frame, or one of the following values:

- *(char *)NULL.* To pass the contents of the URL to the plug-in instance in the form of a Navigator stream.
- "*_blank*" or "*_new*". To display the contents of the URL in a new Navigator window.
- "*_self*" or "*_current*". To display the contents of the URL in the current window.
- "*_parent*". To display the contents of the URL in the FRAMESET parent. Exactly like "_self" if there isn't a parent.
- "*_top*". To display the contents of the URL in full-screen mode in the current window or the top-most frame.

Figure 10.19 shows an example **CWnd::OnLButtonUp** function that uses the "_new" target window name. The example shown causes a new instance of the Navigator window to open on top of the current one, and the new Navigator instance automatically opens the specified URL.

When the plug-in wants to receive the new stream instead of allowing Navigator to handle it, specify a NULL value for the window parameter. The new stream will be

■■■■■■ **Figure 10.19** Sample code that uses the **NPN_GetURL** Navigator function.

```
void CMainDialog::OnLButtonUp( UINT nFlags, CPoint point )
{
        CString csGetURL;
        char *sGetURL;


        csGetURL = "http://www.science.org/";


        if(point.y > 10 && point.y < 200)
        {
                if(point.x > 10 && point.x < 500)
                {
                        sGetURL = csGetURL.GetBuffer(csGetURL.
                        GetLength());
                        NPN_GetURL(nppInstance, sGetURL, "_new");
                }
        }
}
```

■■■■■■

provided to the plug-in through **NPP_NewStream, NPP_WriteReady,** and **NPP_Write** plug-in functions.

You may find that **NPN_GetURL** with a NULL window parameter doesn't work when you specify a URL that includes a filename whose file extension is something other than *html* (such as http://www.science.org/gatt.zip). If you encounter this problem, try creating an HTML file with an <EMBED> tag like the following:

```
<EMBED SRC=gatt.zip>
```

Then, specify the HTML file in the URL instead. The **NPN_GetURL** function should always work with a NULL window parameter and a URL that references an HTML file. One of the most exciting ways to use the **NPN_GetURL** function is to specify a *javascript:* URL along with a NULL window parameter. When a URL begins with *javascript:*, it indicates that the command or series of JavaScript lines specified in the URL should be executed immediately by Navigator. For example, the URL **javascript:document.location;** will cause Navigator to display the URL of the active Web page. Give this a try by typing the URL in your Navigator Location field. A dynamic result like the one shown in Figure 10.20 is generated.

Many other JavaScript commands, object properties, and functions will work in a javascript: URL. When such a URL is used in conjunction with the **NPN_GetURL Navigator** function, a stream is generated and either displayed by Navigator or sent to your plug-in, depending on the value of the window parameter. Often, your plug-in code will receive and parse the stream generated, as in the case of **javascript:document.location,** to collect some type of information that JavaScript makes accessible. For example, the following code snippet will create a new stream formatted as HTML that contains the URL of the current Web page.

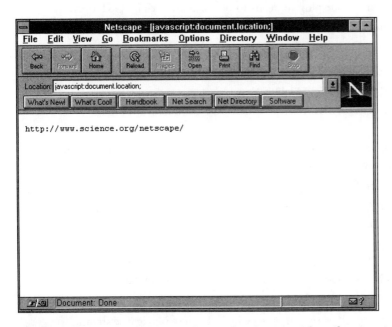

Figure 10.20 Use **javascript:document.location** to retrieve the URL of the current Web page.

```
CString csURL;
csURL = "javascript:document.location;";
NPN_GetURL(nppInstance, csURL.GetBuffer(csURL.GetLength()), (char *)NULL);
```

Note that the stream generated by this code will contain HTML-formatted text like the following:

```
<TITLE>javascript:document.location;</TITLE><PLAINTEXT>http://www.science.org
/netscape/
```

Your plug-in will need to parse the contents of the HTML stream to produce a meaningful result. Other uses are also possible, such as activating functions in the JavaScript history object to traverse the history list automatically.

NPError NPN_PostURL(NPP instance, const char* url, const char* window, uint32 len, const char* buf, NPBool file)

Call **NPN_PostURL** when your plug-in needs to perform an HTTP POST operation to a particular URL and receive the result of the POST in the form of a stream. Parameters to **NPN_PostURL** are:

- *NPP instance.* Identifies the plug-in instance. This NPP structure is considered a *handle* to the plug-in instance.
- *const char* url.* The URL to which the POST command should be directed.
- *const char* window.* Determines the way Navigator (or the plug-in) will handle the stream.
- *uint32 len.* Specifies the length of the data in char *buf.
- *const char* buf.* Contains data to be POSTed to the specified URL. The length of the data in char *buf should be specified in the uint32 len parameter.
- *NPBool file.* TRUE if char *buf contains the name of a local file that contains data to be POSTed. FALSE if char *buf contains the data to be POSTed instead of a reference to a local file.

The window parameter specifies the target to which the new Navigator stream should be directed. It can contain either the name of an existing frame, to direct display of the POST output to a particular frame, or one of the following values:

- *(char *)NULL.* To pass the POST result to the plug-in instance in the form of a Navigator stream.
- *"_blank"* or *"_new"*. To display the POST result in a new Navigator window.
- *"_self"* or *"_current"*. To display the POST result in the current window.
- *"_parent"*. To display the POST result in the FRAMESET parent. Exactly like "_self" if there isn't a parent.
- *"_top"*. To display the POST result in full-screen mode in the current window or the top-most frame.

Plug-in API Version 0.6 note: Netscape Navigator 2.0 handled the **NPN_PostURL** function in an odd way. You could say that there was a bug in **NPN_PostURL** as of the writing of this book. The problem with **NPN_PostURL** was that Navigator 2.0 added two new-line characters preceding the character buffer *char *buf*. If your plug-in provided a URL of http://www.science.org/cgi-bin/post-query and the following value in char *buf:

```
"Content-type: application/x-www-form-urlencoded\nContent-length: 25\n\n
FirstName=Jason&Test=data\n"
```

then Navigator supplied the following (incorrect) POST request to the HTTP server:

```
POST /cgi-bin/post-query HTTP/1.0
Connection: Keep-Alive
User-Agent: Mozilla/2.0 (WinNT; I)
Host: www.science.org
Accept: image/gif, image/x-xbitmap, image/jpeg, image/pjpeg, */*

Content-type: application/x-www-form-urlencoded
Content-length: 25

FirstName=Jason&Test=data
```

Notice the double-new line (causing a single blank line) after the Accept: line and before the first line of buf (Content-type:). The double-new-line in this situation is strictly incorrect HTTP syntax, and the HTTP server will not recognize the POST command.

The double-new line provided by Navigator 2.0 was a problem only if you tried to provide Request-Line information in the buf parameter. The solution was to provide all Request-Line information in the url parameter instead and use buf *only* for the Entity-Body (i.e., x-www-form-urlencoded data of specified length). The only trick to this was that you needed to include an additional HTTP/1.0 indicator immediately following the URL and immediately preceding the desired Request-Line content. Figure 10.21 shows an example of this technique.

When the code in Figure 10.21 was used, Navigator would supply the following POST request to the HTTP server:

```
POST /cgi-bin/post-query HTTP/1.0
Content-type: application/x-www-form-urlencoded
Content-length: 25 HTTP/1.0
Connection: Keep-Alive
```

Figure 10.21 Sample code that uses the **NPN_PostURL** Navigator function.

```
NPError npeTmp;
CString csURL = "http://www.science.org/cgi-bin/post-query";
csURL += " HTTP/1.0\n";
csURL += "Content-type: application/x-www-form-urlencoded\n";
csURL += "Content-length: 25\n";


CString csBody = "FirstName=Jason&Test=data\n";


npeTmp = NPN_PostURL(nppInstance, csURL.GetBuffer(csURL.GetLength()),
         (char *)NULL, (uint32)csBody.GetLength(),
         csBody.GetBuffer(csBody.GetLength()), FALSE);
```

```
User-Agent: Mozilla/2.0 (WinNT; I)
Host: www.science.org
Accept: image/gif, image/x-xbitmap, image/jpeg, image/pjpeg, */*


FirstName=Jason&Test=data
```

Notice the duplicate HTTP/1.0 indicator. According to the HTTP specification, the duplicate HTTP/1.0 indicator won't cause a problem for the HTTP server as it parses the command. This problem is most likely fixed now that a version of Navigator newer than 2.0 is available. We hope that the example given here helps to explain whatever solution Netscape cooked up to solve this problem in the current version of the plug-in API.

Another option available in version 0.6 of the plug-in API that may still work the same in the current release of Navigator was to use a temporary file instead of providing data in char *buf. To POST data from a temporary file, the contents of char *buf must be the full path and name of the temporary file, and the NPBOOL file parameter must be TRUE. Figure 10.22 shows an example of the NPN_PostURL function used to POST the contents of a temporary file named c:\temp\post.txt that contains the following data:

```
Content-type: application/x-www-form-urlencoded
Content-length: 25
```

▆▆▆▆▆▆ **Figure 10.22** Sample code that uses the **NPN_PostURL** Navigator function to post from a file.

```
CString csURL = "http://www.science.org/cgi-bin/post-query";
CString csBuf = "c:\\temp\\post.txt";


NPN_PostURL(nppInstance, csURL.GetBuffer(csURL.GetLength()),
(char *)NULL,
        (uint32)csBuf.GetLength, csBuf.GetBuffer(csBuf.GetLength()),
        TRUE);
```

```
FirstName=Jason&Test=data
```

Note that Navigator deletes the file after sending its contents. As you begin to work with the **NPN_PostURL** function in its current form, you'll want to reference the HTTP specification to ensure that the HTTP command sent by your plug-in is a valid one.

NPError NPN_NewStream(NPP instance, NPMIMEType type, NPStream stream)*

Call **NPN_NewStream** to create a new stream of the specified MIME type. The stream is handled by Netscape and is displayed using the current window. Parameters are:

- *NPP instance.* Identifies the plug-in instance. This NPP structure is considered a handle to the plug-in instance.
- *NPMIMEType type.* Contains the MIME type (**content-type/subtype** pair) of the new stream.
- *NPStream* stream.* Identifies the stream instance. This NPStream structure is considered a handle to the stream.

NPN_NewStream creates a new stream of data from the plug-in of the specified MIME type. The stream is interpreted by Netscape in the current window. Note that this function is currently useful only for instances of type NPBackground.

NPError NPN_DestroyStream(NPP instance, NPStream stream, NPError reason)*

Call **NPN_DestroyStream** to close and delete an existing stream for the plug-in instance.

- *NPP instance.* Identifies the plug-in instance. This NPP structure is considered a *handle* to the plug-in instance.
- *NPStream* stream.* Identifies the stream instance. This NPStream structure is considered a *handle* to the stream.
- *NPError reason.* Indicates to Navigator what the reason is for destroying the stream.

The possible reasons for deleting a stream are:

- NPRES_NETWORK_ERR. A network error occurred.
- NPRES_USER_BREAK. The user requested that the stream be closed.
- NPRES_DONE. Plug-in is done with the stream.

NPError NPN_RequestRead(NPStream* stream, NPByteRange* rangeList)

Call **NPN_RequestRead** to request that a range of bytes be read on a seekable stream.

- *NPStream* stream*. Identifies the stream instance. This NPStream structure is considered a *handle* to the stream.
- *NPByteRange* rangeList*. A pointer to the NPByteRange structure that identifies a range within the seekable stream.

The NPByteRange structure has the following format:

```
typedef struct _NPByteRange
{
    int32               offset;    /* negative offset means from the end */
    uint32              length;
    struct _NPByteRange*  next;
} NPByteRange;
```

The return value of NPN_RequestRead equals 1 if an error occurred.

int32 NPN_Write(NPP instance, NPStream* stream, int32 len, void* buffer)

Call **NPN_Write** to write data to a stream, typically one created by a call to **NPN_NewStream**. Parameters are:

- *NPP instance*. Identifies the plug-in instance. This NPP structure is considered a *handle* to the plug-in instance.
- *NPStream* stream*. Identifies the stream instance. This NPStream structure is considered a *handle* to the stream.
- *int32 len*. Specifies the length of the data buffer void *buffer.
- *void *buffer*. Points to the data buffer that the plug-in wants to send over the stream.

The **NPN_Write** function is typically used with streams created through a call to NPN_NewStream. NPN_Write enables your plug-in to send data over a stream rather than receive data as in the **NPP_Write** API function.

void* NPN_MemAlloc(uint32 size)

Call **NPN_MemAlloc** to allocate a block of memory owned by Navigator. Specify the size of the memory block in the single parameter:

- *uint32 size.* Specifies the size of the memory block to allocate.
- **NPN_MemAlloc** returns a pointer to the allocated memory block. Figure 10.24 shows an example taken from the **NPP_Destroy** function.

Remember to call **NPN_MemFree** to free the allocated memory when your plug-in is done with it.

void NPN_MemFree(void* ptr)

Call **NPN_MemFree** to free Navigator memory previously allocated through a call to **NPN_MemAlloc**. The single parameter to **NPN_MemFree** is:

Figure 10.23 Sample code that uses the **NPN_MemAlloc** Navigator function.

```
// Save data for the plug-in instance so that next time
// the same URL is

// accessed, Navigator will provide this data (in
// *saved) during NPP_New

NPSavedData* savedData = (NPSavedData*)
NPN_MemAlloc(sizeof(NPSavedData));

char* myData = (char*) NPN_MemAlloc(15);

strcpy(myData, "Here it is.\n");


savedData->len = 15;

savedData->buf = (void*) myData;


*save = savedData;
```

▰▰▰▰▰ **Figure 10.24** Sample code that uses the **NPN_MemFree** Navigator function.

```
// NPP_New code snippet
instance->pdata = NPN_MemAlloc(sizeof(PluginInstance));


// NPP_Destroy code snippet
NPN_MemFree(instance->pdata);
```

▰▰▰▰

- *void* ptr.* Reference to the beginning of a memory block previously allocated with **NPN_MemAlloc**.

NPN_MemFree must be called once for each call to **NPN_MemAlloc**.

uint32 NPN_MemFlush(uint32 size)

Call **NPN_MemFlush** from a Macintosh plug-in to free a specific amount of memory. The single parameter is:

- *uint32 size.* Specifies the number of bytes of memory to free.

The **NPN_MemFlush** function returns the number of bytes freed.

This section covered the plug-in API as it existed with the release of Netscape Navigator 2.0. Some of the functions will definitely change a bit as bugs are worked out and as the final version of the plug-in API is developed by Netscape. In spite of its evolving nature, the plug-in API version 0.6 and plug-ins created using it have proven to be stable, exciting developments that enable LiveObject multimedia Web applications. Future enhancements to the plug-in API promise to add even more ability and technical potential for the cutting edge of Web interactivity.

The next chapter shows you how to build plug-ins using the Netscape plug-in SDK and deploy them as an extension to your Web site. The essentials of the Netscape plug-in architecture that you learned in this chapter should be applicable to building a plug-in for any operating system. However, the detailed instructions presented in the next chapter will be directly applicable only toward building a plug-in with the Microsoft Windows Win32 API and the Microsoft Foundation Classes.

BUILDING A

NETSCAPE

INLINE PLUG-IN

Creating your own Netscape inline plug-in, whether for general use on the Web or just for use at your site, is the best way to implement a new MIME content type. Plug-in content types provide the most power, flexibility, and performance of all Web content development options. Because plug-ins are compiled, platform-dependent programs, there are no limits to what plug-in content types can do. When you build a plug-in, you directly extend the ability of the Netscape Navigator (and any other program that supports the Netscape plug-in architecture) and create new potential for your Web applications.

The details of the plug-in API were covered in Chapter 10. This chapter explores the basics of building a plug-in using the SDK provided by Netscape. Each section in this chapter gives a platform-independent overview of the programming technique applicable in the section, followed by an example of code designed to work with the Microsoft Foundation Classes and the Win32 Windows API. Because the requirements of a Unix or Macintosh plug-in are essentially the same as the requirements of a Windows plug-in, porting the concepts, and to a certain extent even the example code, presented in this chapter should be fairly easy.

Programming
with the Netscape Plug-in SDK

Download the Netscape plug-in SDK from the Netscape Web site. The plug-in SDK provides the shell of a plug-in module in a file called NPSHELL.CPP. Make a copy of NPSHELL.CPP to modify for use in your plug-in. None of the other files provided in the SDK should be modified. To build a plug-in using the SDK, you need a C or C++ compiler. Depending on the platform for which you are building a plug-in, the compiler will be used to create either a DLL, a *shared object*, or a *shared library*.

Recall from Chapter 10 that Netscape Navigator provides to your plug-in module a platform-dependent window handle that your plug-in should use for its display. The simplest type of plug-in is one that does not require any user interaction. It simply renders a display using the window handle supplied by Navigator and responds to any resize events indicated when Navigator calls the **NPP_SetWindow** function. In the case of such a simple plug-in, your code doesn't need to bother with window subclassing or other window procedure manipulation; it just writes information to the Navigator window. Most plug-ins, however, benefit greatly from the ability to respond to mouse clicks or other window events. The following discussion of building a plug-in using the SDK assumes that your plug-in module is designed to handle window events and therefore needs to subclass the Navigator window.

Handling Plug-in
Instance Initialization

The plug-in module must be able to handle multiple instances of the same plug-in MIME type. Toward this end, the Netscape SDK NPSHELL.CPP file implements a nifty linked-list strategy that is able to dynamically grow the size of the list to handle a variable number of simultaneous plug-in instances. We don't like the linked-list approach. Instead, we use the **CPtrArray** Microsoft Foundation Class to dynamically grow an array of pointers to plug-in instances. This means that all of the code shown in Figure 11.1 can be chopped out of the NPSHELL.CPP file to make way for the simpler dynamic array approach.

▬▬▬▬▬ **Figure 11.1** Remove this code from NPSHELL.CPP if you don't use
a linked-list for plug-in instances.

```
PluginInstance* g_pHeadInstanceList = NULL;


// Associate the hWnd with pInstance by setting the hWnd member of the
// PluginInstance struct.  Also, add the PluginInstance struct to the
// list if necessary
static void AssociateInstance(HWND hWnd, PluginInstance* pInstance)
{
    pInstance->hWnd = hWnd;


    // add this PluginInstance to the list if it's not already
    if(g_pHeadInstanceList != NULL) { // anything in the list?
        if(g_pHeadInstanceList != pInstance) { // its not first in the
                                               // list
            PluginInstance* pInst = g_pHeadInstanceList;
            while(pInst->pNext != NULL) {
                if(pInst->pNext == pInstance)
                    return; // found it, done
                pInst = pInst->pNext;
            }
            // didn't find it, add it
            pInst->pNext = pInstance;
        }
    }
    else // list is empty, just add it
        g_pHeadInstanceList = pInstance;
}


// Find the PluginInstance associated with this hWnd and return it
static PluginInstance* GetInstance(HWND hWnd)
{
    for(PluginInstance* pInstance = g_pHeadInstanceList;
        pInstance != NULL;
```

Continued...

```
        pInstance = pInstance->pNext) {
            if(pInstance->hWnd == hWnd)
                return pInstance; // found it, done
    }
    return NULL;
}
```

Further, the PluginInstance structure, whose original form is shown in Figure 11.2, can be greatly simplified. The Netscape plug-in SDK provides this structure as a way to store information about a plug-in instance so that the instance can be associated later with the correct array item stored in memory.

Figure 11.2 The original PluginInstance structure as found in the plug-in SDK.

```
// *Developers*: Use this struct to hold per-instance
//               information that you'll need in the
//               various functions in this file.
//

typedef struct _PluginInstance PluginInstance;
typedef struct _PluginInstance
{
    NPWindow*       fWindow;
    HWND            hWnd;
    uint16          fMode;
    FARPROC         lpfnOldWndProc;
    NPSavedData*    pSavedInstanceData;
    PluginInstance* pNext;
} PluginInstance;
```

Since we don't like using the linked-list approach to handling a variable number of simultaneous plug-in instances, our PluginInstance structure is shown in Figure 11.3. The only thing that we need to store in this structure for each plug-in instance is the array index of the instance within the array of pointers. When our plug-in module needs to access the attributes or functions of a plug-in instance later, it simply uses the value stored in iArrayIndex to determine which pointer to dereference.

Figure 11.4 shows how to create a new plug-in instance using the dynamic pointer array approach. Notice that the plug-in instance itself is an object of type CMainDialog. CMainDialog is a dialog class inherited from Cdialog that encapsulates all of the code for the display and management of a single plug-in instance. By using the new operator to create a new CMainDialog object and storing a pointer to the new object in our dynamic pointer array, we implement a very simple strategy for handling many simultaneous plug-in instances simultaneously. Notice also that the iArrayIndex element of our PluginInstance array is set to the zero-based array index of the new CMainDialog object. By adding attributes and member functions to the CMainDialog class, we can easily extend the abilities and instance data of our inline plug-in.

Although it's not easy to see this in Figure 11.4 because we tried to present a simpler version of the source code, our pointer array is actually an instance variable of the CWinApp-derived class. If you use the source code shown exactly as it appears here, you'll need to make the pointer array a global variable instead or create your own CWinApp-derived class and place the majority of Figure 11.4 in a member function of your new CWinApp class.

■■■■■■■■ **Figure 11.3** Our modified PluginInstance structure contains an array index identifier.

```
typedef struct _PluginInstance
{
    NPWindow*        fWindow;
    int              iArrayIndex;


} PluginInstance;
```

■■■■■■■ **Figure 11.4** Add a new instance to your plug-in array in the **NPP_New** function.

```
//-----------------------------------------
// NPP_New:
//-----------------------------------------
NPError NP_LOADDS
NPP_New(NPMIMEType pluginType,
                NPP instance,
                uint16 mode,
                int16 argc,
                char* argn[],
                char* argv[],
                NPSavedData* saved)
{
        if (instance == NULL)
                return NPERR_INVALID_INSTANCE_ERROR;


        CString csUserAgent;


        csUserAgent = NPN_UserAgent(instance);
        if(csUserAgent.Find("Mozilla") == -1)
                MessageBox(NULL,"This plug-in works better with
Netscape Navigator",
                        "Warning",MB_OK);


        instance->pdata = NPN_MemAlloc(sizeof(PluginInstance));
        PluginInstance* This = (PluginInstance*) instance->pdata;
        if (This != NULL)
        {
                This->fWindow = NULL;


                // *Developers*: Initialize fields of your plugin
```

```
// instance data here.  If the NPSavedData is non-
// NULL, you can use that data (returned by you from
// NPP_Destroy to set up the new plugin instance.

CString csMimeTest;
prepplugParamStruct ppsParam;
csMimeTest = pluginType;

if(csMimeTest == csOurPluginMimeType)
{
int iArraySize, iArrayIndex, a;
CMainDialog *cmdlgTmp;

iArraySize = instanceArray.GetSize();
iArrayIndex = iArraySize;     // store array index
This->iArrayIndex = iArrayIndex;
iArraySize = iArraySize + 1; // add one to array
instanceArray.SetSize(iArraySize,1);

cmdlgTmp = new CMainDialog(NULL);
instanceArray.SetAt(iArrayIndex,cmdlgTmp);

cmdlgTmp->nppInstance = instance;
cmdlgTmp->iShowRecvParam = 0;
cmdlgTmp->csNameArray.SetSize(argc,1);
cmdlgTmp->csValueArray.SetSize(argc,1);
for(a=0;a < argc;a++)
{
        cmdlgTmp->csNameArray[a] = argn[a];
        cmdlgTmp->csValueArray[a] = argv[a];
}
```

Continued...

```
                    cmdlgTmp->m_hWnd = (HWND)NULL;

                    ASSERT(cmdlgTmp->m_hWnd == (HWND)NULL);

                }

                else    // this plug-in DLL isn't designed to

                {           // handle the MIME type supplied

                        return NPERR_GENERIC_ERROR;

                }


        return NPERR_NO_ERROR;

        }

        else

        {

                return NPERR_OUT_OF_MEMORY_ERROR;

        }

}
```

Initializing Plug-in Display

Your plug-in code must wait until Navigator calls **NPP_SetWindow** to initialize the
display of a plug-in instance. A sample **NPP_SetWindow** function is shown in Figure
11.5. Notice how the array index stored previously in the PluginInstance structure is
used to get a pointer to the correct CMainDialog object in the following line:

```
cmdlgTmp = (CMainDialog *)instanceArray.GetAt(This->iArrayIndex);
```

■■■ **Figure 11.5** Initialize plug-in display and handle window resizing in
NPP_SetWindow.

```
//----------------------------------------
// NPP_SetWindow:
//----------------------------------------
```

```
NPError NP_LOADDS
NPP_SetWindow(NPP instance, NPWindow* window)
{

        if (instance == NULL)
                return NPERR_INVALID_INSTANCE_ERROR;


        PluginInstance* This = (PluginInstance*) instance->pdata;


        //
        // *Developers*: Before setting fWindow to point to the
        // new window, you may wish to compare the new window
        // info to the previous window (if any) to note window
        // size changes, etc.
        //

        if (!window)
                return NPERR_GENERIC_ERROR;


        if (!instance)
                return  NPERR_INVALID_INSTANCE_ERROR;


        if (!This)
                return NPERR_GENERIC_ERROR;


        if (!window->window && !This->fWindow) // spurious entry
                return NPERR_NO_ERROR;


        if (!window->window && This->fWindow)
        {    // window went away
                return NPERR_NO_ERROR;
        }
```

Continued...

```
        if (!This->fWindow && window->window)
        {    // First time in -- no window created by plugin yet
                This->fWindow = window;


                CMainDialog *cmdlgTmp;
                cmdlgTmp = (CMainDialog *)instanceArray.GetAt(This-
>iArrayIndex);

                if (!(cmdlgTmp->SubclassWindow((HWND)window->window)))
                {
                        MessageBox(NULL,"SubclassWindow
Failed","Error",MB_OK);
                }
                else
                {
                        cmdlgTmp->PrepareDialog();
                        cmdlgTmp->Invalidate(TRUE);
                        cmdlgTmp->UpdateWindow();
                }
        }
        return NPERR_NO_ERROR;
}
```

■■■■

When you use an array instead of a linked list, finding the right plug-in instance object is greatly simplified.

Note that the sample code shown in Figure 11.5 uses the **SubclassWindow** function to replace the Navigator window procedure with the window procedure created for the CMainDialog object. This causes window event messaging to be handled by the message loop present in the CMainDialog object instead of the one present within Navigator. Once window sub-classing is complete, the CMainDialog object is told to display itself with a call to our custom function **PrepareDialog**. The PrepareDialog code is shown in Figure 11.6.

Figure 11.6 Prepare the display of your plug-in instance in a function like **PrepareDialog**.

```
void CMainDialog::PrepareDialog()
{
        CRect rectTmp;

        rectTmp.SetRect(10,10, 250, 50);
        stMessage = new CStatic();
        stMessage->Create("Plug-in Instance Initialized and Display
Prepared.",WS_CHILD|WS_VISIBLE,
                                    rectTmp,this,65535);

        rectTmp.SetRect(10,100,250,160);
        cbOK = new CButton();
        cbOK->Create("OK",BS_PUSHBUTTON, rectTmp,this, IDC_BUTTON1);
}
```

Finally, your plug-in code should expect to receive the MIME content for the plug-in instance as a Navigator stream. Refer to Chapter 10 for details on the Navigator stream functions and for more examples of source code for each of the functions in the plug-in API. You can also visit the SCIENCE.ORG Guide to Building Netscape Inline Plug-ins on the Web for the most up-to-date information on programming with the Netscape plug-in SDK. The address is:

http://www.science.org/netscape/plug-ins/

12

SHOCKWAVE

Shockwave is one of the most exciting Netscape plug-ins available. It was developed by Macromedia for viewing animations generated with the Macromedia Director software, which has become the standard for generating animations with an estimated 250,000 users. Shockwave now allows you to include these interactive multimedia animations in your Web pages.

Check out Macromedia's home page where you'll find information about Director and the other Macromedia software enabling you to design multimedia content for your Web applications. You can even download some of the Macromedia products like the Shockwave inline plug-in and the Afterburner converter. For more information or to download Shockwave contact:

http://www.macromedia.com/

Shockwave

Shockwave is a plug-in that extends the basic capabilities of the Netscape Navigator so that it now displays Macromedia Director movies. The Director movies, actually scripted animations, have already been used in many Web pages around the Internet. These applications range from full-length animations to small animated bullet points on a Web page.

Deepforest is an interesting band specializing in cultural music. You can see a unique example of interesting Web content at its Macromedia site. The Deepforest example demonstrates a complete multimedia experience, with a Macromedia Director production combining sound with user-activated animations.

http://www.macromedia.com/Gallery/Shockwave/Custom/Deepforest/deepforest.html

One of the hottest uses of multimedia to date has been game development because games represent the ultimate in user activity. Macromedia enables interactivity with the multimedia animations you create. There are already numerous games developed with Macromedia Director and integrated in Web pages.

http://www.macromedia.com/Gallery/Shockwave/Games/Lockgame/lock.html

The days of static, unmoving, and unexciting company logos and banners are gone. Using Macromedia Director, you can generate small animated company logos or banners or even integrate animated bullet points and icons into your Web pages.

http://www.macromedia.com/Gallery/Shockwave/Banners/Isn/index.html

Everyone interested in unexplained phenomena and government cover-up has spent a Friday night at home watching the X-Files. Now the X-Files is on the Internet. You can visit the following URL that features a X-Files Macromedia Director production (Figure 12.1).

http://www.hmg.com/staff/rick/x/

The X-Files production is a very successful integration of Director-generated content with a Web site. Users can click on different areas of the animation displayed by Shockwave and view different animations. Rather than access one large file, requiring several minutes to download, users can interactively navigate to different smaller animations. The experience still feels like a large production.

Anyone who enjoys popping bubble packing will love the following URL.

http://www.mackerel.com/bubble.html

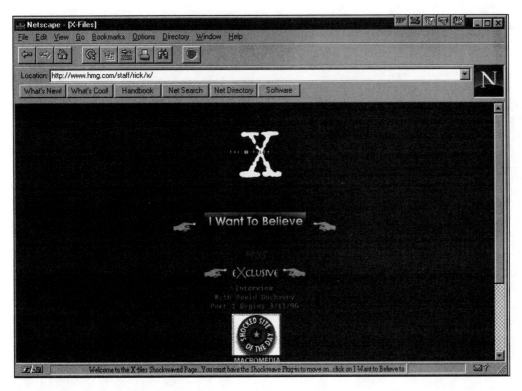

Figure 12.1 The X-Files page is an excellent example of creating interactive multimedia Web content.

The Virtual Bubble Wrap game is a truly inventive application of a Macromedia Director production (Figure 12.2). The game provides user interactivity, sound response to user input, and a small file size for quick download—and it's authentically annoying.

These examples clearly illustrate the compelling Web content you can now create using Macromedia Director combined with your own ingenuity.

Director

Multimedia animation has become an important part of displaying content on the World Wide Web, and Director has been the premier multimedia content creator on

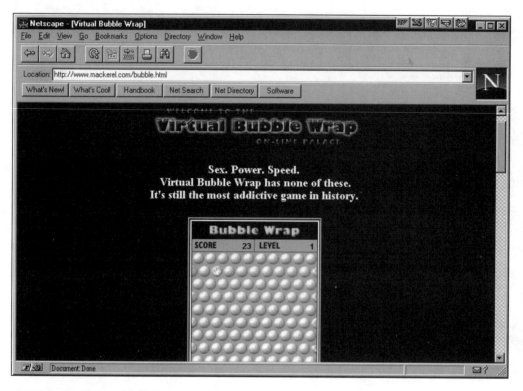

■■■■■ **Figure 12.2** Pop the bubbles to your heart's content.

both the Macintosh and Window platforms. Most of the multimedia CDs now on the market have been created using Director, which is aptly named because with it you direct a cast acting on a stage. The cast of characters may include animated sprites, digital video clips, and still graphic images. Directing a production is always more than simply directing the cast on the stage. Director also includes a very flexible sound editing system. You now direct the score as well as the cast. As every good actor knows, if the background doesn't work and the props aren't right, the production can be off. Director lets you create wonderful scenery for your productions.

Director comes complete with a full multimedia and interactive programming language known as Lingo. This language helps direct the Macromedia Director movie and provides the ability to interact with the cast and background.

The music group called the Cranberries was one of the first groups to release a music CD that also contained multimedia information, and its multimedia presentation was generated with Director. You can create an endless number of applications for the animations using the Director software.

- Sales presentations
- How-to-assemble product guides
- Training presentations
- Games

To create exciting animations you need the tools and the talent. Director provides the tool capabilities, ready to be combined with your talent. There are several key tool windows available in Director that you will use to create animations.

- Stage
- Score
- Cast
- Control panel

The stage is where all the action takes place, just as it would be in a theatre on Broadway. Here is where you bring together the cast and the scenery and play out the script. Figure 12.3 illustrates an example of an application loaded in Macromedia Director and displayed in the stage window.

There wouldn't be much of a play without a script. The score is the script used to create Macromedia Director productions. The Score window is where you designate when members of the cast enter and leave the stage in your production. Figure 12.4 shows the typical Score for a sample production.

Here you see the frames of the production displayed along the top of the window. Below the frames are the objects that have been added to the production. All the elements from sounds to Lingo scripts and the cast members are present in the Score window to appear in the production.

The Internal Cast window is where you can see each of the cast members used in the production. Here you can have graphical images and Lingo script commands. Figure 12.5 shows the Internal Cast window for a sample production.

The window for each sprite also features icons that you can click on to edit the appearance or Lingo script for a chosen sprite. Place a cast member in the production by dragging it into desired frame number of the Score window.

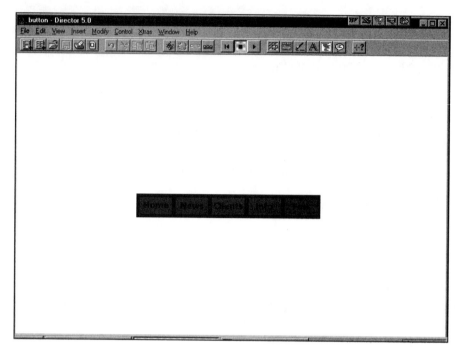

Figure 12.3 Modify and view the animation in the main stage window.

Once you've made your production, you can play it. Choose the **Play** button on the Control Panel window to see what a magnificent production you've created (Figure 12.6).

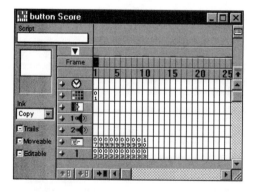

Figure 12.4 Click on the top script bar to open the Script window in the Score window.

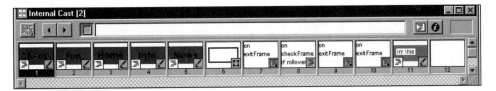

Figure 12.5 Select the pen icon to edit the appearance of a sprite or select the script icon to edit the Lingo script.

Figure 12.6 Use the VCR buttons to review your Macromedia Director production.

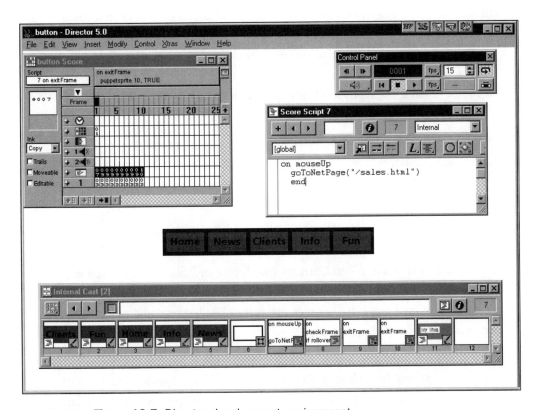

Figure 12.7 Director development environment.

Here are the steps to create a Macromedia Director production.

1. Choose the **File|New** menu selection and enter the name of the production.

2. Open the various tools. Select the **Window** menu selection and open the Score, Internal Cast, Control panel, and paint windows.

3. Select an empty cast member, and then create the desired sprite with the paint tools.

4. Drag the various cast members to the desired frame location in the Score window.

5. Write the interactive Lingo script commands for specific frames and sprites.

6. Play the production using the control panel.

7. Save the completed Macromedia Director production.

Interactive Web Lingo

Most people would rather have their Web content be interactive multimedia presentations that people can't stop using rather than dull animations that people watch only once. Lingo provides the capabilities to make the sprites in your animations interact with the user: buttons that dynamically change when the user moves the mouse pointer over them or sprites in a game that follow wherever the user moves the mouse pointer. These potential applications and more can be down with some of the simple Lingo commands available.

The creation of Shockwave and its emergence as one of the premier animation viewers on the Internet have prompted Macromedia to develop Net-specific Lingo commands. These commands give hyperlink capability to the animations you create and allow them to obtain Net-related information.

Most Web sites feature a control bar that displays information with various buttons, which also serve as hyperlinks to other locations. Wouldn't it be nice to feature animated buttons or control bars on your Web site? These buttons could be small animations that represent specific topics. The Info button could show an animation of a phone ringing, for instance, while the Help button could be an animation of a fire fighter putting out a house fire.

The animation is simple enough to generate with Director, but these buttons still must have hyperlink functionality. The solution to creating hyperlink capability is the Lingo command known as GoToNetPage. With this simple command you can make a chosen cast member be a hyperlink to another Web page. The Lingo script needed to implement this command could be as simple as the following example.

```
on mouseUp
        goToNetPage "http://www.science.org"
end
```

With this command the user would be sent to the indicated URL when a mouseUp event occurred to the designated cast member.

You could also launch other Director animations. The GoToNetMovie command allows you to specify other Director animations that you want to play when they are triggered by a desired user event. Table 12.1 describes all the other Lingo commands that you can incorporate in the productions you produce for the Web.

These Net-specific Lingo commands allow you to integrate your animations with the Web. Check the Macromedia site to keep informed about future Net-specific Lingo commands that become available.

■■■■■ Table 12.1 Additional Net-Specific Lingo

Command	Description
netDone()	Returns false until the asynchronous network operation is completed.
netError()	Returns an empty string until the asynchronous network operation is completed. If the operation was unsuccessful, this function will return a string describing the error. If the operation was successful, it will return the string "OK."
netAbort	Aborts the network operation.
netTextResult()	Returns text result of an operation.
netMIME()	Returns the MIME file type.
netOperationID	Returns an ID so that simultaneous asynchronous operations can take place.
preLoadNetThing()	Loads a file into the local disk cache.
netLastModDate()	Returns the last date string from the HTTP header.

Afterburner

After you create your Macromedia Director production, use Afterburner to "burn" or compress the file. Afterburner is the compressor program used to compress the Director movie that you have created so that the animation can be easily downloaded as Web content. When the Afterburner program is run, the animation with the DIR file extension is converted into the compressed file with a DCR file extension. When you provide this animation in your Web application, you must first configure your server to provide the proper MIME type. The MIME.TYPES file on the HTTP server should have the application/x-director MIME file with the DCR file extension. Only then can users view your Director animations with the Shockwave inline plug-in.

The Shockwave Developer's Guide can be found at the following URL.

http://www.macromedia.com/WHATEVER/

This guide can answer a variety of problems that you may have when you use the Afterburner post-processor.

Keep in Mind

When you deploy your Director animations to be viewed with the Shockwave plug-in, remember not everyone has a T1 connection. Don't get too carried away in adding so many elements to your animation that the result is a a significantly large file size. Larger file size means longer download, and longer download may mean losing many users' attention. Here are several key points to observe when you create your Macromedia Director productions.

- Sound is important to create a true multimedia animation, but sound can add a considerable amount to the file size of the animation.
- Delete unused cast members.
- Use the draw utilities in Director to generate all objects and text.

Embedding Content in HTML

Provide the DCR animation files you've created after you configure the MIME.TYPES file on your HTTPserver so that it can provide this type of MIME file. Add the following MIME file type.

```
application/x-director   dcr
```

After configuring your server to provide the Director animations, you must include the proper <EMBED> tag in the Web source file. Here is an example of the typical <EMBED> tag used to include a Director animation in Web source file.

```
<EMBED   SRC="awesome.dcr"   ALIGN=CENTER   HEIGHT=250   WIDTH=200>
```

Now anyone with the Shockwave inline plug-in installed can view the Macromedia Director content you place in your Web site.

INSTALLING

AND CONFIGURING

NETSCAPE

LIVEWIRE PRO

Installation and configuration of Netscape LiveWire can be very simple or very frustrating, depending on the way that your computer and network are currently configured. This appendix exists to guide you through the process of installing and configuring LiveWire Pro on a Windows NT system. It should help to get you up and running as quickly as possible and, most importantly, point out a few pitfalls to avoid so that your installation goes smoothly. We begin with the Netscape FastTrack HTTP server then cover LiveWire. Finally, we cover the most challenging and problem-plagued installation step, getting Informix OnLine working on your NT system.

Installing the Netscape FastTrack Server

When you begin installing the Netscape FastTrack server, one of the first steps is to specify the host name of the machine on which you wish to install FastTrack. Figure A.1 shows the window used to enter this value during the install process. It is

Figure A.1 Enter the fully qualified domain name of your host.

extremely important that the host name you enter here match precisely the fully qual-ified domain name (FQDN) of the host.

We can't emphasize enough the need to enter a valid FQDN for the computer on which you're installing FastTrack. Further, if your host is known by many names, it isn't sufficient to enter just *one* of the FQDNs by which the host is known on the network; you must enter the FQDN that is returned by your domain nameserver when the host's primary IP address is resolved to a host name. See Figure A.2 for an example of the response that nslookup gives under such a condition. Notice that the FQDN supplied in Figure A.1 matches exactly the FQDN returned by the domain nameserver in Figure A.2. Even though the computer whose IP address is 204.94.74.210 is known by many names on the network, the name *titanium.sci-ence.org* is the one that must be used.

If you enter anything other than the real FQDN as the name of your host, the Informix OnLine Database Server will not function properly. If you aren't sure what host name is returned when your domain nameserver receives a lookup request by IP address, find out before going any further in the installation process.

If you find that the FQDN returned by your domain nameserver doesn't match the FQDN that you are currently using or would like to use for your server, the domain

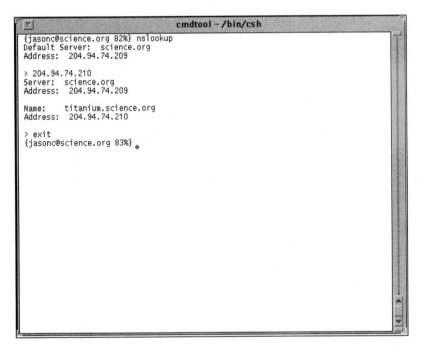

```
┌──────────────────────────────────────────────────┐
│ ▽                    cmdtool – /bin/csh             │
├──────────────────────────────────────────────────┤
│ {jasonc@science.org 82%} nslookup                  │
│ Default Server:  science.org                        │
│ Address:  204.94.74.209                             │
│                                                     │
│ > 204.94.74.210                                     │
│ Server:  science.org                                │
│ Address:  204.94.74.209                             │
│                                                     │
│ Name:    titanium.science.org                       │
│ Address:  204.94.74.210                             │
│                                                     │
│ > exit                                              │
│ {jasonc@science.org 83%} ◆                          │
│                                                     │
│                                                     │
└──────────────────────────────────────────────────┘
```

Figure A.2 Determine the FQDN of your computer by looking up the host name by IP address.

name entry for your computer needs to be changed. If you have access to the nameserver and can configure it yourself, edit the **/etc/named.boot** file (or equivalent) so that it contains a line like the following for the host whose IP address is **204.94.74.210**:

```
primary 210.74.94.204.in-addr.arpa db.204.94.74.210
```

This line tells the nameserver that host name lookups for the IP address **204.94.74.210** can be resolved by looking in the file **db.204.94.74.210**. Notice that each quad of the dotted-quad IP address appears backwards following the word **primary,** but the IP address is written normally at the end of the line when the db filename is specified. The db filename is arbitrary; the reverse-dotted-quad IP address immediately following the word primary must appear reversed as shown in this example. The file **db.204.94.74.210** contains the following:

```
210.74.94.204.in-addr.arpa.  IN  SOA titanium.science.org. root.science.org.
( 10 10800 3600 604800 86400 )

IN  NS  ns.science.org.

IN  PTR  titanium.science.org.
```

You should need to reconfigure only your nameserver if it doesn't provide the right FQDN in response to a host name lookup by IP address. If you can't reconfigure your nameserver easily, just use the FQDN returned by the lookup even if it isn't the one you prefer to use. Next, enter an administrative user name and password in the window shown in Figure A.3. Remember the name and password that you enter here; you'll need to supply both later to administer the server.

Next, choose a document root directory for the FastTrack server. The document root directory is the directory searched by default when the HTTP server receives a request from a Web browser for a particular item. Every item served by your HTTP server must either be located in the document root directory (or one of its subdirectories) or be one of the LiveWire objects registered with the Application Manager. See Figure A.4 for an example.

When you finish configuring your FastTrack server, Netscape Navigator is automatically launched to view the default server home page created by the installation process (see Figure A.5). If the install succeeds, the FastTrack HTTP server is now running on your NT system.

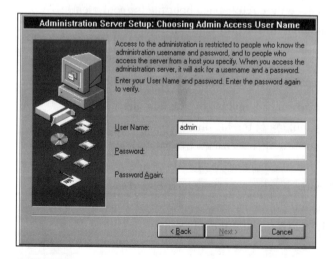

■■■■■ **Figure A.3** Enter an administrative user name and password.

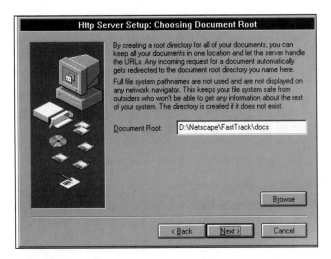

Figure A.4 Enter the document root directory for the HTTP server.

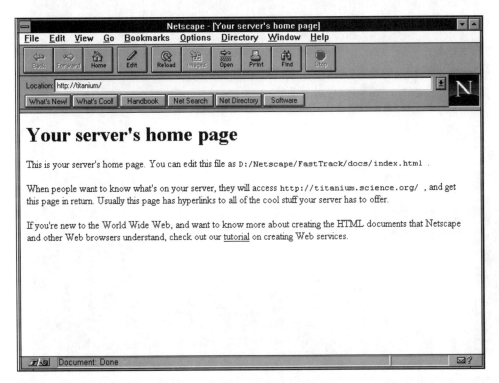

Figure A.5 Finish installing FastTrack then view your server's home page to test out the server.

Your server's home page is located in the document root directory that you specified for your server. To modify the home page, either edit the **index.html** file found in your document root directory or replace the /index.html item with a LiveWire object of the same name. Installing LiveWire is explained next.

Installing Netscape LiveWire

The first step in installing Netscape LiveWire is to supply the name of the HTTP server that will be used with LiveWire. The default server name displayed in the window shown in Figure A.6 is probably correct, though you can verify the name of your HTTP server by going to the control panel and choosing **Services**.

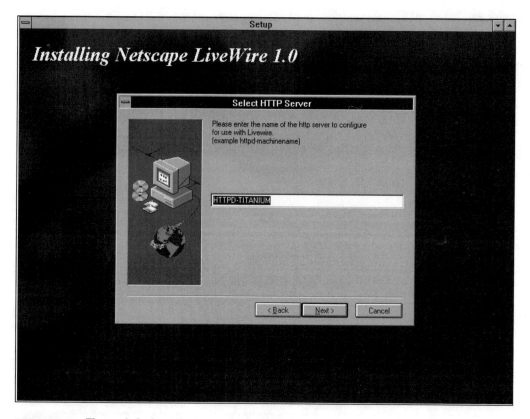

■■■■■■ **Figure A.6** Specify the name of the HTTP server to use with LiveWire.

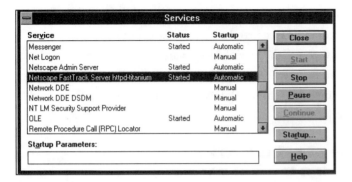

▬▬▬▬▬ **Figure A.7** Verify the name of your HTTP service using the NT services control panel.

If you just installed the FastTrack server, you'll see a Services entry like the one shown in Figure A.7. FastTrack is installed as an NT service. You'll see the name of your FastTrack HTTP server service when you scroll through the list of NT services running on your computer.

Next you need to once again provide the fully qualified domain name (FQDN) of the computer on which LiveWire will be run (see Figure A.8). Be certain that you enter the same FQDN in this step as you did while installing FastTrack in the previous section.

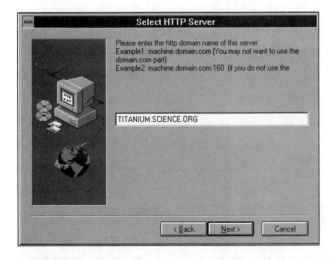

▬▬▬▬▬ **Figure A.8** Enter the FQDN of your NT machine.

Next, choose the destination directory in which you want to install LiveWire. Then reboot your computer when prompted to do so. LiveWire is now installed. Turn to Part 1 of this book to learn how to use the LiveWire software tools including the Navigator Gold editor for creating and modifying Web page source files. Read on to find out how to install the Informix OnLine Database Server and get it working with LiveWire and the JavaScript database object.

Installing the Informix OnLine Database Server

First, go buy another large hard drive (seriously), unless you already have an NTFS file system with a lot of disk space available. Format it as an NTFS file system. You can install Informix only on an NTFS file system, and you'll need a lot of disk space for a typical installation. When you begin installing Informix, the first screen you see is shown in Figure A.9.

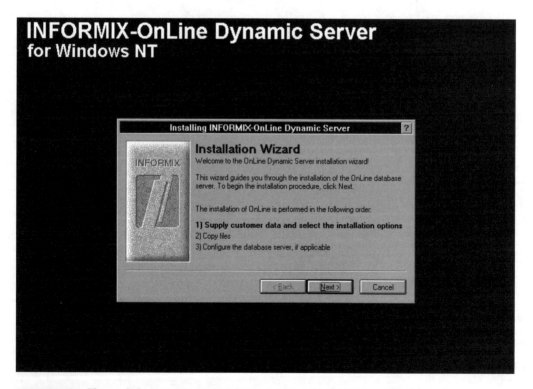

■■■■■■ **Figure A.9** Use the Installation Wizard to install Informix.

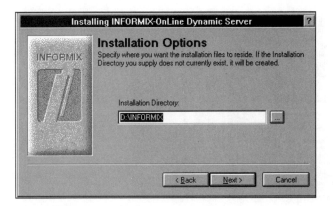

▬▬▬▬▬ **Figure A.10** Select an installation directory for Informix.

Provide information about yourself and your company as requested by the Installation Wizard until you reach the Installation Options screen shown in Figure A.10. The Installation Directory is the directory in which you would like to install the Informix server software. If you enter a directory that does not yet exist, Installation Wizard will create it for you before installing Informix.

When prompted for Role Separation, as shown in Figure A.11, either check or uncheck the **Enable Role Separation** box. Role Separation is the ability to divide the various types of database administration tasks among multiple people on the network. We prefer Role Separation because it provides the greatest flexibility in database management, so we suggest that you turn on Role Separation.

▬▬▬▬▬ **Figure A.11** Enable or disable Role Separation as desired.

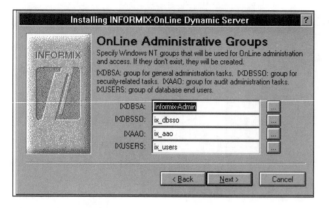

Figure A.12 Enter administrative groups for each task.

If you choose to enable Role Separation, the Installation Wizard will prompt you to enter the OnLine Administrative Groups as shown in Figure A.12. The default groups' names will work for your installation unless you have existing groups that you would like to use for each group of administrative tasks.

Now specify the user name and password for the Auditing Administrator user account as shown in Figure A.13.

Next create a Security Administrator user account as shown in Figure A.14.

Figure A.13 Create an Auditing Administrator user account and enter a password.

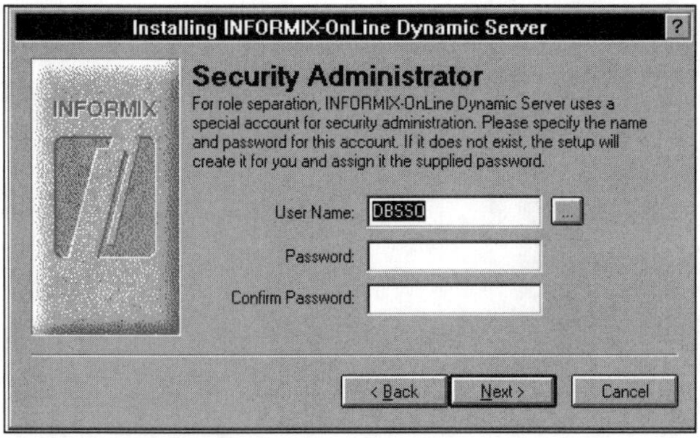

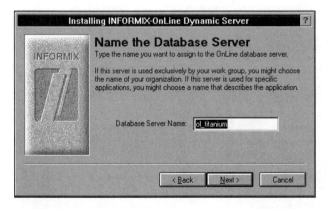

Figure A.14 Create a Security Administrator user account and enter a password.

Give the Database Server a name in the window shown in Figure A.15. The name that you give to your Informix Database Server will be used later any time that you need to specify the name of the server. For example, the JavaScript database object provides a connect method that needs to know the name of the database server in order to connect. The default server name is *ol_* followed by the name of your host, such as *ol_titanium* in this example. Note that naming your Database Server is not the same as creating a database. You'll have an opportunity later to create databases and tables on the server and assign different names to each.

Figure A.15 Give the Informix Database Server a name.

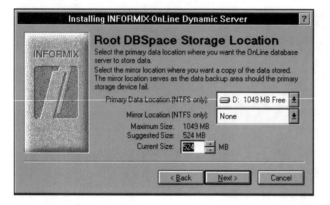

Figure A.16 Specify the size and location of the Informix Root DBSpace.

Next you need to specify the size and location of the Root DBSpace for the server. The Informix Database Server requires an NTFS file system for its DBSpace and recommends that you allocate about half of your available disk space to database storage (see Figure A.16).

If you have a tape device that you would like to use for database backup, you can configure Informix to use it in the screen that appears next (not shown here). When prompted for a new password for the Informix user account, as shown in Figure A.17, enter something other than the default.

Finally, select an SQLHOSTS Registry Machine as shown in Figure A.18. Click on the **Finish** button to complete installation of the Informix Database Server.

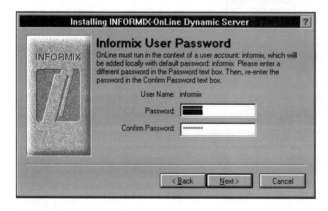

Figure A.17 Change the Informix user password.

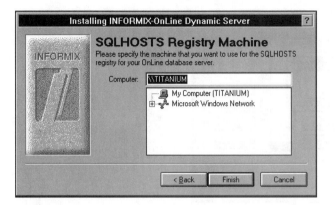

▪▪▪▪▪▪▪▪▪ **Figure A.18** Set the SQLHOSTS Registry Machine.

The Installation Wizard will now complete the installation for you. When it finishes, you are given the option of starting the server now or waiting until later. If any problems arise in either the installation or the execution of the server, Informix will provide instructions on how to determine the cause of the problem. Note that if the host name configured in your TCP/IP setup does not match the fully qualified domain name returned by your domain nameserver, the Informix Database Server will not execute successfully. Be certain that your domain nameserver is configured correctly and that the TCP/IP setup of your NT machine accurately reflects the fully qualified domain name returned by the nameserver.

Now that Informix is installed on your computer, you need to make a change to the Windows NT Service configuration of your HTTP server. In order to work correctly with Informix, the Netscape FastTrack HTTP server should be set up to execute on behalf of one of the users on the NT system. Figure A.19 shows what your new NT Service configuration should look like when configured to log on as a particular user.

Next, install the Informix client software. The Informix client software provides a run-time ESQL/C facility that is used by the JavaScript database object to access the Informix server. Installing the client software is easy—just follow the installation prompts. The first installation screen is shown in Figure A.20.

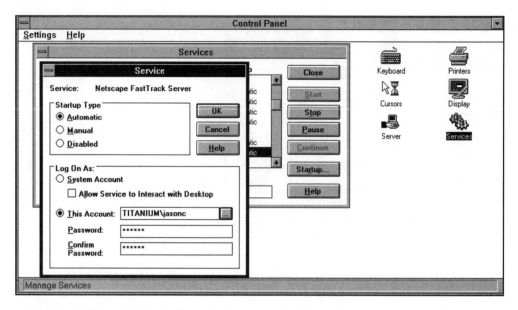

Figure A.19 Configure the Netscape FastTrack Server to log on as an NT user.

Respond to each of the installation steps with the information requested and then click **OK** when you reach the last installation screen (see Figure A.21).

With everything installed and the initial configuration done, you can now turn your attention to preparing LiveWire to work with the Informix Database Server. The steps involved are described next.

Configuring Informix to Work with LiveWire

LiveWire is designed to work with many databases through the JavaScript database object provided by the LiveWire object framework. In order for LiveWire to access the Informix database, however, the ESQL/C client software must first be configured, and at least one application database must exist to which the database object can connect. When you install the Informix Client software, an application called Setnet is supplied in the BIN directory. Run the Setnet application to access the screen shown in Figure A.22.

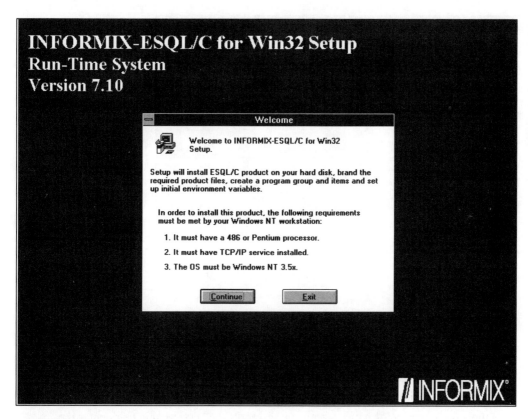

Figure A.20 Install the Informix ESQL/C Client software.

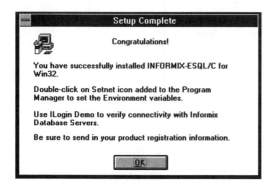

Figure A.21 Complete the installation of ESQL/C Client software.

Informix - Setnet

Environment Information

InformixServer ol_titanium   Edit Server Information   From File

InformixDir D:\INFORMIX\ESQLC   Edit NLS Information   To File

DbPath _____   DbMoney _____   Save Reg

DbLang _____   DbDate _____   Cancel

InformixConTime _____   DbTime _____   Help

InformixConRetry _____   DbTemp _____   About

☐ DelimIdent   ☐ DbAnsiWarn

■■■■■ **Figure A.22** Run the Informix Client Configuration program called Setnet.

In the **InformixServer** field on the Setnet window, enter the name of your Informix Database Server. The sample screen shown contains the server name ol_titanium. The name entered in the **InformixServer** field should match the Database Name assigned during installation of the Informix Database Server. Now click on **Edit Server Information** to access the screen shown in Figure A.23, which enables you to supply additional information about the server. In the **Servicename** field, enter the

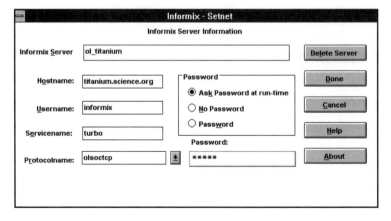

■■■■■ **Figure A.23** Supply the rest of the Informix server information required by Setnet.

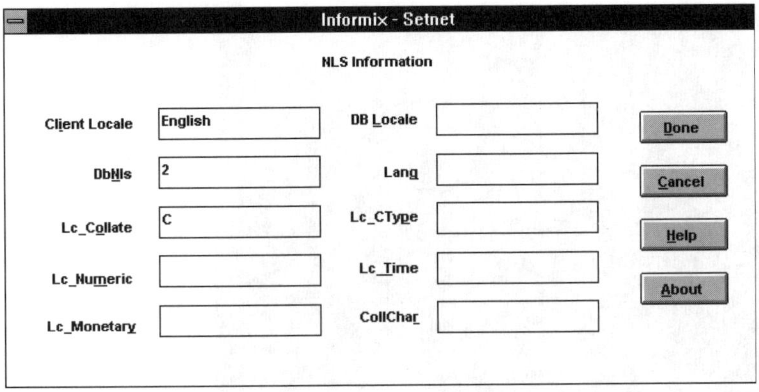

Figure A.24 Enter NLS information in Setnet.

word turbo, and in the **Protocolname** field enter olsoctcp. Click **Done** when you are finished entering Informix Server Information.

From the main Setnet window, click on the **NLS Information** button. In the NLS Information window, shown in Figure A.24, enter **English** for the *Client Locale*, the number **2** for *DbNls*, and the letter C for *Lc_Collate*.

Click **Save Reg** when you're finished configuring the Informix Client software using Setnet. Now create a database and try out LiveWire database access. Netscape supplies a sample Web application with a built-in database access called Video. The Video application requires a LiveWire database on the Informix server. Supplied with your copy of LiveWire should be a ZIP filenamed **lwdata.zip.** Unzip the lwdata file and then run the DBAccess utility provided when you installed the Informix server. The DBAccess icon takes you to a Command Prompt and sets up several environment variables that will enable you to access the Informix Database Server using the DBAccess utility. Once the Command Prompt appears on your screen, change directory to the directory in which you unzipped lwdata. Then type the **dbaccess** command to start the DBAccess utility. DBAccess is shown in Figure A.25.

It's important to change directory to lwdata before typing the dbaccess command. Once DBAccess appears on your screen, press the letter C or move the cursor to the

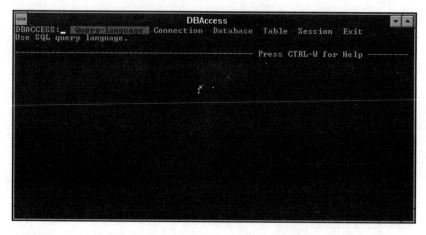

■■■■■■ **Figure A.25** Start DBAccess in the lwdata directory.

right and choose **Connection**. The Connection window is shown in Figure A.26, prompting you to select a Database Server. Press **Enter** to select the highlighted server.

DBAccess will prompt you for the user name under which you want to connect to the server. Type **informix** and press **Enter** (see Figure A.27). You will then be prompted for the Informix user password. Enter the password that you chose during installation of the Informix Database Server.

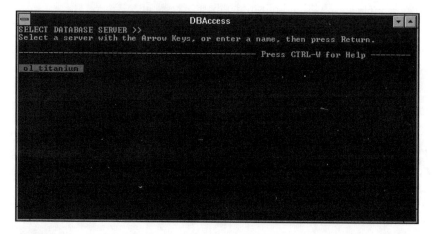

■■■■■■ **Figure A.26** Connect to the Informix Database Server in DBAccess.

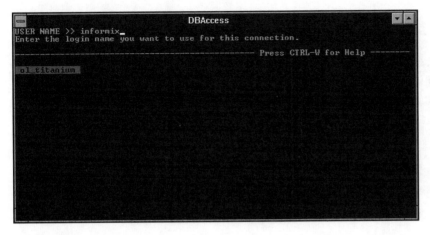

Figure A.27 Enter the Informix user name when prompted.

If you entered the right password for the Informix user account, you will next be prompted to select a Database (see Figure A.28). Choose the sysmaster database, or press **Enter** if it's already highlighted. The sysmaster database is the Informix system database, and you must first select it before you can create a new database.

Return to the DBAccess main menu and select **Query Language** to access the SQL screen shown in Figure A.29. Move the cursor to the right, highlight the **Choose** option, and press **Enter**.

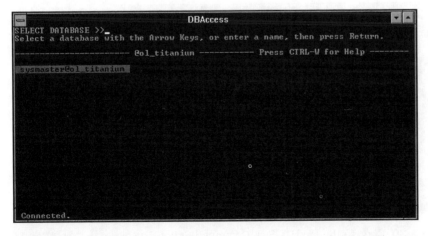

Figure A.28 Choose to connect to the sysmaster database.

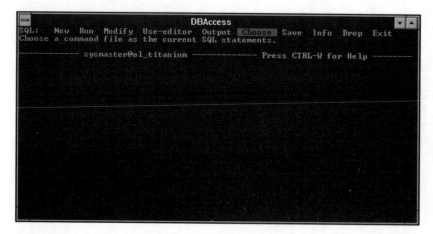

Figure A.29 Select the Choose option in the Query Language menu.

In the CHOOSE window, shown in Figure A.30, select the RWTUT SQL script and press **Enter**. The RWTUT script is provided as part of the **lwdata.zip** file, and it contains the SQL commands necessary to create the LiveWire database and fill it with data for the Video Web application.

Select the **Run** option in the SQL menu to execute the RWTUT script (see Figure A.31). The script will create a new database for you called *livewire* and fill it with data for the Video sample Web application.

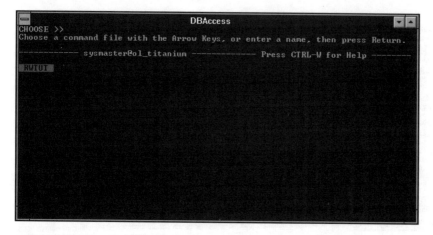

Figure A.30 Choose the RWTUT SQL Command Script.

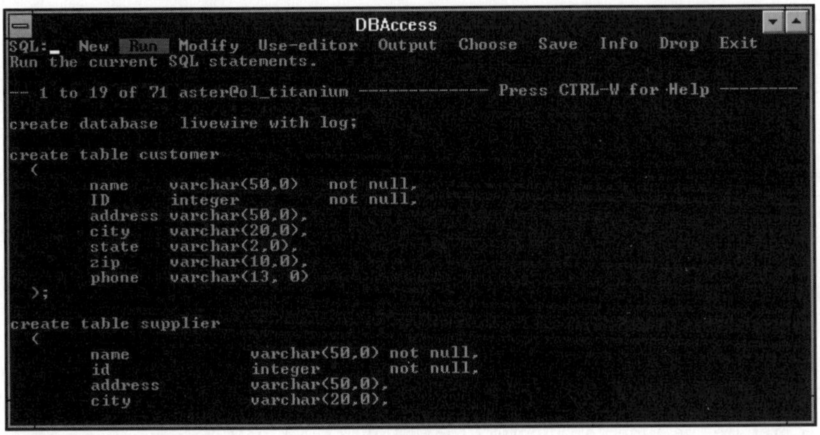

Figure A.31 Run the RWTUT Command Script to create the livewire database.

Before the sample Video application will work with the new Livewire database, you must make a change to the Start.html file located in the LiveWire\samples\video directory. Open **Start.html** in a text editor, as shown in Figure A.32, and change the

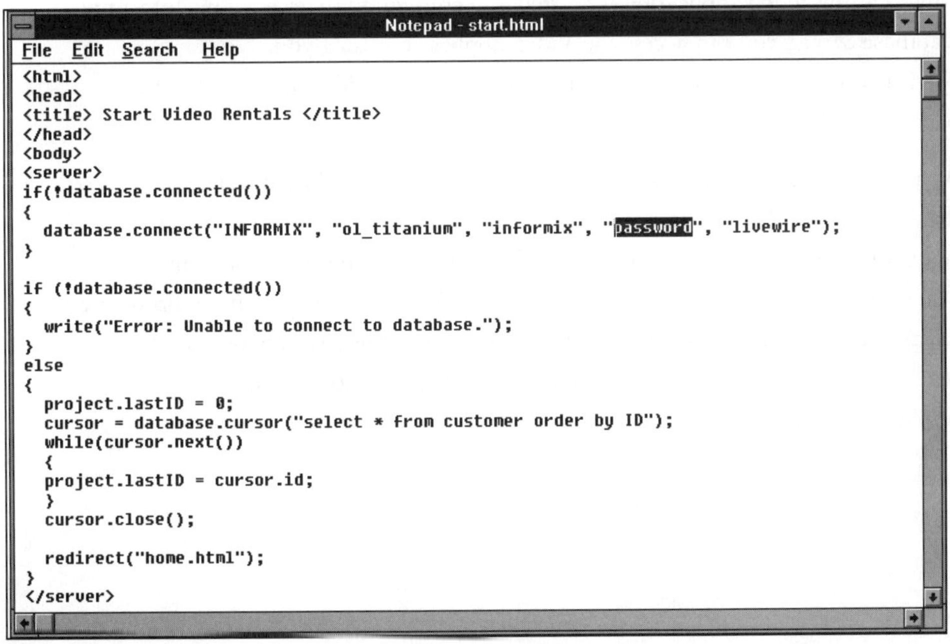

Figure A.32 Change Start.html so that it connects to the right database.

JavaScript line that connects to the database. The first parameter supplied to the JavaScript **database.connect** function should be INFORMIX in all capital letters. The next parameter is the name of your Database Server; in this example, the name is ol_titanium. The third and fourth parameters specify the user account and password to use when connecting to the database. For the Video application, use the Informix user account and supply the Informix user password. The final parameter is the name of the database to which to connect. The RWTUT script created a database named *livewire,* so that should be the final parameter.

Now execute the batch filenamed **build.bat** located in the LiveWire\samples\video directory. The **build.bat** file invokes the LiveWire Build WEB utility, as shown in Figure A.33, to prepare the Video application for use with the LiveWire server.

Now access the LiveWire Application Manager, as shown in Figure A.34, so that you can restart the Video application and make it accessible through LiveWire. Click on the **Restart** link for the Video application.

Figure A.35 shows the response from Application Manager when the Video application is successfully restarted.

Now that the Video application is started and configured to access your Informix Database Server, you can access the Video application using your Netscape Navigator to see how it works. Figure A.36 shows the Video application's main page.

As a final step in installing and configuring LiveWire, you should restrict access to the Application Manager to only authorized users. As of the writing of this Appendix, we couldn't figure out how to restrict access to the Application Manager. However, Netscape will certainly provide such a feature in the production release of LiveWire. We suggest you find and use it; otherwise, anyone on the Internet will be able to mess with your LiveWire applications through the Application Manager.

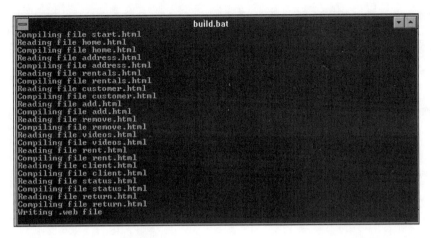

Figure A.33 Execute **build.bat** to prepare the Video Application for LiveWire.

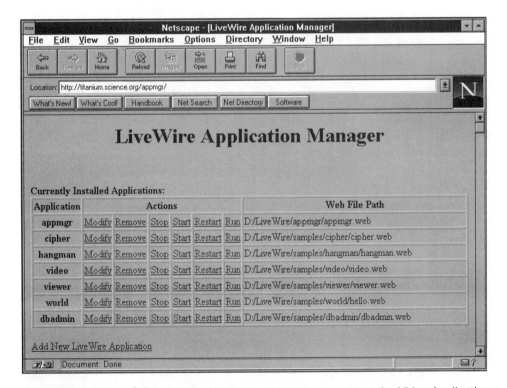

Figure A.34 Access Application Manager to restart the Video Application.

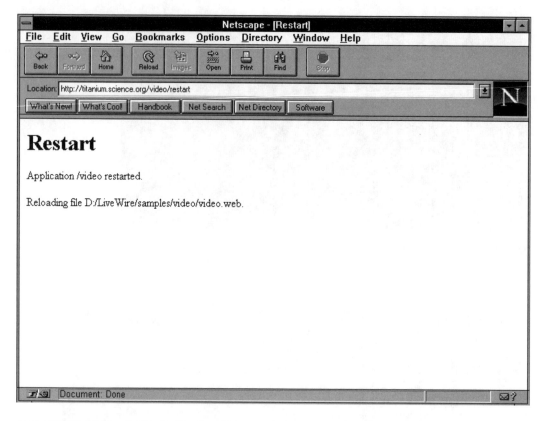

█████████ **Figure A.35** Application Manager informs you that the application has been
restarted.

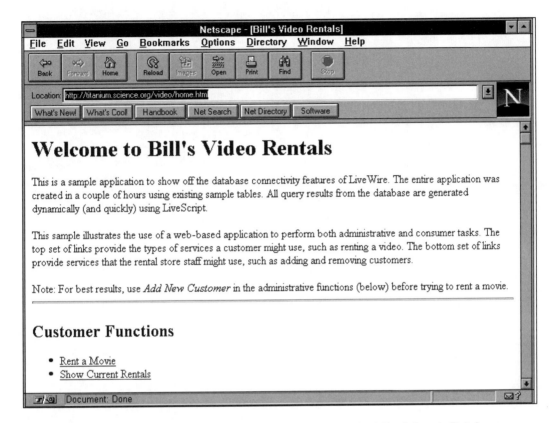

Figure A.36 The Video Application can now contact the Informix Database Server.

THE transferRNA

PLUG-IN

Until now, sending files to someone via the Internet was a problem. Innovators at SCIENCE.ORG, a science and technology think tank, both saw and experienced the problem of file transfer first hand; so they developed the transferRNA plug-in as an answer to many of the file transfer difficulties. Before transferRNA, some of the challenges you faced when trying to send or receive files over the Internet were:

- E-mail clients were incompatible.
- There was no guaranteed delivery of files via e-mail.
- Some e-mail servers have a file size limit.
- Novice users were confused by e-mail decoding strategies such as uudecode and BinHex.
- To use FTP, one of the parties had to run an FTP server.
- Running an FTP server is a security risk.
- Novice and advanced users often accidentally send binary files in text mode rather than binary mode.

- Using FTP is difficult for novice Internet users.
- One could not deliver files from an FTP site without setting up user accounts with passwords.
- "Invisible" incoming directories on FTP sites are difficult to use and confusing to novices.
- Most World Wide Web clients don't support the ability to send a file to an FTP server.

Netscape plug-ins, like the ones you read about in Chapter 9, expand the abilities of Netscape Navigator. Even though Navigator supports FTP file send and receive capabilities, not all the difficulties of file sending with FTP have been solved. Person-to-person file transfer is still a problem unless one or both people are running FTP servers. transferRNA expands the capabilities of Netscape Navigator by allowing person-to-person file transfer without leaving the Netscape Navigator. In fact, you can embed the transferRNA plug-in right in your Web page. One really clever way to use transferRNA is to embed it on the same page as a chat applet (Figure B.1). While chatting, chatters can send files back and forth to each other without missing one precious word of chat. They never have to leave the page they're on or switch to a separate application. Netscape Navigator integrates the two technologies into the same user interface. Navigator is the glue that keeps it all together on the Web.

Using transferRNA

The transferRNA plug-in, often known as tRNA for short, is installed as a Netscape plug-in. Whenever your Netscape Navigator encounters the "application/x-transferRNA" MIME type, transferRNA is launched. There are two ways to activate your tRNA plug-in:

1. Load a local file with a .RNA file extension. The file can be completely empty, but it must exist on your local drive and have the .RNA extension. Using the **Open File** menu selection of Navigator, you can launch the tRNA plug-in.

2. Contact a site on the Internet that is serving the tRNA MIME type as part of a Web page. (See serving transferRNA for more information on how you can provide this type of resource.)

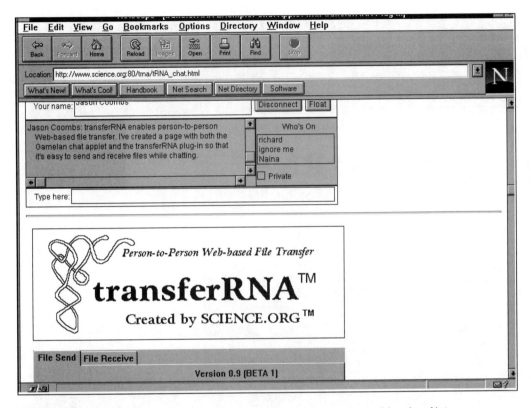

▮▮▮▮▮▮ **Figure B.1** Embed the transferRNA plug-in together with other Netscape technologies to create powerful Web pages.

Sending Files with transferRNA

Once transferRNA is loaded, you are presented with a simple-to-use tab control. The plug-in starts with the **Send** tab selected by default (see Figure B.2).

Follow these steps to send files with tRNA.

1. Make sure the intended recipient is currently running transferRNA and is connected to the Internet.

2. Click the large **File to Send** button in the middle of the **Send** tab. A file open dialog appears where you can select the file to send. The filename will appear on the button after a file is selected.

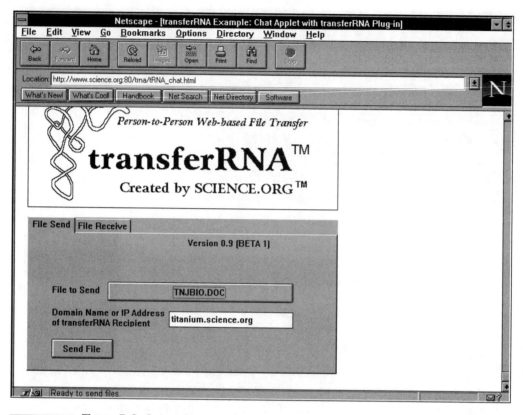

Figure B.2 Select files to send by clicking the large **File to Send** button in the center of the **Send** tab.

3. Enter the address of the recipient in the box provided. You can enter the full machine and domain name of the recipient or an IP address. In Figure B.2 titanium.science.org is a machine at SCIENCE.ORG.

4. Click the **Send File** button.

Receiving Files with transferRNA

To receive files using transferRNA you only need to be running the plug-in. When a file is received by tRNA, your plug-in will automatically switch to the **Receive** tab. You will see the file you've received in the list box (see Figure B.3). To move the file to a directory for permanent storage on your computer, click the **Copy** button. A

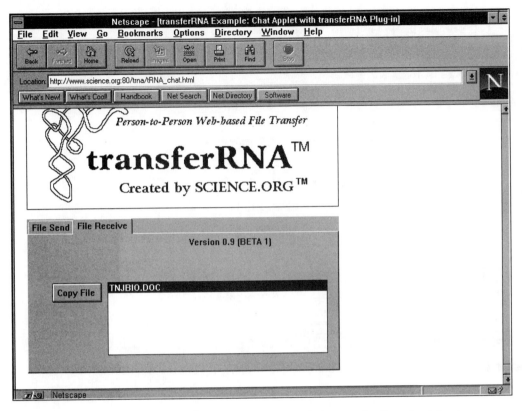

▬▬▬▬ **Figure B.3** transferRNA automatically switches to the **Receive** tab when a
file is loaded in the list box.

Save File dialog will appear, allowing you to save this file to a new directory. The
transferRNA incoming directory is a temporary storage area. Files must be copied
from this directory if you wish to save them.

Where to Get transferRNA

transferRNA is *free*. It has no expiration, evaluation period, or bothersome time-
out. Once you download and install tRNA, you have an unlimited license to use it
for the rest of your life. transferRNA is the product of research at SCIENCE.ORG,
a non-profit research company. Download the transferRNA program by contacting
the SCIENCE.ORG server: http://www.science.org/transferRNA/, Figure B.3.

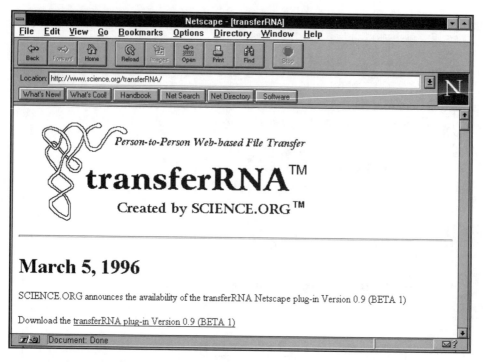

■■■■■■ **Figure B.4** Download the transferRNA plug-in from the SCIENCE.ORG server.

Contact this page for continued updates to the transferRNA program. At the time this book was written, transferRNA was in beta. The final release will have complete instructions on installing transferRNA as a Netscape plug-in. You will also find that this page includes a link that is a valid transferRNA MIME type for testing your plug-in once it's installed.

Create a local file with the extension .RNA and set a Netscape bookmark to that file. This makes launching your transferRNA plug-in very simple. To create a file, you can use Notepad to save a file with a .RNA extension.

Serving transferRNA

Your LiveWire Web system will be enhanced with the ability to use server transferRNA files from Web pages. You will have to modify the MIME type file on your Web server to support the transferRNA MIME type. See Chapter 9 for instructions on modifying this file on your server.

Once your server is modified to be able to deliver the transferRNA MIME type, you can begin embedding the transferRNA plug-in into your Web pages. Use the following syntax for adding the plug-in within the HTML of your Web source files.

```
<embed src="transfer.rna" height=450 width=600 ShowRecvPage="0"></embed>
```

Make sure you have a file called **transfer.rna** available. Remember that the contents of the .RNA file are inconsequential: it's the file extension that triggers the plug-in.

Now, for the first time, you can embed software in your Web pages that gives your Web viewers the ability to have two-way file transfer with you. This service is a must for intranets. File transfer in most companies is either nonexistent or not used. transferRNA is an instantaneous answer to moving files around your company. There are no security problems, administration issues, user support questions, or lost, damaged, or missing e-mail attachments. transferRNA is a simple and elegant solution to in-company and worldwide file transfer.

INDEX

A

<A> tag. *See* Anchor
Absolute link, 41
Absolute URLs, 29
Active X controls, 187
Ad hoc query, 158
Adobe Acrobat, 13, 309, 314
Adobe Amber inline plug-in, 13, 309–311
AdSpace applet, 224, 226
Afterburner, 418–419
Alert method, 116
Amber plug-in. *See* Adobe Amber inline plug-in
Anchor, 91, 92. *See also* Internal anchor
    <A> tag, 38, 48
    array, 92
Animation. *See* Java applet animation
    components, 256
    creation, 260
Animation inline plug-ins, 306–309
ANSI standard, 159
Answer set, 164
API. *See* Live 3D; Platform-independent API;
    Platform-specific API; Plug-in API
    functions, 341, 353, 354, 357, 364, 372, 373
    stream functions, 367

Applet
    animation, 252
    debugging, 185–188
    execution, functions, 184
    modification, 191
    security features, 184–185
    viewing, 185–188
<APPLET> tag, 180–183, 188, 189, 195, 198,
    200–203, 218, 223, 225
Application Manager, 2, 5–6, 67–70, 143,
    267, 442
Application parameters, 69
Applications
    adding, 68–69
    managing, 69–70
Arrays, 80
ASAP WebShow, 311–312
ASAP WebShow content, deploying, 313–316
ASCII characters, 91
ASSERT, 347–350
.AU sound files, 261
Audio plug-ins, 296–306
Audio streaming, 287, 301
Author to Java, 261–264
Auto commit, 170

Autocad Viewer, 322
Automatic link maintenance, 62
AVI plug-in, 352

B

Back-end CGI script, 120
Back-end processing, 7
Backquotes, embedding. *See* JavaScript
Back-ticks, 122
BIN directory, 434
Binary large objects (BLObs), 11
    fields, linking, 169
    HTML images, 169
    insertion. *See* Database
    support, 168–169
Bitmaps (BMP), 321
BLObs. *See* Binary large objects
BMP. *See* Bitmaps
<BODY> tag, 45, 48, 79
Boolean operator, 151
Borland, 277
Break <BR>, 143
Browser environment, 25
Build WEB utility, 3–5, 52, 63–67. *See also*
      Command-line Build WEB utility
    running. *See* Command line
Button, 91, 92–93
ButtonPLUS applets, 232
ButtonPLUS2, 198–201
Byte code format, 12
ByteServe, 310

C

Cafe, 277. *See also* Sun Microsystems
Cafe applet, 195
Cafe chat utility, 194
Cafe Del Sol, 232
Cafe Java applet, 192–194
    deploying, 194–196
Calculations, 116–117
CallC() function, 127
Carberry conversion machine, 319–320
Catalog server, 72
CGMs. *See* Computer graphic metafiles
Chaco Communications, 325
Char* argn[], 356–360
Char* argv[], 356–360
Character type, 155
Checkbox, 91, 93–94
Child frame, 98, 99
Child table, 156
.Class files, 264
Client cookies, 13, 133–134
    examination. *See* Server
Client JavaScript application, 27

Client object, 132–137, 144
    lifetime, 136–137
    maintenance, 133–137
    properties, 132–133
Client URL encoding, 134
Client Web browser, 130
Client/server application development tool, 51
Client/server databases, 156
Client/server Javascript, 119–148
    applications, 51
Client-side JavaScript, 8–10, 150
Client-side Web applications development, 8
Client-to-server connection, 137
.CMV animation files, 252
COD files, 321
Columns, 154–155
Command line
    Build WEB utility, running, 65–67
Command-line Build WEB utility, 64–67
Command-link syntax, 65
Commenting. *See* JavaScript
Commerce server, 5, 7, 72
Common Gateway Interface (CGI), 10, 19
    file, 330
    program, 65, 78, 103, 119
    programming, 75
    scripts, 7, 120, 334. *See also* Back-end CGI
      script
Communications server, 5, 7
Compression/decompression code, 320
Computer graphic metafiles (CGMs), 318
    file format, 320
Computer-generated animation, 306
Condition statements, 78. *See also* JavaScript
    program flow control, 82–85
Const char* fname, 369–370
Const char* message, 384–385
Const char* NPN_UserAgent, 382–383
Const char* url, 385–392
Const char* window, 385–392
Content Manager, 242
CONTROL, 300, 301, 319
Corel WEB.MOVE, 250–264
    file opening, 252–253
    tips, 261
    toolbars, 253–260
Counter, 85
Crescendo, 329
    MIDI inline plug-in, 305–306
Cross-platform support, 12
Cursor object, 164–167
Cursors. *See* Database
    row insertion, 166–167
    usage. *See* Information
Cyberspace, 133

D

Data handling, 158–163
Data navigation, 164–166
Data transfer scheme, 134
Database
    BLObs insertion, 168–169
    column types, 163
    connection, 150–153
    cursors, 164–167
    information deletion, 161
    information insertion, 160
    information retrieval, 161–163
    object, 139–140, 150–156, 173
    query, 163
    security, 150
    status codes, 174–175
    updating, 160–161
    usage. *See* LiveWire
    values, returning. *See* Web Page
Database error handling, 173–175
Database management system (DBMS), 73,
    149–152, 154, 163, 168, 171, 174
    manual, 155
    program, 159
    vendor, 151, 159
Database object sample application, 175–178
Database server. *See* Informix OnLine Database
    Server
Database.execute() method, usage, 158–159
Databases, introduction, 149
Date, 91, 94–95
DBAccess, 437–439
DBAdmin, 157
DBMS. *See* Database management system
DCR animation files, 418
DCR file, 418
Debug() function, 126, 144–147
Debugging, 147
Defined() function, 125
Demo applets, 188–191
Dimension X, 239, 249
Director. *See* Macromedia director
.DLL file, 127, 280–282, 338, 345, 353
Document, 91, 95–96
Document editing, publishing, 44
Document presentation, 287
Document viewing, 287, 309–317
Document-generating software, 309
DOS box, 266
DOS prompt, 240
DOS window, 186
Drag-and-drop capability, 17

E

Elements, 96–97
    array, 91
E-mail, 21–24
    address, 197
    client, 24, 447. *See also* MIME-enabled e-mail
        client
    Netscape Navigator Gold configuration, 20–21
    window, 21
<EMBED> tag, 283, 284, 293, 295, 296, 300,
    305, 306, 311, 314, 316, 320, 325, 332,
    356, 359, 360, 386, 419
Embedded SQL, 11
Error handling. *See* Database error handling
Error-handling routine, 174
Escape(), 90
ESQL/C
    client software, 434
    facility. *See* Run-time ESQL/C facility
Eval(), 91
Event handlers, 88, 89, 91, 93–95, 98, 104,
    108, 111
Event processing. *See* JavaScript
Event programming, 88–89
Events, 75, 77
Excel, 314, 317
Expiration default, 136
Export HTML, 244–249
Expressions, creation. *See* Operators
External editors, 44–49
External HTML, 31
External link tester, 3
External links, 60

F

FastTrack HTTP server, 427, 433
FastTrack Server. *See* Netscape FastTrack Server
Fields, linking. *See* Binary large objects
FIGleaf, 318–319
File and director manager, 3
File object, 140–143
File transfer protocol (FTP), 23, 62
    account, 26
    capability, 18, 25–27
    client, 4, 19, 336
    file, 448
    logons, 100
    passwords, 100
    resource, 125
    server, 20, 26, 44, 447, 448
    site, 44, 198, 232
    URL, 26
    URL type, 4

Firewalls, 285–286
Flush() function, 126–127
Folder icon, 61
Form, 91, 97–98
    array, 97
Form elements/tags, JavaScript addition, 48–49
Form inputs, 138
<FORM> tag, 45, 46, 77, 79, 922
Forms. *See* Netscape Navigator Gold
Formula One/NET plug-in, 317
Foundational objects, 95
FQDN. *See* Fully qualified domain name
Frame, 91, 98–99. *See also* Child frame; Parent
    frame
<FRAME> tag, 47, 98
Frames. *See* Netscape Navigator Gold
<FRAMESET>, 48, 98, 99, 113, 385, 389
FreeTEA, 239, 240, 242, 244
FTP. *See* File transfer protocol
Fully qualified domain name (FQDN), 422, 427
Functions, creation, 85–88

G
Gamelan, 233
Gamelan chat applet, 196–198
GIF. *See* Graphics Interchange Format
Gopher, 23, 62
Graphic files, 66
Graphical animation, 287
Graphics Interchange Format (GIF), 318
    images, 13
Guestbook applet, 203–218
Guru Template Web site configuration, 57
Guru Template window, 54
Gurus(s), 58. *See also* Site Manager

H
<HEAD>, 79, 87, 115
    tags, 87, 95
Hidden, 91, 99
    objects, 99
History, 91, 100–102
HREF, 38
HTML. *See* Hypertext markup language
HTML-formatted text, 388
HTTP, 41
    header, 127
HTTP Communications, 7
HTTP POST, 388
HTTP protocol, 19, 128, 137
HTTP request, 383
HTTP server, 9, 18, 27, 59, 60, 72, 333, 334, 390,
    421, 424, 426. *See also* FastTrack HTTP
    server; Netscape HTTP server
HTTP specification, 392

HTTP syntax, 390
HTTP server, 418
HWND, 351
HWND window handle, 350
Hyperlink functionality, 416
Hyperlinks, 14, 17, 19, 22, 23, 28, 31, 34, 43, 60,
    69, 192, 224, 280, 416
    creation, 38–41
    image usage, 40
Hypertext link, 92, 102
Hypertext markup language (HTML), 2, 17, 79,
    93, 95, 97, 98, 102, 105, 106, 110, 111,
    244, 305, 336, 387, 453. *See* Export
    HTML; External HTML
    attribute, 123
    code, 30, 121, 180
    content, embedding, 418–419
    document, 87, 88, 114, 137, 314
    editor, 44–47, 49. *See also* What You *See* Is
        What You Get
    extensions, 279, 332
    filename, 186
    files, 47, 62, 122, 188, 249, 261, 309, 386
    form, 5, 92
    format, 124
    functions, 114, 115
    guru, 38
    images. *See* Binary large objects
    JavaScript, embedding, 86–88, 122–123
    pages, 9, 78, 138
    source code, 44, 45, 188, 250, 261, 263
    stream, 388
    syntax, 111, 162
    table, 157, 162
    tag feature, 46
    tag icons, 45
    tag syntax, 27
    tag(s), 30, 42, 44, 48, 87, 88, 122
        insertion, 45
    tag-syntax authoring, 3
    Web page, 75

I
IANA. *See* Internet Assigned Numbers Authority
Icons, 17, 34, 35, 291, 304. *See also* Folder icon;
    Link icon; Netscape icon
IDE, 18, 30
Illustra, 139, 150
Image editors, 31
Image enhancement, 287, 317–322
ImageMap applet, 189–191
Images, 34. *See also* Binary large objects;
    Hyperlinks; Hypertext markup language
    applets. *See* ScrollingImages applet
    creation, 40–42

editing, 40–42
usage. *See* Hyperlinks
IMG SRC, 123
<IMG> tag, 11, 40, 169, 180
Information
   cursor usage, 167
   deletion. *See* Database
   insertion. *See* Database
   retrieval. *See* Database
   updating, cursor usage, 167
Informix, 73, 139, 150
   configuration, 434–445
Informix OnLine Database Server, 422
   installation, 428–434
In-house applications, 135
Inktomi, 158
Inline plug-in architecture. *See* Netscape inline
   plug-in
Inline plug-in content, 57
Inline plug-in enhancement, 19
Inline plug-ins, 18, 279–332. *See also* Animation
   inline plug-ins; Video inline plug-ins
   deploying, 283–286
Instance initialization. *See* Plug-in instance
   initialization
Int* netscape_major, 380–382
Int* netscape_minor, 380–382
Int* plugin_major, 380–382
Int* plugin_minor, 380–382
Int16 argc, 356–360
Int16 NPP_HandleEvent, 378–379
Int32 len, 373–374, 393–394
Int32 NP_LOADDS NPP_Write, 373–374
Int32 NPN_Write, 393–394
Int32 offset, 373–374
Integrated Data Systems, 325
Intel, 238
Interactive Web lingo, 416–417
Internal anchor, 38, 39
Internal links, 60
Internet, 28, 158, 281, 294, 297, 305, 306
   connection, 288
   operating system, 337
Internet Assigned Numbers Authority (IANA), 335
Internet database programming, 10
Internet Explorer, 383
Internet Relay Chat (IRC)
   applet, 192, 264
   Java applet, 194–196
   server requirements, 196
   utility, 192–198
Internet tools, 19–20
InterVU, 293
Intranet system, 285

Invalid links, 5
   repair, 62–63
IP address, 41, 71, 137, 422–424. *See also* Server
IRC. *See* Internet Relay Chat
IS file, 7
ISMAP parameter, 169

J

JACK. *See* Java Animation Construction Kit
Java Animation Construction Kit (JACK), 239
Java applet animation, 237–264
Java applet creation tools, 237–277
Java applet sites, 232–233
Java applets, 10–13, 18, 19, 57, 138, 179–235,
   237, 328. *See* Cafe Java applet; Plug-ins
   placement. *See* Web Page
   types, 191–234
   usage, timing, 233–234
Java Developer Team, 188
Java Developer's Kit (JDK), 185–191, 204, 232,
   237, 239
   compiler, 191
Java interoperability, 327
Java language, 233
Java pop-up window, 198, 217
Java Sound applet, 218–224
Java source code, 191
Java visual development tools, 264–277
Java-enabled Web browser, 12
JavaScript, 18, 19, 64, 77, 332. *See* Client/server
   Javascript; Client-side JavaScript; Server-side
   JavaScript
   addition. *See* Form elements/tags
   applications, 113, 157, 264. *See also* Client
      JavaScript application; Server JavaScript
      application
   authoring tool, 2
   backquotes, embedding, 123
   basics, 77–88
   built-in functions, 90–91
   code, 27, 30, 57, 120
   commenting, 86
   condition statements, 78–85
   creation, 42–43
   database access, 10–11
   database object, 428, 431
   embedding. *See* Hypertext markup language
   event processing, 44
   files, 66
   function, 88, 89
   language, 8–9
   null values, 163
   objects, 79, 150
      programming, 90

operators, 78–85
output, 88
program, 78, 93, 99, 112, 113, 117, 126, 134, 151
programming, 124
server functions, 124–127
SQL, execution, 157–158
standard objects, 91–113
statement, 123
string, 163
values, 163
variables, 78–85
wiring, 148
writing, 75–118
JCK file, 241, 244, 245, 249
JDK. *See* Java Developer's Kit
JFactory, 12, 264–277
additions, 277
application compiling/making, 266
application testing, 265–266
controls, addition, 267
starting, 264–265
JIT compiler. *See* Just-in-time compiler
Joint Photographic Experts Group (JPEG), 318
images, 13
JPEG 6.0, 320
JPEG. *See* Joint Photographic Experts Group
JPG graphic file, 168
Just-in-time (JIT) compiler, 237–238

L

Latte, 277
Library error, 173
Lightning Strike compression utility, 321
Lightning Strike inline plug-in, 320–321
Lingo, 13
commands. *See* Net-specific Lingo commands
script, 413, 416
Link, 91, 102. *See also* Absolute link; Relative link
Link icon, 40
Link management, 60–63
Link object, 102
Link tag, 62
Linking. *See* Binary large objects
Link-management tags, 58
Links, 34. *See also* External links; Internal links; Invalid links
viewing, 61–62
Live3D, 325–328
API, 328
viewing, VRML content deployment, 328
LiveObject, 395
LiveObject Web content, 2

LiveWire, 1, 3–6, 13, 14, 20, 51–73, 434–445
Application Manager, 65
applications, building, 7–11
architecture, 15
compiler, 63
database, usage, 149–178
development, 18
installation, 426–428
object framework, 9–10
objects, 127–128
Pro. *See* Netscape LiveWire Pro
server, 52
site, 5
Site Manager user interface, 4
software tools, 2–7
source files, usage, 121–122
system, 120
utility, 63
Local links, 28
Location, 91, 103. *See* URL location
array, 103
Lock(), 126
Loops, program flow control, 82–85

M

Macintosh, 342, 397, 412
event types, 378
OS, 342
plug-ins, 343
Macromedia director, 11, 13–15, 307, 308, 409–418
Macromedia logos, 307
Mail server, 72–73
MAILTO, 62
MAKE file, 4
Math, 91, 103–104
MDI microhelp status bar, 384
Menu-driven interface, 3
Message pump, 343
Message-sending interface, 22
Methods, 76
MFC. *See* Microsoft Foundation classes
Microsoft Foundation classes (MFC), 343–352, 395, 397
MIDI files, 306
MIME. *See* Multipurpose Internet mail extension
MIME files, 24, 287, 297, 319
server configuration, 284–285
MIME-enabled e-mail client, 73
MIME-type content, 367
MIME.TYPES, 284, 285, 292, 295, 304, 316, 322, 418
file, 325

.MLB file, 258
Mosaic browser, 317
Moving Worlds, 327
MPEG file, 295, 296
MPEG videos, 293–295
Multimedia capabilities, 185
Multimedia Web content, production, 11–15
Multipurpose Internet mail extension (MIME), 13,
    19, 23, 334
  architecture, 335
  content, 279, 280, 407
  file, 452
  files. See MIME files
  file types, 282, 283, 285, 286, 288, 293, 295,
      297, 301, 302, 304, 306–311, 313, 316,
      320–322, 324–326, 330, 331
  instances, 363
  type, 22, 169, 284, 335–337, 341, 366, 392,
      418, 448, 453. See also Plug-in MIME
      type
  types, 337, 397
  usage. See Web extension
  workbook/formula, 317
.MWF files, 252

N

Name/value pairs, 134
Navigator, 91, 104
  browser, 25, 42
Navigator functions, calling. See Plug-ins
Navigator Gold. See Netscape Navigator Gold
Net-related information, 416
Netscape cookie protocol, 135
Netscape FastTrack Server, 2
  installation, 421–426
Netscape HTTP server, 128
Netscape icon, 145
Netscape inline plug-in, 11, 13
  architecture, understanding, 333–395
  building, 397–407
Netscape LiveWire. See LiveWire
Netscape LiveWire Pro, 73
  configuration, 421–445
  installation, 421–445
Netscape Navigator, 279, 281, 307, 310, 312,
    329, 330, 334, 338, 340, 398
  browser, 282, 293, 317
  client, 324
  functions, 357, 359
  window, 294
Netscape Navigator 2.0, 77, 180, 309, 318, 382,
    390, 395

Netscape Navigator Gold, 2–4, 13, 17–49, 52, 61,
    62, 67, 119
  browser environment, 18–27
  configuration. See E-mail; News
  document properties, 32–34
  editor environment, 27–49
  editor preferences, 31–32
  editor window, 27–44
  forms, creation, 45–47
  frames, addition, 47–48right click, 43–44
  WYSIWYG toolbar, usage, 34–38
Netscape Navigator menu, 100
Netscape objects, 113–117
Netscape plug-in API, 13, 382
Netscape plug-in SDK, 344
  programming, 398–407
Netscape security, 20
Netscape server, 131, 281
  systems, 7
Netscape Web server, 70
Net-specific Lingo commands, 416, 417
Network communication, 12
Network drive, 54
Network security, 72
Network-enabled word processor, 336
News, Netscape Navigator Gold configuration,
    20–21
News server, 7, 72
NNTP, 19, 21
<NOEMBED>, 332
<NOFRAMES>, 48
NPBool file, 388–392
NPBool seekable, 366–369
NPByteRange* rangeList, 393
NPError NP_LOADDS, 356–373
NPError NPN_DestroyStream, 392–393
NPError NPN_GetURL, 385–388
NPError NPN_NewStream, 392
NPError NPN_PostURL, 388–392
NPError NPN_RequestRead, 393
NPError NPP_Initialize(void), 355
NPError reason, 370–373, 392–393
NPMIMEType type, 366–369, 392
NPP instance, 356–379, 382–394
NPP_Destroy(NPPInstance), 360–363, 370–373
NPP_New(NPMIMEType pluginType, 356–360
NPP_NewStream, 366–369
NPPrint* printinfo, 374–378
NPP_SetWindow(NPP Instance), 363–366
NPSavedData** save, 360–363
NPSavedData* saved, 356–360
NPStream* stream, 366–374, 392–394

NPWindow* window, 363–366
NTFS file system, 428, 432

O

Object attributes, 90
Object linking and embedding (OLE)
    controls, 287
    objects, 314
    OLE/OCX controls, 322–325
Object manager, 267
Object sample application. *See* Database object
    sample application
Object-orientation guru, 90
Objects, 75, 77. *See also* JavaScript
    creation, 79–80
OCX. *See* Object linking and embedding
    controls, 19
ODBC, 139, 150, 151
OLE. *See* Object linking and embedding
OLTP. *See* On-line transaction processing
ONETAG, usage, 183–184
On-line production, 64
On-line transaction processing (OLTP), 11,
    170–173
Openscape, 324–325
Operators, 91. *See also* Boolean operator;
    JavaScript
    expressions, creation, 80–82
<OPTION> tag, 106, 108
Options array, 107
Optima++, 277
Oracle, 139, 150

P

Paint Shop Pro, 314
Parameter case-sensitivity, 200
Parent frame, 98, 99
Parent table, 156
Passing values. *See* URLs
Password, 91, 104–105
PC World, 312
PDF. *See* Portable Document Format
Platform-independent API, 333
Platform-independent compiled byte code, 11
Platform-specific API, 180
Platform-specific window, 339, 363
Plug-in API, 337, 380–382, 391, 395. *See also*
    Netscape plug-in API
    concepts, demystifying, 341–352
    function calls, handling, 353–379
    functions, 341
    specification, 359
    understanding, 338–395

Plug-in code, 368, 370, 404, 407
Plug-in development tool, 352
Plug-in display, initialization, 404–407
Plug-in instance initialization, handling, 398–404
Plug-in MIME type, 13, 360, 361
Plug-in module, 368
Plug-in SDK, 338, 352, 380. *See also* Netscape
    plug-in SDK
Plug-ins. *See* Audio plug-ins; Inline plug-ins; Very
    important plug-ins
    challenges, 281–283
    combination, 328–329
    installation, 280–283
    Java applets, additions, 329
    Navigator functions, calling, 379–395
    user problems, 329–332
Poetry CreatOR2 applet, 230–231
Point-and-click interface, 32
POP, 21
Portable Document Format (PDF)
    documents, 310
    files, 309, 311
POST, 388–391. *See also* HTTP POST
POST request, 9
PowerBuilder, 237
PowerPoint, 314
Powersoft, 277
PreVU video plug-in, 293–296
Program flow control. *See* Condition statements;
    Loops
Progressive Networks, 297
Project object, 131–132, 144
Protocol prefix, 41
Proxy server, 72
Pull mode, 367

Q

Quicktime movie, 284, 285, 314

R

Radio, 91
    buttons, 105–106
RAM file, 299
RAS. *See* Row Address Strobe
RDBMS. *See* Relational database management
    system
Real Audio plug-in, 284
RealAudio, 297–299
    Encoder, 299
    inline plug-in content, deploying, 299–301
Redirect() function, 125
RegisterC() function, 127
Relational database, 155

Relational database management system (RDBMS), 73, 149
Relationships, 155–156
Relative link, 41
Remote links, 28
Request object, 133, 137–139
    properties, 137–139
Request properties, 138
Reserved words, 117
Reset, 91
    button, 106
Restart, shortcut, 70
Result set, 164
RFC 822, 334
RFC 1521, 334
RGB value, 32
Role separation, 429, 430
RollbackTransaction(), 171
Row Address Strobe (RAS), 318
Rows, 154–155
    insertion. *See* Cursors
RPM file, 299
Run-time ESQL/C facility, 433
RWTUT, 440, 442

S

<SCRIPT>, 42, 129
    tag, 86, 87
Scrolling, 224–229
    advertisements. *See* Web site
ScrollingImages applet, 188–189
Select, 91
SELECT statement, usage, 163
Selection list, 106–108
Server
    authorization, 144
    client cookies, examination, 134–135
    configuration. *See* MIME files
    cookies, 135
    IP address, 135
    object, 128–130
    software. *See* VDOLive server software
<SERVER>, 10, 42, 49, 1229
Server JavaScript application, 27
Server object, 125, 144
<Server> tag, 10
    usage, 122–123
Server-generated URLs, 134, 136
Servers, 70–73. *See also* Catalog server; Commerce server; FastTrack server; Mail server; News server; Proxy server
Server-side JavaScript
Server-side scripting, 8
Server-side Web applications development, 8

Shockwave, 11, 13–15, 329, 409–419
    inline plug-in, 307
Short cookies, 135, 136
Short URL encoding, 136
Shread object (.SO) file, 127
.SITE file, 64, 65
Site Manager, 4–5, 52–63
    Gurus, 52
Sizzler animations, deploying, 308–309
Sizzler inline plug-in, 307–308
SMTP, 19, 21
    Internet protocol, 218
.SO file. *See* Shread object file
Software Publishing Corporation (SPC), 311, 312
Softsource, 322
Solaris, 65
    machines, 68
Space Invaders Java applet, 231–232
SPC. *See* Software Publishing Corporation
Spin control, 257
Sports Ticker Java, 226–229
Spy utility, 339
SQL. *See* Structured Query Language
SQLHOSTS Registry Machine, 432
SQLTable(), 158, 162
SQLTable() method, 140, 157
SRC attribute, 283
State structure, 133
Status codes. *See* Database
STD 11, 334
Storage compartment, 80
String, 91, 108–109
Structured Query Language (SQL), 7, 149, 156, 158, 164. *See also* Embedded SQL
    commands, 440
    execution. *See* JavaScript
    introduction, 156–158
    keyword values, 160
    screen, 439
    statement, 159–161, 166
Submit, 91
    button, 110
Subscriber database, 153
SuiteSpot, 70, 71
    server package, 7
Sun Microsystems, 7, 11, 188, 232, 237, 239
    Cafe, 232–233
Sybase, 139, 150
Symantec, 277

T

Tables, 153–154
Tagged Image File Format (TIFF), 318
TCP. *See* Transmission Control Protocol

TCP/IP, 433
TCP/SMTP, 203
TEA. *See* The Easy Animator
Text, 91, 110–111
TextArea, 91, 111–112
The Easy Animator (TEA), 239–249. *See also*
   FreeTEA
TIFF. *See* Tagged Image File Format
Timeout, 99
Time-out function, 26
<TITLE>, 59
Toolbars. *See* Corel WEB.MOVE
ToolVox
   incorporation. *See* Web site
   inline plug-in, 301–302
Totally Hip Software, 308
TourGuide applet, 201–203
Trace utility, 144–147
Tracing, 144–147
Transaction processing. *See* On-line transaction
   processing
TransferRNA
   files, receiving, 450–451
   files, sending, 449–450
   getting, 451–452
   plug-in, 447–453
   serving, 452–453
   usage, 448–451
Transmission Control Protocol (TCP), 286
   ports, 299

U

UDP. *See* User Datagram Protocol
Uint16 mode, 356–360
Uint16* stype, 366–369
Uint32 len, 388–392
Unit32 NPN_MemFlush, 395
Uint32 size, 394, 395
Unescape(), 91
Uniform Resource Identifier (URI), 68
Unix, 334, 397
Unlock(), 126
Unsubclassing, 344
URI. *See* Uniform Resource Identifier
URLs, 24, 25, 62, 67, 68, 71, 103, 114, 120, 124,
   125, 134, 138, 185, 192, 194, 195, 198,
   201–217, 219, 228, 230–232, 234, 242,
   277, 280, 288–291, 293, 301, 302, 307,
   308, 311, 312, 318, 320, 321, 325, 327,
   329, 338, 359, 360, 366, 379, 385–387,
   389, 410. *See also* Absolute URLs; File
   transfer protocol; Server-generated URLs
URL addresses, 23, 28, 183, 224
URL entry field, 282

URL location, 21, 39, 239, 296, 322, 330
URL passing values, addition, 138–139
URL type. *See* File transfer protocol
URL encoding. *See* Client URL encoding; Short
   URL encoding
User Datagram Protocol (UDP), 285–286, 299
   ports, 299
User inputs, validation, 114–116
UUEncoding, 23

V

VARCHAR, 11
Variables. *See* JavaScript
   creation, 79
VBX controls, 323
VCR buttons, 259
VCR controls, 250
VDO content, 289
VDOLive, 286–290
VDOLive Personal Tools, 292
VDOLive server, 291
   software, 290–293
VDOnet, 288, 291
VDOServer, 292
Very important plug-ins (VIPs), 286–332
Video inline plug-ins, 287–296
Video streaming, 287
VIPs. *See* Very important plug-ins
Virtual Bubble Wrap, 411
Virtual machine, 11
Virtual Reality Modeling Language (VRML), 287
   content, deploying. *See* Live3D
   worlds, 307, 326–328
Virtual reality worlds, 325–328
Visual C++, 237, 339
Visual Components, 317
Visual dBASE, 151
Void* buffer, 373–374, 393–394
Void* event, 378–379
Void NP_LOADDS NPP_Print, 374–378
Void NP_LOADDS NPP_StreamAsFile, 369–370
Void* NPN_MemAlloc, 394
Void NPN_MemFree, 394–395
Void NPN_Status, 384–385
Void NPN_Version, 380–382
Void NPP_Shutdown(void), 355–356
Void* ptr, 394–395
VOX file, 302–305
VR Scout, 325
VREALM, 325
VREAM, 325
VRML. *See* Virtual Reality Modeling Language
VTS file, 317

W

Watcom, 151
WAV audio file, 303
.WAV files, 252, 299, 302, 303
Web application, 1–2, 51, 70, 77, 121, 126, 128, 152, 158, 225, 291, 409
    running, 143–144
Web browser, 9, 17, 40, 53, 67, 68, 104, 119, 128, 152, 184, 235, 382. *See also* Client Web browser; Java-enabled Web browser
Web client, 121
Web content, 255, 321, 410, 411, 418. *See also* LiveObject Web content; Multimedia Web content
    development options, 397
Web developers, 27
Web documents, 27, 28, 30, 32, 34, 42, 43, 48, 77, 112, 225
Web environment, 281
Web extension, MIME usage, 334–337
.WEB file, 2, 58, 60, 63, 64, 66, 120
Web functionality, 22, 24
Web lingo. *See* Interactive Web lingo
Web Page/pages, 17, 21, 30, 31, 38–41, 45, 46, 49, 51, 52, 76, 92, 96, 97, 101, 103, 115, 120, 121, 124, 169, 184, 188, 198, 219, 226, 228–230, 233–235, 238, 261, 263, 280, 283, 298, 307, 323, 328–330, 374, 375, 387, 409, 410, 453. *See* Hypertext markup language
    content, 114
    database values, returning, 162
    Java applets, placement, 180–185
    source file, 130
Web publishers, 35
    service, 44
Web publishing, 51
Web resources, 35
Web server, 97, 151
Web site, 53, 72, 179, 182, 195, 201, 233, 234, 249, 264, 287, 295, 296, 301, 302, 305, 307, 309, 311, 317, 320, 331
    configuration. *See* Guru Template Web site configuration
    management, 54–60

scrolling advertisements, 224–226
ToolVox incorporation, 302–305
Web source files, 62, 66, 129, 181, 223, 225, 300, 305, 322, 453
WEB utility. *See* Build WEB utility; Command-line Build-WEB utility
Weblinks, 310
WEB.MOVE. *See* Corel WEB.MOVE
What You *See* Is What You Get (WYSIWYG), 42
    HTML editor, 17
    toolbar, usage. *See* Netscape Navigator Gold
Window, 91
    object, 112–113, 171
Window event messaging, 342–344
Windows API function, 349
Windows Explorer, 26
Windows machines, 68
Windows mouse, 77
Windows NT, 291, 334, 424, 433
Windows 95, 146, 234
Winzip program, 240
Word, 314
WordPerfect, 314
WordPower software, 313
World Wide Web (WWW), 1, 9, 11, 13, 21, 100, 178, 335, 337, 411
    server software, 119
Write() function, 124–125
WYSIWYG. *See* What You *See* Is What You Get
WWW. *See* World Wide Web

X

X Windows, 342
XDB, 151
X-Files production, 410

Y

Yahoo!, 158